THE
MOVING
FRONTIER

DR. LOUIS B. WRIGHT is the distinguished historian who directed the Folger Shakespeare Library in Washington, D.C. for more than twenty years. ELAINE W. FOWLER is his long-time researcher and collaborator. Together they edited *West and By North*, the companion volume to this book.

When the Great Explorers Series was conceived, Vilhjalmur Stefansson, one of the great explorers of our time, and his wife, Evelyn, were chosen as general editors. After her husband's death in August 1962, Mrs. Stefansson, who was librarian of the Stefansson Collection at the Baker Library of Dartmouth, continued her work on the series. In 1964 she married John Nef, the historian and writer who founded the Committee on Social Thought at the University of Chicago and its allied Center for Human Understanding. The Nefs live in Washington, D.C.

THE GREAT EXPLORERS SERIES

CONCEIVED BY

Vilhjalmur Stefansson

GENERAL EDITOR

Evelyn Stefansson Nef

WRIGHT, Louis Booker and Elaine W. Fowler, eds. The moving
frontier; North America seen through the eyes of its pioneer discoverers. Delacorte, 1972. 348p map (The great explorers series)
70-38895. 10.00
Here is the fifth and final volume of this series, conceived more than 10
years ago by Vilhjalmur Stefansson. It is also the second in this series
to be edited by Wright and Fowler. *West and by north* (CHOICE, May
1972) contained sources on the exploration of North America by sea;
this one concentrates on inland exploration, "from barrier to land of
opportunity," from Spaniards in the 16th-century Southeast to the
Alaskan frontier of the 1860s. That is a lot of time and space to cover
in 335 pages, and the volume's most serious flaw is its fundamental
superficiality. Its subject matter deserves at least four volumes. The
documentary materials are well chosen, however, thoughtfully edited,
accompanied by eight maps and an index. The brief concluding essay,
"A nation in motion," will give the book a certain timeliness as a
companion to G. W. Pierson's forthcoming *The moving American*
(1973).

NORTH AMERICA SEEN THROUGH THE EYES
OF ITS PIONEER DISCOVERERS

THE
MOVING
FRONTIER

Edited, annotated, and introduced by
LOUIS B. WRIGHT
and
ELAINE W. FOWLER

DELACORTE PRESS

Library of Congress Cataloging in Publication Data
Wright, Louis Booker, 1899–   comp.
The moving frontier.
(The Great explorers series)
Bibliography: p.
1. America—Discovery and exploration.
2. Explorers. I. Fowler, Elaine W., joint comp. II. Title.
E121.W7   973.1   70–38895

MAPS BY *Andrew Mudryk*

Contents

CONTENTS

List of Maps

Preface

AS the wife of Vilhjalmur Stefansson, who was twice president of the New York Explorers Club, I often saw our house filled with a variety of explorer types of all sizes, ages, nationalities, abilities, and temperaments. For more than two decades I had a wonderful opportunity to observe, compare, and mentally record much about their varied personalities.

Personality is a subject I love to speculate about. What exactly does it consist of? How does it develop? What are the most important factors in its formation? How can we explain why some people are irreparably wounded by a catastrophe that strengthens others? Why do some people lead while the rest are content to follow? Why are some people able to solve formerly insoluble problems while others resent having to consider anything novel? Speculating about the answers is endless and delicious.

A famous lecturer (could it have been Robert Ingersoll?) once said, "My brain may not be the *best* brain in the world, but it is so conveniently located for home use." Stefansson was a great polar explorer and scholar, albeit a controversial figure to some. I don't say he was the *best* polar explorer in the world, but he was so conveniently located for home use as far as observation and comparison were concerned.

The recurring puzzle of why explorers have always been willing to leave comfort and family to journey with danger and death in a foreign world is really no puzzle at all. Since the beginning of recorded history (and probably long, long before), where man's lot was harsh, he was willing because of need to believe in the miraculous. If he was hungry, he dreamt of food; if poor, of riches; if on a low rung of the social ladder, of nobility;

if despised, of love; and so on. To make a difficult life bearable, hope springs eternal; and we have a way of thinking, inherited from early childhood, that helps us to believe in magic. Each believes against all logic that he can do the impossible, and that he will be *the* lucky one—ask any gambler, raffle purchaser, numbers player or a man with a hot tip on the third race at Aqueduct. The fact that once in a great, rare while he *does* do the impossible or *does* find himself lucky fuels the fires of belief. I believe this irrational response to a rational need is an important ingredient in the personality of every explorer, from Leif Erikson to Neil Armstrong.

Trying to isolate the single most important ingredient of an explorer's personality I am reminded of Henry James's confession to his mother that he possessed "a ferocious ambition." Explorers as well as novelists are ambitious men. They assign (don't we all?) noble reasons to their actions—for God, country, honor, mankind, and, since the eighteenth century, science.

On the basis of my personal observations and highly unscientific hunches, it seems to me that all explorers, like other human beings, respond to that familiar basic psychological spur, a desire-need for the opposite of what they feel. It is a lively energy source that catches, combines with, and utilizes the current events of their time, place, and history.

Oh, we are wise and know the difference between reasons assigned and real! The other face of the noble-goal coin was often low and vile, but not always. On the reverse of the "for country" coin was gold and silver badly needed for the royal coffers; in the name of God and Church, men were killed and enslaved but sometimes protected. Opening a great new land usually meant killing the rightful, at first peaceful, inhabitants in order to do so. Land for men without land, furs for men who wore none, tobacco for nonsmokers who saw the commercial possibilities. What a tangled, coarsely woven tapestry it is that depicts the exploration of our continent—beautiful and ugly, the color often rude, but the scale grand. The loveliness of unspoiled nature everywhere; for unlike civilized man, so-called primitive man respected and did not despoil his habitat.

The *Great Explorers Series* is a kind of mirror in which to find and see ourselves. We look for examples to follow, and for likenesses and opposites too, to confirm and shore up our dwindling beliefs. In an increasingly depersonalized world we need reminders of the existence of personal worth. In the terrifying and wonderful struggle between man and hostile nature we can recharge our ego batteries. To live, albeit vicariously, with brave men, to participate in astonishing deeds, to test oneself even if only in imagination—how useful and pleasant an occupation!

The Moving Frontier is volume five of the *Great Explorers Series.* In it, Louis B. Wright and Elaine W. Fowler present the matching twin to *West and by North,* its distinguished predecessor. That book told of the discovery of North America by sea; *The Moving Frontier* tells of the exploration by land of our continent in the way traditional to the series, "through the eyes of its discoverers." It is the last of the planned volumes in this series which was conceived more than a decade ago. What changes have been seen since then! In the interval there have been landings on the moon and satellites transmitting instant color television from China. Our population has exploded and we are in real danger of destroying the natural world. Archaeology has multiplied man's age on earth, giving evolutionary theories, at last, sufficient time to evolve, and man is no longer the only toolmaking animal: chimps are, too. Our ancient ancestors have been shown to be sophisticated observers of the phases of the moon and seasons (according to Alexander Marshak's fascinating work). The latter would have been no surprise to Stefansson, who lived with Stone Age Eskimos and knew them to be far from the simple "savage" that it pleases some of us to imagine.

As general editor of this series I found pleasure in my work, and I have been educated by my editors. Warm thanks go to all the contributors, and to Nancy Gross at the Delacorte Press for her patience and understanding. And so, farewell.

—Evelyn Stefansson Nef

A Note on Sources

WHEREVER possible we have tried to use the earliest readable narrative of the particular exploration discussed in this story of the discovery of the interior of North America. So voluminous is the literature that we have had to omit many accounts of genuine interest, but we have included, we hope, enough of the most important narratives to give a comprehensive picture of North American exploration from the beginning until the whole continent was known and mapped.

The most comprehensive general treatment of westward movement, which includes early exploring expeditions, is Ray Allen Billington's *Westward Expansion: A History of the American Frontier* (New York, 1949). Billington also provides an extensive bibliography of the subject which the reader will find useful. In addition, the volumes in the series *Original Narratives of Early American History* (New York, 1906–1916), under the general editorship of J. Franklin Jameson with specific editors for the separate volumes, provide well-chosen excerpts from the most important explorations.

We have given the specific sources from which excerpts are taken in the annotations to the chapters. Some additional references may be helpful. John B. Brebner, *The Explorers of North America, 1492–1806* (New York, 1933) is concise and accurate. John A. Caruso, *The Southern Frontier* (Indianapolis, 1963) gives a detailed account of de Soto's wanderings. The Spanish expeditions in the West are treated in detail in various works by Herbert E. Bolton, particularly *Coronado, Knight of Pueblos and Plains* (Albuquerque, 1949). A classic work on the French explorers is Francis Parkman, *Pioneers of France in the New World* (Boston,

1865). Also useful is Clarence Vandiveer, *The Fur-Trade and Early Western Exploration* (Cleveland, 1929).

Early English efforts to cross the mountain barrier from the East are described in Clarence W. Alvord and Lee Bidgood, *The First Explorations of the Trans-Allegheny Region by the Virginians, 1650–1674* (Cleveland, 1912). Much information about the penetration of the Southeast will be found in Verner W. Crane, *The Southern Frontier, 1670–1732* (Durham, N.C., 1928). A discussion of land speculation in the West as a motive for exploration will be found in Thomas P. Abernethy, *Western Lands and the American Revolution* (New York, 1937). Information about exploration of western Pennsylvania and adjacent regions is available in Solon J. Buck and Elizabeth H. Buck, *The Planting of Civilization in Western Pennsylvania* (Pittsburgh, 1939). A useful work on western expeditions is E. W. Gilbert, *The Exploration of Western America, 1800–1850, an Historical Geography* (Cambridge, 1933).

Many editions of the Lewis and Clark journals are available. The most complete is that edited by Reuben G. Thwaites, *Original Journals of the Lewis and Clark Expedition, 1804–1806* (8 vols., New York, 1904–1905). We have taken our excerpts from the earliest printed edition, brought together by Nicholas Biddle and completed by Paul Allen, *History of the Expedition Under the Command of Captains Lewis and Clark . . .* (2 vols., Philadelphia, 1814). Thwaites has also edited a vast collection of western travel narratives, *Early Western Travels, 1748–1846* (32 vols., Cleveland, 1904–1907). Much information about western exploration by the mountain men will be found in a classic work by Hiram M. Chittenden, *The American Fur Trade of the Far West* (3 vols., New York, 1902). A contemporary account of early western trade routes is Josiah Gregg, *Commerce of the Prairies, or The Journal of a Santa Fe Trader . . .* (2 vols., New York, 1844).

A succinct account of Arctic exploration, including a chapter on Bering, is given by Jeannette Mirsky in *To the Arctic!* (New York, 1948). See also *Here Is Alaska* (New York, 1943) and *Within the Circle, Portrait of the Arctic* (New York, 1945) both by Evelyn Stefansson.

Note to the Reader

THROUGHOUT these narratives we have modernized spelling and punctuation to make the texts more comprehensible, but we have not altered proper names, either of places or individuals. Eccentric spelling may indicate original pronunciations. We have not altered any obsolete words. Instead, we have added a gloss in brackets where the meaning may not be clear. Similarly, we have tried, where possible, to indicate modern place names in brackets. A few place names have defied research and must be left unidentified.

Where we have abbreviated texts quoted, we have indicated elisions by three dots. We have tried to make as accurate as possible the versions of the original texts reprinted here.

—L. B. W.
E. W. F.

March 6, 1971

THE
MOVING
FRONTIER

1

Introduction: From Barrier
To Land of Opportunity

THE discovery of America was an accident in the search for a route to the Spice Islands, China, India, and the riches of the whole fabulous East that had long excited European imaginations. For many years the effort to find a passage through the troublesome land barrier occupied the efforts of explorers, who regarded the New World as a frustrating annoyance. Columbus himself believed that he had reached the outskirts of Cathay, outlying islands off Japan, or some other hitherto unknown portion of Asia. Although the search for a sea route through the barrier continued for decades, the discovery of gold and other valuable commodities in America changed European attitudes toward the New World. If it was a handicap to Far Eastern commerce, at least it was worthwhile in itself.

Columbus had brought back some gold and pearls, which foretold further wealth to be found in the mysterious land. The penetration of Mexico by Hernán Cortés in 1519 and the seizure of the Aztecs' vast treasure acted like a virus to inflame the gold fever of the Spaniards. In the meantime gold and many pearls had been found along the coast of the Spanish Main, in what is now Panama, and elsewhere. Thirteen years after Cortés entered Mexico, Francisco Pizarro captured Atahualpa, leader of the Incas in Peru, and gained an immense treasure of gold and silver, the greatest yet found. News of all this wealth in America ran through Europe with incredible rapidity—as news of gold strikes always travels with mysterious speed—and soon Spaniards, Frenchmen, Germans, and any adventurer who could contrive, legally or illegally, to get to the New World was dreaming of treasure to be found equal to that of Mexico and Peru. The search for gold and silver prompted the first interior exploration of America.

The early explorers, knowing little or nothing about the Indian cultures in the New World, reasoned that treasure found in Mexico and Central and South America might be duplicated in North America. Who knew what the unknown reaches of the land, stretching no man knew how far, might offer? Legends, tales and rumors were bandied about in the new Spanish settlements to the south and in every village and town of Spain. No dusty farm in Estremadura was too remote for its denizens to have heard of the deeds of the most sensational of the adventurers from their region, the Pizarro brothers. Daring Spaniards could think of nothing more glorious than to search for treasure in the New World. And with a curious religiosity, probably induced by long wars against the infidel Moors, they equated their search with the will of God and believed that they could carry salvation to the heathen, even at the points of their swords.[1] Even in North America, many decades later, missionary efforts would have a bearing on exploration. Our ancestors saw no conflict between gain and goodness, religion and profit.

Although the first Spanish adventurers sought quick wealth and had no firm notions of an imperial domain in America, they soon saw the value of permanent settlement. Here was wealth in minerals and other commodities to be exploited, and they quickly established colonies. From New Spain (Mexico) adventurers went out to probe the land to the north. Earlier, of course, explorers had come from the Spanish settlements in the Caribbean, but the most enduring efforts to investigate North America came from Mexico. At first the explorers were chiefly interested in discovering treasure—quick wealth—but the gold seekers were followed by missionaries and permanent settlers. For example, in both New Mexico and California the missions established by the friars did much to win and hold those regions as principalities for the Spanish empire.

When the early Spanish explorers of North America discovered that they were unlikely to find hoards of treasure such as Cortés

[1] *For further explanation of the mixed motives of the Spanish and other adventurers, see Louis B. Wright,* Gold, Glory, and the Gospel (*New York, 1970*).

had taken from Montezuma, their interest flagged. But it never completely died. The rulers of Spain were determined to cling to every bit of territory they discovered, and to that end the Viceroy of New Spain had orders to encourage settlements to the north and to exclude foreign interlopers. Spain was conscious of its imperial destiny, and its explorers were instructed to remember that they were serving both God and king. They had long since forgotten that the New World was merely a nuisance standing in the way of ships bound for the Far East. The mines of New Mexico and the cattle of California were justification for the labors of many intrepid adventurers who had opened those lands to Spanish settlement.

What Spain had accomplished in the New World, other countries might hope to emulate, even at the expense of antagonizing the greatest land power in Europe. The French were particularly jealous of the Spanish monopoly of the New World and were determined to ignore it and seize some portion of America for themselves. Long before English seamen began to prey on Spanish ships, French corsairs from Saint Malo and other ports were raiding settlements on the Spanish Main and seizing treasure ships. For a time, they established themselves in competition with the Portuguese on the coast of Brazil. As early as 1535 Jacques Cartier of Saint Malo penetrated the interior of North America by sailing up the St. Lawrence River as far as the site of Montreal. The information that he gained from the Indians whetted the appetites of Frenchmen for further exploration of the region. Although the thought of gold had not disappeared from the explorers' minds —all of them had been enjoined to search for mines and signs of precious minerals—a new source of wealth was becoming apparent. The Indians were hunters and trappers, and they had quantities of furs that could be had for trifling amounts of European trade goods. Furs were needed to keep Europeans warm in their miserably heated houses and to dress aristocrats in fashionable garments. Hitherto most furs had come at a high price from the Baltic region and from Russian sources. Here was an impelling motive for trade with the Indians, and the French made the most of it.

For two and a half centuries after Cartier's voyage up the St. Lawrence River, the French carried on a profitable trade with Indians in the Northwest. Their explorers found the first routes to the westernmost points on the Great Lakes and beyond. They also followed the tributaries of the Ohio and Mississippi river systems and sought to establish themselves in the upper Mississippi valley. French traders often married Indian squaws, learned Indian languages and Indian ways, and became commercial missionaries of France throughout the Northwest. In the course of time the French and the English fought bitter wars over the Indian trade and over territories both claimed. Not until the last third of the eighteenth century did the English finally win supremacy over their formidable French political and commercial rivals in North America.

French policy did not encourage rapid settlement of farmers and permanent residents in New France. The Indian fur trade, with the enormous wealth that it brought to a few, was the underlying concern of French officialdom. The principal settlements such as Montreal and Quebec were considered outposts of trade and French military power rather than municipalities that would grow and flourish in their own right. Only late in the history of New France was there much concern for the *habitants* of the country. This was the chief weakness of French colonial policy; in the end it gave the edge to the English in the conflict for possession of Canada.

Nevertheless, the French were unrivaled in their capacity to carry on trade with the Indians, and long after France had ceased to be a power in North America, the skill of their woodsmen and traders endured. French guides—woodsmen ignorant of letters but learned in the ways of the wilderness—helped Englishmen and Americans to explore the great reaches of the continent.

If the English were not slow to realize the importance of the New World, they were dilatory in their efforts to claim a portion of North America. To be sure, John Hawkins, Francis Drake, and others had raided the Spanish settlements, captured treasure ships and sailed along the southern coast of North America, but that is about all they did. The most consistent propagandists for empire were Richard Hakluyt, the preacher-compiler of voyages; Sir Humphrey Gilbert, who dreamed of colonies in Newfoundland and on the mainland; and his half-brother, Sir Walter Raleigh. Both Gilbert and Raleigh tried to establish colonies but failed. They lacked sufficient experience, sufficient capital and clear government support. Furthermore, the time was not ripe for English expansion into the New World, for by the later years of Queen Elizabeth's reign England was at war with Spain. The Armada crisis of 1588 explains in part the failure to support or rescue Raleigh's "Lost Colony" on Roanoke Island.

In the sixteenth century whatever knowledge the English had of North America came principally from French and Spanish sources and from cursory examinations of the coast by Hawkins, Drake, and Raleigh's captains. Not until 1607 did the English establish a permanent settlement in North America, at Jamestown. In the meantime King James I had made peace with the Spaniards. Although Spain did not openly concede that the English—or anyone else—had any right to settle in North America, it was generally understood that land "not occupied by any Christian prince" was available for settlement. Possession by heathen did not count. They could be annihilated or baptized, and their land could be taken.

Although the English, like all those who had preceded them, hoped at first to find gold, they soon realized that the precious metal was elusive. Here and there they found Indians wearing copper ornaments, which led them to think they might discover gold mines too. But at last they had to settle for other forms of treasure. Captain John Smith was one of the earliest explorers to suggest that fish and furs were valuable commodities that would enrich his fellow countrymen. He was also one of the first to explore the interior of the region claimed by the English, as he pushed up the rivers of the Chesapeake Bay region and saw the possibilities in the territory now embraced by Virginia, Maryland, and Delaware.

The first settlers at Jamestown could find no other lading for their returning ships but sassafras, a shrub whose roots and bark European doctors used to make an infusion believed to cure syphilis and other ailments. But they soon discovered another commodity that ultimately would bring the English more wealth than the Spanish had found in Mexico and Peru. This was a weed that the Indians dried and smoked—tobacco. The Virginia species of tobacco was bitter and astringent, but in 1614 John Rolfe (remembered now as the husband of Pocahontas) obtained some seeds of a sweeter variety from the West Indies or South America. Since this new variety could be grown in Virginia, the prosperity of the region was assured.

Since tobacco quickly exhausts the soil, before many years Virginians were eager for fresh land. The search for better farming land led to exploration of the interior. Furthermore, the Virginians had learned the value of furs obtained from the Indians, and before the end of the seventeenth century enterprising traders sent their pack trains into the back country, at least to the foothills of the Alleghenies. By the early eighteenth century these traders had crossed the mountain barrier. One of the early promoters of this trade was the first William Byrd, who, like many of these men, was secretive because he did not want others to discover the sources of his furs. Hence we have little definite information about these early explorations.

After the English had settled in New England and the Carolinas, traffic with the Indians became increasingly important. As traders from the little colony at Plymouth went into the back country to barter with the Indians, they quickly learned that furs were more profitable than farming. Settlers in the Connecticut Valley frequently combined farming, fur trading, and exploration of the interior. From Charleston, South Carolina, dealers in deerskins penetrated the uplands and followed what were called "Indian trading paths" to the mountains and the land of the Cherokees. What they learned about the interior led to later settlements in the upcountry.

Some of the first cowboys in America were Scots who settled in what is now upper South Carolina, where wild pea vines made rich pasture for cattle. Their settlement is remembered in the name of a town, Cowpens, where a famous battle was fought during the Revolutionary War. Before the middle of the eighteenth century, English traders and explorers in the hinterland were making contact with the French in the Ohio valley. Soon the battle for possession of the region was joined. George Washington's first important assignment was to take a message from Governor Dinwiddie of Virginia to the French in the Ohio valley ordering them to get out. They did not heed him. But the journal of Washington's exploratory journey was published in Alexandria in 1754 as propaganda for English seizure of the land from the French.

The Dutch, with a keenly developed sense of the profits from trade, were not willing to be frozen out of North America by any rivals. Their long subjection to Spain, followed by their wars for liberation, prevented any expansion overseas until the seventeenth century, but they quickly made up for lost time after their truce with Spain. In the Far East the Dutch East India Company became a rival of the British East India company. In North America the Dutch West India Company sought to exploit the fur trade. They employed an English captain, Henry Hudson, who in 1609 found the river that bears his name. In his ship the *Half Moon* Hudson sailed up the great river to a point just below the site of Albany. This voyage opened up a great land to the Dutch, who in the next half century developed a prosperous colony centered at New Amsterdam, later called New York. Dutch traders explored the upper tributaries of the Hudson and the New York lake system. They also explored the Delaware River and its tributaries, and took over the Swedish colony that had been established in the region of modern Wilmington, Delaware.

The seventeenth century was an era of exploration and settlement of the land east of the Mississippi, with some Spanish and French penetration beyond. By the eighteenth century the Spaniards held Florida, lower Alabama, and the mouth of the Mississippi, and had outposts in New Mexico and California. The French had the upper Mississippi and the Great Lakes region. The English were competitors for the Ohio valley. All of these sections had been visited by white men, and some settlements had been established.

Even before 1763, when the Peace of Paris made England the ruler of what had been New France, land hunger and land speculation reached fever pitch in the English colonies along the Atlantic seaboard. Everybody was seeking to acquire western lands. Companies were organized to buy up huge tracts through treaties with the Indians or through deals with colonial governments that claimed western territories. As early as 1747 Virginia land speculators organized the Ohio Company to be followed in the next half century by many other companies dealing in land beyond the Alleghenies. The charters of some colonies granted them land from their Atlantic borders westward to "the Great South Sea"—the Pacific Ocean. It is true that when the charters were granted, the English government had not the faintest notion how far away the South Sea lay. It was a general belief at the time that the American continent was a narrow strip of land.

In spite of the danger from the Indians and the French, daring pioneers swarmed into the hinterland and filtered into valleys of the Alleghenies. After the elimination of the French the migration westward swelled until the English became alarmed lest their rich fur trade with the Indians might be disturbed. To protect the Indian hunting grounds the British government, on October 7, 1763, issued a royal proclamation forbidding settlers to establish themselves beyond a line roughly following the crest of the Alleghenies. Later, it was implied, when the Indian problem could be solved—precisely how, no one knew—settlers might be allowed beyond the line. But for the time being migration westward was legally blocked. The Proclamation of 1763 made westward migration illegal but it did not stop it. Squatters continued to move over the mountains and build their cabins in the clearings. The Proclamation of 1763 soon became a dead letter as Colonial governments winked at its violation. The governor of Virginia even declared that he had never heard of it. Pressure to move west continued to build up; though Indian wars, notably Pontiac's Conspiracy, might wipe out frontier settlements, emigrants who believed they could outwit the red men were not deterred even by burning cabins and tomahawked women and children.

Before the Revolution men of property in the East, especially in Virginia, Maryland and Pennsylvania, were looking westward and staking out claims for themselves in the Indian country of western Pennsylvania, Ohio, Tennessee and Kentucky. George Washington, for example, who as a young explorer and surveyor on the frontier had learned about the fertile land to the West, was a speculator in this real estate.

Guides and surveyors hired by land speculators carried out much of the exploration of the western country. For instance, Richard Henderson of North Carolina, who dreamed of creating a great barony for himself in the West, hired Daniel Boone, a noted hunter, to search out promising tracts in Kentucky and report to him. In the spring of 1769 Boone and a colleague named John Finley discovered an easy route over the mountains via the Cumberland Gap and in the next two years explored the bluegrass country of Kentucky. By 1776 settlers were swarming through the Cumberland Gap and the peopling of the first "Wild West" was under way.

After the Revolution land hunger and the pressure for western expansion accelerated the search for fresh lands and new routes to the portion of the continent claimed by the United States. The Lewis and Clark expedition which mapped a route up the Missouri River, over the Rockies, and down the Columbia River to the Pacific, was planned during Jefferson's administration, when these areas were not yet part of the Union. But by the time the expedition was on its way the United States had bought the Louisiana Territory from France.

The need for land for settlement in the West explains nineteenth-century exploration. By the middle years of the century immigrants from most of the countries of western Europe were pouring into the United States, and by the end of the century the nations of eastern Europe, especially Russia, Poland and the Austro-Hungarian Empire, were sending their millions. To Europeans oppressed by poverty or misrule, America, which had once been regarded as a barrier to commerce and progress, became a land of glittering opportunity. The explorers who discovered roads and trails and opened the way to the vast heart of America were benefactors of mankind.

The revolution in transportation resulting from the building of railroads, especially the transcontinental lines, made exploration of routes over the plains and mountains necessary. The California Gold Rush of 1849 and the following decade merely accelerated curiosity about the West and made further exploration essential.

Much of this western exploration was informal and unofficial and left no written record. Trappers, hunters, and adventurers learned about trails and passed on their information by word of mouth. Official missions sent out by the government utilized these guides and set down their information in formal reports complete with maps and graphs. Some other useful accounts were written by men whose sole purpose in exploring the West was adventure.

The literature of the exploration of North America is enormous. Much of it is informative, entertaining, and exciting, and editors become bewildered trying to make a choice of material that illustrates the gradual penetration and mapping of the huge land that stretches from the Atlantic to the Pacific. In the present volume we have tried to select the earliest documents that illustrate westward expansion and knowledge about the new country. Many fascinating accounts exist that space will not permit us even to mention. But the documents cited here will at least provide the reader with some conception of the struggle to conquer a great land and to seek out its most distant reaches, even to the newest of its acquisitions in Alaska.

Spanish Gold Seekers
in the Southeast

THE discovery of vast hoards of gold and silver by Hernán
Cortés in Mexico and Francisco Pizarro in Peru whetted the
appetites of other would-be *conquistadores* to discover realms of
gold for themselves in the vast unclaimed lands of the New World.
Even before these two conquerors had shown the way to untold
wealth, pioneering Spaniards had made some efforts to discover
gold in North America. The first was Juan Ponce de León, who
conquered Puerto Rico and was named governor of that island in
1509. Indians told him stories of a fabulous island called Bimini,
where gold, delicious fruits, and all that man might desire could
be found in abundance. Furthermore, the island had a fountain
which had the virtue of restoring youth to any old man who drank
from it or bathed in it.

On February 23, 1512, Ponce de León received from King Ferdinand of Spain a commission to find and colonize this island, over
which he would rule as governor. In the spring of 1513 he set out
on a voyage of discovery which did not result in finding Bimini
and the Fountain of Youth but did bring him to the coast of a land
that he called La Florida after the Spanish name for the Easter
Feast, Pascua Florida, for it was on Easter, April 2, 1513, that he
sighted the coast.

The precise spot where Ponce de León made his first landfall is
a matter of controversy. It may have been somewhere in the
southern part of the peninsula, near Indian River. At any rate, he
proceeded northward until he reached the region around the
mouth of the Saint Johns River. Finding the coast unpropitious,

he turned south and sailed around the tip of Florida to present-day Charlotte Harbor, on the west coast (south of Tampa Bay). He then returned to Puerto Rico while one of his captains continued the search. Not until 1521 did Ponce de León make a determined effort to colonize Bimini or Florida. In that year he set out with 200 men in two ships and landed on the west coast, either at Charlotte Harbor or Tampa Bay. But Indians attacked the landing party in force and Ponce de León received an arrow wound. Forced to withdraw, he sailed away and landed in Cuba, where he died. Thus ended the first effort to explore and colonize the southeastern portion of what was to become the United States.

In the meantime two other Spaniards had made tentative efforts to expore the coastline of this region. In 1519 Alonso Alvárez de Pineda had sailed along the west coast of Florida and the coasts of Mississippi, Louisiana, and Texas, trading with the Indians and picking up false information about great hoards of gold in the interior. In 1520 Lucas Vásquez de Ayllón sailed along the Atlantic coast as far north as the Cape Fear River in North Carolina. He found no gold but brought back 150 Indian slaves to work in the mines and fields of the Caribbean islands.

When Ponce de León died, Ayllón hurried to Spain to obtain from King Ferdinand a commission to colonize and govern Florida or some other area of the mainland. An Indian named Chicora, whom he took along, reported immense quantities of gold and gems to be had in what is now the Carolinas. Chicora also told of men there with tails so long and rigid that they had to dig holes for their tails before they could sit at ease. With some 500 men Ayllón returned in 1526 to a spot perhaps on the Pee Dee River in eastern South Carolina. But disease, starvation, and Indian hostility forced the evacuation of the colony after Ayllón himself died. Only about 150 survivors got back to Hispaniola.

The next Spaniard to search for another Mexico in North America was Pánfilo de Narváez, a man born to misfortune. He had helped to conquer Cuba but had reaped few of the rewards. When Cortés took control of Mexico in his own name instead of acting on behalf of his superior, Diego de Velásquez, governor of Cuba, Narváez had gone to Mexico to arrest Cortés, but his army deserted him and joined Cortés. In fighting with Cortés' men, Narváez lost an eye and was taken prisoner. Undaunted by his bad luck, he later petitioned Charles V for a grant of land and received the right to conquer and colonize a vague region between Mexico and Florida.

On June 17, 1527, Narváez put out from Sanlúcar de Barrameda, Spain, with 600 colonists and fighting men in five ships. The ill star under which he was born continued to influence his fortunes, for he lost two ships and 60 men in a hurricane off Cuba and more men by desertion at Hispaniola. He finally reached Tampa Bay in April 1528 with 300 followers. Of these only four were to survive to reach civilization again. They were Álvar Núñez Cabeza de Vaca, Andrés Dorantes de Carrança, Alonzo del Castillo Maldonado, and a black slave of Dorantes', one Estéban.

Disaster was the fate of Narváez from the beginning of the expedition. Plagued by illness, lack of food, Indian attacks, and disaffection within his own ranks, he floundered in the swamps of the Gulf Coast without finding gold or other valuables. Tempted by stories of gold at a town in the interior called Apalachee, he pushed north to a point near present Tallahassee. But his dreams of finding another Tenochtitlán such as greeted Cortés when he looked down from the heights over Mexico City, were dashed when Apalachee turned out to be a collection of huts in a heavily forested region. Some much-needed corn and a few deerskins were the only booty worth taking.

Resting for 25 days in the deserted Indian huts, the Spaniards made inquiries about the resources of the country and learned from captured Indians that a town called Aute, some nine days' journey toward the coast, might at least supply corn and beans. Giving up hope of gold, they set out in search of food, but were harassed along the way by Indian bowmen whose accuracy appalled the miserable explorers, whose armor was insufficient to protect them.

Aute, not far from St. Marks on Apalachee Bay, proved just another collection of huts, but its fields supplied corn, beans, and pumpkins now mature enough to eat, for it was the beginning of August 1528.

Narváez had given up the dream of finding a golden city on the mainland of Florida. Even the hope of survival depended upon getting the desperate remnant of his expedition back to Mexico. The only feasible way appeared to be by sea, but he had sent away the ships that brought him and had neither tools nor equipment to build and fit out vessels strong enough to transport nearly 250 men. Nevertheless, the Spaniards in desperation set to work to build boats with such tools as they could improvise. Swords had to serve as axes. From spurs and stirrups they fashioned nails. Vines could be used for cordage. The green timber had to be caulked with the bark and fiber of palmetto trees, whose fronds supplied crude deck covers against the burning tropical sun. For sails the men used their shirts and other bits of clothing. Water casks for a sea voyage were essential, for without water the men would die of thirst. To make containers for water they killed their remaining horses and used the hides for waterskins. Although green horsehides could be used for water vats for a time, they soon rotted and spilled the stinking water, which had long since become unpalatable.

Five boats, rickety and crazy, were at last launched, and the men set out across the Gulf of Mexico for an uncertain destination; not one crew member was skilled in navigation. Miraculously they reached Pensacola Bay, where they found food, but on October 27, 1528, Indians made a furious onslaught and wounded many of them. Putting out from Pensacola, they crossed the mouth of the Mississippi River without actually seeing it. But they dipped fresh water from the sea and realized from the current that a great river was flowing into the Gulf.

After this point the five boats were scattered and the expedition disintegrated. Narváez was drowned west of the Mississippi delta, and some of his men were marooned on land. Others drifted out to sea and were never heard of again. The boat of Cabeza de Vaca grounded on an island off the Texas shore west of Galveston, which the survivors named the Island of Misfortune. After friendly Indians had supplied them with food, they tried to launch their boat again. Stripping, they placed their clothes on board as they tried to push their craft through the surf, but the boat capsized, drowning several men. The remainder scrambled ashore stark naked in the early November cold. Once more the friendly but astonished Indians rescued them and built fires to warm the unclothed strangers.

A little later, Cabeza de Vaca learned that the boat occupied by Castillo Maldonado and Dorantes had also beached nearby, and their crew joined forces with Cabeza de Vaca's men but had no clothes for them. The Spaniards, scattered among various Indian tribes, all passed a miserable winter of semi-starvation.

One group of five in an isolated hut on the coast engaged in cannibalism but none of the five lived to tell the tale. By spring, only
15 men survived of the 80 who had landed on the Texas coast, and
they then found themselves slaves of the Indians who had at first
befriended them.

Cabeza de Vaca, however, was an ingenious man and managed
to gain a reputation as a healer. He capitalized on the arts of the
medicine man so successfully that soon Indians were coming from
far and near to be treated—and were willing to pay the doctor's
bills with deerskins and other objects that could be bartered for
food. After five years Cabeza de Vaca learned that Castillo, Dorantes, and Estéban were still alive, slaves of another nearby tribe.
The four men met and planned an escape that ultimately took
them across the southern border of Texas, into the present Mexican
states of Chihuahua and Sonora, and finally to Spanish settlements
on the Gulf of California in Sinaloa. This was the spring of 1536,
eight years after they had first landed on the west coast of Florida.
The courage and ingenuity of these four men constitute an epic
in the history of human survival. The arts of the medicine man, as
developed by Cabeza de Vaca and amplified by his companions,
especially the black man, Estéban, doubtless explain their ability
to make their way unmolested through warlike Indian tribes.
When they were first sighted by Spaniards in Sinaloa they were
naked, and the white men were sunburned nearly as black as
Estéban. As soon as they were identified and had a chance to tell
of their adventures, they were fêted and treated like the heroes
they were. Their tale helped to inspire other explorers to push into
the interior of the North American continent.

In 1537 Cabeza de Vaca returned to Spain and applied for a
commission as commander of an expedition to conquer Florida.
One would have thought that the memory of the mud, mosquitoes,
palmetto thickets, and warlike Indians would have cured him of
any desire to go back, but, like scores of other adventurers in this
age, Cabeza de Vaca continued to dream of rich cities to be taken
—if only they could be found. By the time Cabeza de Vaca petitioned the Emperor Charles V, that potentate had already granted
a patent for Florida to Hernando de Soto, and Cabeza de Vaca had
to content himself with an appointment as governor and captain-
general of Paraguay.

A far more competent leader than Narváez, Hernando de Soto

had been with Francisco Pizarro at the capture of the Inca Atahualpa in Peru. Rich with spoils from Peru, de Soto returned to
Spain and lived at court like a very great grandee; he was said to
have lent money to the Emperor himself. So it was small wonder
that Charles V named him governor of Cuba and Florida and
promised him a marquisate out of the territory he expected to
conquer. Remembering Peru, de Soto believed that he would find
another Cuzco somewhere in the wilds of North America.

Since the bounds of Florida, as the term was understood at that
time, extended from Mexico to Newfoundland and to an inde-
terminate distance in the west, perhaps including present-day
Texas and Oklahoma, the Viceroy of Mexico, Antonio de Mendoza, worried lest de Soto's grant might encroach on territory he
himself hoped to claim north of the Mexican border. Stories were
already circulating in Mexico about the fabled Seven Cities of
Cíbola, and the adventures of Cabeza de Vaca and his three companions added to the fever for further discovery. But while Mendoza and his cohorts were planning explorations from the west,
de Soto organized an expedition to probe the mainland from the
east.

De Soto's reputation was sufficiently high to induce hundreds
of Spaniards and Portuguese to volunteer for his expedition. On
April 6, 1538, he sailed from Sanlúcar de Barrameda with ten
ships carrying more than 600 fighting men and colonists, including
the wives of several officers, de Soto's wife among them. The flo-
tilla reached Santiago de Cuba in May, and de Soto spent the next
year preparing equipment and seeking additional recruits. At last,
on May 18, 1539, the expedition sailed from Havana and on May
25 landed at Tampa Bay. The force included 213 horses, which
terrified the Indians, who had never seen such beasts. One patrol
of horsemen, sent out to seize Indians who might be used as
guides, brought back a Spaniard, named Juan Ortiz, who had been
with Narváez and had been captured and enslaved by the Indians.
Now naked and sunburned and knowing several Indian languages,
he could pass for an Indian himself. Ortiz proved invaluable as an
interpreter in the remaining years before he died.

De Soto's exploration covered an enormous area and for many
years remained the most extensive reconnaissance by white men in
North America. Pushing northward across Florida, de Soto followed the track of Narváez to Apalachee (Tallahassee), then

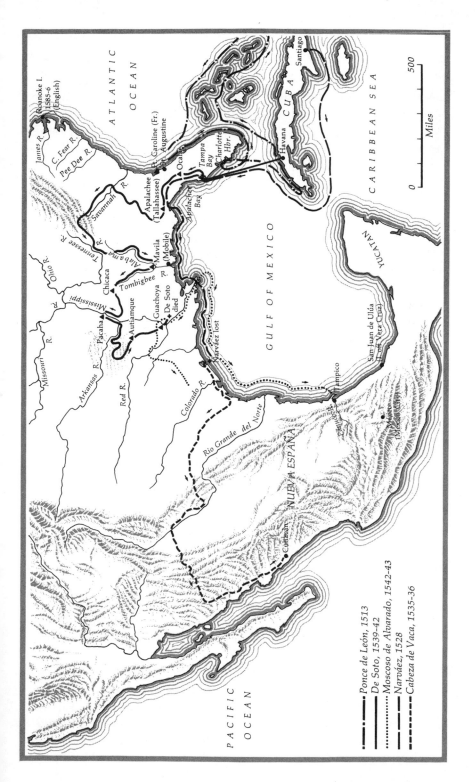

Early Spanish Explorations of North America

PACIFIC
OCEAN

ATLANTIC
OCEAN

CARIBBEAN SEA

GULF OF MEXICO

500

Miles

0

Roanoke I.
1585–6
(English)

James R.
C. Fear R.
Pee Dee R.
Savannah R.
Caroline (Fr.)
St. Augustine
Ocali
Apalachee
(Tallahassee)
Apalachee Bay
Tampa
Bay
Charlotte Hbr.

Havana

CUBA

Santiago

YUCATAN

Tennessee R.
Ohio R.
Missouri R.
Arkansas R.
Mississippi R.
Red R.
Colorado R.
Alabama R.
Tombigbee R.

Chicaca
Pacaha
Autiamque
Guachoya
De Soto
died
Mavila
(Mobile)

Narváez lost

Rio Grande del Norte

Tampico
San Juan de Ulúa
(I. of Vera Cruz)
Pánuco
México
(Mexico City)

NUEVA ESPAÑA

Culiacán

—·—·— Ponce de León, 1513
———— De Soto, 1539–42
·········· Moscoso de Alvarado, 1542–43
— — — Narváez, 1528
– – – – Cabeza de Vaca, 1535–36

moved on through the territory that is now Georgia into South and North Carolina to Tennessee. From there he turned south through Alabama to the vicinity of Mobile. Leaving this region, he again proceeded north through the future state of Mississippi to a point south of what is now Memphis, Tennessee, where he crossed the Mississippi River into Arkansas. After wandering over a large portion of Arkansas and reaching a point west of Fort Smith near the Oklahoma border, he turned back and followed the Arkansas and Ouachita rivers through Arkansas, eventually to reach a point on the Mississippi in upper Louisiana. There de Soto died. But the remnant of his force, after trying to reach Mexico by making a journey westward into Texas, returned to the Mississippi and floated down to the Gulf, and thence around the coast to the mouth of the Pánuco River in Mexico. Such was the epical march of this would-be conquistador and his men, driven by the dream of rich cities filled with gold. The territory through which they wandered for three years comprised some 350,000 square miles.

De Soto, a determined and forceful leader, managed to inspire his men to endure incredible hardships. Ruthless and cruel, he slaughtered Indians mercilessly when it suited his purposes, and he commandeered countless slaves to carry his army's baggage. Women slaves were taken along as concubines for his men; some of the handsome Indian women taken in Alabama became the permanent consorts of survivors of the expedition and later brought up families in Mexico. De Soto himself was supplied with a harem of Indian"wives."

To serve as a part of the commissary, de Soto took along a herd of swine. For the first year or more he refused to let them be killed for he wanted them to breed. But as the swine multiplied, the soldiers were eventually allowed to feed on pork. In the meantime they had developed a taste for dogs, which the Indians sometimes provided.

But living off the land proved difficult. Whenever they could, de Soto's men plundered Indian settlements for corn, beans, pumpkins, persimmons and any other foods they could find. Occasionally Indians supplied them with venison, wild turkeys and fish, but since news of the Spaniards' cruelty usually preceded them, they could not count on friendly contacts and abundant supplies such as Cortés had found in Mexico. For the most part, the supplies that de Soto got came from plunder or extortion under threat. To be rid of the dreaded invaders, the Indians invariably told de Soto of riches to be found at some distant point beyond the local tribe's territory. Thus the Spaniards kept following the will-o'-the-wisp of treasure which they never found.

Account of de Soto by the "Gentleman of Elvas"

[*One of de Soto's companions on the journey across the southern portion of North America was a Portuguese aristocrat who wrote an account of the journey. He signed it simply a "gentleman of Elvas," a town due east of Lisbon near the Spanish province of Badajoz. This work, first published at Évora in 1557, was translated by Richard Hakluyt and published in London in 1609 as* Virginia Richly Valued by the Description of the Main Land of Florida, Her Next Neighbor. *A second English edition was published in 1611 as* The Worthy and Famous History of the Travels, Discovery, and Conquest of That Great Continent of Terra Florida. *In 1851 William B. Rye edited it for the Hakluyt Society. The excerpts reprinted here have been taken from Hakluyt's 1611 edition.*]

Chapter I

Captain [Hernando de] Soto was the son of a squire of Xerez [Jérez de los Caballeros] of Badajoz [a province of southwest Spain near the Portuguese border]. He went into the Spanish Indies when Peter Arias of Avila [Pedro Arias de Ávila, also known as Pedrarias, the man responsible for the execution of Balboa] was governor of the West Indies. And there he was without anything else of his own save his sword and target [shield]. And for his good qualities and valor Peter Arias made him captain of a troop of horsemen, and by his commandment he went with Fernando [Francisco] Pizarro to the conquest of Peru; where (as many persons of credit reported, which were there present), as well at the taking of Atabalipa [Atahualpa], lord of Peru, as at the assault of the city of Cuzco and in all other places where they found resistance, wheresoever he was present he passed all other captains and principal persons. For which cause, besides his part of the treasure of Atabalipa, he had a good share; whereby in time he gathered an hundred and fourscore thousand ducats together, with that which fell to his part, which he brought into Spain. Whereof the Emperor borrowed a certain part, which he repaid again with 60,000 rials of plate [Spanish *reales de plata*, or pieces of eight] in the rent of the silks of Granada, and all the rest was delivered him in the contractation house [Casa de Contratación, or House of Trade] of Seville. He took servants, to wit: a steward, a gentleman usher, pages, a gentleman of the horse, a chamberlain, lackeys, and all other officers that the house of a nobleman requireth. . . . He married with Donna Isabella de Bovadilla, daughter of Peter Arias Avila, Earl of Punno en Rostro. The Emperor made him the governor of the isle of Cuba and Adelantado, or President, of Florida, with a title of marquis of certain part of the lands that he should conquer.

Chapter II

. . . They made their rendezvous with the Adelantado [de Soto] in Sevilla. . . . The like did Núñez de Tovar and Lewis de Moscoso. . . . From Badajoz there went Peter Calderón and three kinsmen of the Adelantado. . . . And from Elvas went Andrew de Vasconcelos . . . and Alvaro Fernandez [possibly the author of this narrative]. And out of Salamanca and Jaén and Valencia and Albuquerque and from other parts of Spain many people of noble birth assembled at Seville; insomuch that in Saint Lucar [Sanlúcar de Barrameda] many men of good account which had sold their goods remained behind for want of shipping, whereas for [voyages to] other known and rich countries they are wont to want men. . . . His kinsmen Christopher de Spindola and Baltasar de Gallegos went with Soto. Baltasar de Gallegos sold houses and vineyards and rent corn and ninety ranks of olive trees in the Xarafe [olive district, Aljarafe, meaning "hilly area"] of Seville. He had the office of Alcalde Mayor, and took his wife with him. And there went also many other persons of account with the President, and had the offices following by great friendship, because they were offices desired of many. . . .

Chapter III

The Portugales departed from Elvas the 15 of January [1538] and came to Seville the 19 of the same month. . . . The Adelantado departed from Seville to Saint Lucar with all the people which were to go with him. And he commanded a muster to be made, at which the Portugales showed themselves armed in very bright armor, and the Castellans [Castilians] very gallant with silk upon silk, with many pinkings and cuts. The Governor, because these braveries [fineries] in such an action did not like him, commanded that they should muster another day, and everyone should come forth with his armor; at the which the Portugales came as at the first, armed with very good armor. The Governor placed them in order near unto the standard which the ensign-bearer carried. The Castellans for the most part did wear very bad and rusty shirts of mail, and all of them headpieces and steel caps, and very bad lances. And some of them sought to come among the Portugales. So those passed and were counted and enrolled which Soto liked and accepted of, and did accompany him into Florida; which were in all six hundred men. He had already bought seven ships, and had all necessary provision aboard them. He appointed captains, and delivered to every one his ship, and gave them in a roll [scroll] what people every one should carry with them.

Chapter IV

In the year of our Lord 1538, in the month of April, the Adelantado delivered his ships to the captains which were to go in them; and took for himself a new ship and good of sail, and gave another to Andrew de Vasconcelos, in which the Portugales went. . . . They arrived at the Antilles, in the isle of Cuba, at the port of the city of Sant Iago [Santiago de Cuba] upon Whitsunday. As soon as they came thither, a gentleman of the city sent to the seaside a very fair roan horse, and well furnished, for the Governor, and a mule for Donna Isabella; and all the horsemen and footmen that were in the town came to receive him at the seaside. The Governor was well lodged, visited, and served

of all the inhabitants of that city, and all his company had their
lodgings freely. . . .

Chapter VI

The Governor sent from S. Iago his nephew Don Carlos with
the ships, in company of Donna Isabella, to tarry for him at
Havana, which is an haven in the west part toward the head of
the island, 180 leagues from the city of Saint Iago. The Governor
and those which stayed with him bought horses and proceeded on
their journey. . . .

Chapter VII

. . . On Sunday the 18 of May, in the year of our Lord 1539,
the Adelantado or President departed from Havana in Cuba with
his fleet, which were nine vessels: five great ships, two caravels,
and two brigantines. They sailed seven days with a prosperous
wind. The 25 day of May, the day de Pasca de Spirito Santo
(which we call Whitsun Sunday), they saw the land of Florida;
and because of the shoals they came to an anchor a league from
the shore. On Friday the 30 of May they landed in Florida
[Tampa Bay area], two leagues from a town of an Indian lord
called Ucita. . . . The town was of seven or eight houses. The
lord's house stood near the shore, upon a very high mount made
by hand for strength. At another end of the town stood the
church, and on the top of it stood a fowl made of wood, with
gilded eyes. . . .

Chapter IX

. . . Thirty leagues from thence dwelt an Indian lord which
was called Paracossi, to whom Mococo and Ucita, with all the
rest of that coast, paid tribute, and [it was reported] that he per-
adventure might have notice of some good country; and that his
land was better than that of the seacoast and more fruitful and
plentiful of maize; whereof the Governor received great conten-
ment and said that he desired no more than to find victuals that
he might go into the mainland, for the land of Florida was so
large that in one place or other there could not choose but be
some rich country. . . .

Chapter X

From the port de Spirito Santo [Bay of Espíritu Santo, now Tampa Bay], where the Governor lay, he sent the Alcalde Mayor, Baltasar de Gallegos, with fifty horsemen and thirty or forty foot-men to the province of Paracossi to view the disposition of the country and inform himself of the land farther inward, and to send him word of such things as he found. Likewise he sent his ships back to the island of Cuba that they might return within a certain time with victuals. . . .

He left Captain Calderón at the port with thirty horsemen and seventy footmen, with provision for two years, and himself with all the rest marched into the mainland and came to the Para-cossi, at whose town Baltasar de Gallegos was; and from thence with all his men took the way to Cale [present-day Ocala]. . . .

Chapter XXI

Upon Wednesday, the 15 of March 1541, after the Governor had lodged eight days in a plain half a league from the place which he had wintered in—after he had set up a forge and tempered the swords which in Chicaça [approximately half-way between present-day Oxford and Greensboro, Mississippi] were burned, and made many targets, saddles, and lances—on Tuesday night at the morning watch many Indians came to assault the camp in three squadrons, every one by themselves. Those which watched gave the alarm. The Governor with great speed set his men in order in other three squadrons, and, leaving some to defend the camp, went out to encounter them. The Indians were overcome and put to flight. . . . There were some taken, by whom the Governor informed himself of the country through which he was to pass. . . .

Chapter XXII

. . . Because in the town where the Governor lodged there was small store of maize, he removed to another, half a league from Rio Grande [the Mississippi River], where they found plenty of maize. And he went to see the river, and found that near unto it was great store of timber to make barges, and good situation of ground to encamp in. Presently he removed himself thither. They made houses and pitched their camp in a plain field a crossbow shot from the river. And thither was gathered all the maize of the towns which they had lately passed. They began presently to cut and hew down timber, and to saw planks for barges. . . .

In thirty days' space, while the Governor remained there, they made four barges. . . . And, because the stream was swift, they went a quarter of a league up the river along the bank, and, crossing over, fell down with the stream and landed right over against the camp. Two stones' cast before they came to land, the horsemen went out of the barges on horseback to a sandy plot of very hard and clear ground, where all of them landed without any resistance. As soon as those that passed first were on land on the other side, the barges returned to the place where the Governor was; and within two hours after sunrising all the people were over.

The river was almost half a league broad. If a man stood still on the other side, it could not be discerned whether he were a man or no. The river was of great depth and of a strong current; the water was always muddy; there came down the river continually many trees and timber, which the force of the water and stream brought down. There was great store of fish in it of sundry sorts, and the most of it differing from the fresh-water fish of Spain. . . .

Chapter XXIV

. . . There was a fish which they call *bagres* [Mississippi catfish]: the third part of it was head, and it had on both sides the gills, and along the sides great pricks like very sharp awls; those of this kind that were in the lakes were as big as pikes; and in the river there were some of an hundred, and of an hundred and fifty, pounds weight; and many of them were taken with the hook. . . .

Chapter XXVIII

Upon Monday the 6 of March 1542 [on the return journey], the Governor departed from Autiamque [winter quarters near

the site of Camden, Arkansas] to seek Nilco [on the lower Ouachita River, Louisiana], which the Indians said was near the great
river [Mississippi], with determination to come to the sea and
procure some succor of men and horses; for he had now but three
hundred men of war and forty horses, and some of them lame,
which did nothing but help to make up the number; and for want
of iron they had gone above a year unshod; and, because they
were used to it in the plain country it did them no great harm.
John Ortiz died in Autiamque, which grieved the Governor very
much because that without an interpreter he feared to enter far
into the land, where he might be lost. . . .

Wednesday the 29 of March the Governor came to Nilco. He
lodged with all his men in the cacique's town, which stood in a
plain field, which was inhabited for the space of a quarter of a
league; and within a league and half-a-league were other great
towns wherein was great store of maize, of French beans, of
walnuts, and prunes. This was the best country that was seen
in Florida, and had most store of maize, except Coça [Coosa, on
Coosa River, Alabama] and Apalache [Tallahassee, Florida]. . . .

Within few days the Governor determined to go to Guachoya
[perhaps near Ferriday, Louisiana] to learn there whether the
sea were near or whether there were any habitation near where
he might relieve his company while the brigantines were making,
which he meant to send to the land of the Christians. As he passed
the river of Nilco [Ouachita?], there came in canoes Indians of
Guachoya up the stream. And when they saw him, supposing
that he came to seek them to do them some hurt, they returned
down the river and informed the cacique thereof; who, with all
his people, spoiling the town of all that they could carry away,
passed that night over to the other side of Rio Grande, or the
great river [the Mississippi]. The Governor sent a captain with
fifty men in six canoes down the river, and went himself by land
with the rest. He came to Guachoya upon Sunday the 17 of April;
he lodged in the town of the cacique, which was enclosed about
and seated a crossbow shot distant from the river. . . .

Chapter XXIX

. . . The Governor fell into great dumps [depression] to see
how hard it was to get to the sea; and worse, because his men

and horses every day diminished, being without succor to sustain themselves in the country; and with that thought he fell sick . . . being evil handled with fevers, and was much aggrieved that he was not in case to pass presently the river. . . . The Indians of Guachoya came every day with fish, in such numbers that the town was full of them. . . .

Chapter XXX

. . . And touching the governor which he commanded they should elect, he [Baltasar de Gallegos] besought him that it would please his lordship to name him which he thought fit, and him they would obey. And presently he named Luys de Moscoso de Alvarado, his captain-general. And presently he was sworn by all that were present and elected for governor. The next day, being the 21 of May 1542, departed out of this life the valorous, virtuous, and valiant captain, Don Fernando de Soto, Governor of Cuba and Adelantado of Florida; whom fortune advanced, as it useth to do others, that he might have the higher fall. He departed in such a place, and at such a time, as in his sickness he had but little comfort; and the danger wherein all his people were of perishing in that country, which appeared before their eyes, was cause sufficient why every one of them had need of comfort, and why they did not visit nor accompany him as they ought to have done. Luys de Moscoso determined to conceal his death from the Indians because Ferdinando de Soto had made them believe that the Christians were immortal.

III

Search for the "Seven Cities"
and Quivira

GOLD fever raged like a plague among the Spaniards and sent almost as many of them to their deaths as would a genuinely pathological ailment. While de Soto was wandering over thousands of square miles from the east, other Spaniards were probing the southwest. The Viceroy of Mexico, Antonio de Mendoza, heard continuing rumors of rich cities in the interior and was beside himself lest someone outside his jurisdiction should find them first. Tales reached him of the Seven Cities of Cíbola, where the inhabitants made their ordinary utensils of gold and where the precious metal was so common that the populace showed no interest in it. The Indians also told of Quivira, another city farther away, which soon lured explorers into the distant waste. Spaniards who remembered Tenochtitlán and Cuzco, reached after long marches across unpromising lands, were ready to believe that similar sources of wealth might lie waiting across the mountains, deserts, and plains in the north. Antonio de Mendoza was not one to overlook an opportunity.

When Cabeza de Vaca and his three companions returned from their years of wandering across the continent, their own stories grew with the telling and the Indians who accompanied them added circumstantial details. Mendoza was eager to enlist these explorers in another foray into the wilderness, but Cabeza de Vaca, as we have seen, wanted an empire of his own and was unwilling to go out as an agent of Mendoza. Castillo, having had enough of wandering, married a well-to-do widow and settled down in Mexico. Not long afterward, Dorantes also found a widow to his liking and did likewise. Of the four wanderers, only the Negro, Estéban, was willing to undertake another venture into the unknown, for he had acquired confidence in his powers as a medicine man.

But another recruit was available, a friar intent upon Christianizing the Indians, one Fray Marcos de Niza, a Franciscan from Nice, as his name indicates. After some experience in Peru, he arrived in Mexico in 1537 and in 1538 obtained permission to engage in missionary work in the north. In the same year Mendoza appointed Francisco Vásquez de Coronado governor of New Galicia, the northernmost province of New Spain (Mexico). These two, the friar and the governor, made momentous explorations into territory that eventually became part of the southwestern United States.

The first journeys into the interior were made by Fray Marcos and Estéban. With a commission from the Viceroy, they set out in March 1539 to spy out the land to the north and to carry the gospel message to the heathen. Fray Marcos went soberly clad in the dun-colored robes of a Franciscan, but Estéban was resplendent in the regalia of a medicine man, with bells on his arms and ankles and a gourd rattle adorned with feathers that he had obtained from Indians on his earlier journey across Texas. Had he known the symbolism of the gourd, he would have left it in Mexico. On his march Estéban was flanked by two magnificent greyhounds. His appearance was calculated to impress any Indians he might meet.

The two pushed northwest to the head of the Gulf of California. At that point Fray Marcos decided to send Estéban on ahead; apparently the friar's flamboyant partner was already scandalizing the cleric by demanding too many women from the Indians. At any rate, Marcos concluded that Estéban would serve better as an advance party; if he discovered anything of importance, he was instructed to send back a cross, the size of which would signify the importance of what he had found. Pleased to be on his own, Estéban pushed forward.

Stories of the Seven Cities continued to filter back to Marcos, and he was encouraged when a messenger came from Estéban bearing a cross as large as a man. Surely this indicated a momentous discovery. Soon another Indian arrived bearing a second cross and a message from Estéban urging Marcos to hurry on.

From the upper reaches of the Sonora River the friar entered what is now Arizona. Indians told him that Cíbola, or something that sounded like that name, lay 30 days' journey to the northwest and that it was one of seven rich cities. This was exciting news indeed, and the friar made all speed. Soon after entering Arizona, however, he met messengers bearing bad news. Estéban had sent his magic gourd to the chief of Cíbola, but it had had the opposite effect than the one he intended. After consulting among themselves, the inhabitants of Cíbola had set upon Estéban's party, shot arrows at them, and killed Estéban. The gourd, it has been surmised, was a war symbol, probably from Comanche Indians in Texas, or had been so interpreted by the Zuñis, whom Estéban found in the town he believed to be Cíbola.[1] Marcos induced Indian guides to lead him to a point within sight of the town; there he piled up stones, erected a cross, and claimed the land in the name of the Viceroy and Emperor Charles V. That done, he made haste to return to Mexico.

Although Estéban was dead, Fray Marcos had actually seen one of the Seven Cities, an Indian town built with stone houses. The report he took back to the governor of New Galicia and the Viceroy kindled a fresh zeal to find the fabulous realm. So excited was Antonio de Mendoza that he wanted to lead an expedition himself but he finally decided to place Coronado in command. Since so important an undertaking would warrant an adequate complement of men and sufficient equipment, the Viceroy did not stint in supplying Coronado. When the army was mustered at Compostela, New Spain, in February 1540, it numbered 336 men, most of them mounted cavalrymen, and some 1,500 horses and mules. In addition Coronado took along several hundred Indians as servants and herdsmen.

While Coronado's expedition was being organized, the Viceroy sent out a reconnaissance party under Melchior Díaz to check on Fray Marcos' report. Díaz did not get as far as Cíbola but he brought back accounts from Indians of towns with stone and mud houses, of plentiful turquoise, but no evidence of gold whatever. This negative report, kept secret from the expedition, was somewhat disheartening but did not discourage Coronado.

[1] *The hazard of the gourd was reported by Fray Marcos. A translation of his account can be found in George P. Hammond and Agapito Rey,* Narratives of the Coronado Expedition (*Albuquerque, 1940*).

The Viceroy ordered two ships under the command of Hernando de Alarcón to proceed from a port north of Acapulco up the Gulf of California and as far as possible up the river at the head of the Gulf. These ships were to carry supplies which, it was hoped, could reach Coronado who was to follow a route paralleling the Gulf.

The excitement generated by the hope of finding the Seven Cities had attracted some of the most adventurous men in New Spain. Not all were Spaniards: the muster roll included five Portuguese, two Italians, a Frenchman, a Scot, and a German. Several priests, including Fray Marcos, went along to carry the gospel message, for Coronado intended both to conquer and to Christianize the inhabitants of the magical realm he believed to lie beyond the mountains and deserts northeast of Sonora. Unlike de Soto, Coronado hoped also to conciliate the Indians rather than to terrify them by cruelty, and he gave strict orders not to mistreat the natives.

Tracing a route northwestward along the Gulf of California, Coronado found the going rough and difficult. Fray Marcos had given an optimistic account of the terrain, but Coronado found to his sorrow that his story had no foundation in fact. A month after leaving the last outpost of civilization at Culiacán, the party had not yet reached the borders of what is now the United States. In fact, they were already exhausted and out of food on the lower reaches of the Sonora River. Alarcón's two supply ships could not be found on the coast, and as he now turned northeastward up the Sonora River valley, Coronado had to depend on whatever food he could obtain. Several men died from eating poisonous herbs, but in spite of hardships and discouragement, the expedition pushed on across mountains and desert through what is now Arizona to reach the Little Colorado River. They were now approaching Cíbola, and, remembering that the Indians had killed Estéban, Coronado proceeded with caution. At last they came in sight of the fabled city, but it was no Tenochtitlán. Nobody looking at the drab huddle of stone and adobe of this Indian pueblo would have thought that it was a fairy city like something described in *Amadis of Gaul,* as Bernal Díaz had reported on first looking down on the Valley of Mexico. Though consumed with disappointment, Coronado's men still thought the inhabitants might have stores of gold and turquoise hidden in their quarters;

at least they would have supplies of corn and beans, more immediately needed than gold. The town had to be taken.

Coronado had tried to make a peaceable entry, but when he was met with arrows, he ordered the place stormed. The Indians resisted stoutly, and their arrows and stones caused many casualties—Coronado himself was wounded by arrows and knocked unconscious by a stone. But his men drove the Indians out and settled down to lick their wounds and recuperate in the first of the Seven Cities, more accurately called Háwikuh than Cíbola. They found an abundance of corn, beans, and squash but no treasure of any kind. Perhaps farther on they would come upon the gold they sought. Always farther ahead beckoned the gleam of gold.

The pueblo Coronado had taken was the westernmost of a string of settlements, perhaps seven, that Zuñi Indians occupied along the river that takes its name from their tribe, in the border regions of Arizona and New Mexico. Their territory lay southwest of Gallup, New Mexico, between the present-day city of Albuquerque and the Grand Canyon. These pueblos, subdued by Coronado, yielded no treasure, not even any quantity of turquoise which the Indians evidently had hidden away.

From a base that Coronado established on the Sonora River, Melchior Díaz led another reconnaissance group and discovered the mouth of the Colorado River at the head of the Gulf of California. He also found fastened to a tree a message from Alarcón saying he had reached that point on the river but, finding no trace of Coronado, had turned back. Díaz was injured in a hunting expedition on the far side of the Colorado, and died three weeks later.

Coronado heard of another string of Indian towns, actually the pueblos of Indians we now call the Hopis, northwest of his own headquarters among the Zuñis, and sent one of his captains, Pedro de Tovar, to see what these towns had to offer. After a short fight the Hopis surrendered, but Tovar found no treasure there. He did, however, bring back a report of a great river farther west, and Coronado sent out another reconnaissance party under García López de Cárdenas who brought back word of a vast gorge at the bottom of which flowed a great river. He had found the Grand Canyon.

Two Indian chiefs from a tribe farther to the east visited Coronado unexpectedly at Cíbola and suggested that they would welcome the Spaniards to their town of Cicúye, which we know as Pecos, southeast of Santa Fe, New Mexico. One of these chiefs had an unusual growth of hair on his face, and Coronado's men at once dubbed him "Bigotes" or "Whiskers." He would have an important influence on the future of the expedition.

To check on Whiskers' stories, Coronado sent another captain, Hernando de Alvarado, with instructions to return after 80 days. Beginning his reconnaissance at the end of August 1540, Alvarado made a difficult crossing of lava beds to the east to reach the fortress pueblo of Acoma, perched on a high rock south of the San Jose River, New Mexico. Fortunately the inhabitants were not hostile and provided the explorers with corn and turkeys, as well as some turquoise and buffalo meat. The Spaniards now began to hear of great herds of "cattle" farther east and they were shown some skins of these animals, the buffalo of the plains. On September 7 they reached the river we now call the Rio Grande and made camp in what the Indians told them was the region of Tiguex, just north of the site of modern Albuquerque.

The Indians in that area proved friendly, and Alvarado, guided by Bigotes, visited the pueblos upstream on the Rio Grande as far as the present town of Taos. The priest who accompanied him, Juan Padilla, set up crosses and was pleased that the Indians were eager to decorate them with flowers and feathers. He considered them ripe for Christian salvation. At last they turned back and headed for Cicúye, Bigotes' own pueblo. There the whiskered guide declared that he had traveled enough and proposed to rest. But he allowed Alvarado to take along as guides for further exploration two Plains Indians whom he held as slaves, one named Sopete and the other called by the Spaniards simply "the Turk" because of his appearance. They had come from the region now known as Kansas and beyond. Sopete called his town Quivira, and both Indians told of its wonders. Their descriptions fired the Spaniards once more with hopes of a great discovery. The Turk told Alvarado that in Quivira he would find gold, silver, jewels, and anything he might desire. He also declared that Bigotes had a huge golden bracelet taken in Quivira.

From a point that he had reached on the Canadian River Alvarado decided to turn back. The evidence from the Turk of gold in Quivira made it imperative that he get to Coronado with the news. Furthermore, he wanted to see—or take—that golden bracelet the Turk swore Bigotes possessed. Alvarado had already seen some astonishing sights, including great herds of buffalo, "monstrous beasts," so numerous that he could only compare them with the fish of the sea. On his return to Cicúye, Alvarado put Bigotes and other chiefs in chains and baited them with his dogs when they did not produce the golden bracelet—which, as it turned out, existed only in the Turk's imagination. With this mistake, Alvarado sowed the seed of hostility among previously friendly tribesmen.

During the winter of 1540–41 Coronado brought the main portion of his force to the Tiguex region on the Rio Grande and wintered there. Relations with the Indians deteriorated into open war, and two pueblos were besieged and captured with considerable losses on both sides. After the first was partially burned and taken, Cárdenas burned many prisoners at the stake and his horsemen ran down and lanced others. Amicable relations with the Pueblo Indians on the Rio Grande were now a thing of the past.

The Turk's stories of the riches of Quivira had grown with the telling, and Coronado and his captains were in a fever to be off to these new discoveries. As the Turk continued to embroider his descriptions, he reported that the king of Quivira sailed on a great lake in vessels propelled by both sails and oars and that the very oarlocks were made of solid gold. So plentiful was the precious metal that the Spaniards would not be able to load it all on their horses. The king also lived in a palace hung with fine cloths and kept greyhounds so ferocious that no enemy dared approach him. Many other tales poured from the vivid imagination of the Turk. Beyond Quivira lay other rich lands, Harahey and Guaes, where gold and silver were more plentiful even than in Quivira. Convinced that they were on the verge of discovering lands that would make Montezuma's realm look poor, the Spaniards waited impatiently for spring and on April 23, 1541, they set out on the long march to the east where they believed they would find untold wealth.

The route followed roughly the trail that Alvarado had already marked and continued in an easterly direction into the Panhandle of Texas. Coronado, bewildered and lost on the vast plains of Texas, turned southeast on the advice of the Turk, though his other Indian guide, Sopete, insisted that the Turk was lying and

that Quivira lay to the northeast. Thirty-seven days after leaving
the pueblos on the Rio Grande the expedition found itself in
broken land cut by deep canyons, with a rugged escarpment to
the east. Descending what they called the "Deep Barranca,"
known today as Palo Duro Canyon, southeast of Amarillo, Texas,
Coronado conferred with Tejas Indians at their village and received confirmation that he was far south of Quivira. The Turk
had led the Spaniards on a fool's errand, and for this trickery he
soon found himself in chains.

After a council with his captains, Coronado decided to proceed
northward in search of Quivira with thirty picked horsemen, a
few foot soldiers, and Indian servants, some forty men in all. The
rest of the army would return to the pueblos. On June 1, 1541,
the party set out from Palo Duro Canyon. The remainder of the
expedition waited, hoping that the commander would soon send
word of a profitable discovery, but when, after two weeks, they
had heard no such news, they headed back to the Rio Grande.
Twenty-five days later they reached the pueblos, found that the
Indians had fled, and settled down in a pueblo called Alcanfor.

Meanwhile Coronado was plodding northward across the high
plains that parallel the great escarpment. He passed the sites of
the modern Texas towns Amarillo, Fritch, Borger and Spearman,
then went on across the Oklahoma Panhandle by Hardesty and
Tyrone into Kansas, passing Liberal, Kismet and Ford, where he
crossed the Arkansas River, naming it "the River of Quivira." This
Arkansas crossing later became famous as the ford used on the
Santa Fe Trail.

As he followed the Arkansas downstream, somewhere between
Kinsley and Larned, Kansas, Coronado encountered Quivira Indians on a buffalo hunt. His guide, Sopete, belonged to a tribe in
this region and could communicate with the Quivirans. Because
rumors had reached Coronado that there were Christians—perhaps survivors of the Narváez expedition—in Quivira and in the
more distant Harahey, he sent a letter ahead asking if they needed
help. Then he pressed on, eager to reach the fabulous place,
though he had already learned that he could not expect a wealthy
city. Following the curve of the Arkansas River, he passed the
site of Great Bend and continued eastward across some of the
river's tributaries to arrive on July 6, 1541, at the first villages of
the Quivira Indians.

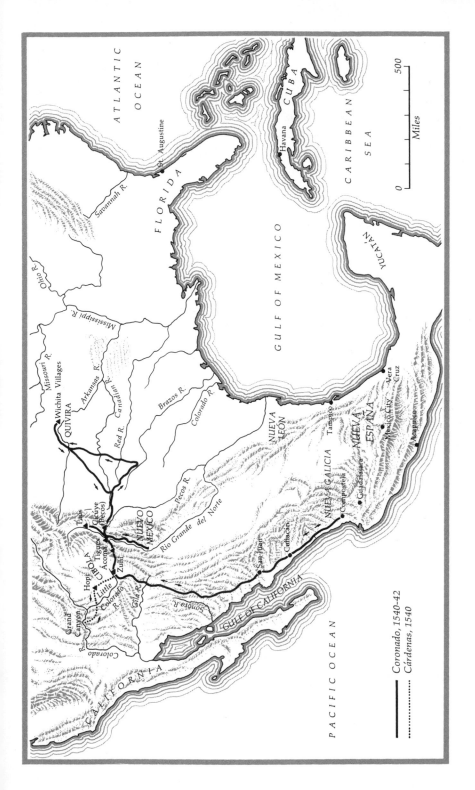

Coronado's Explorations of the Southwest

ATLANTIC OCEAN

CUBA

CARIBBEAN SEA

500

Miles

0

St. Augustine

FLORIDA

Havana

GULF OF MEXICO

YUCATÁN

Ohio R.

Savannah R.

Mississippi R.

Missouri R.

Arkansas R.

Red R.

Canadian R.

Brazos R.

Colorado R.

Wichita Villages

QUIVIRA

NUEVA LEÓN

Tampico

NUEVA ESPAÑA

Vera Cruz

Mexico City

Acapulco

Pecos R.

NUEVA GALICIA

Guadalajara

Compostela

Rio Grande del Norte

NUEVO MEXICO

Taos

Cicuye (Pecos)

San Juan

Culiacán

Hopi

CIBOLA

Tiguex

Acoma

Zuñi

Little Colorado R.

Gila R.

Sonora R.

GULF OF CALIFORNIA

Grand Canyon

Colorado R.

CALIFORNIA

PACIFIC OCEAN

Coronado, 1540–42
Cárdenas, 1540

Exploring for about 25 days among the Quivirans, Coronado got as far east as Lindsborg, Kansas, the terminus of the expedition. Here were no rich cities, not even the sort of well-built pueblos he had found on the Rio Grande, but only round huts thatched with grass and half-naked Indians of the Wichita tribe, who emerged to greet the Spaniards. This was Quivira, which they had struggled so long to reach. Their disappointment was bitter. Though they claimed the endless plains for Spain, they found no negotiable wealth and would go back to Mexico poorer than they came. The Turk, whose imaginative lies had sent them on this long journey to the American plains, paid with his life; caught urging the Quivirans to massacre the Spaniards, he was garroted and secretly buried.

Turning their faces westward, Coronado and his men now sought the quickest way back to the pueblos on the Rio Grande. Following the Arkansas River to the ford (site of the town of Ford), they went southwest across the Oklahoma and Texas Panhandles, South of US route 56 into New Mexico, and thence to the Pecos River and Tiguex, where they planned to spend the winter. During the long months, when food grew scarce and morale was low, some of the Spaniards grumbled that other Indians besides the Turk had told of gold in lands beyond Quivira. Insisting that Coronado lead them back to renew the search, they exacted a promise that he would do so in the spring. But, seriously injured in a fall from his horse and remembering a soothsayer's prediction that he would have a fall in a strange land from which he would never recover, Coronado now wanted above all things to get back to his wife in New Spain. In April 1542, just over two years after their departure from New Spain, the army began its return march. A few friars were left on the Rio Grande to spread the gospel and perhaps to hold the country for Spain. In midsummer of 1542, Coronado, broken in health, reached Mexico City to report to the Viceroy. He brought no wealth of any kind to compensate Mendoza for the 60,000 pesos spent on the expedition. But he had penetrated a continent and in later years his discoveries would give Spain a claim to vast territories in North America.

Castañeda's Report of Coronado's Expedition

[*When Coronado left Culiacán in Sinaloa on his famous expedition in search of the Seven Cities of Cíbola and Quivira, one of his private soldiers was Pedro de Castañeda, a colonist of Culiacán. Castañeda survived to return to his home in Culiacán, where, perhaps 20 years afterwards, he wrote down his recollections of the exploration. This account is the most important of the surviving narratives of the venture. Castañeda's original manuscript has disappeared, but a copy made at Seville in 1596 exists in the New York Public Library. A translation of this manuscript was made in 1896 by George Parker Winship and published in the* Fourteenth Annual Report of the Bureau of Ethnology (*Washington, 1896*). *Later reprints are available, including excerpts in* Spanish Explorers in the Southern United States, 1528–1543, *edited by Frederick W. Hodge and T. H. Lewis in "Original Narratives of Early American History" (New York, 1907). The most complete account of Coronado in English is by Herbert E. Bolton,* Coronado, Knight of Pueblos and Plains (*Albuquerque, New Mexico, 1949*). *Briefer accounts will be found in Stephen Clissold,* The Seven Cities of Cíbola (*New York, 1962*) *and Charles Norman,* Discoverers of America (*New York, 1968*). *Excerpts from Castañeda's narrative follow:*]

Chapter IV

.   .   .   .

The noble viceroy arranged with the friars of the order of Saint Francis so that Friar Marcos was made father provincial, as a result of which the pulpits of that order were filled with such accounts of marvels and wonders that more than 300 Spaniards and about 80 natives of New Spain collected in a few days. There were so many men of such high quality among the Spaniards that such a noble body was never collected in the Indies, nor so many men of quality in such a small body, there being 300 men. Francisco Vázquez Coronado, governor of New Galicia, was captain-general, because he had been the author of it all. The good viceroy Don Antonio did this because at this time Francisco Vázquez was his closest and most intimate friend, and because he considered him to be wise, skillful, and intelligent, besides being a gentleman. Had he paid more attention and regard to the position in which he was placed and the charge over which he was placed, and less to the estates he left behind in New Spain, or, at least, more to the honor he had and might secure from having such gentlemen under his command, things would not have turned out as they did. When this narrative is ended, it will be seen that he did not know how to keep his position nor the government that he held.

Chapter VI

Of how all the companies collected in Compostela and set off on the journey in good order.

When the viceroy Don Antonio de Mendoza had fixed and arranged everything as we have related, and the companies and captaincies had been arranged, he advanced a part of their salaries from the chest of His Majesty to those in the army who were in greatest need. And as it seemed to him that it would be rather hard for the friendly Indians in the country if the army should start from Mexico [city], he ordered them to assemble at the city of Compostela, the chief city in the New Kingdom of Galicia [frontier province of Spanish Mexico at this time], 110 leagues from Mexico, so that they could begin their journey there with everything in good order. There is nothing to tell about what happened on this trip, since they all finally assembled at Compostela by Shrovetide, in the year (fifteen hundred and) forty-one [actually 1540].

After the whole force had left Mexico, he ordered Don Pedro de Alarcón to set sail with two ships that were in the port of La Natividad [Navidad, north of Acapulco] on the south seacoast, and go to the port of Xalisco [Jalisco, between Compostela and Tepic] to take the baggage which the soldiers were unable to carry, and thence to sail along the coast near the army, because he had understood from the reports that they would have to go through the country near the seacoast and that we could find the harbors by means of the rivers, and that the ships could always get news of the army; which turned out afterward to be false, and so all this stuff was lost, or, rather, those who owned it lost it, as will be told farther on. After the viceroy had completed all his arrangements, he set off for Compostela accompanied by many noble and rich men. . . .

All were very glad when he arrived, and he made an examination of the company and found all those whom we have mentioned. He assigned the captains to their companies, and, after this was done, on the next day after they had all heard mass, captains and soldiers together, the viceroy made them a very eloquent short speech, telling them of the fidelity they owed to their general and showing them clearly the benefits which this expedition might afford, from the conversion of those peoples as well as in the profit of those who should conquer the territory, and the advantage to His Majesty and the claim which they would thus have on his favor and aid at all times. After he had finished, they all, both captains and soldiers, gave him their oaths upon the Gospels in a missal that they would follow their general on this expedition and would obey him in everything he commanded them, which they faithfully performed, as will be seen. The next day after this was done the army started off with its colors flying. The viceroy, Don Antonio, went with them for two days, and there he took leave of them, returning to New Spain with his friends.

Chapter X

Of how the army started from the town of Señora, leaving it inhabited, and how it reached Cíbola, and of what happened to Captain Melchior Diaz on his expedition in search of the ships and how he discovered the Tison (Firebrand) [i.e., Colorado] river.

After Melchior Diaz and Juan Gallego had arrived in the town of Señora [settlement on the Sonora River], it was announced that the army was to depart for Cíbola; that Melchior Diaz was to remain in charge of that town with eighty men; that Juan Gallego was going to New Spain with messages for the viceroy; and that Friar Marcos was going back with him because he did not think it was safe for him to stay in Cíbola, seeing that his report had turned out to be entirely false, because the kingdoms that he had told about had not been found, nor the populous cities, nor the wealth of gold, nor the precious stones which he had reported, nor the fine clothes, nor other things that had been proclaimed from the pulpits. When this had been announced, those who were to remain were selected and the rest loaded their provisions and set off in good order about the middle of September on the way to Cíbola following their general.

. . . After the army had gone Captain Melchior Diaz took twenty-five of the most efficient men, leaving in his place one Diego de Alcaraz, a man unfitted to have people under his command. He took guides and went toward the north and west in search of the seacoast. After going about 150 leagues, they came to a province of exceedingly tall and strong men—like giants. . . . On account of the great cold, they carry a firebrand (tison) in the hand when they go from one place to another, with which they warm the other hand and the body as well, and in this way they keep shifting it every now and then. On this account the large river which is in that country was called Rio del Tison (Firebrand River) [the Colorado]. It is a very great river and is more than two leagues wide at its mouth; here it is half a league across.

Here the captain heard that there had been ships at a point three days down toward the sea. When he reached the place where the ships had been, which was more than fifteen leagues up the river from the mouth of the harbor, they found written on a tree: "Alarcón reached this place; there are letters at the foot of this tree." He dug up the letters and learned from them how long Alarcón had waited for news of the army and that he had gone back with the ships to New Spain because he was unable to proceed farther, since this sea was a bay which was formed by the Isle of the Marquis [Cortéz], which is called California, and it was explained that California was not an island, but a point of the mainland forming the other side of that gulf.

After he had seen this, the captain turned back to go up the river, without going down to the sea to find a ford by which to cross to the other side, so as to follow the other bank. After they had gone five or six days, it seemed to them as if they could cross on rafts. For this purpose they called together a large number of the natives, who were waiting for a favorable opportunity to make an attack on our men, and when they saw that the strangers wanted to cross, they helped make the rafts with all zeal and diligence so as to catch them in this way on the water and drown them or else so divide them that they could not help one another.

While the rafts were being made, a soldier who had been out around the camp saw a large number of armed men go across to a mountain, where they were waiting till the soldiers should cross the river. He reported this, and an Indian was quietly shut up in order to find out the truth, and when they tortured him he told all the arrangements that had been made. These were that when our men were crossing and part of them had got over and part were on the river and part were waiting to cross, those who were on the rafts should drown those they were taking across and the rest of their force should make an attack on both sides of the river. If they had had as much discretion and courage as they had strength and power, the attempt would have succeeded.

When he knew their plan, the captain had the Indian who had confessed the affair killed secretly, and that night he was thrown into the river with a weight, so that the Indians would not suspect that they were found out. The next day they noticed that our men suspected them and so they made an attack, shooting showers of arrows, but when the horses began to catch up with them and the lances wounded them without mercy and the musketeers likewise made good shots, they had to leave the plain and take to the mountain, until not a man of them was to be seen. The force then came back and crossed all right, the Indian allies and the Spaniards going across on the rafts and the horses swimming alongside the rafts, where we will leave them to continue their journey.

To relate how the army that was on its way to Cíbola got on: Everything went along in good shape since the general had left everything peaceful, because he wished the people in that region to be contented and without fear and willing to do what they were ordered. In a province called Vacapan [on Gulf of California, south of Sonora River] there was a large quantity of prickly pears, of which the natives make a great deal of preserves. They gave this preserve away freely, and, as the men of the army ate much of it, they all fell sick with a headache and fever, so that the natives might have done much harm to the force if they had wished. This lasted regularly twenty-four hours. . . .

Three days after we entered the wilderness we found a horn on the bank of a river that flows in the bottom of a very steep, deep gully, which the general had noticed and left there for his army to see, for it was six feet long and as thick at the base as a man's thigh. It seemed to be more like the horn of a goat than of any other animal. It was something worth seeing. The army proceeded and was about a day's march from Cíbola when a very cold tornado came up in the afternoon, followed by a great fall of snow, which was a bad combination for the carriers. The army went on till it reached some caves in a rocky ridge, late in the evening. The Indian allies, who were from New Spain and for the most part from warm countries, were in great danger. They felt the coldness of that day so much that it was hard work the next day taking care of them, for they suffered much pain and had to be carried on the horses, the soldiers walking.

After this labor the army reached Cíbola, where their general was waiting for them with their quarters all ready, and here they were reunited, except some captains and men who had gone off to discover other provinces.

Chapter XI

How Don Pedro de Tovar discovered Tusayán or Tutahaco. . . .

While the things already described were taking place, Cíbola being at peace, the General Francisco Vázquez found out from the people of the province about the provinces that lay around it, and got them to tell their friends and neighbors that Christians had come into the country whose only desire was to be their friends and to find out about good lands to live in, and for them to come to see the strangers and talk with them. They did this, since they know how to communicate with one another in these regions, and they informed him about a province with seven villages of the same sort as theirs, although somewhat different. They had nothing to do with these people. This province is called Tusayán [province of the Hopis]. It is twenty-five leagues from Cíbola. The villages are high and the people are warlike.

The general had sent Don Pedro de Tovar to these villages with seventeen horsemen and three or four foot soldiers. Juan de Padilla, a Franciscan friar, who had been a fighting man in his youth, went with them. When they reached the region they entered the country so quietly that nobody observed them, because there were no settlements or farms between one village and another and the people do not leave the villages except to go to their farms, especially at this time when they had heard that Cíbola had been captured by very fierce people who traveled on animals which ate people. This information was generally believed by those who had never seen horses, although it was so strange as to cause much wonder. Our men arrived after nightfall and were able to conceal themselves under the edge of the village, where they heard the natives talking in their houses. But in the morning they were discovered and drew up in regular order, while the natives came out to meet them with bows, and shields, and wooden clubs drawn up in lines without any confusion. The interpreter was given a chance to speak to them and give them due warning, for they were very intelligent people, but nevertheless they drew lines and insisted that our men should not go across these lines toward their village. . . .

Chapter XV

Of why Tiguex revolted, and how they were punished, without being to blame for it.

It has been related how the general reached Tiguex [slightly north of Albuquerque, New Mexico, on the Rio Grande], where he found Don García Lopez de Cárdenas and Hernando de Alvarado, and how he sent the latter back to Cicúye [Pecos, New Mexico] where he took the Captain Whiskers and the governor of the village, who was an old man, prisoners. The people of Tiguex did not feel well about this seizure. . . .

Besides what I have just said, one whom I will not name, out of regard for him, left the village where the camp was and went to another village about a league distant. And seeing a pretty woman there, he called her husband down to hold his horse by the bridle while he went up; and as the village was entered by the upper story, the Indian supposed he was going to some other part of it. While he was there the Indian heard some slight noise, and then the Spaniard came down, took his horse, and went away. The Indian went up and learned that he had violated, or tried to violate, his wife, and so he came with the important men of the town to complain that a man had violated his wife, and he told how it happened. When the general made all the soldiers and the persons who were with him come together, the Indian did not recognize the man, either because he had changed his clothes or for whatever other reason there may have been, but he said that he could tell the horse because he had held his bridle, and so he was taken to the stables and found the horse and said that the master of the horse must be the man. He denied doing it, seeing that he had not been recognized, and it may be that the Indian was mistaken in the horse; anyway, he went off without getting any satisfaction. The next day one of the Indians, who was guarding the horses of the army, came running in saying that a companion of his had been killed, and that the Indians of the country were driving off the horses toward their villages. The Spaniards tried to collect the horses again, but many were lost, besides seven of the general's mules.

The next day Don García Lopez de Cárdenas went to see the villages and talk with the natives. He found the villages closed by palisades and a great noise inside, the horses being chased as in a bull fight and shot with arrows. They were all ready for fighting. Nothing could be done because they would not come down on the plain, and the villages are so strong that the Spaniards could not dislodge them. The general then ordered Don García Lopez de Cárdenas to go and surround one village with all the rest of the force. This village was the one where the greatest injury had been done and where the affair with the Indian woman occurred. Several captains who had gone on in advance with the general . . . took the Indians so much by surprise that they gained the upper story, with great danger for they wounded many of our men from within the houses. Our men were on top of the houses in great danger for a day and a night and part of the next day, and they made some good shots with their crossbows and muskets. The horsemen on the plain with many of the Indian allies from New Spain smoked them out from the cellars into which they had broken, so that they begged for peace.

Pablo de Melgosa and Diego Lopez, the alderman from Seville, were left on the roof and answered the Indians with the same signs they were making for peace, which was to make a cross. They then put down their arms and received pardon. They were taken to the tent of Don García, who, according to what he said, did not know about the peace and thought that they had given themselves up of their own accord because they had been conquered. As he had been ordered by the general not to take them alive, but to make an example of them so that the other natives would fear the Spaniards, he ordered 200 stakes to be prepared at once to burn them alive. Nobody told him about the peace that had been granted them, for the soldiers knew as little as he, and those who should have told him about it remained silent, not thinking that it was any of their business.

Then when the enemies saw that the Spaniards were binding them and beginning to roast them, about a hundred men who were in the tent began to struggle and defend themselves with what there was there and with the stakes they could seize. Our men who were on foot attacked the tent on all sides, so that there was great confusion around it, and then the horsemen chased those who escaped. As the country was level, not a man of them remained alive, unless it was some who remained hidden in the village and escaped that night to spread throughout the country the news that the strangers did not respect the peace they had made, which afterward proved a great misfortune. After this was over, it began to snow, and they abandoned the village and returned to the camp just as the army came from Cíbola.

Chapter [X]VIII

Of Quivira, of where it is and some information about it.

Quivira [central Kansas] is to the west of those ravines, in the midst of the country somewhat nearer the mountains toward the sea, for the country is level as far as Quivira, and there they began to see some mountain chains [Smoky Hills]. The country is well settled. Judging from what was seen on the borders of it, this country is very similar to that of Spain in the varieties of vegetation and fruits. There are plums like those of Castile, grapes, nuts, mulberries, oats, pennyroyal, wild marjoram, and large quantities of flax, but this does not do them any good, because they do not know how to use it. The people are of almost the same sort and appearance as the Teyas. They have villages like those in New Spain. The houses are round, without a wall, and they have one story like a loft, under the roof, where they sleep and keep their belongings. The roofs are of straw. There are other thickly settled provinces around it containing large numbers of men. . . .

The great river of the Holy Spirit (Espiritu Santo) [the Mississippi and Missouri rivers], which Don Fernando de Soto discovered in the country of Florida, flows through this country. It passes through a province called Arache [land of the Apaches], according to the reliable accounts which were obtained here. The sources were not visited, because, according to what they said, it comes from a very distant country in the mountains of the South sea [Pacific Ocean], from the part that sheds its waters onto the plains. It flows across all the level country and breaks through the mountains of the North sea [Atlantic], and comes out where the people with Don Fernando de Soto navigated it. This is more than 300 leagues from where it enters the sea. On account of this, and also because it has large tributaries, it is so mighty when it enters the sea that they lost sight of the land before the water ceased to be fresh.

This country of Quivira was the last that was seen of which I am able to give any description or information. Now it is proper for me to return and speak of the army, which I left in Tiguex, resting for the winter so that it would be able to proceed or return in search of these settlements of Quivira, which was not accomplished after all, because it was God's pleasure that these discoveries should remain for other peoples and that we who had been there should content ourselves with saying that we were the first who discovered it and obtained any information concerning it, just as Hercules knew the site where Julius Caesar was to found Seville or Hispales. May the all-powerful Lord grant that His will be done in everything. It is certain that if this had not been His will Francisco Vázquez would not have returned to New Spain without cause or reason, as he did, and that it would not have been left for those with Don Fernando de Soto to settle such a good country, as they have done, and besides settling it to increase its extent, after obtaining, as they did, information from our army.

Captain Jaramillo Tells of the Pueblos

[*One of Coronado's captains, Juan Jaramillo, wrote an account of the expedition many years after the events, but his memory was accurate and his narrative provides useful details about distances and places. An English translation of Jaramillo by George P. Win-*

ship was included in the Fourteenth Annual Report of the Bureau of Ethnology (*Washington, 1896*). *Excerpts from Jaramillo's account follow:*]

. . . We went to another river, which we called the Bermejo, or Red river [the Little Colorado], in two days' journey in the same direction, but less toward the northeast. Here we saw an Indian or two, who afterward turned out to be from the first settlement of Cíbola. From here we came in two days' journey to the said village, the first of Cíbola. The houses have flat roofs and walls of stone and mud, and here was where they killed Steve, or Estevanillo, the Negro who had come with Dorantes from Florida and returned with Friar Marcos de Niza. In this province of Cíbola there are five little villages besides this, all with flat roofs and of stone and mud, as I described. The country is cold, as is shown by the houses and hothouses (*estufas*) they have. From this first village of Cíbola, facing the northeast and a little less, on the left hand, there is a province called Tusayán, about five days off, which has seven flat-roofed villages, with as good as or better food supply than these, and even a larger population; and they also have the skins of cows and of deer, and cloaks of cotton, as I said.

All the waterways we found up to this Cíbola—and I don't know but what a day or two beyond—the rivers and streams, run into the south sea [Pacific], and those from beyond here into the north sea [Gulf of Mexico].

From this first village of Cíbola, as I have said, we went to another in this same province which was about a short day's journey off, on the way to Tiguex. It is nine days of such marches as we have made from this settlement of Cíbola to the river of Tiguex [Rio Grande]. Halfway between, I do not know but it may be a day more or less, is a village of earth and dressed stone, in a very strong position, which is called Tutahaco. All these Indians, except the first in the village of Cíbola, received us well. At the river of Tiguex there are fifteen villages within a distance of about twenty leagues, all with flat-roofed houses of earth, and not stone, after the fashion of mud walls. There are other villages besides these on other streams which flow into this, and three of these are, for Indians, well worth seeing, especially one that is called Chia, and another Uraba, and another Cicúique [or Cicúye: Pecos]. Uraba and Cicúique have many houses, two stories high. All the rest, and these also, have corn and beans and melons, skins, and some long robes of feathers which they braid, joining the feathers with a sort of thread; and they also make them of a sort of plain weaving with which they make the cloaks with which they protect themselves. They all have hot rooms underground, which, although not very clean, are very warm. They raise and have a very little cotton, of which they make the cloaks of which I have spoken above. This river comes from the northwest and flows about southeast, which shows that it certainly flows into the north sea.

[*The search for the Seven Cities ended in dust and disappointment. No fabulous cities of gold existed in the uplands of what is now New Mexico or on the plains of Kansas. The explorers who survived the great adventure returned to New Spain, some to seek adventure elsewhere, some to live out their lives in the settlements there. But while the Spaniards consolidated their position in Mexico, the memory of the land to the north lingered.*

[*Finally, in 1598 Juan de Oñate with some 400 colonists moved into New Mexico and made a settlement 30 miles northwest of the present site of Santa Fe. In later years New Mexico would become a focal point for trade with the English-speaking region of the North American continent, and the Santa Fe Trail would attract some of the toughest and most daring pioneers of the Old West.*]

Probing the Chesapeake Bay Region and the Mountains Beyond

W HILE de Soto and Coronado were exploring the southern region of what would become the United States, the English were concerned with problems nearer at hand and had not yet laid claim to any portion of the New World. A few seamen from Bristol and other ports made tentative explorations along the North American coast but no effort was yet made to investigate the interior of the land barrier.

[The French under Jacques Cartier had made a more systematic investigation of the Canadian coast and, in 1534–36, Cartier followed the St. Lawrence to the rapids of Lachine. This was the deepest penetration into North America yet made by non-Spanish explorers.[1]

[After the English made their first permanent settlement at Jamestown in 1607, however, they naturally wanted to know something about the hinterland. Like everyone else, they also had been infected with gold fever and had a latent hope that somewhere in the back country they would discover gold mines. Always too there was the prospect that any broad river might lead to an outlet to the South Sea and the way to the Far East.

[When Richard Hakluyt, the indefatigable propagandist for colonization overseas, was drawing up instructions in 1606 for

[1] See West and by North: North America Seen Through the Eyes of Its Seafaring Discoverers in this series.

49

*the Virginia colonists, he insisted that they ought to go inland up
some river to be as safe as possible from sea marauders:* [2]]

As we doubt not but you will have especial care to observe the
ordinances set down by the King's Majesty and delivered unto you
under the Privy Seal, so for your better directions upon your first
landing we have thought good to recommend unto your care these
instructions and articles following.

When it shall please God to send you on the coast of Virginia,
you shall do your best endeavor to find out a safe port in the
entrance of some navigable river, making choice of such a one as
runneth farthest into the land. And if you happen to discover
divers portable rivers, and amongst them any one that hath two
main branches, if the difference be not great, make choice of that
which bendeth most toward the northwest, for that way you shall
soonest find the other sea.

When you have made choice of the river on which you mean to
settle, be not hasty in landing your victuals and munitions, but
first let Captain Newport discover how far that river may be found
navigable, that you make election of the strongest, most wholesome, and fertile place, for if you make many removes, besides the
loss of time, you shall greatly spoil your victuals and your casks
and with great pain transport it in small boats.

But if you choose your place so far up as a bark of fifty tons will
float, then you may lay all your provisions ashore with ease and
the better receive the trade of all the countries about you in the
land. And such a place you may perchance find a hundred miles
from the river's mouth, and the further up the better. For if you
sit down near the entrance, except it be in some island that is
strong by nature, an enemy that may approach you on even
ground may easily pull you out. And if he be driven to seek you a
hundred miles [in] the land in boats, you shall from both sides of
the river where it is narrowest so beat them with your muskets as
they shall never be able to prevail against you.

And to the end that you be not surprised, as the French were in
Florida [on the St. Johns River] by Menéndez and the Spaniard in

[2] *The "Instructions," printed by Edward Arber in* Travels and Works of
Captain John Smith (*Edinburgh, 1910*), I, xxxiii–xxxvii, *are also reproduced
by E. G. R. Taylor in* Original Writings . . . of the Two Richard Hakluyts,
The Hakluyt Society (*London, 1935*), II, 492–96.

the same place by the French, you shall do well to make this double provision. First, erect a little stour [palisade] at the mouth of the river that may lodge some ten men, with whom you shall leave a light boat, that when any fleet shall be in sight they may come with speed to give you warning. Secondly, you must in no case suffer any of the native people of the country to inhabit between you and the seacoast, for you cannot carry yourselves so toward them but they will grow discontented with your habitation and be ready to guide and assist any nation that shall come to invade you. And if you neglect this, you neglect your safety.

When you have discovered as far up the river as you mean to plant yourselves and landed your victuals and munitions, to the end that every man may know his charge you shall do well to divide your sixscore men into three parts, whereof one party of them you may appoint to fortify and build, of which your first work must be your storehouse for victuals. The other you may employ in preparing your ground and sowing your corn and roots. The other ten of these [second] forty you must leave as sentinel at the haven's mouth. The other forty you may employ for two months in discovery of the river above you and on the country about you, which charge Captain Newport and Captain Gosnold may undertake of these forty discoverers. When they do espy any highlands or hills, Captain Gosnold may take twenty of the company to cross over the lands, and carrying a half dozen pickaxes to try if they can find any minerals. The other twenty may go on by river and pitch up boughs upon the bank's side, by which the other boats shall follow them by the same turnings. You may also take with them a wherry, such as is used here in the Thames, by which you may send back to the President for supply of munition or any other want, that you may not be driven to return for every small defect.

You must observe if you can whether the river on which you plant doth spring out of mountains or out of lakes. If it be out of any lake, the passage to the other sea will be more easy. And [it] is like enough that out of the same lake you shall find some spring which run[s] the contrary way toward the East India Sea; for the great and famous rivers of Volga, Tan[a]is [the Don], and Dvina have three heads near joined, and yet the one falleth into the Caspian Sea, the other into the Euxine [Black] Sea, and the third into the Paelonian [probably the White] Sea.

In all your passages you must have great care not to offend the naturals [natives], if you can eschew it, and employ some few of your company to trade with them for corn and all other lasting victuals if you [they?] have any. And this you must do before that they perceive you mean to plant among them, for not being sure how your own seed corn will prosper the first year, to avoid the danger of famine, use and endeavor to store yourselves of the country corn.

Your discoverers that pass overland with hired guides must look well to them that they slip not from them; and for more assurance let them take a compass with them and write down how far they go upon every point of the compass, for, that country having no way nor path, if that your guides run from you in the great woods or desert, you shall hardly ever find a passage back.

And how weary soever your soldiers be, let them never trust the country people with the carriage of their weapons; for if they run from you with your shot, which they only fear, they will easily kill them [you] all with their arrows. And whensoever any of yours shoots before them, be sure they may be chosen out of your best marksmen; for if they see your learners miss what they aim at, they will think the weapon not so terrible and thereby will be bold to assault you.

Above all things, do not advertise the killing of any of your men that the country people may know it. If they perceive that they are but common men and that with the loss of many of theirs they diminish any part of yours, they will make many adventures upon you. If the country be populous, you shall do well also not to let them see or know of your sick men, if you have any, which may also encourage them to many enterprises.

You must take especial care that you choose a seat for habitation that shall not be overburdened with woods near your town, for all the men you have shall not be able to cleanse twenty acres a year, besides that it may serve for a covert for your enemies round about.

Neither must you plant in a low or moist place, because it will prove unhealthful. You shall judge of the good air by the people, for some part of that coast where the lands are low have their people blear-eyed and with swollen bellies and legs. But if the naturals be strong and clean-made, it is a sign of a wholesome soil.

You must take order to draw up the pinnace that is left with you under the fort and take her sails and anchors ashore, all but a small kedge [anchor] to ride by, lest some ill-disposed persons slip away with her.

You must take care that your mariners that go for wages do not mar your trade, for those that mind not to inhabit, for a little gain will debase the estimation of exchange and hinder the trade for ever after; and therefore you shall not admit or suffer any person whatsoever, other than such as shall be appointed by the President and Council there, to buy any merchandises or other things whatsoever.

It were necessary that all your carpenters and other suchlike workmen about building do first build your storehouse and those other rooms of public and necessary use before any house be set up for any private person. And though the workmen may belong to any private persons, yet let them all work together first for the company and then for private men.

And seeing order is at the same price with confusion, it shall be advisably done to set your houses even and by a line, that your street may have a good breadth and be carried square about your marketplace and every street's end opening into it, that from thence, with a few fieldpieces, you may command every street throughout; which marketplace you may also fortify if you think it needful.

You shall do well to send a perfect relation by Captain Newport of all that is done, what height you are seated, how far into the land, what commodities you find, what soil, woods, and their several kinds, and so of all other things else to advertise particularly, and to suffer no man to return but by passport from the President and Council, nor to write any letter of anything that may discourage others.

Lastly and chiefly, the way to prosper and achieve good success is to make yourselves all of one mind for the good of your country and your own, and to serve and fear God, the giver of all goodness, for every plantation which our heavenly father hath not planted shall be rooted out.

[*Following Hakluyt's instructions, Captain Christopher Newport sailed up the James River and landed his passengers in what could be called inland Virginia. At least the settlement, which they named Jamestown, was far enough in the interior to be safe*

*from pirates and from what Newport called the "all devouring
Spaniard." With six fathoms of water under their vessels, the
settlers could tie up their craft to trees on shore.*

[*The broad rivers of Virginia invited exploration of the hinterland. Newport himself took a reconnaissance expedition up the
James as far as the falls at the site of modern Richmond, and
heard stories of great mountains farther to the west. The most
diligent of the early explorers was Captain John Smith, one of
the colony's small governing group, who was chosen "President"
in September 1608. As early as November 1607 he had led an
expedition up the Chickahominy to explore and trade for corn.
Two later expeditions took him into Chesapeake Bay and its
rivers. On his first exploration of the bay he followed the Potomac
River beyond the future site of Washington to a point opposite
the present David Taylor Model Basin. Some earth that he dug
up was "spangled" with gilded specks. Unwittingly Smith may
have stumbled on evidence of gold, for at a later time an effort
was made to mine gold on the banks of the Potomac near this spot.*

[*On a second exploration of Chesapeake Bay Smith probed other
rivers and gained a fair impression of the outlines of today's Maryland. He got as far up the Susquehanna as the falls, which he
named after himself. The Conowingo Dam now occupies the site.
He also pushed up the Elk River to the borders of modern Delaware and investigated the Sassafras River before turning back.
A journey up the Nanticoke River took him into central Delaware
perhaps as far as Laurel. In his barge voyages of exploration
Smith acquired the most accurate knowledge thus far of the lands
watered by the rivers that poured into Chesapeake Bay.*

[*Brief descriptions of Smith's two exploring expeditions in the
Chesapeake Bay region were printed in 1612 as the second part
of Smith's* Map of Virginia *with a separate title page,* The Proceedings of the English Colonies in Virginia. *Portions of these are
reprinted in* Narratives of Early Virginia, 1606–1625, *edited by
Lyon G. Tyler, in "Original Narratives of Early American History"
(New York, 1907). These passages were written by Smith's companions on the expedition and are so noted in the printed version.
Excerpts follow:*]

The Accidents That Happened
in the Discovery of the Bay

. . . The second of June 1608 Smith left the fort to perform his discovery with this company: [List includes Walter Russell, "Doctor of Physic," six Gentlemen, four soldiers, including Anas Todkill, a blacksmith, a fishmonger, and a "fisher."]

These being in an open barge of two tons burden, leaving the *Phoenix* at Cape Henry we crossed the bay to the Eastern Shore and fell with the isles called Smith's Isles [Smith Island]. The first people we saw were two grim and stout savages upon Cape Charles, with long poles like javelins headed with bone. They boldly demanded what we were and what we would, but after many circumstances they in time seemed very kind and directed us to Accomac [30 miles south of the modern town of the same name], the habitation of the werowance [chief or king] where we were kindly treated. This king was the comeliest proper civil savage we encountered. His country is a pleasant fertile clay soil. . . . They spake the language of Powhatan, wherein they made such descriptions of the bay, isles, and rivers that often did us exceeding pleasure.

Passing along the coast, searching every inlet and bay fit for harbors and habitations, seeing many isles in the midst of the bay we bore up for them; but ere we could attain them such an extreme gust of wind, rain, thunder, and lightning happened that with great danger we escaped the unmerciful raging of that oceanlike water. The next day, searching those inhabitable isles (which we called Russell's Isles [probably the islands between Pocomoke Sound and the Bay]) to provide fresh water, the defect whereof forced us to follow the next eastern channel, which brought us to the river Wighcocómoco [Pocomoke]. The people at first with great fury seemed to assault us, yet at last, with songs, dances, and much mirth, became very tractable. But searching their habitations for water, we could fill but three [barricoes, or kegs], and that such puddle [water] that never till then we ever knew the want of good water. We digged and search[ed] many places but ere the end of two days we would have refused two barricoes of gold for one of that puddle water of Wighcocó-moco.

Being past these isles, falling with a high land upon the main, we found a great pond of fresh water, but so exceeding hot that we supposed it some bath. That place we called Point Ployer [named for a friend of Smith's, the Comte de Plouër; possibly Deal Island]. Being thus refreshed, in crossing over from the main to other isles, the wind and waters so much increased with thunder, lightning, and rain that our foremast blew overboard; and such mighty waves overwrought us in that small barge that with great labor we kept her from sinking by freeing out the water. Two days we were enforced to inhabit these uninhabited isles, which (for the extremity of gusts, thunder, rain, storms, and ill weather) we called Limbo [unknown today]. Repairing our foresail with our shirts, we set sail for the main and fell with a fair river on the east called Kuskarawaock [the Nanticoke]. . . .

But finding this eastern shore shallow broken isles and the main for most part without fresh water, we passed by the straits of Limbo for the western shore. So broad is the bay here that we could scarce perceive the great high cliffs on the other side. By them we anchored that night and called them Rickards Cliffs [for Smith's mother's family]. Thirty leagues [or 90 miles; a miscalculation for about 70 miles] we sailed more northward, not finding any inhabitants, yet the coast well watered, the mountains very barren, the valleys very fertile, but the woods extreme thick, full of wolves, bears, deer, and other wild beasts. . . .

When we first set sail some of our gallants doubted nothing but that our Captain would make too much haste home. But having lain not above twelve days in this small barge, oft tired at their oars, their bread spoiled with wet so much that it was rotten (yet so good were their stomachs that they could digest it), [they] did with continual complaints . . . importune him now to return. . . .

—Written by Walter Russell and Anas Todkill

What Happened the Second Voyage
to Discover the Bay

The 20 of July Captain Smith set forward to finish the discovery with twelve men [including Nathaniel Powell, Gentleman, and Anas Todkill, authors of this account]. . . .

The wind being contrary caused our stay two or three days at Kecoughtan [Old Point Comfort], the werowance feasting us with much mirth. . . . The first night we anchored at Stingray Isle [or Point, now Cherry Point]; the next day crossed Patawomecks [Potomac] River and hasted for the river Bolus [Patapsco]. We went not much farther before we might perceive the bay to divide in two heads, and, arriving there, we found it divided in four, all of which we searched so far as we could sail them. . . .

Thus having sought all the inlets and rivers worth noting, we returned to discover the river of Patuxent. These people [the Patuxent Indians] we found very tractable and more civil than any. We promised them, as also the Patawomecks, the next year to revenge them of the Massawomekes. Our purposes were crossed in the discovery of the river of Tappahannock [the Rappahannock, then named for the Tappahannock tribe], for we had much wrangling with that peevish nation; but at last they became as tractable as the rest. It is an excellent, pleasant, well inhabited, fertile, and a goodly navigable river. Toward the head thereof it pleased God to take one of our sick (called M. Fetherstone), where, in Fetherstone's bay we buried him, in the night, with a volley of shot. The rest (notwithstanding their ill diet and bad lodging, crowded in so small a barge, in so many dangers, never resting but always tossed to and again) all well recovered their healths.

Then we discovered the river of Piankatank and set sail for Jamestown. But in crossing the bay in a fair calm, such a sudden gust surprised us in the night, with thunder and rain, as we were half employed in freeing out water, never thinking to escape drowning. Yet running before the wind, at last we made land by the flashes of fire from heaven, by which light only we kept from the splitting shore until it pleased God in that black dark-

ness to preserve us by that light to find [Old] Point Comfort. And arrived safe at Jamestown the 7 of September, 1608. . . .
—By Nathaniel Powell and Anas Todkill.

[*Smith himself, in* A Map of Virginia, *gave a general description of the country that he had explored. Excerpts from his own account follow:*]

Virginia is a country in America that lieth between the degrees of 34 and 44 [45° in the Virginia charter of 1606] of the north latitude. The bounds thereof on the east side are the great Ocean; on the south lieth Florida; on the north, Nova Francia [New France]. As for the west thereof, the limits are unknown. Of all this country we purpose not to speak, but only of that part which was planted by the Englishmen in the year of our Lord 1606 [the Jamestown planters set out from London in December 1606]. And this is under the degrees of 37, 38, and 39.

The temperature of this country doth agree well with English constitutions, being once seasoned to the country. Which appeared by this: that though by many occasions our people fell sick, yet did they recover by very small means and continued in health though there were other great causes not only to have made them sick but even to end their days, etc. The summer is hot as in Spain, the winter cold as in France or England. The heat of summer is in June, July, and August, but commonly the cool breezes assuage the vehemency of the heat. The chief of winter is half December, January, February, and half March. The cold is extreme sharp, but here the proverb is true that no extreme long continueth.

In the year 1607 was an extraordinary frost in most of Europe, and this frost was found as extreme in Virginia. But the next year for eight or ten days of ill weather other fourteen days would be as summer. The winds here are variable, but the like thunder and lightning to purify the air I have seldom seen or heard in Europe. From the southwest came the greatest gusts, with thunder and heat. The northwest wind is commonly cool and bringeth fair weather with it. From the north is the greatest cold, and from the east and southeast, as from the Bermudas, fogs and rains. Sometimes there are great droughts, other times much rain, yet great necessity of neither by reason we see not but that all the

variety of needful fruits in Europe may be there in great plenty
by the industry of men, as appeareth by those we there planted.

There is but one entrance by sea into this country, and that is
at the mouth of a very goodly bay, the wideness whereof is near
eighteen or twenty miles. The cape on the south side is called
Cape Henry in honor of our most noble Prince [eldest son of
James I, who died in 1612, the year this tract was published].
The show of the land there is a white hilly sand like unto the
Downs, and along the shores great plenty of pines and firs. The
north cape is called Cape Charles in honor of the worthy Duke of
York [later Charles I]. Within is a country that may have the
prerogative over the most pleasant places of Europe, Asia, Africa,
or America for large and pleasant navigable rivers; heaven and
earth never agreed better to frame a place for man's habitation
being of our constitutions, were it fully manured and inhabited
by industrious people. Here are mountains, hills, plains, valleys;
rivers and brooks all running most pleasantly into a fair bay
compassed but for the mouth with fruitful and delightsome land.
In the bay and rivers are many isles both great and small, some
woody, some plain, most of them low and not inhabited.

This bay lieth north and south, in which the water floweth near
200 miles and hath a channel for 140 miles of depth betwixt seven
and fifteen fathom, holding in breadth for the most part ten or
fourteen miles. From the head of the bay at the north the land
is mountainous, and so in a manner from thence by a southwest
line, so that the more southward, the farther of[f] from the bay
are those mountains. From which fall certain brooks which after
come to five principal navigable rivers. These run from the northwest into the southeast and so into the west side of the bay, where
the fall of every river is within twenty or fifteen miles one of
another.

The mountains are of diverse natures, for at the head of the
bay the rocks are of a composition like miln [mill]stones; some
of marble, etc.; and many pieces of crystal we found as thrown
down by water from the mountains. For in winter these mountains
are covered with much snow, and when it dissolveth the waters
fall with such violence that it causeth great inundations in the
narrow valleys which yet is scarce perceived being once in the
rivers. These waters wash from the rocks such glistering tinctures
that the ground in some places seemeth as gilded, where both the

rocks and the earth are so splendent to behold that better judgments than ours might have been persuaded they contained more than probabilities. The vesture of the earth in most places doth manifestly prove the nature of the soil to be lusty and very rich. . . .

On the west side of the bay we said were five fair and delightful navigable rivers of which we will now proceed to report. The first of those rivers and the next to the mouth of the bay hath his course from the west and by north. The name of this river they call Powhatan [the James] accor[ding] to the name of a principal country that lieth upon it. The mouth of this river is near three miles in breadth, yet do the shoals force the channel so near the land that a saker [small artillery piece] will overshoot it at point blank. This river is navigable 100 miles; the shoals and soundings are here needless to be expressed. It falleth from rocks far west in a country inhabited by a nation that they call Monacan. But where it cometh into our discovery it is Powhatan. In the farthest place that was diligently observed are falls, rocks, shoals, etc. which makes it past navigation any higher. Thence in the running downward the river is enriched with many goodly brooks which are maintained by an infinite number of small rundles [runnels, i.e., streams] and pleasant springs that disperse themselves for best service as do the veins of a man's body.

From the south there falls into this river, first, the pleasant river of Appomattoc [the Appomattox]. Next, more to the east, are the two rivers of Quiyoughcohannock [Upper and Lower Chippokes creeks in Prince George and Surry counties]. A little farther is a bay wherein falleth three or four pretty brooks and creeks that half entrench the inhabitants of Warraskoyack [Isle of Wight County]. Then the river of Nansemond, and lastly the brook of Chesapeake [Elizabeth River].

From the north side is the river of Chickahominy, the back river of Jamestown; another by the Cedar isle where we lived ten weeks upon oysters; then a convenient harbor for fisher boats or small boats at Kecoughtan that so conveniently turneth itself into bays and creeks that make that place very pleasant to inhabit, their cornfields being girded therein in a manner as peninsulas.

The most of these rivers are inhabited by several nations, or rather families [tribes], of the name[s] of the rivers. They have also in every of those places some governor as their king which they call werowances. In a peninsula on the north side of this river are the English planted in a place by them called Jamestown in honor of the King's most excellent Majesty; upon which side are also many places under the werowances. . . .

In summer no place affordeth more plenty of sturgeon, nor in winter more abundance of fowl, especially in the time of frost. There was once taken fifty-two sturgeons at a draft, at another draft sixty-eight. From the later end of May till the end of June are taken few, but young sturgeons of two foot or a yard long. From thence till the midst of September, them of two or three yards long and few others. And in four or five hours with one net were ordinarily taken seven or eight, often more, seldom less. In the small rivers all the year there is good plenty of small fish, so that with hooks those that would take pains had sufficient.

Fourteen miles northward from the river Powhatan is the river of Pamunkey [the York] which is navigable sixty or seventy miles, but with ketches and small barks thirty or forty miles farther. At the ordinary flowing of the salt water it divideth itself into two gallant branches [the present Pamunkey and the Mattaponi]. . . . Before we come to the third river that falleth from the mountains, there is another river (some thirty miles navigable) that cometh from the inland: the river is called Piankatank; the inhabitants are about some forty serviceable men. The third navigable river is called Tappahannock [Rappahannock]. This is navigable some 130 miles. . . . This river also, as the two former, is replenished with fish and fowl.

The fourth river is called Patawomeck [Potomac] and is six or seven miles in breadth. It is navigable 140 miles and fed as the rest with many sweet rivers and springs which fall from the bordering hills. These hills many of them are planted and yield no less plenty and variety of fruit than the river exceedeth with abundance of fish. This river is inhabited on both sides. . . .

The fifth river is called Patuxent and is of a less proportion than the rest, but the channel is sixteen or eighteen fathom deep in some places. Here are infinite skulls of divers kinds of fish more than elsewhere. . . . Two hundred men was the greatest strength that could be there perceived. But they inhabit together and not so dispersed as the rest. These of all other were found the most civil to give entertainment.

Thirty leagues northward is a river not inhabited yet navigable;

the English call it Bolus [Petapsco River]. . . . At the end of the bay where it is six or seven miles in breadth there fall into it four small rivers, three of them issuing from diverse bogs environed with high mountains. There is one [the Susquehanna] that cometh due north three or four days' journey from the head of the bay and falls from rocks and mountains. Upon this river inhabit a people called Susquehannock. . . .

On the east side the bay is the river of Tockwough [the Sassafras] and upon it a people that can make 100 men, seated some seven miles within the river. . . . More to the south . . . is the river of Kuskarawaock [the Nanticoke] upon which is seated a people with 200 men. After that is the river of Tants Wighcocómoco [the Pocomoke, of the "puddle water"] and on it a people with 100 men. The people of those rivers are of little stature, of another language from the rest, and very rude. . . .

Southward they went . . . to search [for] them there left by Sir Walter Raleigh, for those parts to the town of Chesapeake hath formerly been discovered by Mr. Hariot and Sir Ralph Lane.

Early Penetration of Interior

The first colonists in Virginia were content to cling to the Tidewater region and to settle along the waterways that gave access to oceangoing vessels. But by the mid-seventeenth century Indian traders were pushing into the back country and beginning the westward movement that would not end until two centuries later, when pioneers would gaze across San Francisco Bay. The earliest ventures into the interior did not carry over the mountains; enough virgin country still lay in the foothills. But in time anonymous traders challenged the mountain barrier, and when the first recorded explorers reached the crest of the Alleghenies they found initials carved on trees.

One of the earliest land journeys of exploration into the interior was undertaken in late August 1650 by Edward Bland, Abraham Wood, Sackford Brewster, and Elias Pennant, with an Indian guide. They set out from the site of Petersburg, Virginia, then called Fort Henry, and rode southwest to the fork of the Dan and Staunton rivers at present-day Clarksville, Virginia, not far from the border of North Carolina. Their narrative, *The Discovery of New Britain* (1651), was a promotion tract designed to attract colonists. An address "To the Reader" extolled the climate of "New Britain" as better than Virginia's, though the land lay a mere four or five days' horseback ride from Petersburg. Furthermore, they pointed out, "sugar canes are supposed naturally to be there, or at least if implanted will undoubtedly flourish." They also described the "great store of fish," the quantity of salt "made in the sun without art," the possibility of finding precious minerals, and the productivity of the soil that made it possible to "have two crops of Indian corn yearly whereas Virginia hath but one."

To the north, meanwhile, settlers were establishing bases along the coast from Delaware Bay to Maine. As the region around Boston became too thickly populated, congregations led by their preachers moved out and established new towns. Gradually the coastal lands filled up and settlers began pushing up the river valleys, particularly the rich Connecticut valley. The extermination of hostile Pequot Indians in the Pequot War of 1637 eliminated the immediate danger of Indian attacks and allowed for further expansion. Fur traders led the way to the penetration of the interior and established trading posts on the frontier.

The Dutch made the deepest incursion into the back country from their outpost at Fort Orange on the Hudson, the present site of Albany. They established working relations with the Iroquois Indians and sold them guns to fight off the Algonquins, who obtained their arms from the French in Canada. Dutch and English traders were soon bitter rivals for the profits from furs and narrowly escaped open warfare on more than one occasion. For a time, however, the English did not challenge the Dutch in their more distant forays into the back country but were content to establish trading posts on the lower reaches of the New England rivers. But by the mid-seventeenth century interest in opening new outlets for trade with the Indians to the west was running high both in the colonies and in England. In 1664 the Duke of York sent an expedition that seized the Dutch possessions in the north and changed the name from New Netherlands to New York. One of the objectives was to capture the profitable fur trade with the interior.

In 1668 Médart Chouart, Sieur des Groseilliers, a French explorer and fur trader, outraged at his treatment by the French government, deserted to the English, who gave him a ship, and was sent to open trade in the Hudson Bay region; this venture resulted in the formation of the Hudson's Bay Company. Sir William Berkeley, the governor of Virginia, was closely associated with the noblemen interested in the Hudson's Bay Company and was himself deeply involved in the fur trade with the Indians on the Virginia frontier. Indeed, his concern not to disturb this Indian trade and his failure to protect the farming frontier from Indian attacks was one of the causes of Bacon's Rebellion in 1676.

Other Virginians were also eagerly pursuing the Indian trade, notably William Byrd, founder of the dynasty of that name, and Abraham Wood, who went exploring with Edward Bland in 1650. In time Wood became one of the greatest landowners and Indian traders in Virginia. From captain of the base at Fort Henry he rose to be a major-general. The explorations that Wood fostered are the best documented of the seventeenth century, but his activities were paralleled by others who prudently kept silent about their discoveries, for the routes to the best sources of furs were trade secrets jealously guarded. William Byrd I sent pack trains into the hinterland but he was careful not to reveal too much.

The first efforts by the English to reach trans-Appalachian territory came from Virginia. Abraham Wood was alleged to have discovered the Ohio and Mississippi rivers in the decade 1654–64. This report was made in 1699 in a statement to the Board of Trade in London by Dr. Daniel Coxe, an Englishman who never came to the Colonies but avidly collected documents and information about them. His assertions concerning Wood's discoveries remain a matter of dispute.

Throughout the second half of the seventeenth century interest in the trans-Appalachian region was growing. In 1671 Wood sent out the expedition that made the first recorded crossing of the Appalachian mountains. Another explorer, however, had already made three attempts to investigate the back country. He was a German physician, a somewhat mysterious character named John Lederer, who received authorization in 1669 from Governor Berkeley to make discoveries in the west.

Lederer in 1669–70 led three expeditions through the foothills of Virginia to the Blue Ridge. Twice he reached the summit of the first range of mountains and brought back tall tales of seeing the Atlantic Ocean from the top of a mountain ridge and of en-

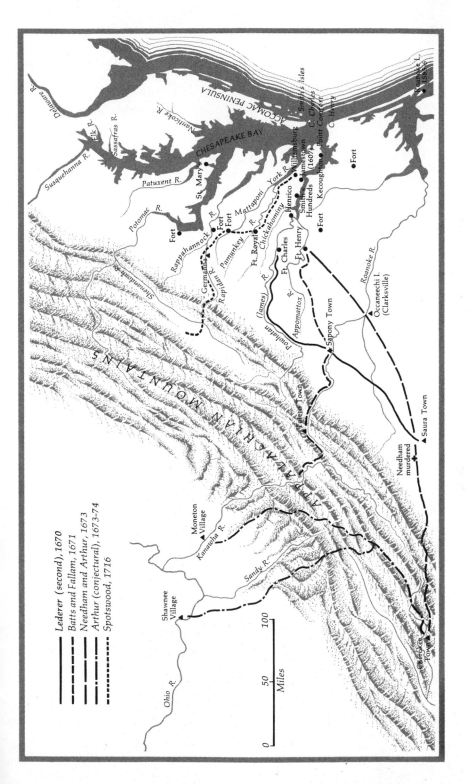

Westward Through the Chesapeake Bay Area to the Appalachian Mountains

Lederer (second), 1670
Batts and Fallam, 1671
Needham and Arthur, 1673
Arthur (conjectural), 1673–74
Spotswood, 1716

countering lions and leopards. After about a year and a half
Lederer left Virginia hastily, probably pursued by creditors, and
he soon drops from sight. But Sir William Talbot's preface "To the
Reader" of Lederer's *Discoveries* (1672) asserts that envious and
prejudiced Virginians had forced Lederer to flee to Maryland,
where Talbot, finding him "a modest ingenious person and a
pretty scholar," decided that "common justice" demanded the
publication of his narrative.

A modern traveler roaring over paved roads from Tidewater
Virginia to the Skyline Drive forgets that this terrain was difficult
to traverse in colonial times when the land was heavily forested
and matted with honeysuckle, grape, and other vines. Men on foot
or mounted on horseback had trouble getting through, and the
natural impediments help to explain the slow pace of explorations
through the Piedmont region. Lederer explains: "The ground is
overgrown with underwood in many places, and that so perplext
and interwoven with vines that who travels here must sometimes
cut through his way. These thickets harbor all sorts of beasts of
prey, as wolves, panthers, leopards, lions, etc. (which are neither
so large nor so fierce as those of Asia and Africa) and small vermin
as wild cats, foxes, raccoons." [3] If other travelers did not see
leopards and lions, many substantiated Lederer's description of
matted vines and heavy underbrush.

Lederer was also impressed and horrified by the snakes of this
region, as well he might have been. At the head of York River his
men killed a rattlesnake "of extraordinary length and thickness,
for I judged it two yards and a half or better from head to tail and
as big about as a man's arm," and, "having killed and opened her,
found there a small squirrel whole." When he wondered how a
snake could catch such a nimble creature, the Indians explained
"that it was usual in these serpents, when they lie basking in the
sun, to fetch down these squirrels from the tops of the trees by
fixing their eyes steadfastly upon them. The horror of which
strikes such an affrightment into the little beast that he has no
power to hinder himself from tumbling down into the jaws of his
enemy." Lederer discounted this story and believed that "these

[3] *Talbot's account of Lederer's journeys is reprinted in* The First Explorations
of the Trans-Allegheny Region by the Virginians, 1650–1674, *edited by
Clarence W. Alvord and Lee Bidgood (Cleveland, Ohio, 1912). See p. 141.*

serpents climb the trees and surprise their prey in their nests." [4] But he was more interested in narrating wonders than in providing geographical data, which perhaps accounts for the fact that his "discoveries" had less impact than others.

Meanwhile General Abraham Wood had been organizing one of the most important of the seventeenth-century expeditions into the Appalachians, sent out from his base at Fort Henry in 1671. The exploring party consisted of Captain Thomas Batts, Robert Fallam, Thomas Wood (perhaps a relative of the General) and an Appomattox Indian chief named Perecute, who went along as guide and proved of immense help. Fallam kept a journal of the expedition that provides accurate information about the territory traversed.

The expedition carried a commission from General Wood "for the finding out of the ebbing and flowing of the waters on the other side of the mountains in order to [make] the discovery of the South Sea." The party set out from Fort Henry on September 1, 1671; by September 13 they had reached the eastern continental divide somewhere beyond the modern city of Roanoke, Virginia, and had found a stream flowing westward from which they drank. They had reached the "western waters" if not the South Sea, and the stream they found, the New River, flowed ultimately into the Ohio. Englishmen had made their presence known in the west and henceforth they would compete with the French for supremacy in the great watershed of the Ohio and the Mississippi.

But they were not the first white men to drink of the western waters. On the way up the Blue Ridge slope they found blazed on a tree the letters "M.A.N I." and into another, "M A," with other symbols that they could not make out.

On September 17 the Batts-Fallam party picked out trees on which they could place their own marks:

Early in the morning we went to seek some trees to mark, our Indians being impatient of longer stay by reason it was like to be bad weather, and that it was so difficult to get provisions. We found four trees exceeding fit for our purpose, that had been half bared by our Indians, standing after one the other. We first proclaimed the King in these words: "Long live Charles the Second, by the grace of God King of England, Scotland, France, Ireland,

[4] Ibid., *pp. 145–46.*

and Virginia and all the territories thereunto belonging, Defender of the Faith, etc.," firing some guns, and went to the first tree which we marked thus with a pair of marking irons for his sacred majesty [symbol of a crown over the initials C R, Charles Rex]. Then the next, W B, for the right honorable Governor Sir William Berkeley; the third thus, A W, for the honorable Major General Wood.

The last tree they marked with their own initials, including "P" for Perecute, the Indian guide, who declared that he would be an Englishman. A cryptic sentence adds: "And on another tree hard by stand these letters one under another: 'TT. NP. VE. R','" whether carved by them or others they do not make clear.[5]

The New River, on which they found themselves, was broader than they expected, "much like the James River at Col. Stagg's [Thomas Stegge, uncle of William Byrd I], the falls much like those falls" (near the site of modern Richmond).

The expedition immediately set out for home, "and when we were on the top of a hill we turned about and saw over against us, westerly, over a certain delightful hill a fog arise and a glimmering light as from water. We supposed there to be a great bay. We came to the Toteras [an Indian settlement] Tuesday night where we found our horses and ourselves well entertained. We immediately had the news of Mr. Byrd and his great company's discoveries three miles from the Tetera's [sic] Town." The discoveries of William Byrd's "great company" remain hidden in the mist that the Batts-Fallam party thought might indicate a bay of the South Sea. The party got back to Fort Henry on October 1, and Fallam concluded his journal with this sentence: "God's holy name be praised for our preservation." [6]

The next expedition sent out by Abraham Wood was led by James Needham, a South Carolina colonist; he had with him an illiterate youth named Gabriel Arthur and eight Indians. Their objective was the discovery of a way to open up trade with the distant Cherokee nation in the mountains of North Carolina and Tennessee.

Setting out from Fort Henry on April 10, 1673, they reached a fortified settlement of Occaneechi Indians on an island in the Roanoke River near modern Clarksville, Virginia. There the In-

[5] Ibid., pp. 191–92.
[6] Ibid., pp. 192–93.

dians made them turn back. The Occaneechi served as middle-men in the trade with more distant Indians and did not want to see the Virginians open direct trade with the Cherokees.

Needham returned to Fort Henry, but in mid-May Wood sent him and his party back to make another attempt to reach the Cherokees. This time they encountered a band of Cherokees whom they joined, and contrived to evade the Occaneechi, cross the Great Smoky Mountains, and reach Cherokee territory in north-eastern Tennessee. Needham discovered that the Cherokees had been trading with the Spaniards in Florida, but, because the Spaniards had attacked a band of Cherokees on a trading expedition to Florida and had enslaved some of them, the Cherokees now regarded the Spaniards as deadly enemies. They therefore welcomed the English. With this good news Needham hurried back to Fort Henry, leaving his companion, Arthur, among the Cherokees to learn their speech.

As soon as Needham could report to Abraham Wood and re-equip himself, he hurried back to the Cherokee country. But his luck had run out. A treacherous Occaneechi Indian murdered him and urged his Cherokee companions to return to their country and kill Arthur. But Arthur's life was spared, though he was forced to join numerous Cherokee war parties that took him over parts of the upper Ohio valley. At last he returned to Fort Henry on June 18, 1674. Unfortunately Arthur lacked the skill of writing and could keep no journal of his adventures. His verbal reports to Wood, however, must have been of great value.

Before the end of the seventeenth century traders were pushing through passes into the new West and developing trade with Indians beyond the mountains. The day was not far distant when Daniel Boone would blaze a trail into the "dark and bloody ground" of Kentucky.

The best known of the early explorations over the mountains was the celebrated expedition led by Governor Alexander Spots-wood in August and September of 1716. His party included a group of Virginia gentlemen, two squads of rangers, servants and Indian guides, making a total of 63 men, among them the historian Robert Beverley and John Fontaine, a Huguenot gentleman who kept a journal. Fontaine's journal reveals a holiday spirit for most of the way, though the party had rough going through tangled vines and brush, and encountered its share of snakes. At one point the briars and brush were so dense that Fontaine reports that their clothes were "torn all to rags." [7]

The route the Spotswood party followed ran from Williamsburg to the Mattaponi River and thence to the Rapidan River, where Spotswood had established a settlement of Germans at a place called Germanna, which was the expedition's base for its venture over the Blue Ridge.

The expedition moved over the mountains at a pass now called Swift Run Gap, which Spotswood's rangers had found the previous spring, and on September 5 reached the crest of the Blue Ridge, where they stopped to celebrate the successful ascent. The group then descended the west side of the mountains and crossed the Shenandoah River (which they called the "Euphrates") in the great Valley of Virginia at a point near modern Elkton.

This journey of investigation over the mountains is one of the most convivial on record. Fontaine, carefully recording the events in his journal, reports the consumption of an incredible quantity of liquor and frequent encounters with rattlesnakes of appalling size. Whether there was any connection between these two facts a later historian cannot say. On September 5, Fontaine writes: "We drank King George's health and all the Royal Family's, at the very top of the Appalachian mountains. . . . I, being somewhat more curious than the rest, went on a high rock on the top of the mountain to see fine prospects, and I lost my gun." The next day Spotswood buried a bottle containing a paper saying that he took possession of the region in the name of George I, King of England. At the conclusion of this ceremony, says Fontaine, "we had a good dinner, and after it we got the men together, and loaded all their arms, and we drank the King's health in champagne, and fired a volley; the Princess' health in burgundy, and fired a volley; and all the rest of the royal family in claret, and fired a volley. We drank the Governor's health and fired another volley. We had several sorts of liquors, viz., Virginia red wine and white wine, Irish usquebaugh, brandy, shrub, two sorts of rum, champagne, canary, cherry punch, water, cider, etc."

Spotswood memorialized the journey by creating the "Trans-

---

[7] *Fontaine's journal is reproduced by Ann Maury, in* Memoirs of a Huguenot Family (*New York, 1872*). *For this and the following passage, see pp. 287–89.*

montane Order" and presenting his companions with golden horse-shoes "to encourage gentlemen to venture backwards and make discoveries and new settlements," according to Hugh Jones, a contemporary historian.[8]

After some pleasant hunting and some more conviviality, the party retraced its steps and was back in Williamsburg on September 17. Fontaine estimates that, counting both the outward journey and the return, they covered 438 miles. Although this was one of the most cheerful exploring expeditions on record, Spotswood had more in mind than a protracted picnic. News of the French infiltration of the back country troubled English settlers in the coastal region, and Spotswood, a military man, realized the danger of having an enemy at one's rear. He was paving the way for English occupation of land beyond the mountains.

[8] *Hugh Jones,* The Present State of Virginia (*London, 1724*), *p. 14.*

The French on
the Great Interior Waterways

THE Virginia traders' concern over the incursion of the French into the hinterland showed a realistic appreciation of a danger that would grow increasingly acute through the first six decades of the eighteenth century. Before the turn of the seventeenth century French fur traders, explorers, and missionaries had already familiarized themselves with the Great Lakes region and the watersheds of the Ohio and the upper Mississippi rivers. Indeed, René Robert Cavelier, Sieur de La Salle, who had set out from Montreal in 1681–82 and floated down the Mississippi to its mouth, had a vision of colonizing the great valley with Frenchmen. Beginning in 1535, when Jacques Cartier, the intrepid sailor from Saint Malo, sailed up the St. Lawrence as far as the site of Montreal searching for a seaway to China, the French had kept up their efforts to explore the waterways beyond the rapids of the St. Lawrence. Cod fishermen drying their catch on land at the mouth of the St. Lawrence soon discovered that the Indians were eager to trade for the white man's products, especially cutlery, blankets and brandy. During the later years of the sixteenth century fishermen and anonymous traders discovered the immense profits from beaver skins and paved the way for fur trading on a scale that would attract national interest.

In 1603 King Henry IV promised a monopoly of the fur trade to a group of aristocrats provided they would establish a colony in Canada. The leader of this group was Aymar de Chastes, the governor of Dieppe, who chose as one of his chief associates Sieur du Pontgravé, a wealthy merchant of Saint Malo. Death soon removed de Chastes and he was succeeded by Pierre du Guast, Sieur de Monts, who pursued the colonial project vigorously. De Monts early recognized the capacity of Samuel de Champlain, a naval officer who had made a voyage to the Caribbean for the Spaniards in 1599–1601 and was on the first expedition sent out by de Chastes to Canada in 1603. On this first voyage Champlain had the title of "Geographer Royal," because an account that he had written of his Caribbean experience had attracted the interest of Henri IV, who gave him this title. On his return from Canada Champlain published in 1604 a narrative of this voyage. Henceforth until the end of his life he proved not only a diligent and observant explorer but an accurate chronicler of what he saw.

In June of 1604 de Monts settled a colony on St. Croix Island in the Bay of Fundy, but the next year the colony moved to a better site at Port Royal on the mainland of Nova Scotia. Champlain saw to it that the French made friends with the Indians, and he himself quickly developed into a diplomat of great skill in dealing with them. He also spent as much time as possible exploring the neighboring terrain, for he had an insatiable curiosity about the geography of the new land in which he found himself.

When de Monts' syndicate in 1607 lost its monopoly of the fur trade to rival intriguers at court, the little colony at Port Royal had to give up and return to France. But Champlain was convinced that a colony, even without a monopoly, could succeed, and in 1608 he returned to Canada with a small group and settled on the site of Quebec. Although its existence at times was precarious, the settlement lasted, and Champlain presided over it for nearly a quarter of a century. As an explorer himself, he led expeditions into the wilderness, and he was instrumental in sending others to seek out distant territories that he could not visit in person.

In the spring of 1609 Champlain accompanied a war party of Hurons, who defeated a band of Iroquois near the site of Crown Point, New York. French gunfire determined the result of the battle, and from this time onward the Iroquois held the French as their enemies. On this journey Champlain discovered the large lake that bears his name. In 1612 he returned to France and succeeded in gaining once more for his syndicate a monopoly of the fur trade. The next year he went exploring again and reached Allumette Island in the Ottawa River. In 1615 he and Étienne

Brulé, with a band of Hurons, reached Georgian Bay on Lake Huron and returned by way of Lake Ontario. In an attack on some Iroquois, Champlain was wounded and had to spend the winter with the Indians. After this he devoted his time principally to the business of the colony and left exploring to others. In 1634 he sent Jean Nicolet on an expedition into Wisconsin. The next year Champlain died at Quebec. His efforts had saved Canada for the French and had opened the way to new lands and new sources of furs in the West.

Champlain's Journal

[*Champlain kept and published elaborate journals of his ex-plorations. A translation of the journals was made by Charles Pomeroy Otis and published by the Prince Society in 1878, 1880 and 1882. Extensive excerpts are to be found in* Voyages of Samuel de Champlain, 1604–1618, *edited by W. L. Grant in "Original Narratives of Early American History" (New York, 1907). The following excerpts describe the discovery of Lake Champlain in 1609 and the attack on the Iroquois which resulted in their endur-ing hostility toward the French.*]

Chapter 9

Departure from the fall of the Iroquois [Richelieu] River. De-scription of a large lake. Encounter with the enemy at this lake; their manner of attacking the Iroquois, and their behavior in battle.

I set out accordingly from the fall of the Iroquois River on the 2d [12th] of July. All the savages set to carrying their canoes, arms, and baggage overland, some half a league, in order to pass by the violence and strength of the fall, which was speedily accomplished. Then they put them all in the water again, two men in each with the baggage; and they caused one of the men of each canoe to go by land some three leagues, the extent of the fall, which is not, however, so violent here as at the mouth, except in some places, where rocks obstruct the river, which is not broader than three hundred or four hundred paces. After we had passed the fall, which was attended with difficulty, all the savages, who had gone by land over a good path and level country, although there are a great many trees, reembarked in their canoes. My men went also by land; but I went in a canoe. The savages made a review of all their followers, finding that there were twenty-four canoes, with sixty men. After the review was completed, we continued our course to an island [Ste. Thérèse, or perhaps Isle aux Noix] three leagues long, filled with the finest pines I had ever seen. Here they went hunting and captured some wild animals. Proceeding about three leagues farther on, we made a halt in order to rest the coming night.

They all at once set to work, some to cut wood, and others to obtain the bark of trees for covering their cabins for the sake of sheltering themselves, others to fell large trees for constructing a barricade on the riverbank around their cabins, which they do so quickly that in less than two hours so much is accomplished that five hundred of their enemies would find it very difficult to dislodge them without killing large numbers. They make no barricade on the riverbank where their canoes are drawn up in order that they may be able to embark, if occasion requires. After they were established in their cabins they despatched three canoes, with nine good men, according to their custom in all their encampments, to reconnoiter for a distance of two or three leagues to see if they can perceive anything, after which they return. They rest the entire night, depending upon the observation of these scouts, which is a very bad custom among them; for they are sometimes while sleeping surprised by their enemies, who slaughter them before they have time to get up and prepare for defense. Noticing this, I remonstrated with them on the mistake they made and told them that they ought to keep watch, as they had seen us do every night, and have men on the lookout, in order to listen and see whether they perceived anything, and that they should not live in such a manner like beasts. They replied that they could not keep watch and that they worked enough in the daytime in the chase, since, when engaged in war, they divide their troops into three parts: namely, a part for hunting scattered in several places; another to constitute the main body of their army, which is always under arms; and the third to act as *avant-coureurs*, to look out along the rivers and observe whether they can see any mark or signal showing where their enemies or friends have passed. . . .

We set out on the next day, continuing our course in the river as far as the entrance of the lake [Lake Champlain]. There are many pretty islands here, low, and containing very fine woods and meadows, with abundance of fowl and such animals of the chase as stags, fallow deer, fawns, roebucks, bears, and others, which go from the mainland to these islands. We captured a large number of these animals. There are also many beavers, not only in this river, but also in numerous other little ones that flow into it. These regions, although they are pleasant, are not inhabited by any savages on account of their wars; but they withdraw as far as possible from the rivers into the interior in order not to be suddenly surprised.

The next day we entered the lake which is of great extent, say eighty or a hundred leagues long, where I saw four fine islands, ten, twelve, and fifteen leagues long [these distances are exaggerated], which were formerly inhabited by the savages, like the River of the Iroquois; but they have been abandoned since the wars of the savages with one another prevail. There are also many rivers falling into the lake, bordered by many fine trees of the same kinds as those we have in France, with many vines finer than any I have seen in any other place; also many chestnut trees on the border of this lake, which I had not seen before. There is also a great abundance of fish of many varieties; among others, one called by the savages of the country *Chaousarou* [the gar, or garpike], which varies in length, the largest being, as the people told me, eight or ten feet long. I saw some five feet long, which were as large as my thigh; the head being as big as my two fists, with a snout two feet and a half long, and a double row of very sharp and dangerous teeth. Its body is, in shape, much like that of a pike; but it is armed with scales so strong that a poniard could not pierce them. Its color is silver-gray. The extremity of its snout is like that of swine. This fish makes war upon all others in the lakes and rivers. . . .

Continuing our course over this lake on the western side, I noticed, while observing the country, some very high mountains on the eastern side [the Green Mountains of Vermont] on the top of which there was snow [probably white limestone instead of snow]. I made inquiry of the savages whether these localities were inhabited, when they told me that the Iroquois dwelt there, and that there were beautiful valleys in these places, with plains productive in grain such as I had eaten in this country, together with many kinds of fruit without limit. They said also that the lake extended near mountains, some twenty-five leagues distant from us, as I judge. I saw, on the south, other mountains, no less high than the first, but without any snow [the Adirondacks]. The savages told me that these mountains were thickly settled and that it was there we were to find their enemies; but that it was necessary to pass a fall [Ticonderoga] in order to go there (which I afterwards saw), when we should enter another lake [Lake George], nine or ten leagues long. After reaching the end of the lake, we should have to go, they said, two leagues by land and pass through a river [the Hudson] flowing into the sea on the Norumbega coast, near [i.e. north of] that of Florida, whither it took them only two days to go by canoe—as I have since ascertained from some prisoners we captured, who gave me minute information in regard to all they had personal knowledge of, through some Algonquin interpreters who understood the Iroquois language.

Now, as we began to approach within two or three days' journey of the abode of their enemies, we advanced only at night, resting during the day. But they did not fail to practise constantly their accustomed superstitions, in order to ascertain what was to be the result of their undertaking; and they often asked me if I had had a dream and seen their enemies, to which I replied in the negative. Yet I did not cease to encourage them, and inspire in them hope. When night came, we set out on the journey until the next day, when we withdrew into the interior of the forest, and spent the rest of the day there. About ten or eleven o'clock, after taking a little walk about our encampment, I retired. While sleeping, I dreamed that I saw our enemies, the Iroquois, drowning in the lake near a mountain, within sight. When I expressed a wish to help them, our allies, the savages, told me we must let them all die, and that they were of no importance. When I awoke, they did not fail to ask me, as usual, if I had had a dream. I told them that I had, in fact, had a dream. This, upon being related, gave them so much confidence that they did not doubt any longer that good was to happen to them.

When it was evening, we embarked in our canoes to continue our course; and, as we advanced very quietly and without making any noise, we met on the 29th of the month the Iroquois, about ten o'clock at evening, at the extremity of a cape [Crown Point,

near Ticonderoga] which extends into the lake on the western
bank. They had come to fight. We both began to utter loud cries,
all getting their arms in readiness. We withdrew out on the water,
and the Iroquois went on shore, where they drew up all their
canoes close to each other and began to fell trees with poor axes,
which they acquire in war sometimes, using also others of stone.
Thus they barricaded themselves very well.

Our forces also passed the entire night [with] their canoes being
drawn up close to each other and fastened to poles so that they
might not get separated and that they might be all in readiness
to fight, if occasion required. We were out upon the water, within
arrow range of their barricades. When they were armed and in
array, they despatched two canoes by themselves to the enemy
to inquire if they wished to fight, to which the latter replied that
they wanted nothing else: but they said that, at present, there
was not much light and that it would be necessary to wait for
daylight so as to be able to recognize each other; and that, as soon
as the sun rose, they would offer us battle. This was agreed to by
our side. Meanwhile, the entire night was spent in dancing and
singing, on both sides, with endless insults and other talk; [such]
as how little courage we had, how feeble a resistance we should
make against their arms, and that, when day came, we should
realize it to our ruin. Ours also were not slow in retorting, telling
them they would see such execution of arms as never before,
together with an abundance of such talk as is not unusual in the
siege of a town.

After this singing, dancing, and bandying words on both sides
to the fill, when day came, my companions and myself continued
under cover, for fear that the enemy would see us. We arranged our
arms in the best manner possible, being, however, separated, each
in one of the canoes of the savage Montagnais [a tribe inhabiting
both banks of the Saguenay]. After arming ourselves with light
armor, we each took an harquebus and went on shore. I saw the
enemy go out of their barricade, nearly two hundred in number,
stout and rugged in appearance. They came at a slow pace toward
us, with a dignity and assurance which greatly amused [or de-
lighted] me, having three chiefs at their head. Our men also
advanced in the same order, telling me that those who had three
large plumes were the chiefs and that they had only these three
and that they could be distinguished by these plumes, which

were much larger than those of their companions, and that I should do what I could to kill them. I promised to do all in my power, and said that I was very sorry they could not understand me, so that I might give order and shape to their mode of attacking their enemies, and then we should, without doubt, defeat them all; but that this could not now be obviated, and that I should be very glad to show them my courage and goodwill when we should engage in the fight.

As soon as we had landed they began to run for some two hundred paces toward their enemies, who stood firmly, not having as yet noticed my companions, who went into the woods with some savages. Our men began to call me with loud cries; and, in order to give me a passageway, they opened in two parts and put me at their head, where I marched some twenty paces in advance of the rest until I was within about thirty paces of the enemy, who at once noticed me, and, halting, gazed at me, as I did also at them. When I saw them making a move to fire at us, I rested my musket against my cheek and aimed directly at one of the three chiefs. With the same shot, two fell to the ground; and one of their men was so wounded that he died some time after. I had loaded my musket with four balls. When our side saw this shot so favorable for them, they began to raise such loud cries that one could not have heard it thunder. Meanwhile, the arrows flew on both sides. The Iroquois were greatly astonished that two men had been so quickly killed, although they were equipped with armor woven from cotton thread and with wood which was proof [effective] against their arrows. This caused great alarm among them. As I was loading again one of my companions fired a shot from the woods, which astonished them anew to such a degree that, seeing their chiefs dead, they lost courage and took to flight, abandoning their camp and fort and fleeing into the woods, whither I pursued them, killing still more of them. Our savages also killed several of them, and took ten or twelve prisoners. The remainder escaped with the wounded. Fifteen or sixteen were wounded on our side with arrow shots; but they were soon healed.

After gaining the victory, our men amused themselves by taking a great quantity of Indian corn and some meal from their enemies, also their armor, which they had left behind that they might run better. After feasting sumptuously, dancing and singing, we returned three hours after with the prisoners. The spot where this attack took place is in latitude 43° and some minutes, and the lake was called Lake Champlain.

Jean Nicolet Gets to Green Bay and Beyond

[*From the beginning of their explorations the French contrived to establish good relations with the Indians. Although Champlain's aid of the Hurons in their attack on the Iroquois made enemies of these Five Nations, the French diligently sought to improve their relations with the Algonquins and the more distant Indians in the West. Champlain encouraged priests to establish missions among the Indians, and he also induced young laymen to live among the Indians to learn their languages and their woodcraft.*

[*The most successful of the missionaries were Jesuits, who, after 1632, had control of all missionary efforts in New France. The missionaries sent in reports to the head of the order, who arranged to have them published in an annual volume, now collected and known as the* Jesuit Relations. *A bilingual version of these reports, edited by Reuben G. Thwaites, was published as* The Jesuit Relations and Allied Documents, 1610–1791 (*Cleveland, Ohio, 1896–1903*). *These reports give vivid accounts of the efforts of the missionaries and their lay colleagues to explore in the interior of the continent.*

[*Jean Nicolet, whom Champlain sent to investigate a region he had heard about in the West, was one of the young men who had gone into the woods to learn from the Indians. His epoch-making journey in 1634 to Green Bay and thence into Wisconsin extended French knowledge of the Great Lakes and the adjacent regions and stirred the French to further exploration. They still believed that these great bodies of fresh water might lead to the Ocean Sea and the Far East. The notion of an easy water route to Asia lingered long in men's hopes and did not vanish until Thomas Jefferson sent Lewis and Clark to search in vain for a convenient portage to a west-flowing navigable river, as we shall see in Chapter IX.*

[*Nicolet proved to be an effective Indian diplomat and was instrumental not only in finding new routes to the interior, but in establishing peace among warring tribes. His expedition to*

Green Bay in 1634 was a peace mission to a tribe then called "People of the Sea," later known as the Winnebago. The French thought that these might indeed be Asiatics, and Nicolet went dressed in a Chinese robe in case these tribesmen turned out to be Chinese or other civilized Asians. A brief account of his journey, included in the Jesuit Relations *of 1642, was written by one of the missionaries, Father Barthélemy Vimont. The pertinent passages follow:]*

The Journey of Jean Nicolet, 1634

I will now speak of the life and death of Monsieur Nicolet, interpreter and agent for the Gentlemen of the Company of New France. He died ten days after the Father [Charles Raymboult] and had lived in this region twenty-five years. What I shall say of him will aid to a better understanding of the country. He came to New France in the year 1618; and forasmuch as his nature and excellent memory inspired good hopes of him, he was sent to winter with the Island Algonquins [known also as Allumettes, a tribe occupying an island in the Ottawa River] in order to learn their language. He tarried with them two years, alone of the French, and always joined the barbarians in their excursions and journeys, undergoing such fatigues as none but eyewitnesses can conceive; he often passed seven or eight days without food, and once, full seven weeks with no other nourishment than a little bark from the trees. He accompanied four hundred Algonquins, who went during that time to make peace with the Hyroquois [Iroquois], which he successfully accomplished; and would to God that it had never been broken, for then we should not now be suffering the calamities which move us to groans, and which must be an extraordinary impediment in the way of converting these tribes. After this treaty of peace, he went to live eight or nine years with the Algonquin Nipissiriniens [the Nipissings], where he passed for one of that nation, taking part in the very frequent councils of those tribes, having his own separate cabin and household, and fishing and trading for himself. He was finally recalled, and appointed agent and interpreter.

While in the exercise of this office, he was delegated to make a journey to the nation called People of the Sea [the Winnebagos] and arrange peace between them and the Hurons, from whom they are distant about three hundred leagues westward. He embarked in the Huron country [the peninsula between Lake Erie and the southern end of Georgian Bay] with seven savages; and they passed by many small nations, both going and returning. When they arrived at their destination, they fastened two sticks in the earth and hung gifts thereon, so as to relieve these tribes from the notion of mistaking them for enemies to be massacred. When he was two days' journey from that nation, he sent one of those savages to bear tidings of the peace, which word was especially well received when they heard that it was a European who carried the message; they despatched several young men to meet the Manitouiriniou—that is to say, "the wonderful man." They meet him; they escort him, and carry all his baggage. He wore a grand robe of China damask, all strewn with flowers and birds of many colors. No sooner did they perceive him than the women and children fled at the sight of a man who carried thunder in both hands—for thus they called the two pistols that he held. The news of his coming quickly spread to the places round about, and there assembled four or five thousand men. Each of the chief men made a feast for him, and at one of these banquets they served at least sixscore beavers. The peace was concluded; he returned to the Hurons, and some time later to the Three Rivers [Trois Rivières on the St. Lawrence], where he continued his employment as agent and interpreter, to the great satisfaction of both the French and the savages, by whom he was equally and singularly loved.

Further Exploration of the Great Lakes Region

[*Jesuit missionaries from their bases in the wilderness continued to push ever westward. In 1643 a mission group reached the northwest tip of Lake Huron and there discovered the strait leading from Lake Superior, which they named Sault de Sainte Marie. In the mid-seventeenth century hostile Iroquois carried their warfare against the Algonquins to the very borders of Quebec and drove the priests from their missions, but before the end of the century missionaries and traders were again exploring the back country and soon had an accurate knowledge of the whole*

Great Lakes region. Some probed the tributaries of the Mississippi and learned about the great river itself.

[Two French traders who displayed extraordinary enterprise, even in that age of daring, were Pierre Esprit Radisson and Médart Chouart, Sieur des Groseilliers. Groseilliers served nine years as a lay assistant to Jesuit missionaries and thus learned at first hand much about Indian life and Indian trade routes. In 1653 he married Radisson's sister Marguerite and thereafter the two men called each other brother. Radisson, who was younger than Groseilliers, did not reach New France until 1651, but he quickly learned about the Indians the hard way, for he was captured by the Iroquois in 1652 while on a hunting trip. For some reason the Iroquois chose not to slaughter him and took him to Albany; there Dutch traders later rescued him and sent him back to his home at Three Rivers (Trois Rivières). In 1657 he accompanied a group of French settlers into Iroquois territory and narrowly escaped capture a second time.

[Despite his hazardous experiences with hostile tribesmen, Radisson was eager to explore the western country and find the sources of the rich cargoes of furs that Indians brought by canoe to Three Rivers and Montreal. Sometime between 1658 and 1660 (the date is not known precisely), he and Groseilliers joined an Indian party returning to the West. They learned much about the interior and made a second journey to the Great Lakes, entered the area that became Minnesota, and perhaps went as far north as Hudson Bay. When they returned in 1660 with canoes laden down with valuable furs, the governor had their cargo confiscated for trading without a license. Nursing their wrath, both men deserted the French and went over to the English. In the expedition that they persuaded an English syndicate to send out in 1668, the ship in which Radisson was embarked had to turn back, but Groseilliers' vessel reached James Bay at the bottom of Hudson Bay. There the English established Fort Charles (later Fort Rupert), which became an important trading post. The shipload of furs that Groseilliers took back convinced the promoters of the value of the fur trade in this area and resulted in their obtaining a charter in 1670 establishing the Hudson's Bay Company.

[The allegiances of these two brothers-in-law wavered and they later rejoined the French and plundered some of the English posts *they had earlier helped to establish. Radisson, however, married an English wife and ended his life as a pensioner of the Hudson's Bay Company. The narratives of his travels and explorations remained in manuscript and were not published until the nineteenth century. Hence they had less influence upon explorers than the Jesuit Relations and other contemporary published narratives.*

[One of the most influential of the French forest diplomats and explorers of the seventeenth century was Nicholas Perrot, who about 1665 began a long career of travel and negotiation with the western Indians, and in 1683 was Indian agent in Wisconsin for the French government. In 1689 he took possession of the whole upper Mississippi valley in the name of the French king. Perrot spent his last years writing his memoirs of the customs, dress, and religion of the North American Indians, a work that was not published until 1864. Although his contemporary influence upon the Indians was of enormous importance to the French, his written work, like Radisson's, had no impact upon the explorations of his day.

[An ardent apostle to the western Indians and an observant explorer was Father Claude Jean Allouez, who was a companion of Nicholas Perrot for a portion of a western journey with the Indians in 1665–1667. Allouez spent seven years learning the Algonquin language and Indian ways before setting out on his first expedition. He founded a mission at Sault Ste. Marie in 1668 and in the following year he visited tribes in Wisconsin, which he made his special field of labor for a decade with headquarters on Green Bay. He was instrumental in establishing other missions, especially one at De Pere, Wisconsin, and another at Fort St. Louis in Illinois. Allouez' reports were summarized in the Jesuit Relations. A description of a difficult journey that he made to Chequamegon Bay of Lake Superior in 1665–67 was first published in the Jesuit Relation for 1668. An excerpt will give some indication of the persistence of priests like Allouez in the face of Indian cruelty and callousness.]

Chapter II
Journal of Father Claude Allouez's Voyage
into the Outaouac [Ottawa] Country
[the region of the upper lakes about Mackinac]

. . . On the eighth of August, in the year 1665, I embarked at
Three Rivers with six Frenchmen, in company with more than
four hundred savages of various nations, who, after transacting
the little trading for which they had come, were returning to
their own country.

The Devil offered all conceivable opposition to our journey,
making use of the false prejudice held by these savages, that bap-
tism causes their children to die. One of their chief men declared
to me, in arrogant and menacing terms, his intention and that of
his people to abandon me on some desert island if I ventured to
follow them farther. We had then proceeded as far as the rapids
of the River des Prairies [the branch of the St. Lawrence forming
the island of Montreal], where the breaking of the canoe that bore
me made me apprehensive of the threatened disaster. We promptly
set about repairing our little vessel; and, although the savages did
not trouble themselves either to aid us or to wait for us, we were
so expeditious as to join them near the Long Sault [of Ottawa
River, about 45 miles above Montreal] two or three days after we
started.

But our canoe, having been once broken, could not long be of
service, and our Frenchmen, already greatly fatigued, despaired
of being able to follow the savages, who were thoroughly accustomed to such severe exertions. Therefore, I resolved to call them
all together, in order to persuade them to receive us separately
into their canoes, showing them that our own was in so bad a
condition as to be thenceforth useless to us. They agreed to this;
and the Hurons promised, although with much reluctance, to
provide for me.

On the morrow, accordingly, when I came down to the water's
edge, they at first received me well, and begged me to wait a very
little while, until they were ready to embark. After I had waited,
and when I was stepping down into the water to enter their canoe,
they repulsed me with the assertion that there was no room for

me, and straightway began to paddle vigorously, leaving me all alone with no prospect of human succor. I prayed God to forgive them, but my prayer was unanswered; for they were subsequently wrecked, and the divine Majesty turned my abandonment on the part of men to the saving of my life.

Finding myself, then, entirely alone, forsaken in a strange land— for the whole fleet was already a good distance away—I had recourse to the blessed Virgin, in whose honor we had performed a novena which gained for us from that Mother of Mercy a very manifest daily protection. While I was praying to her I saw, quite contrary to my hopes, some canoes in which were three of our Frenchmen. I hailed them, and, resuming our old canoe, we proceeded to paddle with all our strength in order to overtake the fleet. But we had long since lost sight of it, and knew not whither to go, it being very difficult to find a narrow detour which must be taken in order to gain the portage of Cat Rapids (as that part is called) [the French name Les Chats is retained today]. We should have been lost had we missed this narrow channel; but it pleased God, owing to the blessed Virgin's intercessions, to guide us directly and almost without our realizing it to this portage. Here, as I saw two more canoes, belonging to the savages, I leaped into the water and hastened to intercept them by land on the other side of the portage, where I found six canoes. "How is this?" said I to them; "do you thus forsake the French? Know you not that I hold Onnontio's voice in my hands and that I am to speak for him, through the presents he entrusted to me, to all your nations?" These words forced them to give us aid, so that we joined the bulk of the fleet toward noon. . . .

No sooner had I embarked than he [an Indian] put a paddle in my hand, urging me to use it and assuring me it was an honorable employment, and one worthy of a great captain. I willingly took the paddle and, offering up to God this labor in atonement for my sins and to hasten those poor savages' conversion, I imagined myself a malefactor sentenced to the galleys; and, although I became entirely exhausted, yet God gave me sufficient strength to paddle all day long, and often a good part of the night. But this application did not prevent my being commonly the object of their contempt and the butt of their jokes; for, however much I exerted myself, I accomplished nothing in comparison with them, their bodies being large and strong and perfectly adapted to such labors. The slight esteem in which they held me caused them to steal from me every article of my wardrobe that they could; and I had much difficulty in retaining my hat, the wide rim of which seemed to them peculiarly fitted for defense against the excessive heat of the sun. And when evening came, as my pilot took away a bit of blanket that I had to serve him as a pillow, he forced me to pass the night without any covering but the foliage of some tree.

When hunger is added to these discomforts it is a severe hardship, but one that soon teaches a man to find a relish in the bitterest roots and the most putrid meat. God was pleased to make me suffer from hunger, on Fridays especially, for which I heartily thank him.

We were forced to accustom ourselves to eat a certain moss growing upon the rocks. It is a sort of shell-shaped leaf which is always covered with caterpillars and spiders; and which, on being boiled, furnishes an insipid soup, black and viscous, that rather serves to ward off death than to impart life.

One morning we found a stag that had been dead four or five days. It was a lucky accident for poor starvelings. I was given a piece of it, and, although its offensive odor deterred some from eating any, hunger made me take my share; but my mouth had a putrid taste, in consequence, until the next day.

Amid all these hardships, whenever we came to any rapids I carried as heavy burdens as I could; but I often succumbed under them, and that made our savages laugh and mock me, saying they must call a child to carry me and my burden. Our good God did not forsake me utterly on these occasions, but often wrought on some of the men so that, touched with compassion, they would, without saying anything, relieve me of my *chapelle* [group of sacred vessels for celebration of the mass] or of some other burden, and would help me to journey a little more at my ease.

It sometimes happened that, after we had carried our loads and plied our paddles all day long, and even two or three hours into the night, we went supperless to bed on the ground or on some rock, to begin over again the next day with the same labors. But everywhere the Divine Providence mingled some little sweetness and relief with our fatigue. . . .

Toward the beginning of September, after coasting along the shores of the Lake of the Hurons, we reached the Sault [Ste. Marie]: for such is the name given to a half-league of rapids that

are encountered in a beautiful river which unites two great lakes—
that of the Hurons, and Lake Superior.

This river is pleasing, not only on account of the islands intercepting its course and the great bays bordering it, but because of
the fishing and hunting, which are excellent there. We sought a
resting place for the night on one of these islands, where our
savages thought they would find provision for supper upon their
arrival; for, as soon as they landed, they put the kettle on the fire,
expecting to see the canoe laden with fish the moment the net was
cast into the water. But God chose to punish their presumption,
and deferred giving any food to the starving men until the following day.

On the second of September, then, after clearing this Sault—
which is not a waterfall, but merely a very swift current impeded
by numerous rocks—we entered Lake Superior. . . .

The form of this lake is nearly that of a bow, the southern
shore being much curved and the northern nearly straight. Fish
are abundant there and of excellent quality; while the water is so
clear and pure that objects at the bottom can be seen to the depth
of six *brasses* [the French *brasse* equaled 5.318 feet].

The savages revere this lake as a divinity, and offer it sacrifices,
whether on account of its size—for its length is two hundred
leagues, and its greatest width eighty [in miles the maximum
measurements are: length, 412; width, 167]—or because of its
goodness in furnishing fish for the sustenance of all these tribes, in
default of game, which is scarce in the neighborhood. . . .

This lake is, furthermore, the resort of twelve or fifteen distinct
nations—coming, some from the north, others from the south, and
still others from the west; and they all betake themselves either
to the best parts of the shore for fishing, or to the islands, which
are scattered in great numbers all over the lake. These peoples'
motive in repairing hither is partly to obtain food by fishing, and
partly to transact their petty trading with one another when they
meet. But God's purpose was to facilitate the proclaiming of the
Gospel to wandering and vagrant tribes—as will appear in the
course of this journal. . . .

Chapter III
Of the Missionary's Arrival and Sojourn
at the Bay of Saint Esprit, Called Chagouamigong
[Chequamegon Bay at Ashland, Wisconsin]

After coasting [westward] a hundred and eighty leagues along the southern shore of Lake Tracy [Superior, named then for Marquis de Tracy, governor-general of New France], where it was our Lord's will often to test our patience by storms, famine, and weariness by day and night, finally, on the first day of October, we arrived at Chagouamigong, whither our ardent desires had been so long directed.

It is a beautiful bay, at the head of which is situated the great village of the savages, who there cultivate fields of Indian corn and lead a settled life. They number eight hundred men bearing arms, but are gathered together from seven different nations, living in peace, mingled one with another.

This large population made us prefer this place to all others for our usual abode, that we might apply ourselves most advantageously to the instruction of these infidels, build a chapel, and enter upon the functions of the Christian religion.

At first we could find shelter only under a bark roof, where we were so frequently visited by these people, most of whom had never seen any Europeans, that we were overwhelmed; and my efforts to instruct them were constantly interrupted by persons going and coming. Therefore I decided to go in person to visit them, each in his cabin, where I told them about God more at my ease, and instructed them more at leisure in all the mysteries of our faith. . . .

Chapter XII
Of the Mission to the Nadouesiouek
[Sioux: Nadoue was Algonquin for enemy]

These are people dwelling to the west of this place, toward the great river named Messipi [Mississippi]. They are forty or fifty leagues from this place, in a country of prairies, rich in all kinds of game. They cultivate fields, sowing therein not Indian corn, but only tobacco; while Providence has furnished them a kind of marsh rye [wild rice] which they go and harvest toward the close of summer in certain small lakes that are covered with it. So well do they know how to prepare it that it is highly appetizing and very nutritious. They gave me some when I was at the head of Lake Tracy, where I saw them. They do not use muskets but only bows and arrows, with which they shoot very skillfully. Their cabins are not covered with bark, but with deerskins, carefully dressed, and sewed together with such skill that the cold does not enter. These people are, above all the rest, savage and wild, appearing abashed and as motionless as statues in our presence. Yet they are warlike, and have conducted hostilities against all their neighbors, by whom they are held in extreme fear. . . .

Toward the northwest there is a nation which eats meat uncooked, being content to hold it in the hand and expose it to the fire, while beyond these people lies the North Sea [North Atlantic]. On this side are the Kilistinons, whose rivers empty into Hutston's Bay [Christinaux, now known as Cree, who roamed plains northwest of Lake Superior to Lake Winnipeg and Hudson Bay]. We have, besides, some knowledge of the savages inhabiting the regions of the south, as far as the sea; so that only a little territory and few people are left to whom the Gospel has not been proclaimed—if we credit the reports often given us by the savages.

Chapter XIII
Of the Mission to the Kilistinouc [Kilistinons, or Cree]

The Kilistinouc have their usual abode on the shores of the North Sea, and their canoes ply along a river emptying into a great bay, which we think is, in all probability, the one designated on the map by the name of Hutson. For those whom I have seen from that country have told me that they had known of a ship; and one of their old men declared to me that he had himself seen, at the mouth of the River of the Assinipoualac [Assiniboine], some peoples allied to the Kilistinouc, whose country is still farther northward.

He told me further that he had also seen a house which the Europeans had built on the mainland out of boards and pieces of wood, and that they held books in their hands, like the one he saw me holding when he told me this. He made mention of another nation, adjoining the Assinipoualac, who eat human beings, and live wholly on raw flesh; but these people, in turn, are eaten by bears [grizzlies] of frightful size, all red, and with prodigiously long claws. It is deemed highly probable that they are lions. . . .

[*In 1669–70 Allouez made a trip to Green Bay and to Indian settlements in that region. His report of that trip in the form of a long letter to the Father Superior written from Green Bay (or, as it was then called, the "Bay of Stinking Waters") was printed in the* Jesuit Relations *in 1671. In view of the present concern over pollution of the lakes, it is interesting that Allouez observed that "the water of this bay and of the rivers is like stagnant ditch-water." Excerpts from his account follow:*]

Chapter XII
Of the Mission of Saint François Xavier
on the "Bay of Stinkards," or rather "of Stinking Waters"

Letter from Father Allouez, who has had charge of this Mission, to the Reverend Father Superior.

My Reverend Father, Pax Christi,

I send to Your Reverence the journal of our winter's campaign, wherein you will find how the Gospel has been proclaimed, and Jesus Christ preached, to peoples that worship only the Sun, or some imaginary idols.

On the third of November [1669], we departed from the Sault, I and two others. Two canoe-loads of Pouteouatamis [Potawatomis] wished to conduct me to their country; not that they wished to receive instruction there, having no disposition for the Faith, but that I might curb some young Frenchmen, who, being among them for the purpose of trading, were threatening and maltreating them.

We arrived on the first day at the entrance to the Lake of the Hurons, where we slept under the shelter of the islands. The length of the journey and the difficulty of the way, because of the lateness of the season, led us to have recourse to Saint Francis Xavier, patron of our mission; this obliged me to celebrate holy mass, and my two companions to receive communion, on the day [December 3] of the feast in his honor, and still further to invoke him, twice every day, by reciting his orison.

On the fourth, toward noon, we doubled the cape which forms the detour [at Detour, Chippewa County, Michigan] and is the beginning of the strait or the gulf of Lake Huron, which is well known, and of the Lake of the Illinois [Lake Michigan], which up to the present time is unknown, and is much smaller than Lake Huron. Toward evening the contrary wind, which was about to cast our canoe upon the shoals of rocks, obliged us rather to finish our journey.

On the 5th, upon waking, we found ourselves covered with snow and the surface of the canoe coated with ice. This little beginning of crosses which our Lord was pleased to allot us invited us to offer ourselves for greater ones. We were compelled to embark with all the baggage and provisions with great difficulty, our bare feet in the water, in order to keep the canoe afloat, which otherwise would have broken. After leaving a great number of islands [the Cheneaux Islands, Mackinac County, Michigan] to the northward, we slept on a little island, where we were detained six days by the bad weather. The snow and frosts threatening us with ice, my companions had recourse to Saint Anne, to whom we entrusted our journey, praying her, together with St. Francis Xavier, to take us under her protection.

On the eleventh we embarked, notwithstanding the contrary wind, and crossed to another island, and thence to the mainland, where we found two Frenchmen with several savages. From them we learned of the great dangers to which we were about to expose ourselves, by reason of the storms that are frequent on this lake, and the ice which would soon be afloat. But all that was not sufficient to shake the confidence that we had reposed in our protectors. After invoking them we launched the canoe, and then doubled successfully enough the cape [Cape St. Ignace] which makes a detour to the west. . . .

On the twenty-ninth [November], as the mouth of the river which we were to enter was frozen over, we were in great difficulty. We thought of making the rest of the journey to the rendezvous by land; but, a furious wind having arisen during the night, we found ourselves enabled, owing to the breaking up of the ice, to continue our voyage. We finished it on the second of December, on the eve of Saint Francis Xavier's day, when we arrived at the place where the French were [possibly near the site of Oconto, Wisconsin]; and they helped us to celebrate his day with the utmost solemnity in our power, thanking him for the succor that he had procured for us during our voyage, and entreating him to be the patron of that mission, which we were about to start under his protection. . . .

In the matter of our sustenance, we have had a good deal of trouble. Scarcely have we found material to make our cabin; all that we have had for food has been only Indian corn and acorns; the few fish that are seen here, and that but seldom, are very poor; and the water of this bay and of the rivers is like stagnant ditch water.

The savages of this region are more than usually barbarous; they are without ingenuity, and do not know how to make even a bark dish or a ladle; they commonly use shells. They are grasping and avaricious to an extraordinary degree, and sell their little commodities at a high price, because they have only what is barely necessary. The season in which we arrived among them was not favorable for us: they were all in a needy condition, and very little able to give us any assistance, so that we suffered hunger. . . .

Of the Mission to the Pouteouatamis [Potawatomis]

On the seventeenth of February [1670] I repaired to the village of the Pouteouatamis, which is eight leagues from this place, on the other side of the lake [probably on the east shore of Green Bay about six miles from the mouth of the Fox River]. After walking all day without halting, we arrived there at sunset, sustained by some small bit of frozen meat that hunger made us eat. On the day after my arrival they made us a present of all the fat of a bear, with many manifestations of affection.

On the nineteenth I assembled the council, and, after relating the news, informed them of the purpose that had brought me to their country, reserving for the following day a fuller discourse on our religion. . . .

On the twenty-third, we set out to return thence; but the wind, which froze our faces, and the snow, compelled us to halt, after we had gone two leagues, and to pass the night on the lake. On the following day, the severity of the cold having diminished, although very little, we continued our journey with much suffering. On my part, I had my nose frozen, and I had a fainting fit that compelled me to sit down on the ice, where I should have remained, my companions having gone on ahead, if, by a divine providence, I had not found in my handkerchief a clove, which gave me strength enough to reach the settlement.

At the opening of the month of March, the great thaws having begun, the savages broke up their settlements to go in quest of the means to sustain life, after being for some time pressed with hunger. . . .

On the 21st of that month, I took the sun's altitude, and found that this was about 46 degrees, 40 minutes; and its elevation from the pole, or the complement of the above, was about 43 degrees, 20 minutes [true latitude is near 44° 31'].

The ice did not break up here until the 12th of April, the winter having been extremely severe this year; and consequently navigation was much impeded.

On the 16th of April, I embarked to go and begin the mission to the Outagamis [Fox Indians, then living near the Fox River], a people of considerable note in all these regions. We slept at the head of the bay [i.e., southern end, at site of Green Bay] at the mouth of the River des Puans [early French name for Fox River deriving from French word *puant*, meaning "stinking"], which we have named for Saint Francis [later renamed for Fox Indians]. On our way we saw clouds of swans, bustards, and ducks. The savages set snares for them at the head of the bay, where they catch as many as fifty in one night, this game seeking in autumn the wild oats [wild rice] that the wind has shaken off in the month of September. . . .

On the twentieth, which was Sunday, I said mass, after voyaging five or six leagues on the lake [Winnebago] after which we came to a river [Upper Fox River] flowing from a lake bordered with wild oats [Lake Butte des Morts]; this stream we followed, and found at the end of it the river [Wolf River] that leads to the Outagamis in one direction, and that which leads to the Machkoutenck [the Mascoutin], in the other. We entered this first stream, which flows from a lake; there we saw two turkeys perched on a tree, male and female, resembling perfectly those of France—the same size, the same color, and the same cry. Bustards, ducks, swans, and geese are in great number on all these lakes and rivers, the wild oats, on which they live, attracting them thither. There are large and small stags, bears, and beavers in great abundance.

On the twenty-fourth [April] after turning and doubling several times in various lakes and rivers, we arrived at the village of the Outagamis. . . .

. . . Six large cabins of these poor people were put to rout this [past] month of March by eighteen Iroquois from Tsonnontouan [i.e., Senecas], who, under the guidance of two fugitive Iroquois slaves of the Pouteouatamis, made an onslaught, and killed all the people, except thirty women whom they led away as captives. As the men were away hunting, they met with but little resistance, there being only six warriors left in the cabins, besides the women and children, who numbered a hundred or thereabout. This carnage was committed two days' journey from the place of our winter quarters at the foot of the Lake of the Ilinioues which is called Machihiganing [Lake Michigan; the attack occurred near the site of Chicago]. . . .

In the evening [of April 26] four savages of the nation of the Oumamis [the Miamis, allies of the Illinois], arrived from a place two days' journey hence, bringing three Iroquois scalps and a half-smoked arm, to console the relatives of those whom the Iroquois had killed a short time before.

On the twenty-seventh, we took our departure, commending to the good angels the first seed sown in the hearts of these poor people, who listened to me with respect and attention. There is a glorious and rich harvest for a zealous and patient missionary. We named this mission after Saint Mark, because on his day [April 25] the Faith was proclaimed there. . . .

On the twentieth [of May], I embarked with a Frenchman and a savage to go to Sainte Marie du Sault, whither obedience called me, leaving all these peoples in the hope that we should see them again next autumn, as I had promised them.

Marquette and Joliet on the Mississippi

[*For many years French* voyageurs *and* coureurs de bois *had heard of a great river flowing south; some perhaps had crossed the upper reaches of this river without recognizing it; others may have gone as far as the mouth of the Ohio; still others had paddled their canoes down various tributaries. Some of the explorers still clung to the hope that this river might lead to the South Sea and show the way to China. In any case, it drained a vast watershed that must be claimed for France.*

[*The government of Louis XIV was determined to claim all the territory its missionaries and its traders had seen or heard about, and to establish its rights to an empire in the New World. To that end a ceremony was planned for the summer of 1671 when Indians from tribes near and far would be invited to the Jesuit mission at Sault Ste. Marie and agents of the royal government of Louis XIV would proclaim his sovereignty over all the lands, rivers, lakes, and people of the region.*

[*In due course the King's representative, Simon François Daumont, Sieur de St. Lusson, accompanied by Nicolas Perrot, Louis Joliet, Father Claude Allouez, other priests, and a small assemblage of* voyageurs *stood before a puzzled gathering of Indians on the banks of the Sault and heard proclaimed, with twig and turf, the authority of Louis XIV over all the land. Father Allouez endeavored to explain in the language of the Indians the intent and meaning of the ceremony. Whatever the Indians may have thought, their delegates had a grand powwow, listened to the hymn singing of the French with wonder, and enjoyed the brandy, bonfire, and dancing that followed.*

[*But having annexed an immense territory, it was desirable to discover its extent and to learn more about the unknown stretches of the empire. Especially was it important to explore the river flowing south. To make this discovery, the French authorities at Quebec chose Louis Joliet (sometimes spelled Jolliet), a native-born Canadian who already had experience on the western waters, and Father Jacques Marquette, a dedicated Jesuit eager to see what souls could be saved along the Mississippi River, about which he had heard from Indians who had visited the Great Lakes missions.*

[Marquette and Joliet set out from the mission of St. Ignace on Mackinac Strait in mid-June 1673 and went to Green Bay and from there up the Fox River to a portage to the Wisconsin River, which led them to the Mississippi. Down the Mississippi, following the west bank, they continued past the mouth of the Arkansas River and determined that the great river flowed into the Gulf of Mexico. They mapped the mouths of both the Missouri and the Ohio rivers. Fearing that they might fall into the hands of Spaniards reported to be on the lower reaches of the Mississippi, they turned back, traveling along the east bank until they reached the Illinois River, which they followed to the site of Chicago. They ended their journey at the mission at De Pere, Wisconsin. Joliet set out to report to the governor of New France at Quebec, and Marquette remained among the Illinois Indians whom he hoped to convert, but died in 1675. In the rapids of La Chine Joliet's canoe overturned and he lost his notes.

[He later put together from memory a brief account of his journey. Marquette wrote a detailed narrative of the expedition. Although an abridged account was published in 1681 in Paris, the full version of Marquette's journal remained in manuscript until the nineteenth century. A definitive edition was published by Reuben G. Thwaites in Jesuit Relations and Allied Documents *in 1899. A useful selection is to be found in* Early Narratives of the Northwest, 1634–1699, *edited by Louise P. Kellogg in "Original Narratives of Early American History" (New York, 1917). Excerpts from Marquette's journal follow:]*

Section 1

Departure of Father Jacques Marquette for the discovery of the Great River called by the savages Missisipi, which leads to New Mexico.

The feast of the Immaculate Conception of the Blessed Virgin [December 8] was precisely the day [in 1672] on which Monsieur Jollyet arrived with orders from Monsieur the Count de Frontenac, our governor, and Monsieur Talon, our intendant, to accomplish this discovery with me. I was all the more delighted at this good news, since I saw that my plans were about to be accomplished; and since I found myself in the blessed necessity of exposing my life for the salvation of all these peoples, and especially of the Ilinois, who had very urgently entreated me, when I was at the Point of St. Esprit [mission at Chequamegon Bay, Lake Superior], to carry the word of God to their country.

We were not long in preparing all our equipment, although we were about to begin a voyage, the duration of which we could not foresee. Indian corn, with some smoked meat, constituted all our provisions; with these we embarked—Monsieur Jollyet and myself, with five men—in two bark canoes, fully resolved to do and suffer everything for so glorious an undertaking.

Accordingly, on the 17th day of May, 1673, we started from the mission of St. Ignace at Michilimakinac [on the north shore of the Strait of Mackinac], where I then was. The joy that we felt at being selected for this expedition animated our courage, and rendered the labor of paddling from morning to night agreeable to us. And because we were going to seek unknown countries, we took every precaution in our power, so that, if our undertaking were hazardous, it should not be foolhardy. To that end, we obtained all the information that we could from the savages who had frequented those regions; and we even traced out from their reports a map [preserved with the MS. journal in St. Mary's College, Montreal] of the whole of that new country; on it we indicated the rivers which we were to navigate, the names of the peoples and of the places through which we were to pass, the course of the great river, and the direction we were to follow when we reached it.

Above all, I placed our voyage under the protection of the Blessed Virgin Immaculate, promising her that, if she granted us the favor of discovering the great river, I would give it the name of the Conception, and that I would also make the first mission that I should establish among those new peoples bear the same name. This I have actually done, among the Ilinois [the Mission of the Immaculate Conception].

Section 2

The Father visits, in passing, the tribes of the Folle Avoine [the Menominees]. What that Folle Avoine is. He enters the Bay des Puants [Bay of Stinking Waters: Green Bay]; some particulars about that Bay. He arrives among the Fire Nation.

With all these precautions, we joyfully plied our paddles on a portion of Lake Huron, on that of the Ilinois [Lake Michigan], and the Bay des Puants [Green Bay].

The first nation that we came to was that of the Folle Avoine. . . . The wild oat [wild rice], whose name they bear because it is found in their country, is a sort of grass, which grows naturally in the small rivers with muddy bottoms, and in swampy places. It greatly resembles the wild oats that grow amid our wheat. The ears grow upon hollow stems, jointed at intervals; they emerge from the water about the month of June, and continue growing until they rise about two feet above it. The grain is not larger than that of our oats, but it is twice as long, and the meal therefrom is much more abundant. The savages gather and prepare it for food as follows: In the month of September, which is the suitable time for the harvest, they go in canoes through these fields of wild oats; they shake its ears into the canoe, on both sides, as they pass through. The grain falls out easily, if it be ripe, and they obtain their supply in a short time. But, in order to clean it from the straw and to remove it from a husk in which it is enclosed, they dry it in the smoke, upon a wooden grating, under which they maintain a slow fire for some days. When the oats are thoroughly dry, they put them in a skin made into a bag, thrust it into a hole dug in the ground for this purpose, and tread it with their feet—so long and so vigorously that the grain separates from the straw, and is very easily winnowed. After this, they pound it to reduce it to flour, or even, without pounding it, they boil it in water, and season it with fat. Cooked in this fashion, the wild oats have almost as delicate a taste as rice has when no better seasoning is added.

I told these peoples of the Folle Avoine of my design to go and discover those remote nations, in order to teach them the mysteries of our holy religion. They were greatly surprised to hear it, and did their best to dissuade me. They represented to me that I should meet nations who never show mercy to strangers, but break their heads without any cause; and that war was kindled between various peoples who dwelt upon our route, which exposed us to the further manifest danger of being killed by the bands of warriors who are ever in the field. They also said that the great river was very dangerous, when one does not know the difficult places; that it was full of horrible monsters, which devoured men and canoes together. . . . Embarking then in our canoes, we arrived shortly afterward at the bottom of the Bay des Puantz, where our Fathers labor successfully for the conversion of these peoples, over two thousand of whom they have baptized while they have been there. . . .

The bay is about thirty leagues in depth and eight in width at its mouth; it narrows gradually to the bottom, where it is easy to observe a tide which has its regular ebb and flow, almost like that of the sea. . . .

We left this bay to enter the river that discharges into it; it is very beautiful at its mouth, and flows gently; it is full of bustards, ducks, teal, and other birds, attracted thither by the wild oats, of which they are very fond. But, after ascending the river a short distance, it becomes very difficult of passage, on account of both the currents and the sharp rocks, which cut the canoes and the feet of those who are obliged to drag them, especially when the waters are low. . . .

On the following day, the tenth of June, two Miamis who were given us as guides embarked with us, in the sight of a great crowd, who could not sufficiently express their astonishment at the sight of seven Frenchmen, alone and in two canoes, daring to undertake so extraordinary and so hazardous an expedition. . . . We knew . . . that the direction we were to follow in order to reach it was west-southwesterly. But the road is broken by so many swamps and small lakes that it is easy to lose one's way, especially as the river leading thither is so full of wild oats that it is difficult to find the channel. For this reason we greatly needed our two guides, who safely conducted us to a portage of 2,700 paces [Portage, Wisconsin], and helped us to transport our canoes to enter that river [the Wisconsin]; after which they returned home, leaving us alone in this unknown country, in the hands of Providence. . . .

The river on which we embarked is called Meskousing [Wisconsin]. It is very wide; it has a sandy bottom, which forms various shoals that render its navigation very difficult. It is full of islands covered with vines. On the banks one sees fertile land, diversified with woods, prairies, and hills. There are oak, walnut, and basswood trees; and another kind, whose branches are armed with long thorns. We saw there neither feathered game nor fish, but many deer, and a large number of cattle. Our route lay to the southwest, and, after navigating about thirty leagues, we saw a spot presenting all the appearances of an iron mine. . . . After proceeding 40 leagues on this same route, we arrived at the mouth of our river; and, at 42 and a half degrees of latitude, we safely entered Missisipi on the 17th of June, with a joy that I cannot express.

Section 4

Of the Great River called Missisipi; its most notable features; of various animals, and especially the pisikious [buffalo] or wild cattle, their shape and nature; of the first villages of the Ilinois, where the French arrived.

Here we are, then, on this so renowned river, all of whose peculiar features I have endeavored to note carefully. The Missisipi River takes its rise in various lakes in the country of the northern nations. . . . Its width is very unequal; sometimes it is three-quarters of a league, and sometimes it narrows to three arpents [about 600 feet]. We gently followed its course, which runs toward the south and southeast, as far as the 42nd degree of latitude. Here we plainly saw that its aspect was completely changed. There are hardly any woods or mountains; the islands are more beautiful, and are covered with finer trees. We saw only deer and cattle, bustards, and swans without wings, because they drop their plumage in this country. From time to time, we came upon monstrous fish, one of which struck our canoe with such violence that I thought that it was a great tree, about to break the canoe to pieces [a catfish, some of which grow very large]. On another occasion, we saw on the water a monster with the head of a tiger, a sharp nose like that of a wildcat, with whiskers and straight, erect ears; the head was gray and the neck quite black [a wildcat]; but we saw no more creatures of this sort. When we cast our nets into the water we caught sturgeon, and a very extraordinary kind of fish. It resembles the trout, with this difference, that its mouth is larger. Near its nose, which is smaller, as are also the eyes, is a large bone shaped like a woman's busk [bone corset stay], three fingers wide and a cubit long, at the end of which is a disk as wide as one's hand. This frequently causes it to fall backward when it leaps out of the water [*polyodon spatula*, a rare river fish]. When we reached the parallel of 41 degrees 28 minutes, following the same direction, we found that turkeys had taken the place of game; and the *pisikious*, or wild cattle [buffalo], that of the other animals. . . . The head is very large; the forehead is flat and a foot and half wide between the horns, which are exactly like those of our oxen, but black and much larger. Under the neck they have a sort of large dewlap, which hangs down; and on the back is a rather high hump. The whole of the head, the neck, and a portion of the shoulders are covered with a thick mane like that of horses; it forms a crest a foot long, which makes them hideous, and, falling over their eyes, prevents them from seeing what is before them. The remainder of the body is covered with a heavy coat of curly hair, almost like that of our sheep, but much stronger and thicker. It falls off in summer, and the skin becomes as soft as velvet. At that season, the savages use the hides for making fine robes, which they paint in various colors. The flesh and the fat of the *pisikious* are excellent, and constitute the best dish at feasts. . . . They are scattered about the prairie in herds; I have seen one of four hundred.

We continued to advance, but, as we knew not whither we were going, for we had proceeded over one hundred leagues without discovering anything except animals and birds, we kept well on our guard. On this account, we make only a small fire on land, toward evening, to cook our meals; and, after supper, we remove ourselves as far from it as possible, and pass the night in our canoes, which we anchor in the river at some distance from the shore. This does not prevent us from always posting one of the party as a sentinel, for fear of a surprise. Proceeding still in a southerly and south-southwesterly direction, we find ourselves at the parallel of 41 degrees, and as low as 40 degrees and some minutes—partly southeast and partly southwest—after having ad-

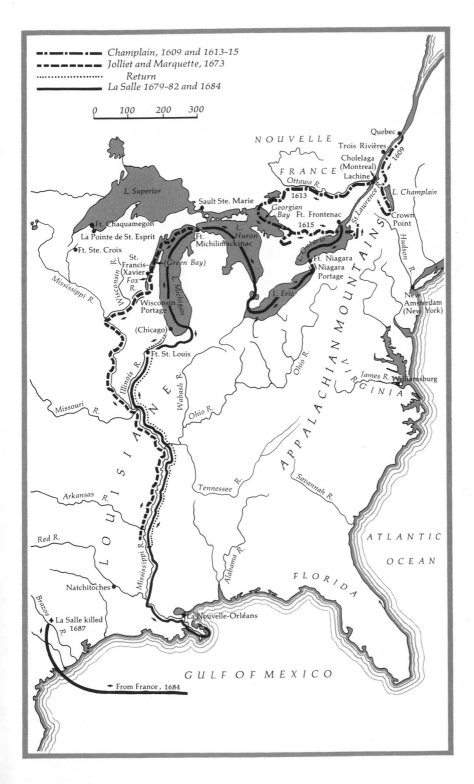

French Explorations of the Great Lakes Region and the Mississippi River

vanced over 60 leagues since we entered the river, without discovering anything.

Finally, on the 25th of June, we perceived on the water's edge some tracks of men, and a narrow and somewhat beaten path leading to a fine prairie. . . . We silently followed the narrow path, and, after walking about two leagues, we discovered a village on the bank of a river, and two others on a hill distant about half a league from the first. Then we heartily commended ourselves to God, and, after imploring His aid, we went farther without being perceived, and approached so near that we could even hear the savages talking. We therefore decided that it was time to reveal ourselves. This we did by shouting with all our energy, and stopped, without advancing any farther. On hearing the shout, the savages quickly issued from their cabins, and having probably recognized us as Frenchmen, especially when they saw a black gown—or, at least, having no cause for distrust, as we were only two men, and had given them notice of our arrival —they deputed four old men to come and speak to us. . . .

I . . . spoke to them first, and asked them who they were. They replied that they were Ilinois; and, as a token of peace, they offered us their pipes to smoke. They afterward invited us to enter their village, where all the people impatiently awaited us. . . .

Section 7

Departure of the Father from the Ilinois. . . . Of the River Pekitanouï [Missouri]. Continuation of the voyage.

We take leave of our Ilinois at the end of June, about three o'clock in the afternoon. We embark in the sight of all the people, who admire our little canoes, for they have never seen any like them.

We descend, following the current of the river called Pekitanouï [Indian word for "muddy"; the Missouri] which discharges into the Mississipy. . . . Sailing quietly in clear and calm water, we heard the noise of a rapid, into which we were about to run. I have seen nothing more dreadful. An accumulation of large and entire trees, branches, and floating islands was issuing from the mouth of the river Pekitanouï with such impetuosity that we could not without great danger risk passing through it. So great was the agitation that the water was very muddy, and could not become clear.

Pekitanouï is a river of considerable size, coming from the northwest, from a great distance; and it discharges into the Missisipi. There are many villages of savages along this river, and I hope by its means to discover the Vermillion or California Sea.

Judging from the direction of the course of the Missisipi, if it continue the same way, we think that it discharges into the Mexican Gulf. It would be a great advantage to find the river leading to the Southern Sea, toward California; and, as I have said, this is what I hope to do by means of the Pekitanouï according to the reports made to me by the savages. . . .

Section 8

Of the new countries discovered by the Father. Various particulars. Meeting with some savages. First news of the sea and of Europeans. . . .

.   .   .   .

Here we began to see canes, or large reeds, which grow on the bank of the river; their color is a very pleasing green; all the nodes are marked by a crown of long, narrow, and pointed leaves. They are very high, and grow so thickly that the wild cattle have some difficulty in forcing their way through them.

Hitherto, we had not suffered any inconvenience from mosquitoes; but we were entering into their home, as it were. This is what the savages of this quarter do to protect themselves against them. They erect a scaffolding, the floor of which consists only of poles, so that it is open to the air in order that the smoke of the fire made underneath may pass through, and drive away those little creatures, which cannot endure it; the savages lie down upon the poles, over which bark is spread to keep off rain. These scaffoldings also serve them as protection against the excessive and unbearable heat of this country; for they lie in the shade, on the floor below, and thus protect themselves against the sun's rays, enjoying the cool breeze that circulates freely through the scaffolding. . . . [The savages] assured us that we were no more than ten days' journey from the sea; that they bought cloth and all other goods from the Europeans who lived to the east; that these Europeans had rosaries and pictures; that they played upon instruments; that some of them looked like me, and had been received by these savages kindly. . . .

This news animated our courage and made us paddle with fresh ardor. We thus push forward, and no longer see so many prairies, because both shores of the river are bordered with lofty trees. The cottonwood, elm, and basswood trees there are admirable for their height and thickness. The great numbers of wild cattle, which we heard bellowing, led us to believe that the prairies are near. We also saw quail on the water's edge. . . .

Section 9

. . . Reasons for not going farther.

.   .   .   .

Monsieur Jolliet and I held another council, to deliberate upon what we should do—whether we should push on, or remain content with the discovery which we had made. After attentively considering that we were not far from the Gulf of Mexico, the basin of which is at the latitude of 31 degrees 60 minutes, while we were at 33 degrees 40 minutes, we judged that we could not be more than two or three days' journey from it; and that, beyond a doubt, the Missisipi River discharges into the Florida or Mexican Gulf, and not to the east in Virginia, whose seacoast is at 34 degrees latitude—which we had passed, without, however, having as yet reached the sea—or to the west in California, because in that case our route would have been to the west, or the west-southwest, whereas we had always continued it toward the south. We further considered that we exposed ourselves to the risk of losing the results of this voyage, of which we could give no information if we proceeded to fling ourselves into the hands of the Spaniards who, without doubt, would at least have detained us as captives. Moreover, we saw very plainly that we were not in a condition to resist savages allied to the Europeans, who were numerous, and expert in firing guns, and who continually infested the lower part of the river. Finally, we had obtained all the information that could be desired in regard to this discovery. All these reasons induced us to decide upon returning; this we announced to the savages, and, after a day's rest, made our preparations for it.

Section 10

Return of the Father and of the French.

After a month's navigation, while descending Missisipi from the 42nd to the 34th degree, and beyond, and after preaching the Gospel as well as I could to the nations that I met, we start on the 17th of July from the village of the Akensea [Arkansas, slightly above the mouth of the Arkansas River near the site of de Soto's death] to retrace our steps. We therefore reascend the Missisipi, which gives us much trouble in breasting its currents. It is true that we leave it, at about the 38th degree, to enter another river [the Illinois], which greatly shortens our road, and takes us with but little effort to the Lake of the Illinois [Lake Michigan].

We have seen nothing like this river that we enter, as regards its fertility of soil, its prairies and woods; its cattle, elk, deer, wildcats, bustards, swans, ducks, parroquets, and even beaver. There are many small lakes and rivers. That on which we sailed is wide, deep, and still, for 65 leagues. In the spring and during part of the summer there is only one portage of half a league. We found on it a village of Illinois. . . . One of the chiefs of this nation, with his young men, escorted us to the Lake of the Illinois, whence, at last, at the end of September, we reached the Bay des Puantz, from which we had started at the beginning of June.

Imperial Designs of La Salle and Duluth

[*Joliet and Marquette had mapped the Mississippi and noted its major tributaries as far as the mouth of the Arkansas River. But much exploration remained to be done before the great drainage system of the Mississippi and its tributaries was fully known. Two explorers were determined to cement the imperial plans of France by continuing the exploration of the Mississippi valley and claiming the whole territory. René Robert, Cavelier de La Salle sought to open up the lower Mississippi to French occupa-*

tion. *Daniel Greysolon, Sieur Duluth, tried to establish the French in possession of the sources of the Mississippi in the north. Their efforts and their explorations were of immense importance to imperial France.*

[*La Salle early in life had been a Jesuit novitiate but left the order and went to Canada. Between the years 1666 and 1687 he explored the Great Lakes region and the whole length of the Mississippi. On a trip to France in 1677 he enlisted an Italian aide named Henri de Tonti (sometimes spelled Tonty) who had served in the French army and lost a hand in battle. The iron attachment that Tonti used in place of the amputated hand astonished the Indians and gave him the reputation of being a great "medicine man."*

[*In 1679 La Salle and Tonti erected a fort at the mouth of the Niagara River. Tonti also built a sailing vessel named the* Griffon *in which they explored the Great Lakes. They established other posts in the region and laid the foundation for an extension of the fur trade with the western Indians.*

[*La Salle's most important voyage of discovery was the journey he and Tonti made in the spring of 1682 to the mouth of the Mississippi. Having viewed the length of the mighty river, he took possession in the name of Louis XIV and gave the name Louisiana to the entire region. In a change of governors of New France, La Salle in 1683 was shorn of his authority on the frontier and returned to France. Received as a conquering hero, he obtained from the king a commission to colonize Louisiana and serve as governor of a territory stretching from the Illinois River to the Spanish possessions in the south. Over this domain he would serve as "viceroy of North America."*

[*On July 24, 1685, La Salle sailed from France with four ships and colonists to make the first settlement in Louisiana. Beset with calamities from the outset, the expedition spent four stormy months reaching the Gulf. One ship was seized by Spanish corsairs; La Salle's poor navigators missed the mouth of the Mississippi and brought up on the coast of Texas at Matagorda Bay, where the colonists eventually went ashore near what is now called Port Lavaca. The ships sailed away for France and left the disconsolate settlers to make the best of their situation.*

[*La Salle evacuated Lavaca and attempted to march overland*

*to the Mississippi. Angry at the leader's arbitrariness and lack of
understanding of their plight, his men mutinied and, on March
19, 1687, near the mouth of the Navasoto River on the Brazos,
they shot La Salle to death. Thus ended the career of an imaginative explorer but a dismal leader of men.*

[La Salle's *colleague Tonti wrote two accounts of his experiences in North America. The second of these narratives, covering
the years 1678–1691, provides a description of La Salle's explorations on the Mississippi. An English translation of this work was
published in London in 1844 in Thomas Falconer's* On the Discovery of the Mississippi. *It has been several times reprinted. A
well-edited version of portions of the narrative is found in* Early
Narratives of the Northwest, 1634–1699, *edited by Louise P. Kellogg in "Original Narratives of Early American History" (New
York, 1917). Excerpts follow:*]

*Memoir Sent in 1693 on the Discovery of the Mississippi
and the Neighboring Nations by M. de La Salle,
from the Year 1678 to the Time of His Death,
and by the Sieur de Tonty to the Year 1691.*

.   .   .   .

We sailed from [La] Rochelle on the 14th of July, 1678, and
arrived at Quebec on the 15th of September following. We
recruited there for some days, and after having taken leave of
M. the Count de Frontenac, governor general of the country,
ascended the St. Lawrence as far as Fort Frontenac, 120 leagues
from Quebec, on the banks of the Lake of Frontenac [Lake On-
tario] which is about 300 leagues around; and after staying there
four days, we embarked in a boat of forty tons to cross this lake,
and on Christmas day we found ourselves opposite a village [of
the Seneca] called Tsonnontouan, to which M. de La Salle sent
some canoes to procure Indian corn for our subsistence. From
thence we sailed toward Niagara, intending to look for a suitable
place above the Falls where a boat might be built. The winds
were so contrary that we could not approach it nearer than nine
leagues, which determined us to go by land. We found there
some cabins of the Iroquois, who received us well. We slept there,

and the next day we went three leagues further up to look for a good place [near the mouth of Cayuga Creek] to build a boat. There we encamped.

The boat in which we came was lost on the coast through the obstinacy of the pilot, whom M. de La Salle had ordered to bring it ashore. The crew and the things in it were saved. M. de La Salle determined to return to Fort Frontenac over the ice, and I remained in command at Niagara with a Recollect Father [Louis Hennepin] and thirty men. The bark was completed in the spring. M. de La Salle joined us with two other Recollect Fathers and several men, to aid in bringing this bark up, on account of the rapids, which I was not able to ascend on account of the weakness of my crew. He directed me to wait for him at the extremity of Lake Erie at a place called Detroit, 120 leagues from Niagara, to join there some Frenchmen whom he had sent off the last autumn. I went in advance in a bark canoe, and when we were near Detroit the ship came up. We got into it, and continued our voyage as far as Missilimakinak [Mackinac] where we arrived at the end of August, having crossed two lakes [Erie and Huron] larger than that of Frontenac. . . .

We went in canoes to the River Chicaou [Chicago], where there is a portage which joins that of the Islinois. The rivers being frozen, we made sledges and dragged our baggage to a point thirty leagues below the village of Islinois, and there, finding the navigation open, we arrived at the end of January [1682] at the River Mississipy [they entered the Mississippi from the Illinois on February 6, 1682]. The distance from Chicaou is estimated at 140 leagues. We descended this river and found, six leagues below, on the right, a great river, which comes from the west [the Missouri]. There are numerous nations above. We slept at its mouth. The next day we went on to the village of the Tamaroas [Tamarois], six leagues off on the left. There was no one there, all the people being at their winter quarters in the woods. We made our marks to inform the savages that we had passed, and continued our route as far as the River Ouabache [the Ohio, below its junction with the Wabash], which is eighty leagues from that of the Islinois. It comes from the east and is more than 500 leagues in length. It is by this river that the Iroquois advance to make war against the nations of the south. . . .

[Tonti was not with La Salle on the disastrous expedition of 1685–87. The following is his reconstruction of the assassination from accounts he procured in 1690.]

M. de La Salle having landed beyond the Mississipy, on the side toward Mexico, about eighty leagues from the mouth of the river [in Victoria County, Texas], and having lost his vessels on the coast, saved a part of the cargo, and began to march along the seashore, in search of the Mississipy. Meeting with many obstacles to his plans on account of the bad roads, he resolved to go to the Islinois by land. So he loaded several horses to carry what was necessary. . . . Finding himself short of provisions, he sent M. de Morangé, his servant, and the Chaouanon [Shawnees] to hunt in a small wood with orders to return in the evening. When they had killed some buffaloes, they stopped to dry the meat. M. de La Salle was uneasy, so he asked the Frenchmen who among them would go and look for them. Du Haut and Lanquetot had for a long time determined to kill M. de La Salle, because, during the journey he had made along the seacoast, he had compelled the brother of Lanquetot, who was unable to keep up, to return to camp, and as he was returning alone he was massacred by the savages. This caused Lanquetot to swear that he would never forgive his brother's death. And as in long journeys there are always many discontented persons in a company, he easily found partisans. He offered, therefore, with them to search for M. de Morangé, in order to have an opportunity to execute their design.

Having found the men, he told them that M. de La Salle was uneasy about them; but, they declaring that they could not set off till the next day, it was agreed to sleep there. After supper they arranged the order of the watch, that it should begin with M. de Morangé; after him was to follow the servant of M. de La Salle, and then the Chaouanon. After they had kept their watch and were asleep, the others massacred them, as persons attached to M. de La Salle. Toward daybreak they heard the reports of pistols, which were fired as signals by M. de La Salle, who was coming with the Recollect Father in search of them. The wretches, suspecting that it was he, lay in wait for him, placing M. du Haut's servant in front. When M. de La Salle came near, he asked where M. de Morangé was. The servant, keeping on his hat, answered that he was behind. As M. de La Salle advanced to remind him of his duty, he received three balls in his head, and fell down dead (March 19, 1687). I do not know whether the Recollect Father could do anything, but it is agreed that he was frightened, and, thinking that he also was to be killed, threw himself on his knees before the murderers, and begged for a quarter of an hour to prepare his soul. They replied that they were willing to spare his life. . . .

Such was the end of one of the greatest men of this age, a man of an admirable spirit, and capable of undertaking all sorts of explorations. . . .

I should not know how to describe the beauty of all the countries that I have mentioned, and, if I had worked them, I would say for what purposes they might be utilized. As for the Mississipy, it might produce every year peltries to the amount of 2,000 crowns, and abundance of lead and of timber for ships. Commerce in silk might be established there, and a port to harbor ships and form a base for the Gulf of Mexico. Pearls will be found, and even if wheat could not be had below, the upper river would furnish it, and one could furnish the islands [French West Indies] with what they need, such as lumber, vegetables, grain, and salt beef.

[A wiser leader than La Salle was Daniel Greysolon, Sieur Duluth, a French soldier and nobleman who ventured into northwest Wisconsin and Minnesota to the country of the powerful Sioux tribes, with whom he formed an alliance. After 1678, when he made his first impact upon the Sioux, for more than two decades Duluth proved an able explorer as well as a forest diplomat of remarkable skill and effectiveness. His influence was responsible for channeling Sioux furs to the French on the St. Lawrence instead of to the English on Hudson Bay. Furthermore he imposed his authority on the frontier with such effectiveness that any Frenchman was safe in Indian country. Duluth, Minnesota, is named after this great French explorer of the seventeenth century. In 1685 he sent a brief report to the minister of marine telling of his travels in the Sioux country. John G. Shea published a translation of this in A Description of Louisiana by Father Louis Hennepin (New York, 1880). His report is also included in Early Narratives of the Northwest. Excerpts follow:]

Memoir of the Sieur Daniel Greyselon du Luth
on the Exploration of the Country of the Nadouecioux
[Sioux Indians], of Which He Gives
a Very Detailed Narrative.

To my Lord the Marquis de Seignelay [Minister of Marine]:
My Lord:

After having made two voyages from here to New France, where everyone believed that it was impossible to explore the country of the Nadouecioux, nor to have any commerce with them, both because of their distance, which is 800 leagues from our settlements, and because they are at war generally with all sorts of tribes, this difficulty caused me to make the resolve to go among them; which I could not put into execution at that time, my affairs having obliged me to come back here; whence . . . I set out to return to Quebec, where I had no sooner arrived than the desire I already had to carry out this plan increased, and I began to take my measures to make myself known on the part of the savages; who having assured me of their friendship, and for proof of it given three slaves whom I had asked of them only in order that they might come with me, I set out from Montreal with them and seven Frenchmen on the first of September of the year 1678, to attempt the exploration of the Nadouecioux and the Assenipoualaks [Assiniboine], who were unknown to us, and to cause them to make peace with all the nations around Lake Superior who dwell in the dominion of our invincible monarch. . . .

In June 1680, not having been satisfied with having made my exploration by land, I took two canoes, with a savage who was my interpreter and with four Frenchmen, to seek a means of making it by water. For this purpose I entered into a river [now called the Brulé, Douglas County, Wisconsin] which has its mouth eight leagues from the extremity of Lake Superior on the south side, where after having cut down some trees and broken through about one hundred beaver dams, I went up the said river, and then made a carry of half a league to reach a lake [Upper Lake St. Croix] which emptied into a fine river, which brought me to the Mississippi, where I learned, from eight lodges of Nadouecioux whom I met, that the Reverend Father Louis Henpin [Hennepin],

Recollect, now at the convent of St. Germain, had with two other Frenchmen been seized and taken away as slaves for more than three hundred leagues by the Nadouecioux themselves.

This news surprised me so much that, without hesitating, I left two Frenchmen with these above-mentioned eight lodges of savages, together with the goods which I had for making presents, and took one of the said savages, to whom I gave a present in order that he should conduct me with my interpreter and two Frenchmen to the place where the said Reverend Father Louis was. And as it was eighty good leagues I went in my canoe two days and two nights, and the next day at ten o'clock in the morning I met him with about 1,000 or 1,100 souls. The want of respect that was being shown to the said Reverend Father provoked me, and I let them know it, telling them that he was my brother, and I put him in my canoe to go with me into the villages of the said Nadouecioux, to which I took him. There, a week after having arrived, I caused a council to be held, setting forth the ill treatment which they had bestowed both upon the said Reverend Father and upon the other two Frenchmen who were with him, seizing them and leading them away as slaves, and even taking the priestly robes of the said Reverend Father. I caused two calumets (which they had danced to us) to be given back to them in recognition of the insult they had done us, these being the things most esteemed among them for pacifying affairs, saying to them that I took no calumets from people who, after having seen me, having received my peace gifts, and having been constantly for a year with Frenchmen, kidnapped them when they were coming to see them.

Each one sought to excuse himself in the council, but their excuse did not prevent me from saying to the Reverend Father Louis that he must come with me toward the Outagamys [the Fox Indians], which he did, I informing him that it would be striking a blow at the French nation in a new exploration to suffer insult of this sort without showing resentment of it, though my plan had been to penetrate then to the sea of the west-northwest coast, which is believed to be the Vermillion Sea [the Pacific], whence the savages who had gone to war in that direction gave salt to three Frenchmen whom I had sent to explore and who brought me some of the said salt, having reported to me that the savages had told them that it was only twenty days' journey from where they were to the discovery of the great lake whose water is not good to drink [possibly Great Salt Lake]. This is what makes me believe that it would not be at all difficult to find it, if one were willing to give permission to go there. Nevertheless I preferred to retrace my steps, letting them know of the just indignation I had against them, rather than remain after the violence they had done to the said Reverend Father and to the two Frenchmen who were with him, whom I put in my canoes, and brought them to the Michelimakinak mission of the reverend Jesuit fathers.

Father Louis Hennepin's Descriptions

[*A colorful narrative of explorations in the Northwest, but not always reliable, was written by this Franciscan Recollect friar, Father Louis Hennepin, and first published in France in 1683 as his* Description de la Louisiane. *Following this came two other works, entitled* Nouveau Voyage (*1696*) *and* Nouvelle Découverte (*1697*).

[*Hennepin's career as an explorer came as a result of meeting La Salle in 1675. Impressed by the priest's charm, La Salle made him his chaplain and sent him with a party commanded by Michel Aco to explore portions of the upper Mississippi Valley. They paddled up the Mississippi into the territory of the Minnesota Sioux where they were captured. While with the Indians Hennepin visited the site of Minneapolis and named the rapids there the Falls of St. Anthony of Padua.*

[*Not content with telling factually what he saw, Hennepin claimed to have gone down the Mississippi to its mouth (which he never did) and to have commanded the expedition led by Aco. Despite such falsities, his narratives are vivid and, in the eyewitness portions, reasonably accurate. An English translation of the* Description de la Louisiane (*edition of 1683*) *was published by John G. Shea as* A Description of Louisiana. By Father Hennepin, Recollect Missionary (*New York, 1880*). *Brief excerpts follow:*]

We embarked to the number of three in our little bark canoe with our portable chapel, a blanket, and a rush mat which served as a bed. This composed our whole outfit. . . .

The Miamis hunt them [buffalo] at the end of autumn in the following manner:

When they see a herd they gather in great numbers and set fire to the grass everywhere around these animals, except some passage which they leave on purpose, and where they take post with their bows and arrows. The buffalo, seeking to escape the fire, are thus compelled to pass near these Indians, who sometimes kill as many as a hundred and twenty in a day, all which they distribute according to the wants of the families; and these Indians, all triumphant over the massacre of so many animals, come to notify their women, who at once proceed to bring in the meat. Some of them at times take on their backs three hundred pounds weight, and also throw their children on top of their load which does not seem to burden them more than a soldier's sword at his side.

. . . The meat of these animals is very succulent. They are very fat in autumn because all the summer they are up to their necks in the grass. These vast countries are so full of prairies that it seems this is the element and the country of the buffalo. There are at near intervals some woods where these animals retire to ruminate, and to get out of the heat of the sun. . . .

Many other kinds of animals are found in these vast plains of Louisiana; stags, deer, beaver, and otter are common there, geese, swans, turtles [from the French *tourtres:* wild pigeons], *poules d'inde* [turkey-hens], parrots, partridges, and many other birds swarm there, the fishery is very abundant, and the fertility of the soil is extraordinary. There are boundless prairies interspersed with forests of tall trees, where there are all sorts of building timber, and among the rest excellent oak full like that in France and very different from that in Canada. The trees are of prodigious girth and height, and you could find the finest pieces in the world for shipbuilding which can be carried on upon the spot, and wood could be brought as ballast in the ships to build all the vessels of France, which would be a great saving to the State and would give the trees in our nearly exhausted forests time to grow again.

Several kinds of fruit trees are also to be seen in the forests and wild grapevines which produce clusters about a foot and a half long which ripen perfectly, and of which very good wine can be made. There are also to be seen fields covered with very good hemp, which grows there naturally to a height of six or seven feet. . . .

This vast continent will be able in a short time to supply all our West India islands with bread, wine, and meat, and our French buccaneers and filibusters [freebooters] will be able to kill wild cattle in greater abundance in Louisiana than in all the rest of the islands which they occupy.

There are mines of coal, slate, iron, and the lumps of pure red copper which are found in various places indicate that there are mines and perhaps other metals and minerals which will one day be discovered, inasmuch as a salt and alum spring has already been found among the Iroquois. . . .

The King may form there an empire which will soon become flourishing, without any foreign power being able to prevent him, and his Majesty by the Religious Ministry of Saint Francis may easily extend the kingdom of Jesus Christ among those many nations, which have hitherto been deprived of the advantages of Christianity, and the French colonies may thence derive great benefits in future.

❧ VI ❧

Journeys in the Middle Colonies
and New England

THE settlers along the Atlantic seaboard from New England
to Delaware slowly filtered into the back country during the
seventeenth century. Many accounts exist of short journeys into
the Indian country but few of these can be called exploring expeditions as such. They were reconnoitering trips to spy out the land
or to develop trade with the Indians.

[The Dutch of course made the deepest penetration into the
interior, thanks to the Hudson River which was accessible to
oceangoing ships as far as Fort Orange (later Albany). From
there Dutch fur traders plunged deeper into the forests, following
watercourses that led them to the Finger Lakes and beyond to
the north and the Susquehanna watershed to the west. They made
contact with the Mohawks, Senecas, and other Iroquois tribes
and developed a profitable trade that the English later took over.

[The early accounts of New Netherland devote much attention
to Indian life, which fascinated the Dutch traders, and to description of the terrain. Perhaps two years after Peter Minuit bought
Manhattan from the Indians in 1626, Isaack de Rasieres, chief
factor of the Dutch West India Company, wrote a letter to Samuel
Blommaert, a director of the company, describing his observations in New Netherland and in the little English colony at
Plymouth, which he had visited. A translation of Rasieres' letter
was printed in the Collections of the New York Historical Society,
II (1849), pp. 339–354, and is reprinted in Narratives of New
Netherland, 1609–1664, edited by J. Franklin Jameson in "Original

Narratives of Early American History" (New York, 1909). Excerpts follow:]

On the 27th of July, Anno 1626, by the help of God, I arrived with the ship *The Arms of Amsterdam,* before the bay of the great Mauritse [Hudson] River, sailing into it about a musket shot from Godyn's Point [Sandy Hook] into Coenraet's Bay [Sandy Hook Bay] (because there the greatest depth is, since from the east point there stretches out a sand bank on which there is only from 9 to 14 feet of water); then sailed on, northeast and north-northeast, to about halfway from the low sand bank called Godyn's Point to the Hamels-Hoofden [Narrows], the mouth of the river, where we found at half ebb 16, 17, 18 feet water, and which is a sandy reef a musket shot broad, stretching for the most part northeast and southwest, quite across, and, according to my opinion, having been formed there by the stream, inasmuch as the flood runs into the bay from the sea, east-southeast; the depth at Godyn's Point is caused by the tide flowing out along there with such rapidity.

Between the Hamels-Hoofden the width is about a cannon's shot of 2,000 [yards]; the depth 10, 11, 12 fathoms. There are tolerably high points, and well wooded. The west point is an island [Staten Island] inhabited by from 80 to 90 savages, who support themselves by planting maize. The east point is a very large island [Long Island] full 24 leagues long, stretching east by south and east-southeast along the seacoast, from the river to the east end of the Fisher's Hook [Montauk Point]. In some places it is from three to four leagues broad, and it has several creeks and bays, where many savages dwell, who support themselves by planting maize and making *sewan* [shell beads used as money], and who are called Souwenos [Siwanoys] and Sinnecox [Shinne-cocks]. It is also full of oaks, elms, walnut and fir trees, also wild cedar and chestnut trees. The tribes are held in subjection by, and are tributary to, the Pyquans [Pequots]. . . . The land is in many places good, and fit for ploughing and sowing. It has many fine valleys, where there is good grass. Their form of government is like that of their neighbors, which is described hereafter.

The Hamels-Hoofden being passed, there is about a league width in the river, and also on the west side there is an inlet [the Kill van Kull], where another river [the Hackensack] runs up about twenty leagues to the north-northeast, emptying into the Mauritse River in the highlands [the headwaters are near the Hudson but do not empty into it], thus making the northwest land opposite to the Manhatas an island eighteen leagues long. It is inhabited by the old Manhatans; they are about 200 to 300 strong, women and men, under different chiefs, whom they call *Sackimas.* This island is more mountainous than the other land on the southeast side of the river, which opposite to the Manhatas is about a league and a half in breadth. At the side of the before-mentioned little river, which we call "Achter Col" [Arthur Kill; i.e., Newark Bay] there is a great deal of waste reedy land; the rest is full of trees, and in some places there is good soil, where the savages plant their maize, upon which they live, as well as by hunting. The other side of the same small river, according to conjecture, is about 20 to 23 leagues broad to the South River [the Delaware] in the neighborhood of the Sancicans [or Sankikans], in so far as I have been able to make it out from the mouths of the savages; but as they live in a state of constant enmity with those tribes, the paths across are but little used, wherefore I have not been able to learn the exact distance; so that when we wish to send letters overland, they (the natives) take their way across the bay, and have the letters carried forward by others, unless one amongst them may happen to be on friendly terms, and who might venture to go there.

The island of the Manhatas extends two [actually four] leagues in length along the Mauritse River, from the point where the Fort "New Amsterdam" is building. It is about seven leagues in circumference, full of trees, and in the middle rocky to the extent of about two leagues in circuit. The north side has good land in two places, where two farmers, each with four horses, would have enough to do without much clearing at first. The grass is good in the forest and valleys, but when made into hay is not so nutritious for the cattle as here [in Holland], in consequence of its wild state, but it yearly improves by cultivation. On the east side there rises a large level field, of from 70 to 80 morgens [a morgen is approximately two acres] of land, through which runs a very fine fresh stream; so that that land can be ploughed without much clearing. It appears to be good. The six farms, four of which lie along the River Hellgate [East River] stretching to the south side of the island, have at least 60 morgens of land ready to be sown with winter seed, which at the most will have been ploughed eight times. But as the greater part must have some manure, inasmuch as it is so exhausted by the wild herbage, I am afraid that all will not be sown; and the more so, as the managers of the farms are hired men. The two hindermost farms, Nos. 1 and 2, are the best; the other farms have also good land, but not so much, and more sandy; so that they are best suited for rye and buckwheat. . . .

Coming out of the river Nassau [the Sakonnet River is probably meant] you sail east-and-by-north about fourteen leagues, along the coast, a half mile from the shore, and you then come to "Frenchman's Point" at a small river where those of Patucxet [name of the region in which Plymouth colony was located] have a house made of hewn oak planks, called Aptucxet [or Manomet, now called Monument, north end of Buzzard's Bay], where they keep two men, winter and summer, in order to maintain the trade and possession. Here also they have built a shallop, in order to go and look after the trade in *sewan*. . . .

From Aptucxet the English can come in six hours, through the woods, passing several little rivulets of fresh water, to New Plymouth, the principal place in the district Patucxet, so called in their patent from His Majesty in England.

New Plymouth lies in a large bay to the north of Cape Cod, or Mallabaer, east and west from the said [north] point of the cape, which can be easily seen in clear weather. Directly before the commenced town lies a sand-bank about twenty paces broad [Plymouth Beach] whereon the sea breaks violently with an easterly and east-northeasterly wind. On the north side there lies a small island [Saquish] where one must run close along, in order to come before the town; then the ships run behind that bank and lie in a very good roadstead. The bay is very full of fish, [chiefly] of cod, so that the governor before named has told me that when the people have a desire for fish they send out two or three persons in a sloop, whom they remunerate for their trouble, and who bring them in three or four hours' time as much fish as the whole community require for a whole day—and they muster about fifty families.

At the south side of the town there flows down a small river of fresh water, very rapid, but shallow, which takes its rise from several lakes in the land above, and there empties into the sea; where in April and the beginning of May, there come so many shad from the sea which want to ascend that river, that it is quite surprising. This river the English have shut in with planks, and in the middle with a little door, which slides up and down, and at the sides with trellice work, through which the water has its course, but which they can also close with slides.

At the mouth they have constructed it with planks, like an eel pot, with wings, where in the middle is also a sliding door, and with trellice work at the sides, so that between the two [dams] there is a square pool, into which the fish aforesaid come swimming in such shoals, in order to get up above, where they deposit their spawn, that at one tide there are 10,000 to 12,000 fish in it, which they shut off in the rear at the ebb, and close up the trellices above, so that no more water comes in; then the water runs out through the lower trellices, and they draw out the fish with baskets, each according to the land he cultivates, and carry them to it, depositing in each hill three or four fishes, and in these they plant their maize, which grows as luxuriantly therein as though it were the best manure in the world. And if they do not lay this fish therein, the maize will not grow, so that such is the nature of the soil.

New Plymouth lies on the slope of a hill stretching east toward the seacoast, with a broad street . . . leading down the hill. . . . The houses are constructed of hewn planks, with gardens also enclosed behind and at the sides with hewn planks, so that their houses and courtyards are arranged in very good order, with a stockade against a sudden attack; and at the ends of the streets there are three wooden gates. In the center, on the cross street, stands the governor's house, before which is a square stockade upon which four patereros are mounted, so as to enfilade the streets. Upon the hill they have a large square house, with a flat roof, made of thick sawn plank, stayed with oak beams, upon the top of which they have six cannon, which shoot iron balls of four and five pounds, and command the surrounding country. The lower part they use for their church, where they preach on Sundays and the usual holidays. They assemble by beat of drum, each with his musket or firelock, in front of the captain's door; they have their cloaks on, and place themselves in order, three abreast, and are led by a sergeant without beat of drum. Behind comes the governor, in a long robe; beside him, on the right hand, comes the preacher with his cloak on, and on the left hand the captain with his side arms, and cloak on, and with a small cane in his hand; and so they march in good order, and each sets his arms down near him. Thus they are constantly on their guard night and day. Their government is after the English form.

. . . Their farms are not so good as ours, because they are more stony, and consequently not so suitable for the plough. They apportion their land according as each has means to contribute to the eighteen thousand guilders which they have promised to those who had sent them out; whereby they have their freedom without rendering an account to any one; only if the King should choose to send a governor general they would be obliged to acknowledge him as sovereign overlord. . . . They have better sustenance than ourselves, because they have the fish so abundant before their doors. There are also many birds, such as geese, herons and cranes, and other small-legged birds, which are in great abundance there in the winter.

The tribes in their neighborhood have all the same customs as already above described, only they are better conducted than ours, because the English give them the example of better ordinances and a better life; and who also, to a certain degree, give them laws, in consequence of the respect they from the very first have established amongst them.

Megapolensis' Account of the Mohawks

[*An enormous tract of land along both banks of the Hudson not far from Fort Orange was acquired between 1630 and 1631 by a rich director of the West India Company, Kilaen van Rensselaer, who named the barony (or patroonship, as it was called) Rensselaerswyck. To minister to the spiritual welfare of settlers on his great estate, and to convert the Indians to Christianity if possible, van Rensselaer sent out in 1642 a learned pastor, Johannes Megapolensis. As a result of his experiences the preacher wrote and sent back to Holland in 1644* Een kort Ontwerp vande Mahakvase Indiaenen (A Short Account of the Mohawk Indians), *which did more than merely tell about the Indians. Megapolensis gave a clear description of the country, its products, and its prospects as well as reporting on the customs of its aboriginal inhabitants. Several versions in English of this description have been published. It appears in* Narratives of New Netherland. *Excerpts follow:*]

A Short Account of the Mohawk Indians, Their Country, Language, Stature, Dress, Religion and Government, Thus Described and Recently, August 26, 1644, Sent Out of New Netherland, by Johannes Megapolensis the Younger, Preacher There.

The country here is in general like that in Germany. The land is good, and fruitful in everything which supplies human needs except clothes, linen, woollen, stockings, shoes, etc., which are all dear here. The country is very mountainous, partly soil, partly rocks, and with elevations so exceeding high that they appear to almost touch the clouds. Thereon grow the finest fir trees the eye ever saw. There are also in this country oaks, alders, beeches, elms, willows, etc. In the forests, and here and there along the water side and on the islands, there grows an abundance of chestnuts, plums, hazel nuts, large walnuts of several sorts and of as good a taste as in the Netherlands, but they have a somewhat harder shell. The ground on the hills is covered with bushes of bilberries or blueberries; the ground in the flat land near the rivers is covered with strawberries, which grow here so plentifully in the fields that one can lie down and eat them. Grapevines also grow here naturally in great abundance along the roads, paths, and creeks, and wherever you may turn you find them. I have seen whole pieces of land where vine stood by vine and grew very luxuriantly, climbing to the top of the largest and loftiest trees, and although they are not cultivated some of the grapes are found to be as good and sweet as in Holland. Here is also a sort of grapes which grow very large, each grape as big as the end of one's finger or an ordinary plum, and because they are somewhat fleshy and have a thick skin we call them *Speck Druyven* [now called "hog grapes"]. If people would cultivate the vines they might have as good wine here as they have in Germany or France. I had myself last harvest a boatload of grapes and pressed them. As long as the wine was new it tasted better than any French or Rhenish Must, and the color of the grape juice here is so high and red that with one wine-glass full you can color a whole pot of white wine.

. . . In the forests is great plenty of deer, which in autumn and early winter are as fat as any Holland cow can be. I have had them with fat more than two fingers thick on the ribs, so that they were nothing else than almost clear fat and could hardly be eaten. There are also many turkies, as large as in Holland, but in some years less than in others. The year before I came here [i.e., 1641] there were so many turkies and deer that they came to feed by the houses and hog pens, and were taken by the Indians in such numbers that a deer was sold to the Dutch for a loaf of bread, or a knife, or even for a tobacco pipe; but now one commonly has to give for a good deer six or seven guilders. In the forests here there are also many partridges, heath hens [now extinct], and pigeons that fly together in thousands, and sometimes ten, twenty, thirty, and even forty and fifty are killed at one shot. We have here, too, a great number of all kinds of fowl, swans, geese, ducks, widgeons [a type of duck], teal, brant, which sport upon the river in thousands in the spring of the year, and again in the autumn fly away in flocks, so that in the morning and evening anyone may stand ready with his gun before his house and shoot them as they fly past. I have also eaten here several times of elks, which were very fat and tasted much like venison; and besides these profitable beasts we have also in this country lions [panthers], bears, wolves, foxes, and particularly very many snakes, which are large and as long as eight, ten, and twelve feet. Among others, there is a sort of snake which we call rattlesnake, from a certain object which it has back upon its tail, two or three fingers' breadth long, and has ten or twelve joints, and with this it makes a noise like the crickets. Its color is variegated much like our large brindled bulls. These snakes have very sharp teeth in their mouth, and dare to bite at dogs; they make way for neither man nor beast, but fall on and bite them, and their bite is very poisonous, and commonly even deadly too. . . .

As for the temperature in this country, and the seasons of the year, the summers are pretty hot, so that for the most of the time we are obliged to go in just our shirts, and the winters are very cold. The summer continues long, even until All Saints' Day [November 1]; but when the winter does begin, just as it commonly does in December, it freezes so hard in one night that the ice will bear a man. Even the rivers, in still weather when there is no strong current running, are frozen over in one night, so that on the second day people walk over it. And this freezing continues commonly three months; for although we are situated here in 42 degrees of latitude, it always freezes so. And although there come warm and pleasant days, the thaw does not continue, but it freezes again until March. Then, commonly, the rivers first begin to open, and seldom in February. We have the greatest cold from the northwest, as in Holland from the northeast. The wind here is very seldom east, but almost always south, southwest, northwest, and north; so also the rain.

Our shortest winter days have nine hours sun; in the summer, our longest days are about fifteen hours. We lie so far west of Holland that I judge you are about four hours [actually 5 hours] in advance of us, so that when it is six o'clock in the morning with us it is ten in the forenoon with you, and when it is noon with us, it is four o'clock in the afternoon with you. . . .

Danckaerts' Journal

[*On June 8, 1679, two Dutch members of a strict Protestant sect known as Labadists, Jasper Danckaerts and Peter Sluyter, left their homes in Friesland at the beginning of a journey that took them over the Atlantic to New York and as far south as Maryland, and thence on their return to Boston and its environs. They were on a reconnaissance trip to search out a place for a settlement of their religionists. This they found in Maryland, and there in Cecil County they brought a small colony of Labadists in 1683. Having made the preliminary arrangements, the two sailed from Maryland for Boston on June 19, 1680 and, after a not-too-favorable opinion of Boston and its inhabitants, they took ship for Europe on July 23. Danckaerts kept a detailed and garrulous journal of their travels and wrote down his opinions of country and people, never bothering to disguise his own religious prejudices. An English translation by Henry C. Murphy was published in Brooklyn in 1867 with the title,* Journal of a Voyage to New York and a Tour in Several of the American Colonies in 1679–80. *A slightly revised and abridged version of the* Journal *was edited by Bartlett B. James and J.*

Franklin Jameson for the "Original Narratives of Early American History" series (New York, 1913). A few descriptive passages follow:]

29th, Friday [September, 1679]. We finished our letters, and intended to go today over to Long Island. . . .

As soon as we had dined we sent off our letters; and this being all accomplished, we started at two o'clock for Long Island. This island is called Long Island, not so much because it is longer than it is broad, but particularly because it is the longest island in this region, or even along the whole coast of New Netherland, Virginia, and New England. It is one hundred and forty-four miles in length, and from twenty-four to twenty-eight miles wide, though there are several bays and points along it, and, consequently, it is much broader in some places than others. On the west is Staten Island, from which it is separated about a mile. . . . The ends of these islands opposite each other are quite high land, and they are, therefore, called the *Hoofden* (Headlands), from a comparison with the Hoofden of the channel between England and France, in Europe. On the north is the island of *Mahatans* and a part of the mainland. On the east is the sea which shoots up to New England, and in which there are various islands. On the south is the great ocean. The outer shore of this island has before it several small islands and broken land, such as *Coninen* [Coney] island, a low sandy island of about three hours' circuit, its westerly point forming with Sandy Hook, on the other side, the entrance from the sea. It is oblong in shape, and is grown over with bushes. Nobody lives upon it, but it is used in winter for keeping cattle, horses, oxen, hogs, and others, which are able to obtain there sufficient to eat the whole winter, and to shelter themselves from the cold in the thickets. . . .

The water by which it [Long Island] is separated from the *Mahatans* is improperly called the East river, for it is nothing else than an arm of the sea, beginning in the bay on the west and ending in the sea on the east. After forming in this passage several islands, this water is as broad before the city as the Y before Amsterdam, but the ebb and flood tides are stronger. There is a ferry for the purpose of crossing over it, which is farmed out by the year and yields a good income as it is a considerable thoroughfare, this island being one of the most populous places in this vicinity. . . . The fare over the ferry is three stuivers in zeewan [less than a half cent] for each person. Here we three crossed over, my comrade, Gerrit, our guide, and myself, in a rowboat, as it happened, which in good weather and tide carries a sail.

. . . We went on, up the hill, along open roads and a little woods, through the first village, called Breukelen [Brooklyn], which has a small and ugly little church standing in the middle of the road.

14th, Tuesday [November 1679]. Having taken leave of all our acquaintances, we set off at ten o'clock this morning in company with Ephraim, his wife, his wife's mother, two of her sisters, and a young brother, who were to accompany her as far as Pescatteway [Piscataway, New Jersey). We stepped into the boat, where we found three horses, two Quakers, and another Englishman. We were not long in starting. The wind was from the west, which is a head wind for sailing to Achter Kol [Newark Bay]. The sky began to be heavily overcast, and the wind to freshen up more, so that we had to tack. Ephraim being afraid the wind might shift to the northwest and blow hard, as it usually does when it is from that quarter, wished to return and would have done so if the skipper had not tried to go ahead more than he did. The tide running out, and the boat advancing but little, and being fearful of the flood tide, which would delay us if it did not drive us back, and as there was room to work with the rudder, I went and took hold of the tiller myself, and brought the boat, with the flood tide, just within the point of Staten Island, where we found a ketch bound for Achter Kol. . . .

3d [December], Sunday. . . . It was, then, on this day and at this plantation [a tract of some 20,000 acres named Bohemia by its owner, a Bohemian] that we made our entry into Maryland, which was so named, I believe, in Queen Mary's time [Henrietta Maria, consort of Charles I] when it was discovered or began to be settled. It is a large territory, but has as yet no fixed boundaries, except only on the south where it is separated from Virginia by a straight line running westerly from [blank] to the river. All north of this line is Maryland, and all south of it Virginia. On the east it is bounded by New Netherland, but that line is undefined; and on the north and west indefinitely by the Indians. . . .

Maryland is considered the most fertile portion of North America, and it were to be wished that it was also the most healthy, though it is more healthy than its neighbor, Virginia, which has to give passage by water through the great bay of [Chesapeake] to Maryland. It is also very rich in fish as well as in all kinds of water fowl. There are few Indians in comparison with the extent of country. . . .

14th, Thursday. While we were waiting for Casparus, we embraced the opportunity to examine his place again, which pleased us in all respects, and was objectionable only because it lay on the road, and was therefore resorted to by every one, and especially by these miserable Quakers. He returned home in the afternoon, and was glad to find us. We spoke to him in relation to a certain tract of land which we wished to look at and Ephraim and his father [Casparus and Ephraim were sons of Augustine Hermans the owner of "Bohemia"] had told us of; and when we heard what it was, it was a part of Bohemia, which we had already tolerably well looked at on our way to Maryland, being that which lies on the creeks and river, and which, on our return and twice losing the way, lay higher up in the woods; but we reserved the privilege in case we should winter on the South River, of riding over it thoroughly on horseback with him and his brother Ephraim [this was the tract, some 15 miles down the Delaware River from Newcastle, on which the Labadists eventually settled]. For the present, time compelled us to see if we could not yet reach the Manathans for the winter; and we were the more induced to the attempt because a servant of Ephraim had arrived this evening by water in a boat, and would be ready to return with it to Newcastle early in the morning. We therefore excused ourselves and let the subject rest. . . .

15th, Friday. It was flood tide early this morning, and our servant slept a little too long, for it was not far from high water when he appeared. We hurried, however, into the boat and pushed on as hard as we could, but the flood stopped running, when we were about halfway. We continued on rowing, and as the day advanced we caught a favorable wind from the west and spread the sail. The wind gradually increasing brought us to Newcastle about eight o'clock among our kind friends again, where we were welcome anew. . . .

All of Maryland that we have seen is high land, with few or no meadows but possessing such a rich and fertile soil as persons living there assured me that they had raised tobacco off the same piece of land for thirty consecutive years. The inhabitants, who are generally English, are mostly engaged in this production. It is their chief staple, and the money with which they must purchase everything they require, which is brought to them from other English possessions in Europe, Africa, and America. There is, nevertheless, sometimes a great want of these necessaries, owing to the tobacco market being low, or the shipments being prevented by some change of affairs in some quarter, particularly in Europe, or indeed to both causes, as was the case at this time, whereby there sometimes arises a great scarcity of such articles as are most necessary, as we saw when there. So large a quantity of tobacco is raised in Maryland and Virginia that it is one of the greatest sources of revenue to the crown by reason of the taxes which it yields. . . .

1680, June 19th, Wednesday. We embarked at noon in the yacht of Mr. *Padechal,* supercargo and captain, residing in Boston. The anchor was weighed at last; but as we had to wait a long time for the governor's yacht, the tide was nearly all spent. The wind was from the northwest. The crew consisted of three men and a boy, besides the captain; but there was another sailor on board who was a passenger. Many persons came to escort the captain, and also a woman, who was going with us; and as soon as they had gone we hastened to leave. The wind being ahead, we tacked and towed until we anchored at Hellgate, almost at flood tide, at four o'clock in the afternoon. . . .

20th, Thursday. It was about ten o'clock in the forenoon before the flood began to make. The wind was southwest, but light. We weighed anchor and towed through Hellgate, when the wind and tide served us until we passed Whitestone (*de witte klip*), as far as which the tide, from the direction of New York, usually reaches. We sailed bravely by and obtained the ebb tide in our favor which carried us this evening beyond Milford.

21st, Friday. We had shot ahead very well during the night, with the wind west and south-southwest, on a course due east, so that by morning we reached the end of Long Island. The governor's yacht—which had to stop at Fisher's island, a little to the leeward of us, which is subject to New England but which the governor is now endeavoring to bring under his authority, and for that purpose had sent his yacht there with letters—left us this morning with a salute. We observed a vessel ahead of us under sail, running before the wind, and we came up to her about nine o'clock. She was a small flute [naval transport] from Milford, laden with horses and bound for Barbadoes. We hailed her, and, as her captain was an acquaintance of our captain and an independent, our captain went on board of her, where he stayed two hours. When he returned we kept our course, and she sailed to the south in order to get to sea. As soon as we reached the end of Long Island they began to throw their fish lines, and continued to catch mackerel all day long. I think the European mackerel are better and fatter. We came to an island called *Maertens Wingaert* [Martha's Vineyard] about four o'clock in the afternoon, having the Elizabeth islands on the larboard and sailing between the two, with our course easterly and a lighter wind. . . .

There was no moon, and the weather was cloudy. We continued sailing onward until two o'clock after midnight, when the captain, going aloft, cried out, "Strike the sails! strike the sails! let them run! let them run! we are on the rocks, let the anchor fall!" This startled me so that I cannot tell how I reached the deck and ran forward. I saw we were indeed close upon a reef of rocks directly before us, and that we were under considerable headway. We did our best to lower the sails and throw the anchor over. The headway was checked some, but the anchor would not hold. We found that the spritsail had caught in the anchor stock in consequence of the hurry in lowering the sail and throwing anchor, but it was some time before we could discover what was the matter and get the anchor loose; it then held fast in three fathoms of water at a musket shot's distance from the reef and about as far from the shore. We lay there until daylight on a lee shore, but fortunately it did not blow hard.

22d, Saturday. As soon as the day broke and we saw where we were, we got under sail again with the wind, the same as before. In sailing between the land, namely *Maertens Wyngaert* and the reef, the course is to the point of the island, running east-southeast in three and two and a half fathoms till you have this point on the side, and then you have passed the reef. We continued on until we reached the westerly point of the island of *Nantocket,* along which we sailed to the easterly point, and thence due north until noon; but the flood tide running in strong, and the vessel not being well steered, we were carried to the west among the shoals.

The weather was rather rough and the atmosphere hazy, so that we could not see far. The shoals were ahead of us, and we had only two fathoms, and even less, of water. The captain and helmsman were confused, and hardly knew where they were. This happened two or three times. In order to avoid the shoals we had to keep to the east. We were fearful we would strike upon them, and it was, therefore, best to look out and keep free of them.

About three o'clock we caught sight of the mainland of Cape Cod, to which we sailed northerly. We arrived inside the cape about six o'clock with a tolerable breeze from the west, and at the same time saw vessels to the leeward of us which had an east wind, from which circumstance we supposed we were in a whirl-wind. These two contrary winds striking against each other, the sky became dark, and they whirled by each other, sometimes the one, and sometimes the other being strongest, compelling us to lower the sails several times. I have never seen such a twisting and turning round in the air as at this time, the clouds being driven against each other and close to the earth. At last it became calm and began to rain very hard, and to thunder and lighten heavily. We drifted along the whole night in a calm, advancing only twelve or sixteen miles.

23d, Sunday. A breeze blew up from the northeast. It was fortunate for us that we arrived inside of Cape Cod yesterday evening before this unfavorable weather, as we would otherwise have been compelled to put back to Rhode Island. We could now still proceed; and we laid our course northwest to Boston. We arrived at the entrance of the harbor at noon, where we found a considerable rolling sea caused by the ebb tide and wind being against each other. There are about thirty islands here, not large ones, through which we sailed, and reached Boston at four o'clock in the afternoon, our captain running with his yacht quite up to his house in the Milk-ditch.

The Lord be praised who has continued in such a fatherly manner to conduct us, and given us so many proofs of his care over us; words are wanting to express ourselves properly, more than occasions for them, which we have had abundantly.

We permitted those most in haste to go ashore before us, and then went ourselves. The skipper received us politely at his house, and so did his wife; but as it was Sunday, which it seems is somewhat strictly observed by these people, there was not much for us to do today. Our captain, however, took us to his sister's, where we were welcome, and from there to his father's, an old corpulent man, where there was a repetition of the worship, which took place in the kitchen while they were turning the spit and busy preparing a good supper. We arrived while they were engaged in the service, but he did not once look up. When he had finished, they turned round their backs and kneeled on chairs or benches. The prayer was said loud enough to be heard three houses off, and also long enough, if that made it good.

This done, he wished us and his son welcome, and insisted on our supping with him, which we did. There were nine or ten persons at the table. It being in the evening, and we strangers, Mr. Padechal requested us to lodge with him this night, as we did, intending in the morning to look out for accommodations. We were taken to a fine large chamber, but we were hardly in bed before we were shockingly bitten. I did not know the cause, but not being able to sleep, I became aware it was bedbugs, in such great numbers as was inconceivable. My comrade, who was very sleepy, fell asleep at first. He tumbled about very much; but I did not sleep any the whole night. In the morning we saw how it was, and were astonished we should find such a room with such a lady.

. . . Cape Cod is a clean coast, where there are no islands, rocks, or banks, and therefore all such laid down on the charts of the great reef of Malebarre and otherwise is false. Indeed, within four, eight, and twelve miles, there is sixty to sixty-five fathoms of water. This cape or coast is about twenty-eight miles long due north; and from thence to Cape Ann it is also due north, but to Boston it is northwest. There are many small islands before Boston, well on to fifty, I believe, between which you sail on to the city. A high one, or the highest, is the first that you meet. It is twelve miles from the city and has a lighthouse upon it which you can see from a great distance, for it is in other respects naked and bare. In sailing by this island you keep it on the west side; on the other side there is an island with many rocks upon and around it, and when you pass by it you must be careful as a shoal pushes out from it which you must sail round. You have then an island in front, in the shape of a battery, which also you leave on the larboard, and then you come in sight of the island upon which the fort stands and where the flag is flown when ships are entering.

That, too, lies to the larboard, and you pass close enough to it for them to hail the ship—what you are, from whence you came, and where you are bound, &c. When you are there you see the city lying directly before you; and so you sail into the bay before the town and cast anchor. There is a high hill in the city, also with a lighthouse upon it, by which you can hold your course in entering.

24th, Monday. We walked with our captain into the town, for his house stood a little one side of it, and the first house he took us to was a tavern.

Journey of Sarah Knight
from Boston to New York, 1704–1705

[*Travel in the early eighteenth century, even in the older settled parts of the East, could be a rugged adventure, even for hardy men. For a woman it could be a genuine hardship. But not all women were deterred from traveling. One who made a memorable journey from Boston to New York in the first decade of the century was Sarah Kemble Knight (1667–1727), a Boston schoolteacher. She was the daughter of a merchant and the wife of a shipmaster, Captain Richard Knight, a widower considerably older than herself. Some sort of business or legal affairs, possibly the settlement of an estate, took her to New York in 1704, a time when the route was both difficult and dangerous. Madam Knight, however, was a woman of spirit, and was equal to the emergency, as her journal makes clear. Her diary of the journey was first published in 1825 as* The Journal of Madam Knight and Rev. Mr. Buckingham, *edited by Timothy Dwight. It was edited by R. P. Keep and reprinted in 1901 as* The Private Journal of Sarah Kemble Knight. *Excerpts follow:*]

Monday, October the second, 1704. About three o'clock afternoon I begun my journey from Boston to New Haven, being about two hundred mile. My kinsman, Captain Robert Luist, waited on me as far as Dedham, where I was to meet the western post.

I visited the Reverd. Mr. Belcher, the minister of the town, and tarried there till evening in hopes the post would come along. But he not coming, I resolved to go to Billings's, where he used to lodge, being 12 miles further. But being ignorant of the way, Madam Belcher, seeing no persuasions of her good spouse's or hers could prevail with me to lodge there that night, very kindly went with me to the tavern, where I hoped to get my guide, and desired the hostess to inquire of her guests whether any of them would go with me. But they being tied by the lips to a pewter engine [i.e., beer mug] scarcely allowed themselves time. . . .

[*There being no volunteers, the hostess offered the services of her son John, at a fee that Mrs. Knight considered exorbitant.*]

I told her no, I would not be accessary to such extortion.

"Then John shan't go," says she. "No indeed, shan't he." And held forth at that rate a long time, [so] that I began to fear I was got among the quaking tribe [i.e., Quakers], believing not a limber-tongued sister among them could outdo Madam Hostess.

Upon this, to my no small surprise, son John arose and gravely demanded what I would give him to go with me.

"Give you?" says I. "Are you John?"

"Yes," says he, "for want of a better." And behold! this John looked as old as my host, and perhaps had been a man in the last century.

"Well, Mr. John," says I, "make your demands."

"Why, half a piece of eight and a dram," says John.

I agreed and gave him a dram [now] in hand to bind the bargain.

My hostess catechised John for going so cheap, saying his poor wife would break her heart. . . .

His [John's] shade [silhouette] on his horse resembled a globe on a gate post. His habit, horse, and furniture, its looks and goings, incomparably answered the rest. Thus jogging on with an easy pace, my guide telling me it was dangerous to ride hard in the night (which his horse had the sense to avoid), he entertained me with the adventures he had passed by late riding and eminent dangers he had escaped so that, remembering the heroes in *Parismus* and the *Knight of the Oracle* [romantic tales then popular], I didn't know but I had met with a prince disguised. . . .

Tuesday, October the third, about 8 in the morning, I with the post proceeded forward without observing anything remarkable; and about two [in the] afternoon arrived at the post's second stage, where the western post met him and exchanged letters.

Here, having called for something to eat, the woman brought in a twisted thing like a cable, but something whiter; and, laying it on the board, tugged for life to bring it into a capacity to spread; which having with great pains accomplished, she served in a dish of pork and cabbage, I suppose the remains of dinner. The sauce was of a deep purple, which I thought was boiled in her dye kettle. The bread was Indian, and everything on the table service agreeable to these. I, being hungry, got a little down. But my stomach was soon cloyed, and what cabbage I swallowed served me for a cud the whole day after.

Having here discharged the ordinary [paid the tavern bill] for self and guide (as I understood was the custom), about three afternoon went on with my third guide, who rode very hard; and, having crossed Providence ferry, we come to a river which they generally ride thro'. But I dare not venture. So the post got a lad and canoe to carry me to t'other side, and he rid thro' and led my horse. The canoe was very small and shallow so that, when we were in, she seemed ready to take in water, which greatly terrified me and caused me to be very circumspect, sitting with my hands fast on each side, my eyes steady, not daring so much as to lodge my tongue a hair's breadth more on one side of my mouth than t'other, nor so much as think on Lot's wife, for a wry thought would have overset our wherry. But was soon out of this pain by feeling the canoe on shore, which I, as soon almost, saluted with my feet. And, rewarding my sculler, again mounted and made the best of our way forwards. . . . The post told me we had near 14 miles to ride to the next stage, where we were to lodge. I asked him of the rest of the road, foreseeing we must travel in the night. He told me there was a bad river we were to ride thro'. . . .

The only glimmering we now had was from the spangled skies, whose imperfect reflections rendered every object formidable. Each lifeless trunk, with its shattered limbs, appeared an armed enemy, and every little stump like a ravenous devourer. Nor could I so much as discern my guide, when at any distance, which added to the terror.

Thus . . . dying with the very thoughts of drowning, I come up with the post, who I did not see till even with his horse. He told me he stopped for me. And we rode on very deliberately a few paces when we entered a thicket of trees and shrubs, and I perceived by the horse's going we were on the descent of a hill which, as we come nearer the bottom, 'twas totally dark with the trees that surrounded it. But I knew by the going of the horse we had entered the water, which my guide told me was the hazardous river he had told me of. And he, riding up close to my side, bid me not fear—we should be over immediately. I now rallied all the courage I was mistress of, knowing that I must either venture my fate of drowning, or be left like the children in the wood. So, as the post bid me, I gave reins to my nag and, sitting as steady as just before in the canoe, in a few minutes got safe to the other side, which he told me was the Narraganset country. . . .

From hence we kept on, with more ease than before. The way being smooth and even, the night warm and serene, and the tall and thick trees at a distance, especially when the moon glared light through the branches, filled my imagination with the pleasant delusion of a sumptuous city filled with famous buildings and churches, with their spiring steeples, balconies, galleries, and I know not what—grandeurs which I had heard of and which the stories of foreign countries had given me the idea of. . . .

Being come to Mr. Havens's, I was very civilly received and courteously entertained in a clean, comfortable house. . . . But I could get no sleep because of the clamor of some of the town topers in next room, who were entered into a strong debate concerning the signification of the name of their country, viz. *Narraganset*. One said it was named so by the Indians because there grew a brier there of a prodigious height and bigness, the like hardly ever known, called by the Indians Narraganset. And quotes an Indian of so barbarous a name, for his author, that I could not write it. His antagonist replied no, it was from a spring it had its name, which he well knew where it was, which was extreme cold in summer and as hot as could be imagined in the winter, which was much resorted to by the natives, and by them called Narraganset (hot and cold), and that was the original of their place's name—with a thousand impertinences not worth notice, which he uttered with such a roaring voice and thundering blows with the fist of wickedness on the table that it pierced my very head. I heartily fretted and wished 'um tongue-tied, but with as little success as a friend of mine once who was, as she said, kept a whole night awake, on a journey, by a country Left. [Lieutenant] and a Sergeant, Insigne, and a Deacon contriving how to bring a triangle into a square. . . .

Wednesday, October 4th. About four in the morning we set out for Kingston . . . with a French doctor in our company. He and the post put on very furiously so that I could not keep up with them, only as now and then they'd stop till they see me. This road was poorly furnished with accommodations for travelers, so that we were forced to ride twenty-two miles by the post's account, but nearer thirty by mine, before we could bait [feed] so much as our horses, which I exceedingly complained of. . . .

Friday, October 6th. I got up very early in order to hire somebody to go with me to New Haven. . . . We advanced on towards Seabrook [Saybrook]. The roads all along this way are very bad, encumbered with rocks and mountainous passages which were very disagreeable to my tired carcass. . . .

Arrived at Saybrook ferry about two of the clock [in the] afternoon, and, crossing it, we called at an inn to bait [restore ourselves]. . . . Landlady comes in with her hair about her ears and hands at full pay scratching. She told us she had some mutton which she would broil, which I was glad to hear. But I suppose forgot to wash her scratchers. In a little time she brought it in. But it being pickled, and my guide said it smelt of head sauce [head souse, or head cheese—boiled pig's feet and heads], we left it, and paid sixpence for our dinners, which was only smell. . . .

Without anything further remarkable, about two a clock [in the] afternoon [October 7] we arrived at New Haven, where I was received with all possible respects and civility. . . . And took some time to rest after so long and toilsome a journey, and informed myself of the manners and customs of the place, and at the same time employed myself in the affair I went there upon. . . .

There are great plenty of oysters all along by the seaside as far as I rode in the colony, and those very good. And they generally lived very well and comfortably in their families. . . .

There are everywhere in the towns as I passed a number of Indians, the natives of the country, and are the most savage of all the savages of that kind that I had ever seen, little or no care taken (as I heard upon inquiry) to make them otherwise. They have in some places lands of their own, and governed by laws of their own making. They marry many wives and at pleasure put them away—and on the least dislike or fickle humor, on either side; saying "Stand away" to one another is a sufficient divorce. . . .

We may observe here the great necessity and benefit both of education and conversation. For these people have as large a portion of mother wit, and sometimes a larger, than those who have been brought up in cities. But for want of improvements render themselves almost ridiculous. . . .

Their chief red letter day is St. Election, which is annually observed, according to charter, to choose their governor: a blessing they can never be thankful enough for, as they will find, if ever it be their hard fortune to lose it. The present governor in Connecticut is the Honorable John Winthrop, Esq., a gentleman of an ancient and honorable family, whose father was governor here sometime before, and his grandfather had been governor of the Massachusetts. This gentleman is a very courteous and affable person, much given to hospitality, and has by his good services gained the affections of the people as much as any who had been before him in that post. . . .

The city of New York is a pleasant, well-compacted place, situated on a commodious river which is a fine harbor for shipping. The buildings [are of] brick generally, very stately and high, though not altogether like ours in Boston. The bricks in some of the houses are of divers colors and, laid in checkers, being glazed look very agreeable. The inside of them are neat to admiration. . . .

They have vendues [auctions] very frequently and make their earnings very well by them, for they treat with good liquor liberally, and the customers drink as liberally and generally pay for't as well by paying for that which they bid up briskly for, after the sack has gone plentifully about—tho' sometimes good pennyworths are got there.

Their diversions in the winter is riding sleighs about three or four miles out of town, where they have houses of entertainment at a place called the Bowery. . . . I believe we met 50 or 60 sleighs that day—they fly with great swiftness and some are so furious that they'll turn out of the path for none except a loaded cart. . . .

Having here transacted the affair I went upon and some other that fell in the way, after about a fortnight's stay there I left New York with no little regret, and Thursday, Dec. 21, set out for

New Haven with my kinsman. . . . Being overtaken by a great storm of wind and snow which set full in our faces about dark, we were very uneasy. . . .

The weather being now fair, Friday the 22nd Dec. we set out for New Rochelle, where, being come, we had good entertainment and recruited ourselves very well. This is a very pretty place, well compact, and good handsome houses, clean, good and passable roads, and situated on a navigable river. . . . Here we rid over a bridge made of one entire stone of such a breadth that a cart might pass with safety and to spare—it lay over a passage cut through a rock to convey water to a mill not far off. Here are three fine taverns within call of each other, very good provision for travelers. . . .

Descending the mountainous passage that almost broke my heart in ascending before, we come to Stamford, a well-compact town but miserable meeting house, which we passed, and thro' many and great difficulties, as bridges which were exceeding high and very tottering and of vast length, steep and rocky hills and precipices (bugbears to a fearful female traveler). . . .

Saturday, Dec. 23, a very cold and windy day, after an intolerable night's lodging, we hasted forward . . . to Fairfield. . . . This is a considerable town and filled, as they say, with wealthy people; have a spacious meeting house and good buildings. But the inhabitants are litigious, nor do they well agree with their minister who (they say) is a very worthy gentleman.

They have abundance of sheep, whose very dung brings them great gain; with part of which they pay their parson's salary. And they grudge that, preferring their dung before their minister. They let out their sheep at so much as they agree upon for a night. The highest bidder always carries them. And they will sufficiently dung a large quantity of land before morning. But were once bit by a sharper who had them a night and sheared them all before morning. . . .

Having finished, though not till February, the man that waited on me to [New] York taking the charge of me, I set out for Boston. We went from New Haven upon the ice (the ferry being not passable thereby) and . . . went onward without anything remarkable till we come to New London and lodged again at Mr. Saltonstall's. . . . I stayed a day here longer than I intended by the commands of the Honorable Governor Winthrop to stay and take a supper with him, whose wonderful civility I may not omit. The next morning I crossed the ferry to Groton . . . and that night lodged at Stonington and had roast beef and pumpkin sauce for supper. . . .

We were now in the colony of the Massachusetts and, taking lodgings at the first inn we come too, had a pretty difficult passage the next day, which was the second of March, by reason of the sloughy ways then thawed by the sun. Here I met Capt. John Richards of Boston, who was going home, so, being very glad of his company, we rode something harder than hitherto. And, missing my way in going up a very steep hill, my horse dropped down under me as dead. This new surprise no little hurt me, meeting it just at the entrance into Dedham, from whence we intended to reach home that night. But was now obliged to get another horse there and leave my own, resolving for Boston that night if possible. But in going over the causeway at Dedham, the bridge being overflowed by the high waters coming down, I very narrowly escaped falling over into the river, horse and all, which 'twas almost a miracle I did not.

Now it grew late in the afternoon and, the people having very much discouraged us about the sloughy way, which they said we should find very difficult and hazardous, it so wrought on me, being tired and dispirited and disappointed of my desires of going home, that I agreed to lodge there that night, which we did at the house of one Draper. And the next day, being March 3rd, we got safe home to Boston.

Benjamin Franklin Reports on Travel from New York to Philadelphia, 1723

[A journey made by Benjamin Franklin in 1723 from New York to Philadelphia throws further light on conditions of travel in the first quarter of the eighteenth century. In later years Franklin was to serve as Postmaster General and preside over a postal system that expedited mail over the roads linking the principal cities in the East.

[Franklin had learned the printer's trade in Boston as apprentice to his half brother James, publisher of The New England

Courant. *Chafing under the master-apprentice relationship within the family, Benjamin quit his brother's service to seek employment in New York. The printer there, "having little to do," told him of a possible opening in Philadelphia. Franklin's autobiography gives a vivid account, reproduced below, of travel between the two cities in the time of his and the country's youth. The original manuscript of the autobiography is preserved in the Huntington Library. Of the many editions available, the most accurate is* Benjamin Franklin's Memoirs, *edited by Max Farrand (San Marino, California, 1949).*]

The inclination I had had for the sea was by this time done away, or I might now have gratified it. But having another profession and conceiving myself a pretty good workman, I offered my services to the printer of the place [New York], old Mr. Wm. Bradford (who had been the first printer in Pennsylvania, but had removed thence in consequence of a quarrel with the Governor, Geo. Keith). He could give me no employment, having little to do and hands enough already. "But," says he, "my son at Philadelphia has lately lost his principal hand, Aquila Rose, by death. If you go thither I believe he may employ you."

Philadelphia was a hundred miles farther. I set out, however, in a boat for Amboy, leaving my chest and things to follow me round by sea. In crossing the bay we met with a squall that tore our rotten sails to pieces, prevented our getting into the kill, and drove us upon Long Island. In our way a drunken Dutchman, who was a passenger too, fell overboard; when he was sinking, I reached through the water to his shock pate and drew him up so that we got him in again. His ducking sobered him a little and he went to sleep, taking first out of his pocket a book which he desired I would dry for him. It proved to be my old favorite author Bunyan's *Pilgrim's Progress* in Dutch, finely printed on good paper with copper cuts, a dress better than I had ever seen it wear in its own language. I have since found that it has been translated into most of the languages of Europe, and suppose it has been more generally read than any other book except, perhaps, the Bible. Honest John was the first that I know of who mixes narration and dialogue, a method of writing very engaging to the reader, who in the most interesting parts finds himself, as it were, admitted into the company and present at the conversation. Defoe has imitated him successfully in his *Robinson Crusoe*, in his *Moll Flanders*, and other pieces; and Richardson has done the same in his *Pamela*, etc.

On approaching the island, we found it was in a place where there could be no landing, there being a great surf on the stony beach. So we dropped anchor and swung out our cable toward the shore. Some people came down to the water edge and hallooed to us, as we did to them, but the wind was so high and the surf so loud that we could not understand each other. There were some canoes on the shore, and we made signs and called to them to fetch us, but they either did not comprehend us or thought it impracticable, so they went off. Night approaching, we had no remedy but to have patience till the wind abated, and in the meantime the boatman and I concluded to sleep if we could, and so we crowded into the scuttle with the Dutchman, who was still wet, and the spray breaking over the head of our boat leaked through to us so that we were soon almost as wet as he. In this manner we lay all night with very little rest; but, the wind abating the next day, we made a shift to reach Amboy before night, having been thirty hours on the water without victuals or any drink but a bottle of filthy rum, the water we sailed on being salt. . . .

In the morning crossing the ferry, I proceeded on my journey on foot, having fifty miles to Burlington where I was told I should find boats that would carry me the rest of the way to Philadelphia.

It rained very hard all the day, I was thoroughly soaked and by noon a good deal tired, so I stopped at a poor inn, where I stayed all night, beginning now to wish I had never left home. I made so miserable a figure, too, that I found by the questions asked me I was suspected to be some runaway servant and in danger of being taken up on that suspicion. However, I proceeded the next day and got in the evening to an inn within eight or ten miles of Burlington, kept by one Dr. Brown.

He entered into conversation with me while I took some refreshment and, finding I had read a little, became very sociable and friendly. Our acquaintance continued all the rest of his life. He had been, I imagine, an itinerant doctor, for there was no town in England or any country in Europe of which he could not give a very particular account. . . . At his house I lay that night, and the next morning reached Burlington, but had the mortification to find that the regular boats were gone a little before and no other expected to go before Tuesday, this being Saturday.

Wherefore I returned to an old woman in the town of whom I had bought some gingerbread to eat on the water and asked her advice; she invited me to lodge at her house till a passage by water should offer, and, being tired with my foot traveling, I accepted the invitation. Understanding I was a printer, she would have had me remain in that town and follow my business, being ignorant of the stock necessary to begin with. She was very hospitable, gave me a dinner of ox cheek with great goodwill, accepting only of a pot of ale in return. And I thought myself fixed till Tuesday should come.

However, walking in the evening by the side of the river, a boat came by which I found was going toward Philadelphia with several people in her. They took me in, and, as there was no wind, we rowed all the way; and about midnight, not having yet seen the city, some of the company were confident we must have passed it and would row no farther; the others knew not where we were, so we put toward the shore, got into a creek, landed near an old fence, with the rails of which we made a fire (the night being cold in October), and there we remained till daylight. Then one of the company knew the place to be Cooper's Creek, a little above Philadelphia, which we saw as soon as we got out of the creek; and arrived there about eight or nine o'clock on the Sunday morning and landed at the Market Street wharf.

VII

The Search for Frontier Land

THE eighteenth century was an era of land speculation when the greed for fresh land in the interior affected every part of the Atlantic seaboard. During the seventeenth century the older settled regions had gradually filled up and cheap land was no longer available in coastal areas. As the population grew, the pressure to push westward over the mountains increased. Traders had long since penetrated the Indian country, as we have seen, and daring squatters were not far behind them. Although Indian wars kept the frontier in turmoil through much of the eighteenth century, not even the hazard of scalping knives kept back pioneers eager to carve out homesteads for themselves in the back country.

The ownership of the hinterland beyond the coastal settlements was a matter of controversy. The charters of seven of the Colonies extended their borders westward to the Great South Sea (the Pacific Ocean), and thus the granting of land in the back country was the privilege of these colonial governments. Even after the Revolution the demand for the cession of this land to the national government posed a serious problem. The question of the ownership of the land by the aborigines did not at first trouble the authorities in London, for custom permitted the occupation of territory not already occupied by "any Christian prince." The Indians were heathen and therefore their land was subject to occupation by Christians. But practical considerations made it desirable for Colonial governments to make deals with the Indians. Pennsylvania, for example, negotiated a number of treaties with the Indians for the purchase of land needed by settlers.

But maps were vague and inaccurate, boundaries even between colonies were not clearly marked, and systematic surveys nonexistent in the early eighteenth century. Nevertheless, Colonial governments or the government in London, by simply marking out spaces on maps, awarded enormous holdings to favorites and speculators of one kind or another. Lord Cornbury, the royal governor of New York, for instance, between 1702 and 1708 gave huge baronies in the Hudson valley to his friends. Earlier Charles II had granted to eight courtiers all of South and North Carolina from sea to sea; they were empowered to rule as lords proprietors. Profits to the owners of these territories depended on their ability to sell smaller holdings to settlers or to other speculators. Consequently, throughout the eighteenth century both private and governmental holders of land carried on a propaganda designed to attract settlers. But not all of the emigrants to the back country bothered to pay for property upon which they settled. Many were simply squatters. They found a limitless supply of unoccupied woodland or grassy plain, and they proceeded to appropriate what they could use. Right of possession, they believed, would serve in place of a title deed.

One way or another the great valleys beyond the first mountain ranges in Pennsylvania, Maryland, and Virginia gradually filled up, as did the Piedmont region of the Carolinas. William Penn proved one of the best promoters of his day, and his advertisements of the virtues of Pennsylvania lured thousands to his proprietary colony. The port of Philadelphia became the gateway for thousands of immigrants who filtered first into nearby valleys and eventually made their way over the mountains and down the great valley of Virginia into the Carolinas. During the last two decades of the seventeenth and the early years of the eighteenth century, swarms of immigrants who had heard of Pennsylvania from Penn's agents poured through Philadelphia. They came principally from England, Ireland, Scotland, and the Rhineland. Scots from Ulster, bitter at economic and other restrictions imposed by the English, came by the shipload. Germans from the Rhine valley, impoverished by incessant war, flocked to this new Promised Land. The first Rhinelanders for the most part were German and Swiss Pietists, Mennonites and related sects, not incompatible with Penn's Quakers. They were followed in the early years of the eighteenth century by many German Lutherans. These industrious and hardworking folk occupied fertile lands in a great arc that stretched from the Delaware at Easton to the Maryland border on the lower Susquehanna. Later Germans pushed farther into the interior in search of good farmlands. By 1727 Germans were moving into the Shenandoah Valley of Virginia, and in 1731 a group of 11 German families founded the town of Winchester. From this time onward the progress down the valley was rapid, and by the mid-century German immigrants into the Carolinas from the mountain valleys met other immigrants moving northward from the coast.

The Scots who came in increasing numbers during the eighteenth century found the best land nearest civilization already occupied by the Germans and had to push farther inland to the frontier. They made ideal frontiersmen, for they were tough, fearless, and convinced that they had a right to any land they could seize from the Indians. Using Scripture to justify their actions, they equated the Indians with the Amalekites, whom they could smite hip and thigh.

Most of this early penetration of the interior came by gradual infiltration. The first settlers were not explorers in the sense that they came for that purpose. Only rarely did they bother to write down their observations. They came not to make reports but to find homesteads. By the mid-century, however, land speculators in Virginia and Maryland, concerned about western lands, organized the Ohio Company and sent out an explorer, Christopher Gist, to make a cursory survey of the territory as far as the present site of Louisville. Unfortunately for the English speculators, the French had already laid claim to much of this territory and created a barrier to English expansion westward toward the Mississippi. Convinced, however, that Englishmen would eventually expel the French from the Ohio valley, speculators in western land never lost interest. Capitalists in the East dreamed of amassing great fortunes from lands that they hoped to obtain west of the mountains.

When the English were finally victorious over the French and obtained all of French North America by the Peace of Paris in 1763, the land speculators received a setback in a new Indian policy drawn up in London by the imperial planners. Fur traders in England were concerned lest immigration into the Indians' hunting grounds would ruin the lucrative trade in furs. A simple expedient would be to forbid further settlement beyond the mountains. Consequently, in October of 1763 the Board of Trade in London got out a map of North America and drew a line roughly coinciding with the crest of the Alleghenies, and the imperial authorities decreed that all land west of the "Proclamation Line" would be an enormous Indian reservation. White settlers were prohibited from going beyond the line and those already there were ordered to move back east. This decree violated the vested interests of the older Colonies and of some of their most influential capitalists. Furthermore, it antagonized every settler who had gone over the mountains. The result was an almost complete disregard of the Proclamation Line, which served merely as one more grievance of the Colonies against the home government.

A more immediate danger on the frontier in this period was the Indian revolt of 1763–64, known as the conspiracy of Pontiac. Hundreds of settlers on the frontier lost their lives as Indians burned homesteads and scalped their victims. An uneasy peace was at last established by Sir William Johnson in a treaty made at Oswego in 1765. But even the hazard of Indian attack did not stop the westward migration for long.

Indeed, after 1763 many new land companies sprang into being and a fresh wave of speculation swept the Colonies. George Washington was one of the most enthusiastic advocates of investment in western lands and sent an agent into the Ohio country to stake out land for him. Richard Henderson, a wealthy North Carolinian, retained Daniel Boone—already known as an experienced woodsman wise in the ways of the Indian country—to search out desirable tracts of land in Kentucky. The story of land speculation and of the maneuverings by the various land companies, the Colonial governments, and the imperial authorities in London in this period would require a separate volume. Suffice it to say that the interest in westward expansion was virtually universal in the Colonies and affected in one way or another all classes. A great amount of detail will be found in Ray A. Billington, *Westward Expansion: A History of the American Frontier* (New York, 1949).

The Virginia and North Carolina Back Country

[*The most readable description of the back country of Virginia and North Carolina was written by William Byrd II of Westover, leader in 1728 of a group of commissioners from Virginia and North Carolina who surveyed the dividing line between the two colonies. Byrd wrote two narratives of his adventures on the frontier, one called* The Secret History of the Line *and the other entitled* The History of the Dividing Line Betwixt Virginia and North Carolina, Run in the Year of Our Lord 1728. *Neither account was published in Byrd's lifetime but both circulated in manuscript among the author's friends.* The Secret History, *in which Byrd gave the participants fictitious names, is shorter by half and franker than the other account. Both versions appear in* The Prose Works of William Byrd of Westover, *edited by Louis B. Wright (Cambridge, Mass., 1966).*

[*Like most of his contemporaries, Byrd was land hungry, and by the time of his death in 1744 he had acquired 179,440 acres, mostly on the Virginia–North Carolina frontier, which he had observed during his survey in 1728. He actively engaged in efforts to lure European immigrants to this domain, which he named "The Land of Eden." He particularly favored German Swiss and in 1737 was responsible for the publication in Berne of a promotion tract by Samuel Jenner entitled* Neu-gefundenes Eden [New-Found Eden], *put together from notes supplied by Byrd. Excerpts from* The History of the Dividing Line *follow:*]

The Quakers flocked over to this country in shoals, being averse to go to Heaven the same way with the bishops. Amongst them were not a few of good substance, who went vigorously upon every kind of improvement; and thus much I may truly say in their praise, that by diligence and frugality, for which this harmless sect is remarkable, and by having no vices but such as are private, they have in a few years made Pennsylvania a very fine country. The truth is, they have observed exact justice with all the natives that border upon them; they have purchased all their lands from the Indians, and though they paid but a trifle for them it has procured them the credit of being more righteous than their neighbors. They have likewise had the prudence to treat them kindly upon all occasions, which has saved them from many wars and massacres wherein the other colonies have been indiscreetly involved. The truth of it is, a people whose principles forbid them to draw the carnal sword were in the right to give no provocation.

Both the French and Spaniards had, in the name of their respective monarchs, long ago taken possession of that part of the northern continent that now goes by the name of Carolina; but, finding it produced neither gold nor silver, as they greedily expected, and meeting such returns from the Indians as their own cruelty and treachery deserved, they totally abandoned it. In this deserted condition that country lay for the space of ninety years, till King Charles II, finding it a derelict, granted it away to the Earl of Clarendon and others by his royal charter dated March 24, 1663. The boundary of that grant toward Virginia was a due-west line from Luck Island (the same as Colleton [Colington] Island), lying in 36 degrees of north latitude, quite to the South Sea.

But afterwards Sir William Berkeley, who was one of the grantees and at that time Governor of Virginia, finding a territory of thirty-one miles in breadth between the inhabited part of Virginia and the above-mentioned boundary of Carolina, advised the Lord Clarendon of it. And His Lordship had interest enough with the King to obtain a second patent to include it, dated June 30, 1665.

This last grant describes the bounds between Virginia and Carolina in these words: "To run from the north end of Currituck Inlet due west to Weyanoke Creek, lying within or about the degree of thirty-six and thirty minutes of northern latitude, and from thence west in a direct line as far as the South Sea." Without question this boundary was well known at the time the charter was granted, but in a long course of years Weyanoke Creek lost its name, so that it became a controversy where it lay. Some ancient persons in Virginia affirmed it was the same with Wicca-con, and others again in Carolina were as positive it was Nottoway River.

In the meantime, the people on the frontiers entered for land and took out patents by guess, either from the King or the Lords Proprietors. But the Crown was like to be the loser by this uncertainty because the terms both of taking up and seating land were easier much in Carolina. The yearly taxes to the public were likewise there less burdensome, which laid Virginia under a plain disadvantage.

This consideration put that government upon entering into measures with North Carolina to terminate the dispute and settle a certain boundary between the two colonies. All the difficulty was to find out which was truly Weyanoke Creek. The difference was too considerable to be given up by either side, there being a territory of fifteen miles betwixt the two streams in controversy. . . .

The quadrant produced by the surveyors of Virginia . . . placed the mouth of Nottoway River in the latitude of 37 degrees, whereas by an accurate observation made since it appears to lie in 36° 30' 30", so that there was an error of near 30 minutes, either in the instrument or in those who made use of it.

Besides, it is evident the mouth of Nottoway River agrees much better with the latitude wherein the Carolina charter supposed Weyanoke Creek (namely, in or about 36° 30'), than it does with Wiccacon Creek, which is about fifteen miles more southerly.

This being manifest, the intention of the King's grant will be pretty exactly answered by a due-west line drawn from Currituck Inlet to the mouth of Nottoway River; for which reason 'tis probable that was formerly called Weyanoke Creek and might change its name when the Nottoway Indians came to live upon it, which was since the date of the last Carolina charter.

The Lieutenant Governor of Virginia, at that time Colonel Spotswood, searching into the bottom of this affair, made very equitable proposals to Mr. Eden, at that time Governor of North Carolina, in order to put an end to this controversy. These, being formed into preliminaries, were signed by both governors and transmitted to England, where they had the honor to be ratified by His late Majesty and assented to by the Lords Proprietors of Carolina.

Accordingly an order was sent by the late King to Mr. Gooch, afterwards Lieutenant Governor of Virginia, to pursue those preliminaries exactly. In obedience thereunto he was pleased to appoint three of the council of that colony to be commissioners on the part of Virginia, who, in conjunction with others to be named by the Governor of North Carolina, were to settle the boundary between the two governments upon the plan of the above-mentioned articles. . . . All the persons being thus agreed upon, they settled the time of meeting to be at Currituck, March 5, 1728.

In the meantime, the requisite preparations were made for so long and tiresome a journey; and because there was much work to be done and some danger from the Indians in the uninhabited part of the country, it was necessary to provide a competent number of men. Accordingly, seventeen able hands were listed on the part of Virginia, who were most of them Indian traders and expert woodsmen.

February 1728

27. These good men were ordered to come armed with a musket and a tomahawk or large hatchet and provided with a sufficient quantity of ammunition. They likewise brought provisions of their own for ten days, after which time they were to be furnished by the government. Their march was appointed to be on the twenty-seventh of February, on which day one of the commissioners met them at their rendezvous and proceeded with them as far as Colonel Allen's. This gentleman is a great economist and skilled in all the arts of living well at an easy expense. . . .

29. They pursued their march through the Isle of Wight and observed a most dreadful havoc made by a late hurricane, which happened in August, 1726. The violence of it had not reached above a quarter of a mile in breadth but within that compass had leveled all before it. Both trees and houses were laid flat on the ground and several things hurled to an incredible distance. 'Tis happy such violent gusts are confined to so narrow a channel, because they carry desolation wherever they go. In the evening they reached Mr. Godwin's, on the south branch of Nansemond River [in Virginia], where they were treated with abundance [of] primitive hospitality.

March 1. This gentleman was so kind as to shorten their journey by setting them over the river. They coasted the northeast side of the Dismal [Swamp] for several miles together and found all the grounds bordering upon it very full of sloughs. The trees that grew near it looked very reverend with the long moss that hung dangling from their branches. Both cattle and horses eat this moss greedily in winter when other provender is scarce, though it is apt to scour [purge] them at first. In that moist soil, too, grows abundance of that kind of myrtle which bears the candleberries. There was likewise here and there a gallbush [inkberry], which is a beautiful evergreen and may be cut into any shape. It derives its name from its berries turning water black, like the galls of an oak. When this shrub is transplanted into gardens, it will not thrive without frequent watering.

The two other commissioners came up with them just at their journey's end, and that evening they arrived all together at Mr. Crawford's, who lives on the south branch of Elizabeth River over against Norfolk. Here the commissioners left the men with all the horses and heavy baggage and crossed the river with their servants only, for fear of making a famine in the town. . . .

7. This morning the surveyors began to run the dividing line from the cedar post we had driven into the sand, allowing near three degrees for the variation. Without making this just allowance, we should not have obeyed His Majesty's order in running a due-west line. It seems the former commissioners had not been so exact, which gave our friends of Carolina but too just an exception to their proceedings. The line cut Dosier's Island, consisting only of a flat sand with here and there an humble shrub growing upon it. From thence it crossed over a narrow arm of the sound into Knott's Island and there split a plantation belonging to William Harding.

The day being far spent, we encamped in this man's pasture, though it lay very low and the season now inclined people to aguish distempers. He suffered us to cut cedar branches for our enclosure and other wood for firing, to correct the moist air and drive away the damps. Our landlady, in the days of her youth, it seems, had been a laundress in the Temple [Middle Temple, London] and talked over her adventures in that station with as much pleasure as an old soldier talks over his battles and distempers and, I believe, with as many additions to the truth.

The soil is good in many places of this island, and the extent of it pretty large. It lies in the form of a wedge: the south end of it is several miles over, but toward the north it sharpens into a point. It is a plentiful place for stock by reason of the wide marshes adjacent to it and because of its warm situation. But the inhabitants pay a little dear for this convenience by losing as much blood in the summer season by the infinite number of mosquitoes as all their beef and pork can recruit in the winter.

The sheep are as large as in Lincolnshire, because they are never pinched by cold or hunger. The whole island was hitherto reckoned to lie in Virginia, but now our line has given the greater part of it to Carolina. The principal freeholder here is Mr. White, who keeps open house for all travelers that either debt or ship-wreck happens to cast in his way.

8. By break of day we sent away our largest piragua [pirogue] with the baggage round the south end of Knott's Island, with orders to the men to wait for us in the mouth of North River. Soon after, we embarked ourselves on board the smaller vessel, with intent, if possible, to find a passage round the north end of the island.

We found this navigation very difficult by reason of the con-tinued shoals and often stuck fast aground; for though the sound spreads many miles, yet it is in most places extremely shallow and requires a skillful pilot to steer even a canoe safe over it. It was almost as hard to keep our temper as to keep the channel in this provoking situation. But the most impatient amongst us stroked down their choler and swallowed their curses, lest, if they suffered them to break out, they might sound like complaining, which was expressly forbid as the first step to sedition. . . .

22. . . . Our surveyors told us they had measured ten miles in the Dismal and computed the distance they had marched since to amount to about five more, so they made the whole breadth to be fifteen miles in all.

23. It was very reasonable that the surveyors and the men who had been sharers in their fatigue should now have a little rest. They were all, except one, in good health and good heart, blessed be God! notwithstanding the dreadful hardships they had gone through. It was really a pleasure to see the cheerfulness wherewith they received the order to prepare to reenter the Dismal on the Monday following in order to continue the line from the place where they had left off measuring, that so we might have the exact breadth of that dirty place. There were no more than two of them that could be persuaded to be relieved on this occasion or suffer the other men to share the credit of that bold undertaking; neither

would these have suffered it had not one of them been very lame and the other much indisposed.

By the description the surveyors gave of the Dismal, we were convinced that nothing but the exceeding dry season we had been blessed with could have made the passing of it practicable. It is the source of no less than five several rivers which discharge themselves southward into Albemarle Sound and of two that run northerly into Virginia. From thence 'tis easy to imagine that the soil must be thoroughly soaked with water or else there must be plentiful stores of it underground to supply so many rivers, especially since there is no lake or any considerable body of that element to be seen on the surface. The rivers that head in it from Virginia are the south branch of Nansemond and the west branch of Elizabeth, and those from Carolina are Northwest River, North River, Pasquotank, Little River, and Perquimans.

There is one remarkable part of the Dismal, lying to the south of the line, that has few or no trees growing on it but contains a large tract of tall reeds. These, being green all the year round and waving with every wind, have procured it the name of the Green Sea. We are not yet acquainted with the precise extent of the Dismal, the whole having never been surveyed; but it may be computed at a medium to be about thirty miles long and ten miles broad, though where the line crossed it, 'twas completely fifteen miles wide. But it seems to grow narrower toward the north, or at least does so in many places.

The exhalations that continually rise from this vast body of mire and nastiness infect the air for many miles round and render it very unwholesome for the bordering inhabitants. It makes them liable to agues, pleurisies, and many other distempers that kill abundance of people and make the rest look no better than ghosts. It would require a great sum of money to drain it, but the public treasure could not be better bestowed than to preserve the lives of His Majesty's liege people and at the same time render so great a tract of swamp very profitable, besides the advantage of making a channel to transport by water carriage goods from Albemarle Sound into Nansemond and Elizabeth rivers in Virginia.

24. This being Sunday, we had a numerous congregation, which flocked to our quarters from all the adjacent country. The news that our surveyors were come out of the Dismal increased the

number very much, because it would give them an opportunity of guessing, at least, whereabouts the line would cut, whereby they might form some judgment whether they belonged to Virginia or Carolina. Those who had taken up land within the disputed bounds were in great pain lest it should be found to lie in Virginia; because this being done contrary to an express order of that government, the patentees had great reason to fear they should in that case have lost their land. But their apprehensions were now at an end when they understood that all the territory which had been controverted was like to be left in Carolina.

In the afternoon, those who were to reenter the Dismal were furnished with the necessary provisions and ordered to repair the overnight to their landlord, Peter Brinkley's, that they might be ready to begin their business early on Monday morning. Mr. Irvin was excused from the fatigue in compliment to his lungs; but Mr. Mayo and Mr. Swann were robust enough to return upon that painful service, and, to do them justice, they went with great alacrity. The truth was, they now knew the worst of it and could guess pretty near at the time when they might hope to return to land again.

25. The air was chilled this morning with a smart northwest wind, which favored the Dismalites in their dirty march. They returned by the path they had made in coming out and with great industry arrived in the evening at the spot where the line had been discontinued. After so long and laborious a journey, they were glad to repose themselves on their couches of cypress bark, where their sleep was as sweet as it would have been on a bed of Finland down.

In the meantime, we who stayed behind had nothing to do but to make the best observations we could upon that part of the country. The soil of our landlord's plantation, though none of the best, seemed more fertile than any thereabouts, where the ground is near as sandy as the deserts of Africa and consequently barren. The road leading from thence to Edenton, being in distance about twenty-seven miles, lies upon a ridge called Sandy Ridge, which is so wretchedly poor that it will not bring potatoes. The pines in this part of the country are of a different species from those that grow in Virginia: their bearded leaves are much longer and their cones much larger. Each cell contains a seed of the size and figure of a black-eyed pea, which, shedding in November, is very good mast for hogs and fattens them in a short time. The smallest of these pines are full of cones which are eight or nine inches long, and each affords commonly sixty or seventy seeds. This kind of mast has the advantage of all other by being more constant and less liable to be nipped by the frost or eaten by the caterpillars.

The trees also abound more with turpentine and consequently yield more tar than either the yellow or the white pine and for the same reason make more durable timber for building. The inhabitants hereabouts pick up knots of lightwood in abundance, which they burn into tar and then carry it to Norfolk or Nansemond for a market. The tar made in this method is the less valuable because it is said to burn the cordage, though it is full as good for all other uses as that made in Sweden and Muscovy [Russia].

Surely there is no place in the world where the inhabitants live with less labor than in North Carolina. It approaches nearer to the description of Lubberland [a fabulous land of ease and plenty] than any other, by the great felicity of the climate, the easiness of raising provisions, and the slothfulness of the people. Indian corn is of so great increase that a little pains will subsist a very large family with bread, and then they may have meat without any pains at all, by the help of the low grounds and the great variety of mast that grows on the high land. The men, for their parts, just like the Indians, impose all the work upon the poor women. They make their wives rise out of their beds early in the morning, at the same time that they lie and snore till the sun has risen one-third of his course and dispersed all the unwholesome damps. Then, after stretching and yawning for half an hour, they light their pipes, and, under the protection of a cloud of smoke, venture out into the open air; though if it happen to be never so little cold they quickly return shivering into the chimney corner. When the weather is mild, they stand leaning with both their arms upon the cornfield fence and gravely consider whether they had best go and take a small heat at the hoe but generally find reasons to put it off till another time. Thus they loiter away their lives, like Solomon's sluggard, with their arms across, and at the winding up of the year scarcely have bread to eat. To speak the truth, 'tis a thorough aversion to labor that makes people file off to North Carolina, where plenty and a warm sun confirm them in their disposition to laziness for their whole lives. . . .

[October] 25. The air clearing up this morning, we were again agreeably surprised with a full prospect of the mountains. They discovered themselves both to the north and south of us on either side, not distant above ten miles, according to our best computation. We could now see those to the north rise in four distinct ledges one above another, but those to the south formed only a single ledge and that broken and interrupted in many places, or rather they were only single mountains detached from each other. One of the southern mountains was so vastly high it seemed to hide its head in the clouds, and the west end of it terminated in a horrible precipice that we called the Despairing Lover's Leap. The next to it, toward the east, was lower except at one end, where it heaved itself up in the form of a vast stack of chimneys. The course of the northern mountains seemed to tend west-southwest and those to the southward very near west. We could descry other mountains ahead of us, exactly in the course of the line though at a much greater distance. In this point of view, the ledges on the right and left both seemed to close and form a natural amphitheater. Thus 'twas our fortune to be wedged in betwixt these two ranges of mountains, insomuch that if our line had run ten miles on either side it had butted before this day either upon one or the other, both of them now stretching away plainly to the eastward of us.

It had rained a little in the night, which dispersed the smoke and opened this romantic scene to us all at once, though it was again hid from our eyes as we moved forward by the rough woods we had the misfortune to be engaged with. The bushes were so thick for near four miles together that they tore the deerskins to pieces that guarded the bread bags. Though, as rough as the woods were, the soil was extremely good all the way, being washed down from the neighboring hills into the plain country. Notwithstanding all these difficulties, the surveyors drove on the line 4 miles and 205 poles.

In the meantime we were so unlucky as to meet with no sort of game the whole day, so that the men were obliged to make a frugal distribution of what little they left in the morning. We encamped upon a small rill, where the horses came off as temperately as their masters. They were by this time grown so thin by hard travel and spare feeding that henceforth, in pure compassion, we chose to perform the greater part of the journey on foot. And as our baggage was by this time grown much lighter, we divided it after the best manner so that every horse's load might be proportioned to the strength he had left. Though after all the prudent measures we could take, we perceived the hills began to rise upon us so fast in our front that it would be impossible for us to proceed much farther.

We saw very few squirrels in the upper parts, because the wildcats devour them unmercifully. Of these there are four kinds: the fox squirrel, the gray, the flying, and the ground squirrel. These last resemble a rat in everything but the tail and the black and russet streaks that run down the length of their little bodies.

26. We found our way grow still more mountainous, after extending the line three hundred poles farther. We came then to a rivulet that ran with a swift current toward the south. This we fancied to be another branch of the Irvin, though some of these men, who had been Indian traders, judged it rather to be the head of Deep River, that discharges its stream into that of Pee Dee, but this seemed a wild conjecture. The hills beyond that river were exceedingly lofty and not to be attempted by our jaded palfreys, which could now hardly drag their legs after them upon level ground. Besides, the bread began to grow scanty and the winter season to advance apace upon us. We had likewise reason to apprehend the consequences of being intercepted by deep snows and the swelling of the many waters between us and home. The first of these misfortunes would starve all our horses and the other ourselves, by cutting off our retreat and obliging us to winter in those desolate woods. These considerations determined us to stop short here and push our adventures no farther. The last tree we marked was a red oak growing on the bank of the river; and to make the place more remarkable, we blazed all the trees around it.

We found the whole distance from Currituck Inlet to the rivulet where we left off to be, in a straight line, 240 miles and 230 poles. And from the place where the Carolina commissioners deserted us, 72 miles and 302 poles. This last part of the journey was generally very hilly, or else grown up with troublesome thickets and underwoods, all which our Carolina friends had the discretion to avoid. We encamped in a dirty valley near the rivulet above-mentioned for the advantage of the canes, and so sacrificed our own convenience to that of our horses. There was a small mountain half a mile to the northward of us, which we had the curiosity to climb up in the afternoon in order to enlarge our prospect. From thence we were able to discover where the two ledges of mountains closed, as near as we could guess about thirty miles to the west of us, and lamented that our present circumstances would not permit us to advance the line to that place, which the hand of Nature had made so very remarkable.

Observations of Two Naturalists

[*The first naturalist explorer of note in America was John Bartram, a Philadelphia Quaker, who was without formal education but became a respected amateur botanist. English noblemen, eager for new plants and trees from America, engaged Bartram to supply them with seeds and seedlings which he obtained on expeditions into the wilderness. His journeys took him to the Great Lakes and as far south as Florida. At Philadelphia he laid out a botanical garden on the Schuylkill River, where he propagated plants obtained in his wilderness searches. This garden became one of the sights of Philadelphia in the eighteenth century and attracted both American and European naturalists.*

[*In the summer and early autumn of 1743 Bartram made a journey to Fort Oswego on Lake Ontario in the company of Lewis Evans, a geographer and surveyor, and Conrad Weiser, a mediator with the Indians. Weiser, who had learned the Mohawk language, was highly respected by the Indians, and was going to a council at Onondaga to smooth out difficulties between the whites and the Iroquois.*

[*Bartram's primary interest was in the flora of the region through which they passed. He made notes of the plants, shrubs, trees, and grasses as well as other features of the terrain. A manuscript of his observations, sent to friends in England, fell into the hands of printers in London who in 1751 brought out* Observations on the Inhabitants, Climate, Soil, Rivers, Productions, Animals, and Other Matters Worthy of Notice Made by Mr. John Bartram in His Travels from Pennsylvania to Onondaga, Oswego, and the Lake Ontario in Canada. To Which is Annexed a Curious Account of the Cataracts at Niagara by Mr. Peter Kalm, a Swedish Gentleman Who Traveled There. *Although the long title, which served as an advertisement for the book, promised somewhat more than the contents supplied, Bartram's comments provide an insight into the things that interested a naturalist. A few excerpts will indicate the nature of the work:*]

July 8th. . . . It were to be wished that the English government in these parts had been more diligent in searching and surveying the heads of their own rivers and the sources of the others that run westwards from the backs of their respective provinces. Yet enough is already known to justify the surmises of Mr. de la Sale [i.e., La Salle], who in his Journal addressed to the Count de Frontenac expresses his fears, lest the English, from their settlements, should possess themselves of the trade on the Mississippi. . . .

The 15th. We set out a N.E. course, and passed by very thick and tall timber of beech, chestnut, linden ash, great magnolia, sugar birch, sugar maple, poplar, spruce, and some white pine, with ginseng and maidenhair; the soil black on the surface, and brown underneath, the stones a brown grit, the way very uneven over fallen trees, abundance of hollow, and heaps of earth, turned up by the roots of prostrate timber: hence it is that the surface is principally composed of rotten trees, roots, and moss, perpetually shaded, and for the most part wet; what falls is constantly rotting and rendering the earth loose and spongy, and this tempts abundance of yellow wasps to breed in it, which were very troublesome to us throughout our journey. On the branches of Susquehanah our course this day was generally east, and we got through this dismal wilderness about two hours before sunset, and came to oak and hickory land, then down a steep hill producing white pine to a creek. . . . We had a fine warm night, and one of the Indians that had so generously feasted us, sung in a solemn harmonious manner, for seven or eight minutes, very different from the common Indian tune, from whence I conjectured it to be a hymn to the great spirit as they express it. . . .

18. This morning we sent an Indian with a string of Wampun to Onondago to acquaint them with our coming and the business we came about, that they might send messengers to the several nations to hasten their deputies to meet them as soon as possible. For this town serves the five nations as Baden does the thirteen cantons of Switzerland, with this difference, that Onondago is at the same time the capital of a canton.

We set out at half an hour after 9, and traveled till 6. This day our general course was N. and N.W., having fine level rich land most of the way, and tall timber oak, birch, beech, ash, spruce, linden, elm . . . and maidenhair in abundance. We lodged by Front Creek in a spacious vale, and it looking like rain, we made us a cabin of spruce bark, but no rain came.

19. We rode over good level land. After, we came to very swampy bottoms, thickets and hills of spruce and white pine. Here were three ridges of steep hills that run nearly E. and W. and with difficulty we rode over their steep cliffs, which projected close to the creek. We were several times obliged to ford it backwards and forwards. Several runs came into the creek on both sides from between the mountains. Now we came to most excellent level ground, than which nothing can be more fruitful, full of tall timber, sugar maple, birch, linden ash, and beech, and shrubs. . . .

21st. . . . We descended easily for several miles over good land producing sugar maples, many of which the Indians had tapped to make sugar of the sap, also oaks, hickory, white walnuts, plums, and some apple trees, full of fruit; the Indians had set long bushes all round the trees at a little distance, I suppose to keep the small children from stealing the fruit before they were ripe. Here we halted and turned our horses to grass, while the inhabitants cleared a cabin for our reception. They brought us victuals, and we dispatched a messenger immediately to Onondago to let them know how near we were, it being within 4 miles. All the Indians, men, women, and children came to gaze at us and our horses, the little boys and girls climbed on the roofs of their cabins, about ten in number, to enjoy a fuller view. We set out about ten, and traveled over good land all the way, mostly an easy descent, some limestone, then down the east hill over ridges of limestone rock, but generally a moderate descent into the fine vale where this capital (if I may so call it) is situated.

We alighted at the council house, where the chiefs were already assembled to receive us, which they did with a grave cheerful complaisance, according to their custom; they shew'd us where to lay our baggage and repose ourselves during our stay with them, which was in the two end apartments of this large house. The Indians that came with us were placed over against us. This cabin is about 80 feet long, and 17 broad, the common passage

6 feet wide; and the apartments on each side 5 feet, raised a foot about the passage by a long sapling hewed square and fitted with joists that go from it to the back of the house; on these joists they lay large pieces of bark, and on extraordinary occasions spread mats made of rushes; this favor we had. . . .

25th. . . . Oswego is an infant settlement made by the province of New York with the noble view of gaining to the crown of Great Britain the command of the 5 [Great] lakes and the dependence of the Indians in their neighborhood, and to subjects the benefit of the trade upon them and of the rivers that empty themselves into them. At present the whole navigation is carried on by the Indians themselves in bark canoes, and there are perhaps many reasons for desiring it should continue so for some years at least; but a good Englishman cannot be without hopes of seeing these great lakes become one day accustomed to English navigation. It is true, the famous fall of Niagara is an insurmountable bar to all passage by water from the lake Ontario into the lake Erie in such vessels as are proper for the secure navigation of either; but besides that bark canoes are carried on men's shoulders with ease, from one to the other, as far as the passage is impracticable, it will be much more easy to carry the goods in wagons from the upper lake into the Huron or Quatoghie lake; the strait is rendered unnavigable by the Saute [i.e., Sault] St. Marie, but a vessel of considerable burthen may sail from the hither end of the Erie lake to the bottom of the lake Michigan, and, for ought we know, through all parts of the 3 middle lakes. These lakes receive the waters of many rivers, that in some places approach so near the branches of the vast river Mississippi that a short land carriage supplies the communication. And here to use the words of a most judicious writer, "He that reflects on the natural state of that continent must open to himself a field for traffic in the southern parts of N. America, and by the means of this river and the lakes, the imagination takes into view such a scene of inland navigation as cannot be paralleled in any other part of the world."

[*The title page of Bartram's* Observations *promised the reader a description of Niagara Falls by Peter Kalm, a Swedish botanist who traveled in North America from 1748 to 1751. An account of his travels appeared in a series of publications between 1753 and 1761. The description of Niagara Falls, printed in the* Observations, *was written as a letter to Bartram dated September 2, 1750. Excerpts follow:*]

A Letter from Mr. Kalm, a Gentleman of Sweden, now on his Travels in America, to his Friend in Philadelphia; containing a particular Account of the Great Fall of Niagara.

Albany, Sep. 2, 1750.

SIR,

After a pretty long journey made in a short time, I am come back to this town. You may remember that when I took my leave of you, I told you I would this summer, if time permitted, take a view of Niagara Fall, esteemed one of the greatest curiosities in the World. . . .

After a fatiguing travel, first on horseback thro' the country of the Six Indian Nations to Oswego, and from thence in a Canoe upon lake Ontario, I came on the 12th of August in the evening to Niagara fort [French fort at site of Niagara Falls, New York]. The French there seemed much perplexed at my first coming, imagining I was an English officer who, under pretext of seeing Niagara Falls, came with some other view; but as soon as I shew'd them my passports they chang'd their behavior and received me with the greatest civility.

Niagara Fall is six French leagues from Niagara Fort. You first go three leagues by water up Niagara river, and then three leagues over the carrying place. As it was late when I arriv'd at the Fort, I could not the same day go to the Fall, but I prepar'd myself to do it the next morning. . . .

Accordingly the next morning, being the 13th of August, at break of day I set out for the Fall. The commandant had given orders to two of the officers of the Fort to go with me and shew me every thing, and also sent by them an order to Monsr. Jonqueire, who had liv'd ten years by the carrying place and knew everything worth notice of the Fall, better than any other person, to go with me and shew and tell me whatever he knew.

A little before we came to the carrying place, the water of Niagara River grew so rapid that four men in a light birch canoe had much difficulty to get up thither. Canoes can go half a league above the beginning of the carrying place, tho' they must work against a water extremely rapid; but higher up it is quite impossible, the whole course of the water for two leagues and a half up to the great Fall being a series of smaller Falls (Whirlpool Rapids) one under another, in which the greatest canoe or Battoe would in a moment be turn'd upside down. We went ashore therefore and walk'd over the carrying place, having besides the high and steep side of the river two great hills to ascend one above the other. Here on the carrying place I saw above 200 Indians, most of them belonging to the Six Nations, busy in carrying packs of furs, chiefly of deer and bear, over the carrying place. You would be surpris'd to see what abundance of these things are brought every day over this place. An Indian gets 20 pence for every pack he carries over, the distance being three leagues.

Half an hour past 10 in the morning we came to the great Fall, which I found as follows: to the river (or rather strait) runs here from S.S.E. to N.N.W. and the rocks of the great Fall crosses it, not in a right line, but forming almost the figure of a semicircle on horse shoe [falls on the Canadian, or western, side are known today as the Horseshoe Falls]. Above the Fall, in the middle of the river is an island, lying also S.S.E. and N.N.W. or parallel with the sides of the river [Goat Island]; its length is about 7 or 8 French arpents [an arpent being 180 feet]. The lower end of this island is just at the perpendicular edge of the Fall. On both sides of this island runs all the water that comes from the lakes of Canada, viz. lake Superior, lake Mischigan, lake Huron, and lake Erie, which you know are rather small seas than lakes, and have besides a great many large rivers that empty their water in them, of which the greatest part comes down this Niagara Fall.

Before the water comes to this island it runs but slowly compar'd with its motion when it approaches the island, where it grows the most rapid water in the world, running with a surprising swiftness before it comes to the Fall; it is quite white, and in many places is thrown high up into the air! The greatest and strongest battoes [bateaux, boats] would here in a moment be turn'd over and over. The water that goes down on the west side of the island is more rapid, in greater abundance, whiter, and seems almost to outdo an arrow in swiftness.

When you are at the Fall and look up the river, you may see that the river above the Fall is everywhere exceeding steep, almost as the side of a hill. When all this water comes to the very Fall, there it throws itself down perpendicular! It is beyond all belief the surprise when you see this! I cannot with words express how amazing it is! You cannot see it without being quite terrified to behold so vast a quantity of water falling headlong from a surprising height! I doubt not but you have a desire to learn the exact height of this great Fall. Father Hennepin supposes it 600 feet perpendicular; but he has gained little credit in Canada. . . . Since Father Hennepin's time this Fall by all accounts that have been given of it has grown less and less; and those who have measur'd it with mathematical instruments find the perpendicular fall of the water to be exactly 137 feet [Canadian Falls are around 155 feet, the American Falls around 165 feet]. . . .

When the water is come down to the bottom of the rock of the Fall, it jumps back to a very great height in the air; in other places it is white as milk or snow; and all in motion like a boiling caldron. You may remember to what a great distance Hennepin says the noise of this great Fall may be heard. All the gentlemen who were with me agreed that the farthest one can hear it is 15 leagues, and that very seldom. When the air is quite calm, you can hear it to Niagara Fort; but seldom at other times, because when the wind blows the waves of Lake Ontario make too much noise there against the shore. They inform'd me that when they hear at the Fort the noise of the Fall louder than ordinary they are sure a northeast wind will follow, which never fails. This seems wonderful, as the Fall is southwest from the Fort, and one would imagine it to be rather a sign of a contrary wind. Sometimes, 'tis said, the Fall makes a much greater noise than at other times; and this is look'd upon as a certain mark of approaching bad weather, or rain; the Indians here hold it always for a sure sign. . . .

From the place where the water falls there rise abundance of vapors, like the greatest and thickest smoke, sometimes more, sometimes less. These vapors rise high in the air when it is calm but are dispers'd by the wind when it blows hard. If you go nigh to this vapor or fog, or if the wind blows it on you, it is so penetrating that in a few minutes you will be as wet as if you had been under water. I got two young Frenchmen to go down to bring me from the side of the Fall at the bottom some of each of the several kinds of herbs, stones, and shells they should find there. They returned in a few minutes, and I really thought they had fallen into the water: they were obliged to strip themselves quite naked, and hang their clothes in the sun to dry. . . .

Several of the French gentlemen told me that when birds come flying into this fog or smoke of the fall they fall down and perish in the water, either because their wings are become wet or that the noise of the fall astonishes them and they know not where to go in the dark. But others were of opinion that seldom or never any bird perishes there in that manner; because, as they all agreed, among the abundance of birds found dead below the fall there are no other sorts than such as live and swim frequently in the water, as swans, geese, ducks, waterhens, teal, and the like. And very often great flocks of them are seen going to destruction in this manner; they swim in the river above the fall, and so are carried down lower and lower by the water; and as water fowl commonly take great delight in being carried with the stream, so here they indulge themselves in enjoying this pleasure so long till the swiftness of the water becomes so great that 'tis no longer possible for them to rise, but they are driven down the precipice and perish. . . .

The French told me they had often thrown whole great trees into the water above, to see them tumble down the Fall. They went down with surprising swiftness but could never be seen afterwards; whence it was thought there was a bottomless deep or abyss just under the Fall. I am also of opinion that there must be a vast deep here. Yet I think if they had watched very well they might have found the trees at some distance below the Fall. The rock of the Fall consists of a grey limestone.

Here you have, Sir, a short but exact description of this famous Niagara cataract: you may depend on the truth of what I write. You must excuse me if you find in my account no extravagant wonders. I cannot make nature otherwise than I find it. I had rather it should be said of me in time to come that I related things as they were and that all is found to agree with my description than to be esteemed a false relater. I have seen some other things in this my journey, an account of which I know would gratify your curiosity. But time at present will not permit me to write more, and I hope shortly to see you.   I am, etc.

PETER KALM

Young George Washington in the Ohio Valley

[In the late autumn of 1753 young George Washington, who had gained experience in the backwoods as a surveyor, was commissioned by Governor Robert Dinwiddie of Virginia to carry a message to the French commander at Fort Le Boeuf at what is now Waterford, Erie County, Pennsylvania. The French had established themselves in territory that the English claimed. The Ohio Company, which had designs on great estates in the region, was disturbed at the invasion of the French; Washington himself was eager for land in this region. Dinwiddie's message was a warning to the French to get out, which they refused to do.

[The following summer, 1754, Dinwiddie sent Washington with 400 men to reinforce a small English outpost at the site of modern Pittsburgh; the French, however, captured the place before Washington could reach it and a little later forced him to surrender at Great Meadows (in Pennsylvania).

[Washington's report of the journey to Fort Le Boeuf between October 31, 1753 and January 16, 1754 describes an expedition of unusual hardship. Fortunately he was accompanied by a skilled frontiersman, Christopher Gist. Governor Dinwiddie had the report immediately printed in Williamsburg with the title The Journal of Major George Washington . . . *(1754). It served as propaganda against the French and helped to arouse the Colonists to the need of preserving the Ohio Valley from their inveterate enemies. Excerpts follow:]*

Wednesday, October 31st, 1753. I was commissioned and appointed by the Honorable Robert Dinwiddie, Esq., Governor, etc. of Virginia, to visit and deliver a letter to the Commandant of the French forces on the Ohio, and set out [from Williamsburg] on the intended journey the same day. The next, I arrived at Fredericksburg and engaged Mr. Jacob Vanbraam to be my

French interpreter; and proceeded with him to Alexandria, where we provided necessaries. From thence we went to Winchester and got baggage, horses, etc., and from thence we pursued the new road to Wills Creek, where we arrived the 14th of November. Here I engaged Mr. Gist to pilot us out, and also hired four others as servitors . . . and in company with those persons left the inhabitants the day following.

The excessive rains and vast quantity of snow which had fallen prevented our reaching Mr. Frazier's, an Indian trader, at the mouth of Turtle Creek on Monongahela [River] till Thursday the 22d. We were informed here that expresses had been sent a few days before to the traders down the river to acquaint them with the French general's death and the return of the major part of the French army into winter quarters.

The waters were quite impassable without swimming our horses, which obliged us to get the loan of a canoe from Frazier. . . . As I got down before the canoe, I spent some time in viewing the rivers and the land in the Fork [the confluence of the Allegheny and Monongahela rivers, site of Pittsburgh], which I think extremely well situated for a fort as it has the absolute command of both rivers. The land at the Point is 20 or 25 feet above the common surface of the water, and a considerable bottom of flat, well-timbered land all around it, very convenient for building. The rivers are each a quarter of a mile or more across, and run here very near at right angles: Allegheny bearing N.E., and Monongahela S.E. The former of these two is a very rapid and swift-running water, the other deep and still without any perceptible fall.

About two miles from this, on the southeast side of the river, at the place where the Ohio Company intended to erect a fort, lives Shingiss, King of the Delawares. We called upon him to invite him to council at the Loggs-Town [near Ambridge, Pennsylvania].

As I had taken a good deal of notice yesterday of the situation at the Forks, my curiosity led me to examine this more particularly; and I think it greatly inferior, either for defense or advantages, especially the latter. For a fort at the Forks would be equally well situated on the Ohio [same as the Allegheny] and have the entire command of the Monongahela, which runs up to our settlements and is extremely well designed for water carriage as it is of a deep still nature. Besides, a fort at the Fork might be built at a much less expense than at the other place. Nature has well contrived this lower place for water defense, but the hill whereon it must stand being about a quarter of a mile in length and then descending gradually on the land side will render it difficult and very expensive to make a sufficient fortification there. . . .

30th [November]. Last night the great men [of the Delawares] assembled to their council house to consult further about this journey and who were to go. The result of which was that only three of their chiefs, with one of their best hunters, should be our convoy. The reason they gave for not sending more . . . was that a greater number might give the French suspicions of some bad design and cause them to be treated rudely; but I rather think they could not get their hunters in.

We set out about 9 o'clock with the Half-King, Jeskakake, White Thunder, and the hunter, and traveled on the road to Venango [Franklin, Pennsylvania], where we arrived the 4th of December without anything remarkable happening but a continued series of bad weather. This is an old Indian town situated at the mouth of French Creek on [the] Ohio. . . .

We found the French colors hoisted at a house from which they had driven Mr. John Frazier, an English subject. I immediately repaired to it, to know where the Commander resided. There were three officers, one of whom, Capt. Joncaire, informed me that he had the command of the Ohio, but that there was a general officer at the near fort [Le Boeuf] where he advised me to apply for an answer. He invited us to sup with them and treated us with the greatest complaisance.

The wine, as they dosed themselves pretty plentifully with it, soon banished the restraint which at first appeared in their conversation and gave a license to their tongues to reveal their sentiments more freely. They told me that it was their absolute design to take possession of the Ohio, and by G—— they would do it. For that, altho' they were sensible the English could raise two men for their one, yet they knew their motions were too slow and dilatory to prevent any undertaking of theirs. They pretend to have an undoubted right to the river from a discovery made by one La Salle 60 years ago. . . .

5th [December]. Rain'd excessively all day, which prevented our traveling. . . .

7th. . . . We found it extremely difficult to get the Indians off today, as every [French] stratagem had been used to prevent their going up with me. . . . At 11 o'clock we set out for the fort, and were prevented from arriving there till the 11th by excessive rains, snows, and bad traveling through many mires and swamps. These we were obliged to pass to avoid crossing the creek, which was impossible, either by fording or rafting, the water was so high and rapid. . . .

13th. The chief officers [at Fort Le Boeuf] retired to hold a council of war, which gave me an opportunity of taking the dimensions of the fort and making what observations I could. . . .

14th. As the snow increased very fast and our horses daily became weaker, I sent them off unloaded . . . to make all convenient dispatch to Venango and there wait our arrival, if there was prospect of the rivers freezing. . . . This evening I received an answer to His Honor the Governor's letter from the Commandant.

15th. The Commandant ordered a plentiful store of liquor, provision, etc. to be put on board our canoe and appeared to be extremely complaisant, though he was exerting every artifice which he could invent to set our own Indians at variance with us to prevent their going till after our departure: presents, rewards, and everything which could be suggested by him or his officers. I can't say that ever in my life I suffered so much anxiety as I did in this affair. . . . As I was very much pressed by the Indians to wait this day for them, I consented, on a promise that nothing should hinder them in the morning.

16th. The French were not slack in their inventions to keep the Indians this day also . . . but I urged and insisted with the [Half-] King so closely upon his word that he refrained and set off with us as he had engaged.

We had a tedious and very fatiguing passage down the [French] Creek. Several times we had like to have been staved against rocks; and many times were obliged all hands to get out and remain in the water half an hour or more getting over the shoals. At one place the ice had lodged and made it impassable by water; therefore we were obliged to carry our canoe across a neck of land a quarter of a mile over. We did not reach Venango till the 22d, where we met with our horses.

This creek is extremely crooked. I dare say the distance between the fort and Venango can't be less than 130 miles, to follow the meanders.

23d. . . . Our horses were now so weak and feeble, and the baggage so heavy (as we were obliged to provide all the necessaries which the journey would require) that we doubted much their performing it. Therefore myself and others . . . gave up our horses for packs, to assist along with the baggage. I put myself in an Indian walking dress and continued with them three days, till I found there was no probability of their getting home in any reasonable time. The horses grew less able to travel every day, the cold increased very fast, and the roads were becoming much worse by a deep snow, continually freezing. Therefore as I was uneasy to get back to make report of my proceedings to His Honor the Governor, I determined to prosecute my journey the nearest way through the woods, on foot. . . .

I took my necessary papers, pulled off my clothes, and tied myself up in a matchcoat [an Indian wrap of Algonquian origin]. Then with gun in hand and pack at my back, in which were my papers and provisions, I set out with Mr. Gist, fitted in the same manner, on Wednesday the 26th.

[*27th.*] The day following, just after we had passed a place called the Murdering Town . . . we fell in with a party of French Indians who had lain in wait for us. One of them fired at Mr. Gist or me, not 15 steps off, but fortunately missed. We took this fellow into custody and kept him till about 9 o'clock at night. Then let him go and walked all the remaining part of the night without making any stop, that we might get the start, so far as to be out of the reach of their pursuit the next day, since we were well assured they would follow our track as soon as it was light. The next day we continued traveling till quite dark and got to the river. . . . We expected to have found the river frozen, but it was not—only about 50 yards from each shore. The ice I suppose had broken up above, for it was driving in vast quantities.

There was no way for getting over but on a raft, which we set about [building] with but one poor hatchet, and finished just after sunsetting. This was a whole day's work. We next got it launched and went on board of it, then set off. But before we were halfway over we were jammed in the ice, in such a manner that we expected every moment our raft to sink and ourselves to perish. I put out my setting pole to try to stop the raft that the ice might pass by, when the rapidity of the stream threw it with so much violence against the pole that it jerked me out into ten feet water. But I fortunately saved myself by catching hold of one of the raft logs. Notwithstanding all our efforts, we could not get the raft to either shore but were obliged, as we were near an island, to quit our raft and make to it.

The cold was so extremely severe that Mr. Gist had all his fingers and some of his toes frozen. And the water was shut up so hard that we found no difficulty in getting off the island on the ice in the morning, and went to Mr. Frazier's. . . .

Tuesday the 1st day of January. . . . This day we arrived at Wills Creek after as fatiguing a journey as it is possible to conceive, rendered so by excessive bad weather. From the first day of December to the 15th there was but one day on which it did not rain or snow incessantly; and throughout the whole journey we met with nothing but one continued series of cold wet weather, which occasioned very uncomfortable lodgings, especially after we had quitted our ten, which was some screen from the inclemency of it.

On the 11th I got to Belvoir [Fort Belvoir, Virginia], where I stopped one day to take necessary rest, and then set out and arrived in Williamsburg the 16th, when I waited upon His Honor the Governor with the letter I had brought from the French Commandant.

Daniel Boone,
Romantic Scout and Explorer

[Of all the early explorers of the trans-Appalachian region, the one best known in popular legend is Daniel Boone—hunter, explorer for the land speculators, Indian fighter and western pioneer. He early became a popular hero, partly as a result of a biographical account of Boone appended to John Filson's The Discovery, Settlement, and Present State of Kentucke (*Wilming-*

ton, Delaware, 1784). *Filson's work attracted immediate attention and was frequently reprinted. A year after its publication in Wilmington it was translated into French and published in Paris. A London reprint, read by Lord Byron, induced him to devote seven stanzas in Canto VIII of* Don Juan *(1823) to Daniel Boone; Byron's praise added to Boone's romantic reputation in Europe. From Filson's time to our own Boone has been a popular hero. A long series on television has attributed incredible adventures to the "long hunter."*

[*Boone was born in 1734 near Reading, Pennsylvania. In 1750–51 his family moved by slow stages through the Shenandoah Valley to Buffalo Lick, North Carolina, on the north fork of the Yadkin River. During General Braddock's ill-fated campaign against Fort Duquesne (later Pittsburgh) in 1755, Boone went along as a teamster and blacksmith and escaped the debacle on one of his horses. A year after Braddock's defeat Boone married Rebecca Bryan, a girl of seventeen with determination to match his; at any rate she refused to agree to Boone's plan to move to Florida, a decision that ultimately sent him to Kentucky.*

[*In the autumn of 1767, with one or two companions, Boone made his first western journey, spending the winter in the Kentucky wilderness and returning in the spring. Abundant game lured Boone and other hunters to the region.*

[*A more extensive exploration of Kentucky began on May 1, 1769, when Boone, John Stuart Finley and four others left North Carolina and crossed the mountains via the Cumberland Gap. They did not return until the spring of 1771. News of the wonders of the western country had already circulated in Virginia and North Carolina, and Colonel Richard Henderson had organized the Transylvania Company to take up land in Kentucky. In March 1775 he employed Boone to lead a party of settlers to Kentucky. At Boonesborough in April they built a stockade as a defense against the Indians. In the autumn of that year Boone moved his own family to Kentucky and brought along 20 more men whom he had recruited.*

[*When Kentucky became a county of Virginia in 1776 Boone was made a captain of militia. Two years later he was captured by a war party of Shawnee Indians but contrived to escape after some four months of servitude. Boone was unfortunate in his later career. Because he had improperly recorded his land holdings in*

Kentucky he was eventually evicted and in disgust moved to the mouth of the Great Kanawha River in West Virginia. Failing to prosper there, sometime in 1798–99 he moved on to Missouri where he spent the rest of his life. He died in 1820, full of years and the conviction that he had really done all the deeds attributed to him by romantic biographers.

[Filson's "life," written in the first person as if by Boone himself, made the hunter's reputation, and since it had such an importance in creating the legend, portions of it have been selected for reproduction here. But Filson himself is obviously the author of the stilted and artificial narrative, couched in language that the uneducated Boone could never have used. Excerpts follow:]

It was on the first of May, in the year 1769, that I resigned my domestic happiness for a time and left my family and peaceable habitation on the Yadkin River in North Carolina to wander through the wilderness of America in quest of the country of Kentucke, in company with John Finley, John Stewart, Joseph Holden, James Monay, and William Cool. We proceeded successfully, and after a long and fatiguing journey through a mountainous wilderness, in a westward direction, on the seventh day of June following we found ourselves on Red River [which crosses the border of present-day Tennessee and Kentucky], where John Finley had formerly been trading with the Indians, and, from the top of an eminence, saw with pleasure the beautiful level of Kentucke. . . .

We found everywhere abundance of wild beasts of all sorts through this vast forest. The buffaloes were more frequent than I have seen cattle in the settlements, browsing on the leaves of the cane, or cropping the herbage on those extensive plains, fearless, because ignorant, of the violence of man. Sometimes we saw hundreds in a drove, and the numbers about the salt springs were amazing. In this forest, the habitation of beasts of every kind natural to America, we practiced hunting with great success until the twenty-second day of December following. . . .

Soon after, I returned home to my family with a determination to bring them as soon as possible to live in Kentucke, which I esteemed a second paradise, at the risk of my life and fortune.

I returned safe to my old habitation, and found my family in happy circumstances. I sold my farm on the Yadkin, and what goods we could not carry with us; and on the twenty-fifth day of September, 1773, bade a farewell to our friends, and proceeded on our journey to Kentucke, in company with five families more, and forty men that joined us in Powel's Valley [Valley of Powell River, between Clinch River and Cumberland Gap], which is one hundred and fifty miles from the now settled parts of Kentucke. This promising beginning was soon overcast with a cloud of adversity; for upon the tenth day of October, the rear of our company was attacked by a number of Indians, who killed six, and wounded one man. Of these my eldest son was one that fell in the action.

Though we defended ourselves, and repulsed the enemy, yet this unhappy affair scattered our cattle, brought us into extreme difficulty, and so discouraged the whole company that we retreated forty miles, to the settlement on Clinch river. . . .

[There] I was ordered to take the command of three garrisons during the campaign which Governor Dunmore carried on against the Shawanese Indians; after the conclusion of which the militia was discharged from each garrison and I, being relieved from my post, was solicited by a number of North Carolina gentlemen, that were about purchasing the lands lying on the S. side of Kentucke River from the Cherokee Indians, to attend their treaty at Wataga [Watauga Settlements, a pioneer waystation, on the Watauga River], in March, 1775, to negotiate with them, and mention the boundaries of the purchase. This I accepted, and at the request of the same gentlemen, undertook to mark out a road in the best passage from the settlement through the wilderness to Kentucke, with such assistance as I thought necessary to employ for such an important undertaking.

I soon began this work, having collected a number of enterprising men, well armed. We proceeded with all possible expedition until we came within fifteen miles of where Boonsborough now stands, and where we were fired upon by a party of Indians that killed two and wounded two of our number; yet, although surprised and taken at a disadvantage, we stood our ground. This was on the twentieth of March, 1775. Three days later, we were fired upon again, and had two men killed and three wounded. Afterwards we proceeded on to Kentucke river without opposition; and on the first day of April began to erect the fort of

Boonsborough at a salt lick, about sixty yards from the river on the S. side. . . .

On the fourteenth day of July, 1776, two of Col. Calaway's daughters and one of mine were taken prisoners near the fort. Immediately pursued the Indians, with only eight men, and on the sixteenth overtook them, killed two of the party, and recovered the girls. The same day on which this attempt was made, the Indians divided themselves into different parties and attacked several forts, which were shortly before this time erected, doing a great deal of mischief. This was extremely distressing to the new settlers. The innocent husbandman was shot down while busy cultivating the soil for his family's supply. Most of the cattle around the stations were destroyed. They continued their hostilities in this manner until the fifteenth of April 1777, when they attacked Boonsborough with a party of above one hundred in number, killed one man, and wounded four. Their loss in this attack was not certainly known to us.

On the fourth day of July following, a party of about two hundred Indians attacked Boonsborough, killed one man, and wounded two. They besieged us forty-eight hours; during which time seven of them were killed, and at last, finding themselves not likely to prevail, they raised the siege, and departed. . . .

On the twenty-fifth of this month a reinforcement of forty-five men arrived from North Carolina, and about the twentieth of August following Col. Bowman arrived with one hundred men from Virginia. Now we began to strengthen, and from hence, for the space of six weeks, we had skirmishes with Indians, in one quarter or other, almost every day.

The savages now learned the superiority of the Long Knife, as they call the Virginians, by experience; being out-generaled in almost every battle. Our affairs began to wear a new aspect, and the enemy, not daring to venture on open war, practiced secret mischief at times. . . .

On the seventh day of February, as I was hunting to procure meat for the company, I met with a party of one hundred and two Indians and two Frenchmen on their march against Boonsborough, that place being particularly the object of the enemy.

They pursued and took me; and brought me on the eighth day to the Licks, where twenty-seven of my party were, three of them having previously returned home with the salt. I, knowing it was impossible for them to escape, capitulated with the enemy, and, at a distance in their view, gave notice to my men of their situation, with orders not to resist but surrender themselves captives.

The generous usage the Indians had promised before in my capitulation was afterwards fully complied with, and we proceeded with them as prisoners to Old Chelicothe [Chillicothe, Ohio], the principal Indian town on Little Miami [River], where we arrived after an uncomfortable journey in very severe weather, on the eighteenth day of February, and received as good treatment as prisoners could expect from savages.

On the tenth day of March following, I, and ten of my men, were conducted by forty Indians to Detroit, where we arrived the thirtieth day and were treated by Governor Hamilton, the British commander at that post, with great humanity.

During our travels, the Indians entertained me well; and their affection for me was so great that they utterly refused to leave me there with the others, although the Governor offered them one hundred pounds Sterling for me, on purpose to give me a parole to go home. . . .

The Indians left my men in captivity with the British at Detroit, and on the tenth day of April brought me toward Old Chelicothe, where we arrived on the twenty-fifth day of the same month. . . . At Chelicothe I spent my time as comfortably as I could expect, was adopted, according to their custom, into a family where I became a son, and had a great share in the affection of my new parents, brothers, sisters, and friends. I was exceedingly familiar and friendly with them, always appearing as cheerful and satisfied as possible, and they put great confidence in me. I often went a hunting with them, and frequently gained their applause for my activity at our shooting, for no people are more envious than they in this sport. . . .

I now began to meditate an escape, and carefully avoided their suspicions, continuing with them at Old Chelicothe until the first day of June following, and then was taken by them to the salt springs on Sciotha [Scioto River], and kept there, making salt, ten days. During this time I hunted some for them, and found the land, for a great extent about this river, to exceed the soil of Kentucke, if possible, and remarkably well watered.

When I returned to Chelicothe, alarmed to see four hundred

and fifty Indians of their choicest warriors, painted and armed in a fearful manner, ready to march against Boonsborough, I determined to escape the first opportunity.

On the sixteenth, before sunrise, I departed in the most secret manner, and arrived at Boonsborough on the twentieth after a journey of one hundred and sixty miles, during which I had but one meal.

I found our fortress in a bad state of defense, but we proceeded immediately to repair our flanks, strengthen our gates and posterns, and form double bastions, which we completed in ten days. In this time we daily expected the arrival of the Indian army; and at length one of my fellow prisoners, escaping from them, arrived, informing us that the enemy had an account of my departure, and postponed their expedition three weeks. . . .

On the eighth, the Indian army arrived, being four hundred and forty-four in number, commanded by Capt. Duquesne, eleven other Frenchmen, and some of their own chiefs, and marched up within view of our fort, with British and French colors flying; and having sent a summons to me, in his Britannick Majesty's name, to surrender the fort, I requested two days' consideration, which was granted.

It was now a critical period with us: we were a small number in the garrison; a powerful army before our walls, whose appearance proclaimed inevitable death, fearfully painted, and marking their footsteps with desolation. Death was preferable to captivity; and if taken by storm, we must inevitably be devoted to destruction. In this situation we concluded to maintain our garrison, if possible. We immediately proceeded to collect what we could of our horses and other cattle, and bring them through the posterns into the fort. And in the evening of the ninth, I returned answer that we were determined to defend our fort while a man was living. . . . Contrary to our expectations, they formed a scheme to deceive us, declaring it was their orders, from Governor Hamilton, to take us captives, and not to destroy us; but if nine of us would come out and treat with them, they would immediately withdraw their forces from their walls and return home peaceably. This sounded grateful in our ears, and we agreed to the proposal.

We held the treaty within sixty yards of the garrison, on purpose to divert them from a breach of honor as we could not avoid suspicions of the savages. In this situation the articles were formally agreed to, and signed; and the Indians told us it was customary with them, on such occasions, for two Indians to shake hands with every white man in the treaty, as an evidence of entire friendship. We agreed to this also, but were soon convinced their policy was to take us prisoners. They immediately grappled us; but, although surrounded by hundreds of savages, we extricated ourselves from them and escaped all safe into the garrison, except one that was wounded through a heavy fire from their army. They immediately attacked us on every side, and a constant heavy fire ensued between us day and night for the space of nine days.

In this time the enemy began to undermine our fort, which was situated sixty yards from Kentucke river. They began at the watermark, and proceeded in the bank some distance, which we understood by their making the water muddy with the clay; and we immediately proceeded to disappoint their design by cutting a trench across their subterranean passage. The enemy, discovering our countermine by the clay we threw out of the fort, desisted from that stratagem. And experience now fully convincing them that neither their power nor policy could effect their purpose, on the twentieth day of August they raised the siege and departed.

VIII

The English Open Old
and New Trade Routes West

Alexander Henry's Travels

AFTER *the victory of the English over the French in 1759–60,
and the final cession of all of Canada to the English by the
Treaty of Paris in 1763, English fur traders moved rapidly into
territory once monopolized by the French. The Indians were slow
to recognize English supremacy because French* coureurs des bois,
*who had long since made friends of the red men, assured them
that their father, the king of France, would soon throw out the
English and restore the old trading posts that had supplied them
with French knives, guns, blankets and brandy. For a time the
Indians were openly hostile to the English. The widespread revolt
that flared along the frontier, known as Pontiac's Conspiracy, kept
the whole back country in turmoil for several years. Even in the
face of Indian hostility, some English traders and explorers pushed
into the interior to make contacts with tribes previously dominated
by the French.*

*[One of the most daring of these English fur traders was Alex-
ander Henry, a native of New Jersey, who on August 3, 1761, set
out from Montreal with a convoy of canoes bound for Mackinac
Strait between Lake Huron and Lake Michigan. The British had
taken over Fort Mackinac (then called Michilimackinac), but they
had not subdued the tribes in the hinterland nor had they consum-
mated peace and trade treaties with them. To all intents and
purposes, the English were still at war with the former Indian
allies of the French, a fact that Henry learned at his peril.*

[*After an arduous and hazardous journey up the Ottawa River to Lake Nipissing and thence up the French River to Georgian Bay and Lake Huron, Henry reached Mackinac in September 1761. Established at Fort Mackinac, with French* coureurs des bois *to serve as his agents, he opened trade with the Chippewa and other Indians of the region. Trade prospered until June 4, 1763, when the Chippewas in a surprise attack captured Fort Mackinac, massacred most of the garrison and took Henry prisoner. He was finally rescued by an Indian chief named Wenniway, who had earlier adopted him as a brother, and was released, after a year, at Fort Niagara. Later, after the conclusion of the peace that ended Pontiac's Conspiracy, Henry was granted a monopoly of the trade in the region around Sault Ste. Marie on Lake Superior. In 1776 he made a journey to the west and hoped to reach the Rocky Mountains, though he got no farther than the Great Plains.*

[*Henry's account of these adventures appeared in a volume printed in London in 1809 with the title* Travels and Adventures in Canada and the Indian Territories Between the Years 1760 and 1776. *His descriptions of methods of building canoes, modes of travel, Indian customs, and life among hostile savages are vivid and dramatic. Excerpts follow:*]

Chapter 2

The inland navigation from Montreal to Michilimackinac may be performed either by the way of Lakes Ontario and Erie or by the river Des Outaouais [Ottawa River], Lake Nipissing, and the river Des Français [French River]; for, as well by one as the other of these routes, we are carried to Lake Huron. The second is the shortest and that which is usually pursued by the canoes employed in the Indian trade.

The canoes which I provided for my undertaking were, as is usual, five fathom and a half in length, and four feet and a half in their extreme breadth, and formed of birch-tree bark a quarter of an inch in thickness. The bark is lined with small splints of cedar-wood; and the vessel is further strengthened with ribs of the same wood, of which the two ends are fastened to the gunwales: several bars, rather than seats, are also laid across the canoe, from gunwale to gunwale. The small roots of the spruce tree afford the *wattap,* with which the bark is sewed, and the gum of the pine tree supplies the place of tar and oakum. Bark, some spare wattap and gum are always carried in each canoe for the repairs which frequently become necessary.

The canoes are worked, not with oars, but with paddles, and, occasionally, with a sail. To each canoe there are eight men; and to every three or four canoes, which constitute a brigade, there is a guide, or conductor. Skillful men, at double the wages of the rest, are placed in the head and stern. They engage to go from Montréal to Michilimackinac and back to Montréal again, the middle men at one hundred and fifty livres and the end men at three hundred livres [French monetary unit worth about 19 cents when replaced by the franc in 1795]. The guide has the command of his brigade, and is answerable for all pillage and loss; and, in return, every man's wages is answerable to him. This regulation was established under the French government.

The freight of a canoe, of the substance and dimensions which I have detailed, consists in sixty pieces, or packages, of merchandise, of the weight of from ninety to a hundred pounds each; and provisions to the amount of one thousand weight. To this is to be added the weight of eight men and of eight bags, weighing forty pounds each, one of which every man is privileged to put on board. The whole weight must therefore exceed eight thousand pounds; or may perhaps be averaged at four tons.

The nature of the navigation, which is to be described, will sufficiently explain why the canoe is the only vessel which can be employed along its course. The necessity, indeed, becomes apparent at the very instant of our departure from Montréal itself.

The Saint Lawrence, for several miles immediately above Montréal, descends with a rapid current over a shallow rocky bed; insomuch that even canoes themselves, when loaded, cannot resist the stream, and are therefore sent empty to Lachine, where they meet the merchandise which they are to carry and which is transported thither by land. Lachine is about nine miles higher up the river than Montréal, and is at the head of the Sault de Saint Louis, which is the highest of the *saults,* falls, or leaps, in this part of the Saint Lawrence.

On the third of August [1761] I sent my canoes to Lachine, and, on the following morning, embarked with them for Michilimackinac. The river is here so broad as to be denominated a lake, by the title of Lake Saint Louis; the prospect is wide and cheerful; and the village has several well-built houses.

In a short time we reached the rapids and carrying place of Saint Anne, two miles below the upper end of the island of Montréal; and it is not till after passing these that the voyage may be properly said to be commenced. At Saint Anne's the men go to confession, and, at the same time, offer up their vows; for the saint from which this parish derives its name, and to whom its church is dedicated, is the patroness of the Canadians in all their travels by water.

There is still a further custom to be observed on arriving at Saint Anne's, and which is that of distributing eight gallons of rum to each canoe (a gallon for each man) for consumption during the voyage; nor is it less according to custom to drink the whole of this liquor upon the spot. The saint, therefore, and the priest were no sooner dismissed than a scene of intoxication began, in which my men surpassed, if possible, the drunken Indian in singing, fighting, and the display of savage gesture and conceit. In the morning we reloaded the canoes and pursued our course across the lake Des Deux Montagnes [Lake of Two Mountains, part of the Ottawa River].

This lake, like that of Saint Louis, is only a part of the estuary of the Outaouais, which here unites itself with the Saint Lawrence. . . .

At ten leagues above the island of Montréal I passed the limits of the cultivated lands on the north bank of the Outaouais. On the south the farms are very few in number, but the soil has every appearance of fertility.

In ascending the Longue Sault, a distance of three miles, my canoes were three times unladen and, together with their freight, carried on the shoulders of the *voyageurs*. The rocky carrying places are not crossed without danger of serious accidents by men bearing heavy burdens.

The Longue Sault being passed, the Outaouais presented, on either side, only scenes of primitive forest, the common range of the deer, the wolf, the bear, and the Indian. The current is here gentle. The lands upon the south are low, and, when I passed them, were overflowed; but on the northern side the banks are dry and elevated, with much meadowland at their feet. The grass in some places was high. Several islands are in this part of the river. Among the fish, of which there are abundance, are catfish of a large size.

At fourteen leagues above the Longue Sault we reached a French fort or trading house, surrounded by a stockade. Attached was a small garden, from which we procured some vegetables. The house had no inhabitant. At three leagues further is the mouth of the Hare River [Gatineau] which descends from the north; and here we passed another trading house. At a few leagues still higher, on the south bank, is the mouth of a river four hundred yards wide, and which falls into the Outaouais perpendicularly from the edge of a rock forty feet high. The appearance of this fall has procured for it the name of the *rideau,* or curtain; and hence the river itself is called the Rideau, or Rivière du Rideau. The fall presented itself to my view with extraordinary beauty and magnificence, and decorated with a variety of colors. . . .

While paddling against the gentle current of Lake des Châts [Lac des Chats, a broad reach of the Ottawa River between Renfrew and Arnprior], we met several canoes of Indians, returning from their winter's hunt to their village at the lake Des Deux Montagnes. I purchased some of their maple sugar and beaver skins in exchange for provisions. They wished for rum, which I declined to sell them; but they behaved civilly, and we parted, as we had met, in a friendly manner. Before they left us they inquired of my men whether or not I was an Englishman, and, being told that I was, they observed that the English were mad in their pursuit of beaver, since they could thus expose their lives for it; "for," added they, "the Upper Indians [Chippewas] will certainly kill him," meaning myself. These Indians had left their village before the surrender of Montréal, and I was the first Englishman they had seen.

In conversation with my men, I learned that the Algonquins of the lake Des Deux Montagnes, of which description were the party that I had now met, claim all the lands on the Outaouais as far as Lake Nipisingue [Nipissing], and that these lands are subdivided between their several families, upon whom they have devolved by inheritance. I was also informed that they are exceedingly strict as to the rights of property in this regard, accounting an invasion of them an offense sufficiently great to warrant the death of the invader. . . .

On the 10th of July, we had reached the Portage du Grand

Calumet, which is at the head of the channels of the same name, and which name is derived from the *pierre à calumet,* or pipe stone, which here interrupts the river, occasioning a fall of water. This carrying place is long and arduous, consisting in a high steep hill over which the canoe cannot be carried by fewer than twelve men. The method of carrying the packages, or pieces as they are called, is the same with that of the Indian women, and which indeed is not peculiar even to them. One piece rests and hangs upon the shoulders, being suspended in a fillet, or forehead band; and upon this is laid a second, which usually falls into the hollow of the neck and assists the head in its support of the burden.

The ascent of this carrying place is not more fatiguing than the descent is dangerous; and in performing it accidents too often occur, producing strains, ruptures, and injuries for life.

The carrying place and the repairs of our canoes, which cost us a day, detained us till the 13th. It is usual for the canoes to leave the Grand Calumet in good repair, the rapids, or shallow rocky parts of the channel (from which the canoes sustain the chief injury) being now passed, the current become gentle, and the carrying places less frequent. The lands above the carrying places and near the water are low; and, in the spring, entirely inundated. . . .

Chapter 8

When I reached Michilimackinac [May 20, 1763] I found several other traders, who had arrived before me, from different parts of the country, and who, in general, declared the dispositions of the Indians to be hostile to the English, and even apprehended some attack. . . . But the commandant, believing this and other reports to be without foundation, proceeding only from idle or ill-disposed persons and of a tendency to do mischief, . . . threatened to send the next person who should bring a story of the same kind a prisoner to Détroit. . . .

Chapter 9

The morning [June 5] was sultry. A Chipeway came to tell me that his nation was going to play at *bag'gat'iway,* with the Sacs or Saäkies, another Indian nation, for a high wager. He invited me to witness the sport, adding that the commandant was to be there and would bet on the side of the Chipeways. In consequence of this information, I went to the commandant and expostulated with him a little, representing that the Indians might possibly have some sinister end in view; but the commandant only smiled at my suspicions.

Baggatiway, called by the Canadians *le jeu de la crosse* [i.e., the game of lacrosse], is played with a bat and ball. The bat is about four feet in length, curved, and terminating in a sort of racket. Two posts are planted in the ground at a considerable distance from each other, as a mile or more. Each party has its post, and the game consists in throwing the ball up to the post of the adversary. The ball, at the beginning, is placed in the middle of the course, and each party endeavors as well to throw the ball out of the direction of its own post as into that of the adversary's.

I did not go myself to see the match which was now to be played without the fort because, there being a canoe prepared to depart on the following day for Montréal, I employed myself in writing letters to my friends; and even when a fellow trader, Mr. Tracy, happened to call upon me, saying that another canoe had just arrived from Détroit and proposing that I should go with him to the beach to inquire the news, it so happened that I still remained to finish my letters, promising to follow Mr. Tracy in the course of a few minutes. Mr. Tracy had not gone more than twenty paces from my door when I heard an Indian war cry and a noise of general confusion.

Going instantly to my window, I saw a crowd of Indians within the fort, furiously cutting down and scalping every Englishman they found. . . .

This was a moment for despair; but the next [moment], a Pani [Pawnee] woman, a slave of M. Langlade's, beckoned me to follow her. She brought me to a door which she opened, desiring me to enter and telling me that it led to the garret where I must go and conceal myself. I joyfully obeyed her directions; and she, having followed me up to the garret door, locked it after me. . . .

Chapter 10

The game of baggatiway, as from the description above will have been perceived, is necessarily attended with much violence and noise. In the ardor of contest, the ball, as has been suggested, if it cannot be thrown to the goal desired, is struck in any direction by which it can be diverted from that designed by the adversary. At such a moment, therefore, nothing could be less liable to excite premature alarm than that the ball should be tossed over the pickets of the fort, nor that having fallen there, it should be followed, on the instant, by all engaged in the game, as well the one party as the other, all eager, all struggling, all shouting, all in the unrestrained pursuit of a rude athletic exercise. Nothing could be less fitted to excite premature alarm—nothing, therefore, could be more happily devised, under the circumstances, than a stratagem like this; and this was, in fact, the stratagem which the Indians had employed, by which they had obtained possession of the fort, and by which they had been enabled to slaughter and subdue its garrison and such of its other inhabitants as they pleased. To be still more certain of success, they had prevailed upon as many as they could, by a pretext the least liable to suspicion, to come voluntarily without the pickets, and particularly the commandant and garrison themselves. . . .

That whole night, or the greater part of it, was passed in mutual condolence; and my fellow prisoners shared my garret. In the morning, being again called down, I found my master, Wenniway [a Chippewa subchief who adopted him as brother], and was desired to follow him. He led me to a small house within the fort where, in a narrow room and almost dark I found Mr. Ezekiel Solomons, an Englishman from Détroit, and a soldier, all prisoners. With these I remained in painful suspense as to the scene that was next to present itself till ten o'clock in the forenoon, when an Indian arrived and presently marched us to the lakeside, where a canoe appeared ready for departure and in which we found that we were to embark.

. . . At noon our party was all collected, the prisoners all embarked, and we steered for the Isles du Castor [Beaver Islands] in Lake Michigan.

Chapter 11

.   .   .   .

We were bound [June 6] as I have said, for the Isles du Castor, which lie in the mouth of Lake Michigan; and we should have crossed the lake but that a thick fog came on, on account of which the Indians deemed it safer to keep the shore close under their lee. We therefore approached the lands of the Otawas and their village of L'Arbre Croche, already mentioned as lying about twenty miles to the westward of Michilimackinac on the opposite side of the tongue of land on which the fort is built.

Every half hour the Indians gave their warwhoops, one for every prisoner in their canoe. This is a general custom, by the aid of which all other Indians within hearing are apprised of the number of prisoners they are carrying.

In this manner we reached Wagoshense [Waugoshance Point], a long point stretching westward into the lake and which the Otawas make a carrying place, to avoid going round it. It is distant eighteen miles from Michilimackinac. After the Indians had made their warwhoop as before, an Otawa appeared upon the beach, who made signs that we should land. In consequence, we approached. The Otawa asked the news and kept the Chipeways in further conversation till we were within a few yards of the land and in shallow water. At this moment a hundred men rushed upon us from among the bushes and dragged all the prisoners out of the canoes, amid a terrifying shout.

We now believed that our last sufferings were approaching; but, no sooner were we fairly on shore and on our legs than the chiefs of the party advanced and gave each of us their hands, telling us that they were our friends, and Otawas, whom the Chipeways had insulted by destroying the English without consulting with them on the affair. They added that what they had done was for the purpose of saving our lives, the Chipeways having been carrying us to the Isles du Castor only to kill and devour us. . . .

Chapter 22

.   .   .   .

On the 18th of June [1764] we crossed Lake aux Claies [Lake Simcoe, between Lake Huron and Lake Ontario], which appeared to be upward of twenty miles in length. At its further end, we came to the carrying place of Toronto [then a French trading post on Lake Ontario near the site of old Fort York and Toronto, Ontario]. Here the Indians obliged me to carry a burden of more than a hundred pounds weight. The day was very hot, and the woods and marshes abounded with mosquitoes; but the Indians walked at a quick pace, and I could by no means see myself left behind. The whole country was a thick forest through which our only road was a footpath, or such as, in America, is exclusively termed an Indian path.

Next morning at ten o'clock we reached the shore of Lake Ontario. Here we were employed two days in making canoes out of the bark of the elm tree, in which we were to transport ourselves to Niagara. For this purpose the Indians first cut down a tree; then stripped off the bark, in one entire sheet of about eighteen feet in length, the incision being lengthwise. The canoe was now complete as to its top, bottom, and sides. Its ends were next closed by sewing the bark together; and a few ribs and bars being introduced, the architecture was finished. In this manner we made two canoes, of which one carried eight men, and the other, nine.

On the 21st we embarked at Toronto and encamped, in the evening, four miles short of Fort Niagara, which the Indians would not approach till morning.

At dawn the Indians were awake, and presently assembled in council, still doubtful as to the fate they were to encounter. I assured them of the most friendly welcome; and at length, after painting themselves with the most lively colors in token of their own peaceable views, and after singing the song which is in use among them on going into danger, they embarked and made for Point Missisaki [Mississaugi], which is on the north side of the mouth of the river or strait of Niagara, as the fort is on the south [approximate site of Youngstown, N.Y.]. A few minutes after, I crossed over to the fort; and here I was received by Sir William Johnson in a manner for which I have ever been gratefully attached to his person and memory.

Thus was completed my escape from the sufferings and dangers which the capture of Fort Michilimackinac brought upon me. . . .

Part the Second

Chapter 1

Under the French government of Canada, the fur trade was subject to a variety of regulations established and enforced by the royal authority; and in 1765, the period at which I began to prose-

cute it anew, some remains of the ancient system were still preserved. No person could go into the countries lying northwestward
of Détroit unless furnished with a license; and the exclusive trade
of particular districts was capable of being enjoyed in virtue of
grants from military commanders.

The exclusive trade of Lake Superior was given to myself by the
commandant of Fort Michilimackinac; and to prosecute it I purchased goods which I found at this post at twelve months' credit.
My stock was the freight of four canoes, and I took it at the price
of ten thousand pounds' weight of good and merchantable beaver.
It is in beaver that accounts are kept at Michilimackinac; but in
defect of this article, other furs and skins are accepted in pay-
ments, being first reduced unto their value in beaver. Beaver was
at this time at the price of two shillings and sixpence per pound,
Michilimackinac currency; otter skins, at six shillings each; marten,
at one shilling and sixpence, and others in proportion.

To carry the goods to my wintering ground in Lake Superior I
engaged twelve men, at two hundred and fifty livres of the same
currency, each; that is, a hundred pounds' weight of beaver. For
provisions I purchased fifty bushels of maize at ten pounds of
beaver per bushel. At this place, specie was so wholly out of the
question that in going to a cantine you took with you a marten's
skin to pay your reckoning.

On the 14th of July, 1765, I embarked for the Sault de Sainte
Marie, where on my arrival I took into partnership M. Cadotte
. . . ; and on the 26th I proceeded for my wintering ground,
which was to be fixed at Chagouemig [Chequamegon Bay, southwest shore of Lake Superior]. . . .

On my arrival at Chagouemig I found fifty lodges of Indians
there. These people were almost naked, their trade having been
interrupted first by the English invasion of Canada, and next by
Pontiac's war.

Adding the Indians of Chagouemig to those which I had
brought with me, I had now a hundred families, to all of whom
I was required to advance goods on credit. At a council which I
was invited to attend, the men declared that unless their demands
were complied with, their wives and children would perish, for
that there were neither ammunition nor clothing left among them.
Under these circumstances I saw myself obliged to distribute
goods to the amount of three thousand beaver skins. This done, the

Indians went on their hunt at the distance of a hundred leagues. A clerk acting as my agent accompanied them to Fond du Lac, taking with him two loaded canoes. Meanwhile, at the expense of six days' labor, I was provided with a very comfortable house for my winter's residence.

Chapter 5

In the beginning of April [1768], I prepared to make maple sugar, building for this purpose a house in a hollow dug out of the snow. The house was seven feet high, but yet was lower than the snow.

On the twenty-fourth I began my manufacture. On the twenty-eighth the lands below were covered with a thick fog. All was calm, and from the top of the mountain not a cloud was to be discovered in the horizon. Descending the next day, I found half a foot of new-fallen snow, and learned that it had blown hard in the valleys the day before; so that I perceived I had been making sugar in a region above the clouds.

Sugar making continued till the twelfth of May. On the mountain we eat nothing but our sugar during the whole period. Each man consumed a pound a day, desired no other food, and was visibly nourished by it.

After returning to the banks of the river wild fowl appeared in such abundance that a day's subsistence for fifty men could without difficulty be shot daily by one; but all this was the affair of less than a week, before the end of which the water, which had been covered, was left naked, and the birds had fled away to the northward.

On the twentieth day of the month the first party of Indians came in from their winter's hunt. During the season some of them had visited one of the factories of the Hudson's Bay Company. Within a few days following I had the satisfaction of seeing all those to whom I had advanced goods return. Out of two thousand skins, which was the amount of my outstanding debts, not thirty remained unpaid; and even the trivial loss which I did suffer was occasioned by the death of one of the Indians, for whom his family brought, as they said, all the skins of which he died possessed, and offered to pay the rest from among themselves—his manes [spirit], they observed, would not be able to enjoy peace while his name remained in my books and his debts were left unsatisfied. . . .

Chapter 10

The Plains, or, as the French denominate them, the Prairies or Meadows, compose an extensive tract of country which is watered by the Elk, or Athabasca, the Sascatchiwaine, the Red River, and others, and runs southward to the Gulf of Mexico. On my first setting out for the northwest I promised myself to visit this region, and I now prepared to accomplish the undertaking. Long journies on the snow are thought of but as trifles in this part of the world.

On the first day of January 1776 I left our fort on Beaver Lake [Saskatchewan near Manitoba border], attended by two men and provided with dried meat, frozen fish, and a small quantity of praline, made of roasted maize, rendered palatable with sugar, and which I had brought from the Sault de Sainte Marie for this express occasion. . . .

Our provisions were drawn by the men upon sledges made of thin boards, a foot in breadth and curved upward in front after the Indian fashion. Our clothing for night and day was nearly the same; and the cold was so intense that, exclusively of warm woolen clothes, we were obliged to wrap ourselves continually in beaver blankets, or at least in ox skins which the traders call buffalo robes. At night we made our first encampment at the head of the Maligne [a tributary of the Athabasca], where one of our parties was fishing with but very indifferent success.

On the following evening, we encamped at the mouth of the same river. The snow was four feet deep; and we found it impossible to keep ourselves warm, even with the aid of a large fire. . . .

From Cumberland House [on south bank of Cumberland Lake, eastern Saskatchewan] I pursued a westerly course, on the ice, following the southern bank of Sturgeon Lake [Cumberland Lake] till I crossed the neck of land by which alone it is separated from the great river Pasquayah, or Sascatchiwaine. In the evening I encamped on the north bank of this river at the distance of ten leagues from Cumberland House.

The depth of the snow and the intenseness of the cold rendered my progress so much slower than I had reckoned upon that

I soon began to fear the want of provisions. The sun did not rise till half past nine o'clock in the morning, and it set at half past two in the afternoon. It is, however, at no time wholly dark in these climates, the northern lights and the reflection of the snow affording always sufficient light for the traveler. Add to this that the river, the course of which I was ascending, was a guide, with the aid of which I could not lose my way. Every day's journey was commenced at three o'clock in the morning.

I was not far advanced before the country betrayed some approaches to the characteristic nakedness of the Plains. The wood dwindled away, both in size and quantity, so that it was with difficulty we could collect sufficient for making a fire, and without fire we could not drink; for melted snow was our only resource, the ice on the river being too thick to be penetrated by the axe.

For the two days succeeding, the depth of the snow and the violence of the winds greatly retarded our journey; but from the ninth to the twelfth the elements were less hostile, and we traveled rapidly. . . .

On the twentieth the last remains of our provisions were expended; but I had taken the precaution to conceal a cake of chocolate in reserve for an occasion like that which was now arrived. Toward evening my men, after walking the whole day, began to lose their strength; but we nevertheless kept on our feet till it was late, and, when we encamped, I informed them of the treasure which was still in store. I desired them to fill the kettle with snow, and argued with them the while that the chocolate would keep us alive for five days at least, an interval in which we should surely meet with some Indian at the chase. Their spirits revived at the suggestion, and, the kettle being filled with two gallons of water, I put into it one square of the chocolate. The quantity was scarcely sufficient to alter the color of the water, but each of us drank half a gallon of the warm liquor by which we were much refreshed, and in its enjoyment felt no more of the fatigues of the day. In the morning we allowed ourselves a similar repast, after finishing which we marched vigorously for six hours. . . .

This day, the twenty-fifth [of January], we found the borders of the Plains reaching to the very banks of the river, which were two hundred feet above the level of the ice. Watermarks presented themselves at twenty feet above the actual level. . . .

Chapter 15

The days being now lengthened, and the snow capable of bearing the foot, we traveled swiftly; and the weather, though cold, was very fine.

On the fifth of April, we arrived, without accident, at Cumberland House. On our way we saw nothing living, except wolves, who followed us in great numbers and against whom we were obliged to use the precaution of maintaining large fires at our encampments.

Mackenzie Crosses North America

[*The first white man known to have crossed the North American continent on an exploring expedition was a Scotsman, Alexander Mackenzie, an officer of the Northwest Company of fur traders. In two journeys he reached both the Arctic and the Pacific oceans, and he established the fact that a land barrier stood in the way of a northwest passage to the Pacific farther south than the Arctic.*

[*Mackenzie, manager of a trading post for the Northwest Company on Lake Athabasca in the present province of Alberta, left that area on June 3, 1789, on his first exploring expedition in search of a water route to the Pacific. Following a river that now bears his name (though Mackenzie called it the "River of Disappointment"), he came on July 12 to the open sea, but it turned out to be the Arctic instead of the Pacific. The point that he reached is now called Mackenzie Bay on the Beaufort Sea.*

[*Mackenzie, however, was convinced that a feasible water route could be found to the Pacific and continued his search. Realizing that he did not have sufficient navigational skill, he went to London for instruction. On his return to Canada he organized another expedition to seek the western water route and, on October 10, 1792, once more started west from Lake Athabasca. On May 11, 1792, an American ship captain, Robert Gray, trading for sea-otter skins on the coast of Oregon, had piloted his vessel, the* Columbia, *through the breakers into the mouth of a great river which he named after his ship. Before Mackenzie left on his*

*second exploring expedition he had heard from traders of Gray's
discovery of a navigable river flowing into the Pacific. Rumors had
long been circulating of a "Great River of the West." Surely,
Mackenzie reasoned, such a river would provide easy access to
the Pacific for boat traffic from the East.*

*[Establishing winter quarters on the Peace River, Mackenzie
waited until the spring of 1793 before resuming his search. On
the western side of the Rocky Mountains he came upon a large
river flowing toward the Pacific. Believing he had found the
Columbia, he followed it to the sea, and, upon the flat surface
of a rock, he wrote in vermilion paint these words: "Alexander
Mackenzie from Canada, by land, the twenty-second of July, one
thousand, seven hundred and ninety-three." Not until 1807 did
Simon Fraser, another explorer, prove that the river Mackenzie
had traced was not the Columbia but one that now bears Fraser's
name.*

*[Mackenzie had proved that waterways could take canoes for
most of the way from Lake Athabasca to the Pacific, even though
the mountain barrier of the Rockies made water traffic that way
difficult. He still hoped that relatively easy portages could be
found, and he dreamed of a river and lake route that would link
the Atlantic and the Pacific.*

*[The narrative of Mackenzie's two exploring expeditions was
published in London in 1801 with the title* Voyages from Montreal, on the River St. Laurence, Through the Continent of North
America, to the Frozen and Pacific Oceans in the Years 1789 and
1793. *. . . Since Mackenzie himself had little education, some
professional writer clearly put the book together from the explorer's rough notes. Interest in the North American west was high
in this period and publishers eagerly sought reports of explorations. Mackenzie's editor managed to retain much factual detail
that he believed would be of general interest. The first part of
the narrative deals with the journey to the Arctic in 1789; the
second portion recounts his adventures on the trip to the Pacific.
Excerpts follow:]*

Chapter 1

We embarked at nine o'clock in the morning (June 3, 1789) at
Fort Chipewyan [northern Alberta] on the south side of the Lake

of the Hills [Lake Athabasca], in latitude 58.40. north, and longitude 110.30. west from Greenwich, and compass has sixteen degrees variation east, in a canoe made of birch bark. The crew consisted of four Canadians, two of whom were attended by their wives, and a German; we were accompanied also by an Indian, who had acquired the title of English Chief, and his two wives in a small canoe with two young Indians, his followers in another small canoe. These men were engaged to serve us in the twofold capacity of interpreters and hunters. . . .

We were also accompanied by a canoe that I had equipped for the purpose of trade and given the charge of it to M. Le Roux, one of the Company's clerks. In this I was obliged to ship part of our provision, which—with the clothing necessary for us on the voyage, a proper assortment of the articles of merchandise as presents to ensure us a friendly reception among the Indians, and the ammunition and arms requisite for defense, as well as a supply for our hunters—were more than our canoe could carry. But by the time we should part company, there was every reason to suppose that our expenditure would make sufficient room for the whole. . . .

Chapter 4

.   .   .   .

Saturday 11 [July]. I sat up all night to observe the sun. At half past twelve I called up one of the men to view a spectacle which he had never before seen; when, on seeing the sun so high, he thought it was a signal to embark, and began to call the rest of his companions, who would scarcely be persuaded by me that the sun had not descended nearer to the horizon and that it was now but a short time past midnight.

We reposed, however, till three quarters after three, when we entered the canoe and steered about northwest, the river [Mackenzie] taking a very serpentine course. About seven we saw a ridge of high land. At twelve we landed at a spot where we observed that some of the natives had lately been. . . . The weather was cloudy, and the air cold and unpleasant. From this place for about five miles the river widens; it then flows in a variety of narrow, meandering channels amongst low islands enlivened with no trees but a few dwarf willows.

At four, we landed where there were three houses, or rather huts, belonging to the natives. The ground plot is of an oval form, about fifteen feet long, ten feet wide in the middle, and eight feet at either end. The whole of it is dug about twelve inches below the surface of the ground, and one half of it is covered over with willow branches, which probably serves as a bed for the whole family. A space in the middle of the other part, of about four feet wide, is deepened twelve inches more, and is the only spot in the house where a grown person can stand upright. One side of it is covered, as has been already described, and the other is the hearth or fireplace, of which, however, they do not make much use. Though it was close to the wall, the latter did not appear to be burned. The door or entrance is in the middle of one end of the house, and is about two feet and an half high and two feet wide, and has a covered way or porch five feet in length; so that it is absolutely necessary to creep on all fours in order to get into, or out of, this curious habitation. There is a hole of about eighteen inches square on the top of it, which serves the threefold purpose of a window, an occasional door, and a chimney.

The underground part of the floor is lined with split wood. Six or eight stumps of small trees driven into the earth, with the root upwards, on which are laid some cross pieces of timber, support the roof of the building, which is an oblong square of ten feet by six. The whole is made of driftwood covered with branches and dry grass; over which is laid a foot deep of earth. On each side of these houses are a few square holes in the ground of about two feet in depth, which are covered with split wood and earth, except in the middle. These appeared to be contrived for the preservation of the winter stock of provisions. In and about the houses we found sledge runners and bones, pieces of whalebone, and poplar bark cut in circles, which are used as corks to buoy the nets, and are fixed to them by pieces of whalebone. Before each hut a great number of stumps of trees were fixed in the ground, upon which it appeared that they hung their fish to dry.

We now continued our voyage, and encamped at eight o'clock. I calculated our course at about northwest, and, allowing for the windings, that we had made fifty-four miles. . . .

The discontents of our hunters were now renewed by the accounts which our guide had been giving of that part of our voyage that was approaching. According to his information, we were to see a larger lake on the morrow. Neither he nor his relations, he said, knew anything about it, except that part which is opposite to, and not far from, their country. The Esquimaux alone, he added, inhabit its shores, and kill a large fish that is found in it, which is a principal part of their food; this, we presumed, must be the whale. He also mentioned white bears and another large animal which was seen in those parts, but our hunters could not understand the description which he gave of it. He also represented their canoes as being of a large construction, which would commodiously contain four or five families. However, to reconcile the English Chief to the necessary continuance in my service, I presented him with one of my capots or traveling coats; at the same time, to satisfy the guide and keep him, if possible, in good humor, I gave him a skin of the moosedeer, which, in his opinion, was a valuable present.

Sunday 12. It rained with violence throughout the night, and till two in the morning; the weather continuing very cold. We proceeded on the same meandering course as yesterday, the wind north-northwest, and the country so naked that scarce a shrub was to be seen. At ten in the morning, we landed where there were four huts, exactly the same as those which have been so lately described. The adjacent land is high and covered with short grass and flowers, though the earth was not thawed above four inches from the surface; beneath which was a solid body of ice. This beautiful appearance, however, was strangely contrasted with the ice and snow that are seen in the valleys. The soil, where there is any, is a yellow clay mixed with stones. These huts appear to have been inhabited during the last winter; and we had reason to think that some of the natives had been lately there, as the beach was covered with the track of their feet. . . .

When we had satisfied our curiosity we reembarked, but we were at a loss what course to steer, as our guide seemed to be as ignorant of this country as ourselves. Though the current was very strong, we appeared to have come to the entrance of the lake. The stream set to the west, and we went with it to a high point at the distance of about eight miles which we conjectured to be an island; but, on approaching it, we perceived it to be connected with the shore by a low neck of land. I now took an observation which gave 69.1 north latitude. From the point that has been just mentioned we continued the same course for the westernmost point of a high island and the westernmost land in sight, at the distance of fifteen miles.

The lake was quite open to us to the westward, and out of the channel of the river there was not more than four feet water, and in some places the depth did not exceed one foot. From the shallowness of the water it was impossible to coast to the westward. At five o'clock we arrived at the island, and during the last fifteen miles five feet was the deepest water. The lake now appeared to be covered with ice for about two leagues distance, and no land ahead, so that we were prevented from proceeding in this direction by the ice and the shallowness of the water along the shore.

We landed at the boundary of our voyage in this direction, and as soon as the tents were pitched I ordered the nets to be set; when I proceeded with the English Chief to the highest part of the island, from which we discovered the solid ice extending from the southwest by compass to the eastward. As far as the eye could reach to the southwestward we could dimly perceive a chain of mountains, stretching further to the north than the edge of the ice, at the distance of upwards of twenty leagues. To the eastward we saw many islands, and in our progress we met with a considerable number of white partridges, now become brown. There were also flocks of very beautiful plovers, and I found the nest of one of them with four eggs. White owls, likewise, were among the inhabitants of the place. But the dead as well as the living demanded our attention, for we came to the grave of one of the natives, by which lay a bow, a paddle, and a spear. The Indians informed me that they landed on a small island about four leagues from hence where they had seen the tracks of two men that were quite fresh; they had also found a secret store of train oil [whale or fish oil], and several bones of white bears were scattered about the place where it was hid. The wind was now so high that it was impracticable for us to visit the nets.

My people could not, at this time, refrain from expressions of real concern that they were obliged to return without reaching the sea; indeed the hope of attaining this object encouraged them to bear, without repining, the hardships of our unremitting voyage. For some time past their spirits were animated by the expectation that another day would bring them to the *Mer d'ouest* [Western

Sea], and even in our present situation they declared their readiness to follow me wherever I should be pleased to lead them.

Journal of a Second Voyage

Chapter 2

.   .   .   .

The month of April [1793] being now past, in the early part of which I was most busily employed in trading with the Indians, I ordered our old canoes to be repaired with bark and added four new ones to them, when, with the furs and provisions I had purchased, six canoes were loaded and dispatched on the 8th of May for Fort Chipewyan. I had, however, retained six of the men who agreed to accompany me on my projected voyage of discovery. I also engaged my hunters, and closed the business of the year for the company by writing my public and private dispatches.

Having ascertained by various observations the latitude of this place [winter quarters on Peace River] to be 56.9 north, and longitude 117.35.15. west, on the 9th day of May . . . the canoe was put into the water: her dimensions were twenty-five feet long within, exclusive of the curves of stem and stern, twenty-six inches hold, and four feet nine inches beam. At the same time she was so light that two men could carry her on a good road three or four miles without resting. In this slender vessel we shipped provisions, goods for presents, arms, ammunition, and baggage to the weight of three thousand pounds, and an equipage of ten people. . . . With these persons I embarked at seven in the evening. My winter interpreter, with another person whom I left here to take care of the fort and supply the natives with ammunition during the summer, shed tears on the reflection of those dangers which we might encounter in our expedition, while my own people offered up their prayers that we might return in safety from it.

Chapter 3

Thursday 9 [*May*]. We began our voyage with a course south by west against a strong current one mile and three quarters, southwest by south one mile, and landed before eight on an island for the night.

Friday 10. The weather was clear and pleasant, though there was a keenness in the air; and at a quarter past three in the morning we continued our voyage, steering southwest three quarters of a mile, southwest by south one mile and a quarter, south three quarters of a mile. . . . The canoe being strained from its having been very heavily laden because so leaky that we were obliged to land, unload, and gum it. As this circumstance took place about twelve, I had an opportunity of taking an altitude, which made our latitude 55.58.48. . . .

From the place which we quitted this morning, the west side of the [Peace] river displayed a succession of the most beautiful scenery I had ever beheld. The ground rises at intervals to a considerable height and stretching inwards to a considerable distance; at every interval or pause in the rise there is a very gently ascending space or lawn, which is alternate with abrupt precipices to the summit of the whole, or, at least as far as the eye could distinguish. This magnificent theatre of nature has all the decorations which the trees and animals of the country can afford it: groves of poplars in every shape vary the scene, and their intervals are enlivened with vast herds of elks and buffaloes, the former choosing the steeps and uplands, and the latter preferring the plains. At this time the buffaloes were attended with their young ones who were frisking about them, and it appeared that the elks would soon exhibit the same enlivening circumstance. The whole country displayed an exuberant verdure; the trees that bear a blossom were advancing fast to that delightful appearance, and the velvet rind of their branches reflecting the oblique rays of a rising or setting sun added a splendid gaiety to the scene which no expressions of mine are qualified to describe. The east side of the river consists of a range of high land covered with the white spruce and the soft birch, while the banks abound with the alder and the willow. The water continued to rise, and the current being proportionably strong, we made a greater use of setting poles than paddles. . . .

Chapter [9]

· · · · · · · · ·

Thursday 18 [July]. . . . Salmon is so abundant in this river [the Fraser] that these people have a constant and plentiful supply of that excellent fish. To take them with more facility they had, with great labor, formed an embankment or weir across the river for the purpose of placing their fishing machines, which they disposed both above and below it. I expressed my wish to visit this extraordinary work, but these people are so superstitious that they would not allow me a nearer examination than I could obtain by viewing it from the bank. The river is about fifty yards in breadth, and by observing a man fish with a dipping net, I judged it to be about ten feet deep at the foot of the fall. The weir is a work of great labor and contrived with considerable ingenuity. It was near four feet above the level of the water at the time I saw it, and nearly the height of the bank on which I stood to examine it. The stream is stopped nearly two thirds by it. It is constructed by fixing small trees in the bed of the river in a slanting position (which could be practicable only when the water is much lower than I saw it) with the thick part downwards; over these is laid a bed of gravel, on which is placed a range of lesser trees, and so on alternately till the work is brought to its proper height. Beneath it the machines are placed, into which the salmon fall when they attempt to leap over. On either side there is a large frame of timber work six feet above the level of the upper water, in which passages are left for the salmon leading directly into the machines, which are taken up at pleasure. At the foot of the fall dipping nets are also successfully employed.

The water of this river is of the color of asses' milk, which I attributed in part to the limestone that in many places forms the bed of the river, but principally to the rivulets which fall from mountains of the same material. . . .

Chapter 11

· · · · · · · · ·

Saturday 20 [July]. We rose at a very early hour this morning, when I proposed to the Indians to run down our canoe or procure another at this place. To both these proposals they turned a deaf ear, as they imagined that I should be satisfied with having come in sight of the sea. Two of them peremptorily refused to proceed; but the other two having consented to continue with us, we obtained a larger canoe than our former one, and though it was in a leaky state, we were glad to possess it.

At about eight we got out of the river, which discharges itself by various channels into an arm of the sea [Strait of Georgia]. The tide was out and had left a large space covered with seaweed. The surrounding hills were involved in fog. The wind was at west, which was ahead of us, and very strong; the bay appearing to be from one to three miles in breadth. As we advanced along the land we saw a great number of sea otters. We fired several shots at them but without any success, from the rapidity with which they plunge under the water. We also saw many small porpoises or divers. The white-headed eagle, which is common in the interior parts, some small gulls, a dark bird which is inferior in size to the gull, and a few small ducks were all the birds which presented themselves to our view.

At two in the afternoon the swell was so high, and the wind, which was against us, so boisterous, that we could not proceed with our leaky vessel. We therefore landed in a small cove on the right side of the bay. Opposite to us appeared another small bay in the mouth of which is an island, and where, according to the information of the Indians, a river discharges itself that abounds in salmon. . . .

When we landed the tide was going out, and at a quarter past four it was ebb, the water having fallen in that short period eleven feet and one half. Since we left the river not a quarter of an hour had passed in which we did not see porpoises and sea otters. Soon after ten it was high water, which rendered it necessary that our baggage should be shifted several times, though not till some of the things had been wetted.

We were now reduced to the necessity of looking out for fresh water, with which we were plentifully supplied by the rills that ran down from the mountains.

When it was dark the young chief returned to us, bearing a large porcupine on his back. He first cut the animal open, and having disencumbered it of the entrails, threw them into the sea; he then singed its skin and boiled it in separate pieces, as our kettle was not sufficiently capacious to contain the whole; nor did he go to rest till, with the assistance of two of my people who happened to be awake, every morsel of it was devoured. . . .

Chapter 13

Saturday 24 [Aug.]. . . . At length, as we rounded a point and came in view of the Fort [on the Peace River] we threw out our flag and accompanied it with a general discharge of our firearms; while the men were in such spirits and made such an active use of their paddles that we arrived before the two men whom we left here in the spring could recover their senses to answer us. Thus we landed at four in the afternoon at the place which we left on the ninth of May.

Here my voyages of discovery terminate. Their toils and their dangers, their solicitudes and sufferings, have not been exaggerated in my description. On the contrary, in many instances language has failed me in the attempt to describe them. I received, however, the reward of my labors for they were crowned with success.

❧ IX ❧

Jefferson Sends Lewis and Clark
to Explore the Continent

O F all the exploring expeditions on the continent of North
America the journey of Lewis and Clark from St. Louis to
the Pacific in 1804–1806 stands out as the most extraordinary
venture of its kind. Carefully planned to the last minute detail, it
was highly successful, for the explorers carried out their mission
with precision, collected scientific data according to instruction,
made valuable geographical observations, and came back with
comprehensive reports that continue to fascinate readers. Among
other things accomplished, they established in the public mind a
new respect for the enormous extent of the continent and the
immense variations in the terrain.

The plan for this expedition originated in the fertile imagination
of Thomas Jefferson who for many years had been eager to send
explorers into the western country. As early as 1792 he had proposed to the American Philosophical Society in Philadelphia that
it send a scientific observer across the Mississippi to report on the
country, its flora and fauna, and its native peoples. Even earlier,
while serving as American minister in Paris, he had encountered
an adventurer named John Ledyard who proposed to cross Siberia, land on the west coast of North America, and proceed on
foot across the continent. In 1786 Jefferson had tried to get permission from the Russians for Ledyard to make the journey but
failed. Even so, Ledyard crossed Russia without any diplomatic
permission and got as far as eastern Siberia before he was captured
and deported.

The proposal to the American Philosophical Society was less

harebrained than Ledyard's scheme, but Jefferson was unfortunate in his choice of a scientist, for he nominated a Frenchman, André Michaux, who, he came to believe, was more interested in spying for France than in observing for the new United States.

But finally, in January 1803 Jefferson as president persuaded Congress to appropriate funds to send a scientific expedition across the continent to the Pacific. One of the objectives would be to find a water route to the western sea. Like many of his contemporaries, Jefferson dreamed of a series of rivers that would lead to a feasible portage over the mountains to a river that would take boats down to the sea. No one imagined that the Rocky Mountains stood as an impassable barrier and that a portage or a canal would be impossible. Jefferson also wanted to make contact with the western Indians and to negotiate a lasting peace that would prevent intertribal warfare and hostility to the United States. Furthermore, English traders had been swarming across the Canadian border and he wanted to establish trading posts that would insure to citizens of the United States a fair share of the Indian trade in the West. But in addition to political, geographical, and economic purposes, the expedition would make scientific observations and collect plant, animal, and mineral specimens.

When the expedition was planned, the purchase of Louisiana was not yet contemplated. It is true that Jefferson was greatly concerned about the free navigation of the Mississippi and was hoping to gain control of New Orleans. On April 18, 1802, he had written a famous letter to the American minister in Paris, Robert Livingston, which stated his views of the importance of the Mississippi for transportation of the products of the Ohio and upper Mississippi valleys. "There is on the globe one single spot, the possessor of which is our natural and habitual enemy," he wrote. "It is New Orleans, through which the produce of three-eighths of our territory must pass to market. . . . France, placing herself in that door, assumes to us the attitude of defiance. . . . The day that France takes possession of New Orleans . . . seals the union of two nations who in conjunction can maintain exclusive possession of the ocean. From that moment we must marry ourselves to the British fleet and nation." In short, Jefferson authorized Livingston to show the letter to Napoleon and to offer to buy New Orleans from France. Spain had controlled New Orleans and all of Louisiana since 1763, when France ceded the territory to

Spain to keep it from falling into the hands of the British, but by the secret treaty of San Ildefonso Napoleon in 1800 had forced Spain to return Louisiana to France. Jefferson was concerned lest France close the port of New Orleans to United States shipping.

When Livingston obtained no answer from Napoleon about the proposal to buy New Orleans, Jefferson sent James Monroe to Paris in March, 1803 to pursue the negotiations. Fortune favored the Americans, for Napoleon had recently lost two expeditionary forces in the West Indies and believed that the British might seize Louisiana. Faced with that possibility, he authorized his foreign minister, Talleyrand, to offer all of Louisiana to the American commissioners, who had the courage to close the deal without further authorization from Washington. They obtained the whole of Louisiana for some 15 million dollars. On June 20, 1803, about ten days before news of the purchase reached the United States, Jefferson completed plans for the exploration of the territory by Lewis and Clark. The acquisition of the vast territory gave greater urgency to the expedition. The Americans would now be exploring territory that their country owned.

To lead the expedition Jefferson appointed his private secretary, a young army captain named Meriwether Lewis. The President permitted Lewis to choose a friend, William Clark, to share the responsibility as joint commander. Clark was commissioned a second lieutenant of artillery but was known as "Captain Clark" and was coequal with Lewis throughout the expedition. Contrary to what might normally be expected, the two men got on well without the least friction. In fact, their skills complemented each other, for Lewis was better educated and a keener scientific observer than his colleague, while Clark was an excellent boatman, a shrewd judge and leader of men, and a wise negotiator with the Indians.

Beginning in the late summer of 1803, Lewis and Clark began to recruit and train personnel for the expedition. They chose a campsite on the east bank of the Mississippi a short distance above St. Louis and there during the autumn and winter they whipped the group into shape. The party consisted of fourteen regular soldiers, nine Kentucky woodsmen, two Frenchmen who knew the river, a French interpreter called Drewyer, and a stout black servant of Clark's named York. These were enlisted for the whole journey. In addition they had a corporal, six soldiers, and nine boatmen who were to go only as far as the Mandan villages on the upper Missouri. Thus the entire group numbered forty-five men. In the Mandan country, they later hired another French interpreter, named Toussaint Charbonneau, who brought along two wives, one of whom, named Sacajawea, was a Shoshone. Without her help the expedition might have failed, for she was able to communicate with her tribe when they reached the Rockies and were in dire need of assistance. Of this group, in the whole journey to the Pacific and back, they lost only one man, Sergeant Floyd, who died of what Clark described in his characteristic spelling as "Biliose Chorlick" [bilious colic].

To convey the party on the rivers they intended to use, they had a 55-foot keelboat, decked fore and aft, and two large pirogues —flat-bottomed batteaux, rowed by oars. The keelboat had 22 oars as well as a sail. At each end were mounted two small cannon called "swivel guns." Watertight lockers between the two decked areas of the keelboat made storage spaces for supplies and Indian trade goods (beads, knives, mirrors, bright cloth, blankets, flags and medals). The Great Father in Washington was sending to his children, at least to some of the chiefs, medals as tokens of his love. So carefully had they planned their space that lead canisters for gunpowder were designed to be melted down into bullets when empty. They carried relatively little food, for they planned to live off the country. Two horses for riders on the banks of the rivers were included for hunting and reconnoitering.

The expedition departed from the base camp on May 14, 1804, and headed up the Missouri River. At first they had considerable difficulty with the boats because of caving banks, snags, and submerged logs. At length, however, they grew skillful in manipulating the boats and made fairly good progress. In good weather with everything favorable they might cover as much as 20 miles upstream, but at other times they were lucky to do half as much.

They frequently saw Indians watching them from the riverbanks, and they made every effort to show their friendliness by giving them gifts and telling of the prosperous trade to come. Occasionally they encountered Indians who were surly but always they managed to avert trouble. Clark's black servant, York, proved of immense interest to the Indians, some of whom rubbed his skin to see if the black would come off. Indian women found him particularly attractive and Lewis commented that they appeared to want "to preserve among them some memorial of this wonderful stranger." Descendants of York may still survive on some of the reservations in the Northwest.

By November 1 the expedition reached the Mandan Indian settlement on the upper Missouri near the site of Bismarck, North Dakota; there they set to work to build cabins for their winter quarters. During the winter they received Indian delegations, engaged in buffalo hunts, and made dugout canoes from cottonwood trees for the rest of the journey. The keelboat was too heavy and bulky to go any farther upstream. When the spring thaw melted the ice in the river, Lewis and Clark sent back the keelboat loaded with specimens, and on April 7, 1805, the remainder of the party, now 32 people, set forth on their westward journey. By May they were in rugged mountain country and encountered their first grizzly bears, creatures they soon learned to respect and fear. They made ever slower progress with their boats and at last had to abandon the heavier of the pirogues, which they buried with some of their equipment against their return that way.

By early August they reached a point where no boat could go any farther by water. Cutting round circles out of cottonwood trees, they made crude wheels, attached them to some of their canoes, and with these contrivances dragged their supplies over mountain trails. They crossed the Continental Divide at Lemhi Pass, 40 or more miles west of the present town of Grant, Montana. Since streams were now flowing west, they began to search for the Columbia River; but they had many weary miles to travel over rough mountains before they reached any navigable stream, much less the Columbia. At last they encountered Shoshone Indians in the mountains of Idaho and, thanks to Sacajawea, bargained for 29 horses. They later bought nine more and made easier progress. Near Lewiston, Idaho, they found the Clearwater River, made dugouts from pine trees, and once more were waterborne. Following the Clearwater and then the Snake rivers, with some rough portages, they reached the Columbia River on October 16, 1805. Their horses were left with friendly Nez Percé Indians near Lewiston. Food had become a problem because game was scarce. They learned to subsist on roots, fish, and dog meat, which some of the party pronounced "sweet."

Floating down the Columbia, shooting the rapids, and surviving as best they could, they all arrived safely at the mouth of the river on November 19. Rain fell incessantly and they were cold, wet, hungry and miserable. Their stockade they named Fort Clatsop, the name of the local Indians. After a wet winter on the Pacific coast, they began their return journey up the Columbia on May 23, 1806, and by the end of June had cleared the worst of the mountains. The party divided into two groups. Lewis led one group to explore the Marias River valley. There he encountered a war party of Gros Ventre Indians, and in the first clash of the expedition they killed two warriors. Knowing that the Indians would soon be on their trail, they put spurs to their horses and raced to join the main party under Clark, which had followed the Yellowstone River to its confluence with the Missouri. With the expedition safely united, they entered their dugouts once more and made rapid progress downstream. As they floated down the Missouri, they met trappers coming upstream. Already the stories of the profits from beaver and other furs were attracting the daring and adventurous. Many of these trappers would become the "mountain men" who would open up new trails through the western mountains.

The expedition reached St. Louis on September 23, 1806, and both Lewis and Clark immediately dispatched letters to President Jefferson telling of the successful culmination of the journey. The President appointed Lewis governor of Louisiana Territory and made Clark superintendent of Indian affairs. In October 1809 Lewis left the Louisiana Territory to make a report to Washington; about 60 miles southwest of Nashville, at a tavern run by a man and his wife named Grinder, he either committed suicide or was murdered. Evidence seems to point to murder.

The Lewis and Clark Journals

[*Both Lewis and Clark kept detailed journals of the expedition. In addition, other literate members of the party were enjoined to keep journals. The original journals were deposited with the American Philosophical Society in Philadelphia. The first official report of the expedition was made to the Congress in a* Message from the President of the United States Communicating Discoveries Made . . . by Captains Lewis and Clark . . . Feb. 19, 1806. *Newspapers published accounts of the journey, and in 1807 a volume appeared in Pittsburgh called* A Journal of the Voyages and Travels of a Corps of Discovery . . . *based on a journal kept by Patrick Gass, one of the sergeants in the expedition, which had been carefuly edited by a schoolteacher. This account was reprinted in London in 1808, in Philadelphia in 1810, and was translated into French and published in Paris in 1810. It had a German edition in 1814.*

[*To provide a fuller and more authoritative account of the most important exploring expedition in the history of the country up to that time, President Jefferson encouraged Nicholas Biddle, a prominent Philadelphian and a man of letters, to compile an edition based on the journals kept by Lewis, Clark, and others, on deposit at the American Philosophical Society. Biddle began the work but was unable to finish it, and a poet and journalist, Paul Allen, completed the task. The work was published in two volumes at Philadelphia in 1814 with the title:* History of the Expedition under the Command of Captains Lewis and Clark to the Sources of the Missouri, Thence Across the Rocky Mountains and Down the River Columbia to the Pacific Ocean. Performed in the Years 1804-5-6. By Order of the Government of the United States. Prepared for the Press by Paul Allen, Esquire. *This version, generally known as the Biddle edition, was several times reprinted both at home and abroad and did much to spread information about the discoveries. Since it was the first official compilation from the journals, passages from it have been chosen for reproduction in the present volume.*

[*Various other editions of the journals have appeared. In 1893 an edition in four volumes was prepared by Elliot Coues with elaborate notes and a useful bibliography. The standard modern edition of the journals was compiled and edited from the original journals by Reuben G. Thwaites as* Original Journals of the Lewis and Clark Expedition, 1804–1806 (8 *vols., New York, 1904–05*). *A recent volume,* American Odyssey: The Journey of Lewis and Clark, *by Ingvard Henry Eide (New York, 1969), provides recent photographs of scenes that survive much as the original explorers saw them. Excerpts from the first Biddle edition follow:*]

Chapter 1

All the preparations being completed, we left our encampment on Monday, May 14th, 1804. This spot is at the mouth of Wood River, a small stream which empties itself into the Mississippi opposite to the entrance of the Missouri. It is situated in latitude 38° 55′ 19″ $\frac{6}{10}$ north, and longitude from Greenwich, 89° 57′ 45″. On both sides of the Mississippi the land for two or three miles is rich and level, but gradually swells into a high pleasant country with less timber on the western than on the eastern side but all susceptible of cultivation. The point which separates the two rivers on the north extends for fifteen or twenty miles, the greater part of which is an open level plain in which the people of the neighborhood cultivate what little grain they raise. Not being able to set sail before four o'clock P.M., we did not make more than four miles, and encamped on the first island opposite a small creek called Cold Water.

[*May 16.*] . . . We set sail at five o'clock. At the distance of a few miles we passed a remarkable large coal hill on the north side called by the French La Charbonniere, and arrived at the town of St. Charles. Here we remained a few days. . . .

Being joined by Captain Lewis, who had been detained by business at St. Louis, we again set sail on Monday, May 21st, in the afternoon, but were prevented by wind and rain from going more than about three miles. . . .

May 23. Two miles from our camp of last night we reached a river emptying itself on the north side called Osage Woman river. It is about thirty yards wide and has now a settlement of thirty or forty families from the United States. About a mile and a half beyond this is a large cave on the south side at the foot of cliffs nearly three hundred feet high overhanging the water, which becomes very swift at this place. The cave is one hundred and twenty feet wide, forty feet deep, and twenty high; it is known by the name of the Tavern among the traders who have written their names on the rock and painted some images which command the homage of the Indians and French. About a mile further we passed a small creek called Tavern creek, and encamped on the south side of the river, having gone nine miles. . . .

May 26. The wind being favorable we made eighteen miles today. . . . In the course of the day we met two canoes loaded with furs which had been two months on their route from the Mahar nation, residing more than seven hundred miles up the river—one large raft from the Pawnees on the river Platte, and three others from the Grand Osage river. . . .

May 31. In the afternoon a boat came down from the Grand Osage river bringing a letter from a person sent to the Osage nation on the Arkansaw river which mentioned that the letter announcing the cession of Louisiana was committed to the flames— that the Indians would not believe the Americans were owners of that country, and disregarded St. Louis and its supplies. . . .

Chapter 4

. . . .

Friday, [*October*] *19.* We set sail with a fine morning and a southeast wind, and at two and a half miles passed a creek on the north side. At eleven and a half miles we came to a lake or large pond on the same side in which were some swans. On both banks of the Missouri are low grounds which have much more timber than lower down the river. The hills are at one or two miles distance from the banks, and the streams which rise in them are brackish, and the mineral salts appear on the sides of the hills and edges of the runs. In walking along the shore we counted fifty-two herds of buffaloe and three of elk at a single view. Besides these we also observed elk, deer, pelicans, and wolves. After seventeen and a half miles we encamped on the north, opposite to the uppermost of a number of round hills forming a cone at the top, one being about ninety, another sixty feet in height, and some of less elevation. Our chief tells us that the calumet bird [golden eagle] lives in the holes formed by the filtration of the water from the top of these hills through the sides. Near to one of these moles, on a point of a hill ninety feet above the plain, are the remains of an old village which is high, strong, and has been fortified; this our chief tells us is the remains of one of the Mandan villages, and are the first ruins which we have seen of that nation in ascending the Missouri. Opposite to our camp is a deep bend to the south, at the extremity of which is a pond. . . .

Chapter 5

Saturday, October 27. At an early hour we proceeded and anchored off the village. Captain Clarke went on shore and, after smoking a pipe with the chiefs, was desired to remain and eat with them. He declined on account of his being unwell; but his refusal gave great offense to the Indians, who considered it disrespectful not to eat when invited, till the cause was explained to their satisfaction. We sent them some tobacco and then proceeded to the second village on the north, passing by a bank containing coal and a second village, and encamped at four miles on the north, opposite to a village of Ahnahaways. We here met with a Frenchman named Jesseaume who lives among the Indians with his wife and children, and who we take as an interpreter. The Indians had flocked to the bank to see us as we passed, and they visited in great numbers the camp, where some of them remained all night. We sent in the evening three young Indians with a present of tobacco for the chiefs of the three upper villages, inviting them to come down in the morning to a council with us. Accordingly the next day,

Sunday, October 28, we were joined by many of the Minnetarees and Ahnahaways from above, but the wind was so violent from the southwest that the chiefs of the lower villages could not come up, and the council was deferred till tomorrow. In the meanwhile we entertained our visitors by showing them what was new to them in the boat; all which, as well our black servant, they called "great medicine," the meaning of which we afterward learnt [see entry under August 17, 1805]. We also consulted the grand chief of the Mandans, Black Cat, and Mr. Jesseaume as to the names, characters, &c. of the chiefs with whom we are to hold the council. In the course of the day we received several presents from the women consisting of corn, boiled hominy, and garden stuffs; in our turn we gratified the wife of the great chief with a gift of a glazed earthen jar. Our hunter brought us two beaver. In the afternoon we sent the Minnetaree chiefs to smoke for us with the great chief of the Mandans, and told them we would speak in the morning.

Finding that we shall be obliged to pass the winter at this

place, we went up the river about one and a half miles today with a view of finding a convenient spot for a fort, but the timber was too scarce and small for our purposes.

Monday, October 29. . . . In the evening the prairie took fire, either by accident or design, and burned with great fury, the whole plain being enveloped in flames. So rapid was its progress that a man and a woman were burnt to death before they could reach a place of safety; another man with his wife and child were much burnt, and several other persons narrowly escaped destruction. Among the rest a boy of the half-white breed escaped unhurt in the midst of the flames. His safety was ascribed to the great medicine spirit, who had preserved him on account of his being white. But a much more natural cause was the presence of mind of his mother, who seeing no hopes of carrying off her son, threw him on the ground, and, covering him with the fresh hide of a buffaloe, escaped herself from the flames; as soon as the fire had passed, she returned and found him untouched, the skin having prevented the flame from reaching the grass on which he lay. . . .

Saturday, [November] 3. We now began the building of our cabins, and the Frenchmen who are to return to St. Louis are building a pirogue for the purpose. We sent six men in a pirogue to hunt down the river. We were also fortunate enough to engage in our service a Canadian Frenchman who had been with the Chayenne Indians on the Black mountains, and last summer descended thence by the Little Missouri. Mr. Jesseaume, our interpreter, also came down with his squaw and children to live at our camp. In the evening we received a visit from Kagohami or Little Raven, whose wife accompanied him, bringing about sixty weight of dried meat, a robe, and a pot of meal. We gave him in return a piece of tobacco, to his wife an axe and a few small articles, and both of them spent the night at our camp. Two beavers were caught in traps this morning.

Sunday 4. We continued our labors: the timber which we employ is large and heavy, and chiefly consists of cottonwood and elm with some ash of an inferior size. Great numbers of the Indians pass our camp on their hunting excursions. The day was clear and pleasant, but last night was very cold and there was a white frost.

Monday 5. The Indians are all out on their hunting parties. A camp of Mandans caught within two days one hundred goats a short distance below us. Their mode of hunting them is to form a large strong pen or fold, from which a fence made of bushes gradually widens on each side; the animals are surrounded by the hunters and gently driven toward this pen, in which they imperceptibly find themselves enclosed and are then at the mercy of the hunters. The weather is cloudy and the wind moderate from the northwest. Late at night we were awaked by the sergeant on guard to see the beautiful phenomenon called the northern light: along the northern sky was a large space occupied by a light of a pale but brilliant white color which, rising from the horizon, extended itself to nearly twenty degrees above it. After glittering for some time its colors would be overcast and almost obscured, but again it would burst out with renewed beauty; the uniform color was pale light but its shapes were various and fantastic: at times the sky was lined with light-colored streaks rising perpendicularly from the horizon and gradually expanding into a body of light in which we could trace the floating columns sometimes advancing, sometimes retreating, and shaping into infinite forms the space in which they moved. It all faded away before the morning. . . .

Thursday, [December] 27th. A little fine snow fell this morning and the air was colder than yesterday, with a high northwest wind. We were fortunate enough to have among our men a good blacksmith, whom we set to work to make a variety of articles. His operations seemed to surprise the Indians who came to see us, but nothing could equal their astonishment at the bellows, which they considered as a very great medicine.

Chapter 7

.   .   .   .

Thursday, [March] 28, [1805]. The day is fair. Some obstacle above has prevented the ice from running. Our canoes are now nearly ready, and we expect to set out as soon as the river is sufficiently clear to permit us to pass.

Friday 29. The weather clear and the wind from N. W. The obstruction above gave way this morning, and the ice came down in great quantities, the river having fallen eleven inches in the course of the last twenty-four hours. We have had few Indians at the fort for the last three or four days as they are now busy in catching the floating buffaloe. Every spring as the river is breaking up the surrounding plains are set on fire, and the buffaloe tempted to cross the river in search of the fresh grass which immediately succeeds to the burning; on their way they are often insulated on a large cake or mass of ice, which floats down the river. The Indians now select the most favorable points for attack, and, as the buffaloe approaches, dart with astonishing agility across the trembling ice, sometimes pressing lightly a cake of not more than two feet square. The animal is of course unsteady and his footsteps insecure on this new element, so that he can make but little resistance, and the hunter, who has given him his death wound, paddles his icy boat to the shore and secures his prey.

Saturday 30. The day was clear and pleasant, the wind N. W. and the ice running in great quantities. All our Indian presents were again exposed to the air, and the barge made ready to descend the Missouri.

Sunday 31. Early this morning it rained, and the weather continued cloudy during the day; the river rose nine inches, the ice not running so much as yesterday. Several flocks of geese and ducks fly up the river.

Monday, April 1, 1805. This morning there was a thunder storm, accompanied with large hail, to which succeeded rain for about half an hour. We availed ourselves of this interval to get all the boats in the water. At four o'clock P.M. it began to rain a second time and continued till twelve at night. With the exception of a few drops at two or three different times, this is the first rain we have had since the 15th of October last. . . .

Wednesday 3. The weather is pleasant, though there was a white frost and some ice on the edge of the water. We were all engaged in packing up our baggage and merchandise.

Thursday 4. The day is clear and pleasant, though the wind is high from N. W. We now packed up in different boxes a variety of articles for the President which we shall send in the barge. They consisted of a stuffed male and female antelope with their skeletons, a weasel, three squirrels from the Rocky Mountains, the skeleton of the prairie wolf, those of the white and gray hare, a male and female blaireau [badger] or burrowing dog of the prairie [prairie dog], with a skeleton of the female, two burrowing squirrels, a white weasel, and the skin of the louservia [*loup-cervier:* Canada lynx], the horns of the mountain ram, or big-horn, a pair of large elk horns, the horns and tail of the black-tailed deer, and a variety of skins, such as those of the red fox, white hare, marten, yellow bear, obtained from the Sioux; also, a number of articles of Indian dress, among which was a buffaloe robe representing a battle fought about eight years since between the Sioux and Ricaras against the Mandans and Minnetarees, in which the combatants are represented on horseback. . . .

Sunday, 7th. . . . Having made all our arrangements, we left the fort about five o'clock in the afternoon. The party now consisted of thirty-two persons. . . . The two interpreters were George Drewyer and Toussaint Chaboneau. The wife of Chaboneau also accompanied us with her young child, and we hope may be useful as an interpreter among the Snake [or Shoshonee] Indians. She was herself one of that tribe, but having been taken in war by the Minnetarees, by whom she was sold as a slave to Chaboneau, who brought her up and afterward married her. One of the Mandans likewise embarked with us in order to go to the Snake Indians and obtain a peace with them for his countrymen. All this party with the baggage was stowed in six small canoes and two large pirogues. We left the fort with fair pleasant weather though the northwest wind was high, and, after making about four miles, encamped on the north side of the Missouri nearly opposite the first Mandan village. At the same time that we took our departure our barge, manned with seven soldiers, two Frenchmen, and Mr. Gravelines as pilot, sailed for the United States loaded with our presents and dispatches. . . .

Chapter 15

Saturday, August 17. . . . On setting out at seven o'clock, Captain Clarke, with Chaboneau and his wife, walked on shore; but they had not gone more than a mile before Captain Clarke saw Sacajawea, who was with her husband one hundred yards ahead, began [sic] to dance and show every mark of the most extravagant joy, turning round him and pointing to several Indians, whom he now saw advancing on horseback, sucking her fingers at the same time to indicate that they were of her native tribe. As they advanced Captain Clarke discovered among them Drewyer dressed like an Indian, from whom he learnt the situation of the party. While the boats were performing the circuit he went toward the forks with the Indians who, as they went along, sang aloud with the greatest appearance of delight.

We soon drew near to the camp, and just as we approached it a woman made her way through the crowd toward Sacajawea, and, recognizing each other, they embraced with the most tender affection. The meeting of these two young women had in it something peculiarly touching, not only in the ardent manner in which their feelings were expressed, but from the real interest of their situation. They had been companions in childhood; in the war with the Minnetarees they had both been taken prisoners in the same battle; they had shared and softened the rigors of their captivity till one of them had escaped from the Minnetarees, with scarce a hope of ever seeing her friend relieved from the hands of her enemies.

While Sacajawea was renewing among the women the friendships of former days, Captain Clarke went on and was received by Captain Lewis and the chief, who, after the first embraces and salutations were over, conducted him to a sort of circular tent or shade of willows. Here he was seated on a white robe; and the chief immediately tied in his hair six small shells resembling pearls, an ornament highly valued by these people, who procured them in the course of trade from the seacoast. The moccasins of the whole party were then taken off, and after much ceremony the smoking began. After this the conference was to be opened, and, glad of an opportunity of being able to converse more intelligibly, Sacajawea was sent for.

She came into the tent, sat down, and was beginning to interpret when in the person of Cameahwait she recognized her brother. She instantly jumped up and ran and embraced him, throwing over him her blanket and weeping profusely. The chief was himself moved, though not in the same degree. After some conversation between them, she resumed her seat and attempted to interpret for us, but her new situation seemed to overpower her, and she was frequently interrupted by her tears. After the council was finished the unfortunate woman learnt that all her family were dead except two brothers, one of whom was absent, and a son of her eldest sister, a small boy who was immediately adopted by her.

The canoes arriving soon after, we formed a camp in a meadow on the left side a little below the forks, took out our baggage, and by means of our sails and willow poles formed a canopy for our Indian visitors. About four o'clock the chiefs and warriors were collected, and after the customary ceremony of taking off the moccasins and smoking a pipe, we expained to them in a long harangue the purposes of our visit, making themselves one conspicuous object of the good wishes of our government, on whose strength as well as its friendly disposition we expatiated. . . . In the meantime our first wish was that they should immediately collect as many horses as were necessary to transport our baggage to their village, where, at our leisure, we would trade with them for as many horses as they could spare.

The speech made a favorable impression. . . . The conference being ended to our satisfaction, we now inquired of Cameahwait what chiefs were among the party, and he pointed out two of them. We then distributed our presents. . . . They had indeed abundant sources of surprise in all they saw: the appearance of the men, their arms, their clothing, the canoes, the strange looks of the Negro, and the sagacity of our dog, all in turn shared their admiration, which was raised to astonishment by a shot from the airgun: this operation was instantly considered as a "great medicine" by which they as well as the other Indians mean something emanating directly from the Great Spirit, or produced by his invisible and incomprehensible agency. The display of all these riches had been intermixed with inquiries into the geographical situation of their country; for we had learnt by experience that to keep the savages in good temper their attention should not be wearied with too much business, but that the serious affairs should be enlivened by a mixture of what is new and entertaining. . . .

After the council was over, we consulted as to our future operations. The game does not promise to last here for a number of days, and this circumstance combined with many others to induce our going on as soon as possible. Our Indian information as to the state of the Columbia is of a very alarming kind, and our first object is of course to ascertain the practicability of descending it, of which the Indians discourage our expectations. It was therefore agreed that Captain Clarke should set off in the morning with eleven men furnished, besides their arms, with tools for making canoes; that he should take Chaboneau and his wife to the camp of the Shoshonees, where he was to leave them in order to hasten the collection of horses; that he was then to lead his men down to the Columbia, and if he found it navigable and the timber in sufficient quantity, begin to build canoes. As soon as he had decided as to the propriety of proceeding down the Columbia or across the mountains, he was to send back one of the men with information of it to Captain Lewis, who by that time would have brought up the whole party and the rest of the baggage as far as the Shoshonee village.

Preparations were accordingly made this evening for such an arrangement. The sun is excessively hot in the daytime, but the nights very cold and rendered still more unpleasant from the want of any fuel except willow brush. The appearances too of game, for many days' subsistence, are not very favorable. . . .

Chapter 17

[*Thursday, October 10, 1805*]. The country at the junction of the two rivers [the Clearwater and the Snake] is an open plain on all sides, broken toward the left by a distant ridge of highland thinly covered with timber: this is the only body of timber which the country possesses, for at the forks there is not a tree to be seen, and during almost the whole descent of sixty miles down the Kooskooskee [Clearwater] from its forks there are very few. This southern branch is in fact the main stream of Lewis's river [the Snake], on which we encamped when among the Shoshonees. The Indians inform us that it is navigable for sixty miles; that not far from its mouth it receives a branch from the south; and a second and larger branch, two days' march up and nearly parallel to the first Chopunnish [Nez Percé] villages, we met near the mountains. This branch is called Pawnashte, and is the residence of a chief who, according to their expression, has more horses than he can count. The river has many rapids near which are situated many fishing camps, there being ten establishments of this before reaching the first southern branch. . . .

At its mouth Lewis's river is about two hundred and fifty yards wide, and its water is of a greenish-blue color. The Kooskooskee, whose waters are clear as crystal, one hundred and fifty yards in width; and after the union the river enlarges to the space of three hundred yards. At the point of the union is an Indian cabin, and in Lewis's river a small island.

The Chopunnish or Pierced-nose nation, who reside on the Kooskooskee and Lewis's rivers, are in person stout, portly, well-looking men; the women are small, with good features and generally handsome, though the complexion of both sexes is darker than that of the Tushapaws. In dress they resemble that nation, being fond of displaying their ornaments. . . .

Volume II

Chapter 2

Wednesday, [October] 23, [1805]. Having ascertained from the Indians and by actual examination the best mode of bringing down the canoes, it was found necessary, as the river [Columbia] was divided into several narrow channels by rocks and islands, to follow the route adopted by the Indians themselves. This operation Captain Clarke began this morning, and, after crossing to the other side of the river, hauled the canoes over a point of land so as to avoid a perpendicular fall of twenty feet. At the distance of four hundred and fifty-seven yards we reached the water, and embarked at a place where a long rocky island compresses the channel of the river within the space of a hundred and fifty yards, so as to form nearly a semicircle. On leaving this rocky island the channel is somewhat wider, but a second and much larger island of hard black rock still divides it from the main stream, while on the left shore it is closely bordered by perpendicular rocks.

Having descended in this way for a mile, we reached a pitch of the river which, being divided by two large rocks, descends with great rapidity down a fall eight feet in height. As the boats could not be navigated down this steep descent, we were obliged to land and let them down as slowly as possible by strong ropes of elk skin which we had prepared for the purpose. They all passed in safety except one, which, being loosed by the breaking of the ropes, was driven down but was recovered by the Indians below. With this rapid ends the first pitch of the great falls, which is not great in point of height and remarkable only for the singular manner in which the rocks have divided its channel.

From the marks everywhere perceivable at the falls it is obvious that in high floods, which must be in the spring, the water below the falls rises nearly to a level with that above them. Of this rise, which is occasioned by some obstructions which we do not as yet know, the salmon must avail themselves to pass up the river in such multitudes that that fish is almost the only one caught in great abundance above the falls. But below that place we observe the salmon trout and the heads of a species of trout smaller than the salmon trout, which is in great quantities and which they are now burying to be used as their winter food. A hole of any size being dug, the sides and bottom are lined with straw, over which skins are laid: on these the fish, after being well dried, is laid, covered with other skins, and the hole closed with a layer of earth twelve or fifteen inches deep.

About three o'clock we reached the lower camp, but our joy at having accomplished this object was somewhat diminished by the persecution of a new acquaintance. On reaching the upper point of the portage we found that the Indians had been encamped there not long since and had left behind them multitudes of fleas. . . .

[*Thursday, October 24*]. . . . We landed at the huts of the Indians, who went with us to the top of this rock, from which we saw all the difficulties of the channel. We were no longer at a loss to account for the rising of the river at the falls, for this tremendous rock stretches across the river to meet the high hills of the left shore, leaving a channel of only forty-five yards wide [the Dalles of the Columbia River], through which the whole body of the Columbia must press its way. The water thus forced into so narrow a channel is thrown into whirls and swells and boils in every part with the wildest agitation. But the alternative of carrying the boats over this high rock was almost impossible in our present situation, and as the chief danger seemed to be not from any rocks in the channel, but from the great waves and whirlpools, we resolved to try the passage in our boats in hopes of being able by dexterous steering to escape. This we attempted and with great care were able to get through, to the astonishment of all the Indians of the huts we had just passed, who now collected to see us from the top of the rock.

The channel continues thus confined within a space of about half a mile, when the rock ceased. We passed a single Indian hut at the foot of it, where the river again enlarges itself to the width of two hundred yards, and at the distance of a mile and a half stopped to view a very bad rapid. This is formed by two rocky islands which divide the channel, the lower and larger of which is in the middle of the river. The appearance of this place was so unpromising that we unloaded all the most valuable articles, such as guns, ammunition, our papers, &c., and sent them by land with all the men that could not swim to the extremity of the rapids. We then descended with the canoes two at a time, and, though the canoes took in some water, we all went through safely; after which we made two miles, and stopped in a deep bend of the river toward the right, and encamped a little above a large village of twenty-one houses. Here we landed, and, as it was late before all the canoes joined us, we were obliged to remain here this evening, the difficulties of the navigation having permitted us to make only six miles. . . .

Chapter 4

.   .   .   .

Saturday [*November*] 23. The rain continued through the night, but the morning was calm and cloudy. The hunters were sent out and killed three deer, four brant, and three ducks. Toward evening seven Clatsops came over in a canoe with two skins of the sea otter. To this article they attach an extravagant value, and their demands for it were so high that we were fearful of reducing our small stock of merchandise, on which we must depend for subsistence as we return, to venture on purchasing. To ascertain however their ideas as to the value of different objects, we offered for one of the skins a watch, a handkerchief, an American dollar, and a bunch of red beads; but neither the curious mechanism of the watch nor even the red beads could tempt him; he refused the offer but asked for tiacomoshack or chief beads, the most common sort of coarse blue-colored beads, the article beyond all price in their estimation. Of these blue beads we have but few, and therefore reserve them for more necessitous circumstances.

Sunday 24. The morning being fair, we dried our wet articles and sent out the hunters, but they returned with only a single brant. In the evening a chief and several men of the Chinnooks came to see us; we smoked with them, and bought a sea-otter skin for some blue beads. Having now examined the coast, it becomes necessary to decide on the spot for our wintering quarters. The people of the country subsist chiefly on dried fish and roots, but of these there does not seem to be a sufficient quantity for our support, even were we able to purchase, and the extravagant prices as well as our small store of merchandise forbid us to depend on that resource. We must therefore rely for subsistence on our arms, and be guided in the choice of our residence by the abundance of game which any particular spot may offer.

The Indians say that the deer is most numerous at some distance above on the river, but that the country on the opposite side of the bay is better supplied with elk, an animal much larger and more easily killed than deer, with a skin better fitted for clothing, and the meat of which is more nutritive during the winter, when they are both poor. The climate too is obviously much milder here than above the first range of mountains, for the Indians are thinly clad, and say they have little snow; indeed since our arrival the weather has been very warm, and sometimes disagreeably so, and dressed as we are altogether in leather. . . .

Tuesday, [December] 3. The wind was from the east, and the morning fair; but, as if a whole day of fine weather was not permitted, toward night it began to rain. Even this transient glimpse of sunshine revived the spirits of the party, who were still more pleased when the elk killed yesterday was brought into camp. This was the first elk we had killed on the west side of the Rocky Mountains, and, condemned as we have been to the dried fish, forms a most nourishing food. After eating the marrow of the shank bones, the squaw chopped them fine and, by boiling, extracted a pint of grease superior to the tallow itself of the animal. . . .

Two of the hunters who set out yesterday had lost their way and did not return till this evening. They had seen in their ramble great signs of elk, and had killed six elk, which they had butchered and left at a great distance. A party [under Captain Lewis] was sent in the morning,

Wednesday, December 4, to carry the elk to a bay some distance below, to which place, if the weather permitted, we would all remove our camp this evening. But the rain which had continued during the night lasted all next day and was accompanied by so high a wind from the southeast and south that we dared not risk our canoes on the water. It was high water at eleven o'clock, when the spring tide rose two feet higher than the common flood tides. We passed the day around our fires, and as we are so situated that the smoke will not immediately leave the camp, we are very much incommoded and our eyes injured by it. No news has yet been received from Captain Lewis, and we begin to have much uneasiness for his safety.

Thursday, December 5. It rained during the whole night, and this morning the rain and high wind compelled us to remain at our camp. Besides the inconvenience of being thus stopped on our route, we now found that all our stores and bedding are again wet with rain. The high water was at twelve o'clock and rose two inches beyond that of yesterday. In the afternoon we were rejoiced at the return of Captain Lewis, who came in a canoe with three of his men, the other two being left to guard six elk and five deer which they had killed. He had examined the coast and found a river a short distance below on which we might encamp during the winter, with a sufficiency of elk for our subsistence within reach. This information was very satisfactory, and we decided on going thither as soon as we could move from the point; but all night and the following day,

Friday 6, it rained, and the wind blew hard from the southwest, so that the sea was still too rough for us to proceed. The high tide of today rose thirteen inches higher than it did yesterday, and obliged us to move our camp to a high situation. . . .

Sunday, [January] 5 [1806]. Two of the five men who had been dispatched to make salt returned. They had carefully examined the coast, but it was not till the fifth day after their departure that they discovered a convenient situation for their manufacture. At length they formed an establishment about fifteen miles southwest of the fort, near some scattered houses of the Clatsop and Killamuck nation, where they erected a comfortable camp and had killed a stock of provisions. The Indians had treated them very kindly, and made them a present of the blubber of the whale, some of which the men brought home. It was white and not unlike the fat of pork, though of a coarser and more spongy texture, and on being cooked was found to be tender and palatable and in flavor resembling the beaver.

The men also brought with them a gallon of the salt, which was white, fine, and very good, but not so strong as the rock salt common to the western parts of the United States. It proves to be a most agreeable addition to our food, and as the saltmakers can manufacture three or four quarts a day, we have a prospect of a very plentiful supply.

The appearance of the whale seemed to be a matter of importance to all the neighboring Indians, and as we might be able to procure some of it for ourselves, or at least purchase blubber from the Indians, a small parcel of merchandise was prepared and a party of the men held in readiness to set out in the morning. As soon as this resolution was known, Chaboneau and his wife requested that they might be permitted to accompany us. The poor woman stated very earnestly that she had traveled a great way with us to see the great water, yet she had never been down to the coast, and now that this monstrous fish was also to be seen, it seemed hard that she should not be permitted to see neither the ocean nor the whale. So reasonable a request could not be denied; they were therefore suffered to accompany Captain Clarke, who,

Monday 6, after an early breakfast set out with twelve men in two canoes. He proceeded down the Netul into Meriwether Bay [now Young's Bay], intending to go to the Clatsop town and there procure a guide through the creeks, which there was reason to believe communicated not only with the bay but with a small river running toward the sea, near where our saltmakers were encamped. Before, however, he could reach the Clatsop village, the high wind from the northwest compelled him to put into a small creek. He therefore resolved to attempt the passage without a guide, and proceeded up the creek three miles, to some high open land where he found a road. He therefore left the canoes and followed the path over three deep marshes to a pond about a mile long and two hundred yards wide.

He kept on the left of this pond, and at length came to the creek which he had crossed on a raft when he had visited Cuscalah's village on the ninth of December. He proceeded down it till he found a small canoe fit to hold three persons, in which the whole party crossed the creek. Here they saw a herd of elk, and the men were divided into small parties and hunted them till after dark, when they met again at the forks of the river. Three of the elk were wounded, but night prevented their taking more than one, which was brought to the camp and cooked with some sticks of pine which had drifted down the creeks. The weather was beautiful, the sky clear, the moon shone brightly, a circumstance the more agreeable as this is the first fair evening we have enjoyed for two months.

Chapter 8

Many reasons had determined us to remain at Fort Clatsop till the first of April. Besides the want of fuel in the Columbian plains, and the impracticability of passing the mountains before the beginning of June, we were anxious to see some of the foreign traders, from whom, by means of our ample letters of credit, we might have recruited our exhausted stores of merchandise. About the middle of March, however, we become seriously alarmed for the want of food: the elk, our chief dependence, had at length deserted their usual haunts in our neighborhood and retreated to the mountains. We were too poor to purchase other food from the Indians, so that we were sometimes reduced, notwithstanding all the exertions of our hunters, to a single day's provision in advance. The men too, whom the constant rains and confinement had rendered unhealthy, might we hoped be benefitted by leaving the coast and resuming the exercise of traveling. We therefore determined to leave Fort Clatsop, ascend the river slowly, consume the month of March in the woody country, where we hope to find subsistence, and in this way reach the plains about the first of April, before which time it will be impossible to attempt crossing them. For this purpose we began our preparations.

During the winter we had been very industrious in dressing skins, so that we now had a sufficient quantity of clothing, besides between three and four hundred pair of moccasins. But the whole stock of goods on which we are to depend, either for the purchase of horses or of food, during the long tour of nearly four thousand miles, is so much diminished that it might all be tied in two handkerchiefs. We have in fact nothing but six blue robes, one of scarlet, a coat and hat of the United States artillery uniform, five robes made of our large flag, and a few old clothes trimmed with riband. We therefore feel that our chief dependence must be on our guns, which fortunately for us are all in good order as we had taken the precaution of bringing a number of extra locks, and one of our men proved to be an excellent artist in that way. The powder had been secured in leaden canisters, and, though on many occasions they had been under water, it remained perfectly dry, and we now found ourselves in possession of one hundred and forty pounds of powder and twice that quantity of lead, a stock quite sufficient for the route homeward.

After much trafficking we at last succeeded in purchasing a canoe for a uniform coat and half a carrot [a twisted bundle of tobacco leaves] of tobacco, and took a canoe from the Clatsops as a reprisal for some elk which some of them had stolen from us in the winter. We were now ready to leave Fort Clatsop, but the rain prevented us for several days from caulking the canoes, and we were forced to wait for calm weather before we could attempt to pass Point William [Tongue Point, Oregon]. In the meantime we were visited by many of our neighbors for the purpose of taking leave of us. The Clatsop Commowool has been the most kind and hospitable of all the Indians in this quarter: we therefore gave him a certificate of the kindness and attention which we had received from him, and added a more substantial proof of our gratitude, the gift of all our houses and furniture. To the Chinnook chief Delashelwilt we gave a certificate of the same kind. We also circulated among the natives several papers, one of which we also posted up in the fort, to the following effect:

"The object of this last is that through the medium of some civilized person who may see the same, it may be made known to the world that the party consisting of the persons whose names are hereunto annexed, and who were sent out by the government of the United States to explore the interior of the continent of North America, did penetrate the same by the way of the Missouri and Columbia rivers, to the discharge of the latter into the Pacific ocean, where they arrived on the 14th day of November 1805, and departed the 23rd day of March, 1806, on their return to the United States, by the same route by which they had come out."

On the back of some of these papers we sketched the connection of the upper branches of the Missouri and Columbia rivers with our route and the track which we intended to follow on our return. This memorandum was all that we deemed it necessary to make; for there seemed but little chance that any detailed report to our government, which we might leave in the hands of the savages to be delivered to foreign traders, would ever reach the United States. To leave any of our men here, in hopes of their procuring a passage home in some transient vessel, would too much weaken our party, which we must necessarily divide during our route; besides that, we will most probably be there ourselves sooner than any trader, who, after spending the next summer here, might go on some circuitous voyage.

The rains and wind still confined us to the fort; but at last our provisions dwindled down to a single day's stock, and it became absolutely necessary to remove. We therefore sent a few hunters ahead, and stopped the boats as well as we could with mud. The next morning,

Sunday, March 23, 1806, the canoes were loaded, and at one o'clock in the afternoon we took a final leave of Fort Clatsop. . . .

Monday, March 24. . . . On resuming our route among the seal islands we mistook our way, which an Indian observing, he pursued us and put us into the right channel [of the Columbia]. He soon, however, embarrassed us by claiming the canoe we had taken from the Clatsops, and which he declared was his property; we had found it among the Clatsops and seized it as a reprisal for a theft committed by that nation; but being unwilling to do an act of injustice to this Indian, and having no time to discuss the question of right, we compromised with him for an elk skin, with which he returned perfectly satisfied. . . .

Chapter 12

.   .   .   .

Wednesday, [May] 14. After sending out some hunters, [we] transported the baggage by means of the canoe, and then drove our horses into the river, over which they swam without accident, although it is one hundred and fifty yards wide, and the current very rapid. We then descended the river about half a mile, and formed our camp on the spot which the Indians had recommended. It was about forty paces from the river, and formerly an Indian habitation; but nothing remained at present but a circle thirty yards in diameter, sunk in the ground about four feet, with a wall round it of nearly three and a half feet in height. In this place we deposited our baggage, and round its edges formed our tents of sticks and grass.

This situation is in many respects advantageous. It is an extensive level bottom, thinly covered with long-leafed pine, with a rich soil, affording excellent pasture, and supplied, as well as the high and broken hills on the east and northeast, with the best game in the neighborhood; while its vicinity to the river makes it convenient for the salmon, which are now expected daily.

As soon as we had encamped, Tunnachemcotoolt and Hohastilpilp, with about twelve of their nation, came to the opposite side and began to sing, this being the usual token of friendship on similar occasions. We sent the canoe for them, and the two chiefs came over with several of the party, among whom were the two young men who had given us the two horses in behalf of the nation. After smoking some time, Hohastilpilp presented to Captain Lewis an elegant gray gelding, which he had brought for the purpose, and was perfectly satisfied at receiving in return a handkerchief, two hundred balls, and four pounds of powder.

The hunters killed some pheasants, two squirrels, and a male and a female bear, the first of which was large and fat and of a bay color; the second meagre, grisly, and of smaller size. They were of the species common to the upper part of the Missouri, and might well be termed the variegated bear, for they are found occasionally of a black, grisly brown, or red color. There is every reason to believe them to be of precisely the same species. Those of different colors are killed together, as in the case of these two, and as we found the white and bay associated together on the Missouri, and some nearly white were seen in this neighborhood by the hunters. Indeed, it is not common to find any two bears of the same color, and if the difference in color were to constitute a distinction of species, the number would increase to almost twenty. Soon after, they killed a female bear with two cubs. The mother was black, with a considerable intermixture of white hairs and a white spot on the breast. One of the cubs was jet black, and the other of a light reddish brown, or bay color. . . .

A large part of the meat we gave to the Indians, to whom it was a real luxury, as they scarcely taste flesh once in a month. They immediately prepared a large fire of dried wood, on which were thrown a number of smooth stones from the river. As soon as the fire went down and the stones were heated, they were laid next to each other, in a level position, and covered with a quantity of branches of pine on which were placed flitches [strips] of the bear, and thus placing the boughs and flesh alternately for several courses, leaving a thick layer of pine on the top. On this heap was then poured a small quantity of water, and the whole covered with earth to the depth of four inches. After remaining in this state about three hours the meat was taken off, and was really more tender than that which we had boiled or roasted, though the strong flavor of the pine rendered it disagreeable to our palates. This repast gave them much satisfaction, for though they sometimes kill the black bear, yet they attack very reluctantly the furious variegated bear, and only when they can pursue him on horseback through the plains and shoot him with arrows. . . .

Chapter 19

. . . .

Monday, September 1. We set out early, but were shortly compelled to put to shore for half an hour till a thick fog disappeared. At nine o'clock we passed the entrance of the Quicurre [the Niobrara], which presents the same appearance as when we ascended, the water rapid and of a milky-white color. . . .

The bottom on the northeast side is very rich, and so thickly overgrown with pea vines and grass, interwoven with grapevines, that some of the party who attempted to hunt there were obliged to leave it and ascend the plain, where they found the grass nearly as high as their heads. These plains are much richer below than above the Quicurre, and the whole country is now very beautiful. After making fifty-two miles against a headwind, we stopped for the night on a sandbar opposite to the Calumet bluff where we had encamped on the first of September, 1804, and where our flagstaff was still standing. We suffered very much from the mosquitoes till the wind became so high as to blow them all away.

Tuesday, 2. At eight o'clock we passed the river Jacques [James River, South Dakota] but soon after were compelled to land in consequence of the high wind from the northeast, and remain till sunset; after which we went on to a sandbar twenty-two miles from our camp of last evening. Whilst we were on shore we killed three buffaloes and four prairie fowls, which are the first we have seen in descending. Two turkies were also killed and were very much admired by the Indians, who had never seen that animal before. The plains continue level and fertile, and in the low grounds there is much white oak and some white ash in the ravines and high bottoms, with lyn [linden] and slippery elm occasionally. During the night the wind shifted to the southwest and blew the sand over us in such a manner that our situation was very unpleasant. It lulled, however, toward daylight, and we then,

Wednesday, 3, proceeded. At eleven o'clock we passed the Redstone. The river is now crowded with sandbars, which are very differently situated now from what they were when we ascended. But notwithstanding these and the head wind, we made sixty miles before night, when we saw two boats and several men on shore. We landed, and found a Mr. James Airs, a partner of a house at Prairie de Chien, who had come from Mackinau by the way of Prairie de Chien and St. Louis with a license to trade among the Sioux for one year. He had brought two canoes loaded with merchandise but lost many of his most useful articles in a squall some time since. After so long an interval the sight of anyone who could give us information of our country was peculiarly delightful, and much of the night was spent in making inquiries into what had occurred during our absence. . . .

Thursday, 4, we left Mr. Airs about eight o'clock, and, after passing the Big Sioux river, stopped at noon near Floyd's bluff [near Sioux City, Iowa]. On ascending the hill we found that the grave of Floyd had been opened, and was now half uncovered. We filled it up and then continued down to our old camp near the Maha village, where all our baggage, which had been wet by the rain of last night, was exposed to dry. There is no game on the river except wild geese and pelicans. Near Floyd's grave are some flourishing black walnut trees, which are the first we have seen on our return. . . .

Tuesday, 16. We set out at an early hour, but the weather soon became so warm that the men rowed but little. In the course of the day we met two trading parties on their way to the Pawnees and Mahas, and, after making fifty-two miles, remained on an island till next morning,

Wednesday, 17, when we passed in safety the island of the Little Osage village. This place is considered by the navigators of the Missouri as the most dangerous part of it, the whole water being compressed, for two miles, within a narrow channel crowded with timber into which the violence of the current is constantly washing the banks. At the distance of thirty miles we met a Captain M'Clellan, lately of the United States' army, with whom we encamped. He informed us that the general opinion in the United States was that we were lost, the last accounts which had been heard of us being from the Mandan villages. Captain M'Clellan is on his way to attempt a new trade with the Indians. . . .

Thursday, 18. We parted with Captain M'Clellan, and within a few miles passed the Grand river [in Missouri], below which we overtook the hunters who had been sent forward yesterday afternoon. They had not been able to kill anything, nor did we see any game except one bear and three turkies, so that our whole stock of provisions is one biscuit for each person; but as there is an abundance of papaws the men are perfectly contented. The current of the river is more gentle than it was when we ascended, the water being lower though still rapid in places where it is confined. We continued to pass through a very fine country, for fifty-two miles, when we encamped nearly opposite to Mine river [where it empties into the Missouri near Booneville, Missouri]. The next morning,

Friday, 19, we worked our oars all day without taking time to hunt, or even landing except once to gather papaws; and at eight o'clock reached the entrance of the Osage river, a distance of seventy-two miles. Several of the party have been for a day or two attacked with a soreness in the eyes, the eyeball being very much swelled and the lid appearing as if burnt by the sun and extremely painful, particularly when exposed to the light. Three of the men are so much affected by it as to be unable to row. We therefore turned one of the boats adrift, and distributed the men among the other canoes when we set out a little before daybreak,

Saturday, 20. The Osage is at this time low and discharges but a very small quantity of water. Near the mouth of Gasconade, where we arrived at noon, we met five Frenchmen on their way to the Great Osage village. As we moved along rapidly we saw on the banks some cows feeding, and the whole party almost involuntarily raised a shout of joy at seeing this image of civilization and domestic life.

Soon after, we reached the little French village of La Charette [village on the Missouri near St. Louis], which we saluted with a discharge of four guns and three hearty cheers. We then landed and were received with kindness by the inhabitants, as well as some traders from Canada who were going to traffic with the Osages and Otoes. They were all equally surprised and pleased at our arrival, for they had long since abandoned all hopes of ever seeing us return.

These Canadians have boats prepared for the navigation of the Missouri which seem better calculated for the purpose than those in any other form. They are in the shape of batteaux, about thirty feet long and eight wide, the bow and stern pointed, the bottom flat, and carrying six oars only; and their chief advantage is their width and flatness, which saves them from the danger of rolling sands.

Having come sixty-eight miles, and the weather threatening to be bad, we remained at La Charette till the next morning,

Sunday, 21, when we proceeded, and, as several settlements have been made during our absence, were refreshed with the sight of men and cattle along the banks. We also passed twelve canoes of Kickapoo Indians going on a hunting excursion. At length, after coming forty-eight miles, we saluted, with heartfelt satisfaction, the village of St. Charles [northwest of St. Louis], and on landing were treated with the greatest hospitality and kindness by all the inhabitants of that place. Their civility detained us till ten o'clock the next morning,

Monday, 22, when, the rain having ceased, we set out for Cold-water creek about three miles from the mouth of the Missouri,

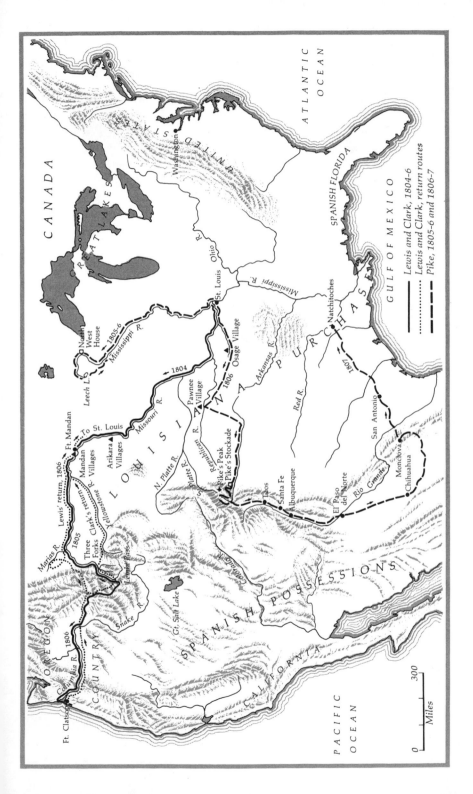

Probing Westward: Lewis and Clark, and Zebulon Pike

where we found a cantonment of troops of the United States, with whom we passed the day, and then,

Tuesday, 23, descended to the Mississippi and round to St. Louis, where we arrived at twelve o'clock and, having fired a salute, went on shore and received the heartiest and most hospitable welcome from the whole village.

X

New Ventures
into the Great West

LEWIS and Cark blazed a trail across the American continent, and the narratives of their adventures excited American imaginations. Land-hungry Easterners and adventurous men of all types began to dream of careers in the western country they had described. As we have seen, Lewis and Clark on their way back to St. Louis met trappers and traders heading for the Indian country. Men were impatient to snatch the riches from trade in virgin territory. For decades to come trappers, traders, hunters, and eventually homesteaders would swarm from St. Louis and other staging areas along the Mississippi until they had penetrated even the most desolate and rugged regions of the West.

While Lewis and Clark were struggling toward the Pacific, another explorer, a brash young army lieutenant named Zebulon Pike, led an expedition seeking the headwaters of the Mississippi. Leaving St. Louis in the late summer of 1805, Pike spent the winter in Minnesota, where he made contact with northern Indians and British traders. He came back with an inaccurate report of the sources of the Mississippi.

Soon Pike was busy organizing another expedition. He had received orders from General James Wilkinson, then military commander in Louisiana, to explore the Southwest. Wilkinson was a scoundrel who had long plotted to separate the West into a new nation. Whether he hoped to use Pike's discoveries for some scheme of his own, one can only conjecture. Less than two months before the return of Lewis and Clark, Pike, on July 15, 1806, led an exploring party from St. Louis on an expedition that took him across the plains into present-day Colorado, New Mexico, northeastern Mexico, Texas, and thence to Louisiana. The journey to Mexico was involuntary, for he was apprehended on the Rio Grande by Spanish forces, taken to Santa Fe and thence to Chihuahua for questioning.

In 1810 Pike published in Philadelphia a narrative of his explorations with a title long enough to symbolize the extent of his journeys: *An Account of Expeditions to the Sources of the Mississippi, and Through the Western Parts of Louisiana to the Sources of the Arkansaw, Kans, La Platte, and Pierre Jaun Rivers; Performed by Order of the Government of the United States During the Years 1805, 1806, and 1807. And a Tour Through the Interior Parts of New Spain When Conducted Through These Provinces by Order of the Captain-General in the Year 1807.* By Major Z. M. Pike.

As a woodsman and an explorer Pike was untrained and inept. Lacking even the elementary knowledge that frontiersmen needed, he reveals in his journals a hasty, impetuous character that ill-suited the task before him. On both of his expeditions his men were miserably equipped and poorly led.

Pike's western expedition, however, accomplished more than the previous journey to Minnesota; he penetrated unknown country, and his account of the trek, printed before the public had had an opportunity to read in detail of Lewis and Clark's discoveries, described an exciting new region. His book was published in England the year after its appearance in Philadelphia and was quickly translated into French, Dutch, and German. His revelation of the potentialities of trade with the Spanish settlements in New Mexico did much to stimulate interest in Santa Fe and contributed to the subsequent development of the Santa Fe trade.

Pike had orders to conduct a group of Indians back to their villages on the upper Missouri and Osage rivers. These included Osage and Pawnee chiefs who had been on a mission to Washington and some Osages who had been redeemed from captivity among the Potawatomis. After negotiating peace treaties among various western tribes, he was to explore the Arkansas and Red rivers, return down the Red River and report to the American outpost at Natchitoches in what is now the state of Louisiana. Interest in this region was acute. Two previous expeditions—one led by

William Dunbar and John Hunter, the other by Thomas Freeman —had tried but failed to reach the sources of the Arkansas and Red Rivers because they had been turned back by Spanish forces. Accordingly, Pike's instructions warned him to "move with great circumspection" when he approached the borders of New Mexico to avoid any clash with the Spaniards.

When Pike left St. Louis for the Southwest he had a command of 21 men and a volunteer surgeon, Dr. John H. Robinson. His second in command, Lieutenant John B. Wilkinson, was to lead a detachment down the Arkansas after they had completed their exploration of the sources of the rivers. The Indians in the party, including women and children, numbered 51.

After delivering the Osages to their villages and the Pawnee chiefs to their habitations on the Republican River, Pike and his men turned south and followed the Arkansas beyond the Great Bend to the Rockies in what is now Colorado. Establishing a camp near Pueblo, Pike made side trips into the Colorado mountains. He discovered but was unable to climb the peak that now bears his name, for by this time it was late November and snow was falling. Nevertheless, with more fortitude than wisdom, Pike pushed on through the mountains in the dead of winter and early in February moved into New Mexico and built a cottonwood stockade on a branch of the Rio Grande. If he knew he had entered Spanish territory, he did not admit it and maintained that he was still within the borders of the United States.

The Spanish authorities at Santa Fe soon heard about him and sent a detachment of 100 cavalrymen to investigate. The upshot was that Pike and his men were conducted to Santa Fe and questioned; later the Spaniards sent them to Chihuahua for further investigation. Although Pike blustered and declared that, if he had strayed into Spanish territory, he had done it inadvertently, he could not convince the Spaniards that his party was concerned only with collecting scientific and geographical information. To the Spaniards he and his party were spies, and, though the Spaniards treated the Americans with courtesy, they did not relax their vigilance. Furthermore, they confiscated all of Pike's papers except a few personal letters and his journal, which he succeeded in hiding. The papers and drawings remained in Mexican archives for more than a century until they were discovered by an American historian and returned to the United States.

Pike's Journal

[*Pike's journal of his winter travels through the Colorado mountains is a narrative of incredible—and unnecessary—hardships.
Ill-clothed and ill-supplied for winter exploration, he and his men
nearly froze and frequently were on the verge of starvation when
game failed them. The most interesting portion of the journal
describes his experiences after he made contact with the Spaniards
in New Mexico and was conducted by his host-captors across
northeastern Mexico and Texas to the Louisiana border. The route
led from Chihuahua southeasterly through the province of Du-
rango by the village of Mapimi, somewhat north of the present
city of Torreon and the towns of Parras de la Fuentes and Saltillo.
Taking a northeasterly road in Nuevo León not far from Mon-
terrey, the party entered Texas in the vicinity of Laredo and followed a trail that took them south of San Antonio and the site
of Austin to Nacogdoches, Texas. From there it was a relatively
easy journey across the Sabine River into Louisiana and thence
to Natchitoches. A few excerpts from Pike's journal will indicate
the nature of his commentary:*]

1st April [1807], *Wednesday.* In the morning Malgares [the
Spanish officer then in command of Pike's escort] dispatched a
courier with a letter to the commandant general Salcedo to inform
him of our approach and also one to his father-in-law.

2d April, Thursday. When we arrived at Chihuahua we pursued
our course through the town to the house of the general. I was
much astonished to see with what anxiety Malgares anticipated
the meeting with his military chief; after having been on the
most arduous and enterprising expedition ever undertaken by
any of His Majesty's officers from these provinces and having
executed it with equal spirit and judgment, yet was he fearful
of his meeting him with an eye of displeasure, and appeared to
be much more agitated than ourselves, although we may be
supposed to have also had our sensations, as on the will of this
man depended our future destiny, at least until our country could
interfere in our behalf. On our arrival at the general's we were

halted in the hall of the guard until word was sent to the general of our arrival, when Malgares was first introduced, who remained some time, during which a Frenchman came up and endeavored to enter into conversation with us but was soon frowned into silence as we conceived he was only some authorized spy. Malgares at last came out and asked me to walk in. I found the general sitting at his desk; he was a middle-sized man, apparently about fifty-five years of age, with a stern countenance, but he received me graciously and beckoned to a seat. He then observed, "You have given us and yourself a great deal of trouble."

Captain Pike: "On my part entirely unsought, and on that of the Spanish government voluntary."

General: "Where are your papers?"

Captain Pike: "Under charge of Lieutenant Malgares," who was then ordered to have my small trunk brought in; which being done, a Lieutenant Walker came in, who is a native of New Orleans, his father an Englishman, his mother a French woman, and spoke both those languages equally well, also the Spanish. . . . This same young gentleman was employed by Mr. Andrew Ellicott as a deputy surveyor on the Florida line between the United States and Spain in the years '97 and '98. General Salcedo then desired him to assist me in taking out my papers. . . .

28th April, Tuesday. In the morning Malgares waited on us and informed us he was to accompany us some distance on the route. After bidding adieu to all our friends, marched at a quarter past three o'clock and encamped at nine o'clock at night at a spring—stony—passed near Chihuahua a small ridge of mountains, and there encamped in a hollow.

This day as we were riding along, Malgares rode up to me and informed me that the general had given orders that I should not be permitted to make any astronomical observations. To this I replied that he well knew I never had attempted making any since I was conducted into the Spanish dominions.

29th April, Wednesday. Arrived at a settlement at eight o'clock —plenty of milk, &c. When about to make my journal Malgares changed color and informed me it was his orders I should not take notes, but added, "You have a good memory, and when you get to Cogquilla you can bring it all up." At first I felt considerably indignant and was on the point of refusing to comply; but thinking for a moment of the many politenesses I had received from his hands, induced me merely to bow assent with a smile, and we proceeded on our route, but had not proceeded far before I made a pretext to halt—established my boy as a vedette, and sat down peaceably under a bush and made my notes, &c. This course I pursued ever after, not without some very considerable degree of trouble to separate myself from the party. . . .

30th April, Thursday. Marched at six o'clock, and at eleven arrived at the river Conchos 24 miles—beautiful green trees on its banks. I was taken very sick at half past ten o'clock.

Arrived at night at a small station on the river Conchos, garrisoned by a sergeant and ten men from the Fort Conchos, fifteen leagues up said river. Distance 43 miles.

1st May, Friday. Marched up the Conchos to its confluence with the river Florada, 15 leagues from where we left the former river, and took up the latter, which bears from the Conchos S. 80° and 50° E. On its banks are some very flourishing settlements, and they are well-timbered. A poor miserable village at the confluence. . . . Came ten miles up the Florada to dinner and at night stopped at a private house. This property or plantation was valued formerly at 300,000 dollars, extending on the Florada from the small place we slept at on the last of April 30 leagues up said river. Distance 45 miles.

Finding that a new species of discipline had taken place, and that the suspicions of my friend Malgares were much more acute than ever, I conceived it necessary to take some steps to secure the notes I had taken, which were clandestinely acquired. In the night I arose, and after making my men charge all their pieces well, I took my small books and rolled them up in small rolls, and tore a fine shirt to pieces and wrapped it round the papers and put them down in the barrels of the guns until we just left room for the tampions, which were then carefully put in; the remainder we secured about our bodies under our shirts. This occupied about two hours, but was effected without discovery and without suspicions. . . .

9th May, Saturday. Marched between four and five o'clock and arrived at Pelia at eight. This is only a station for a few soldiers, but is surrounded by mines. At this place are two large warm springs, strongly impregnated with sulphur, and this is the water

obliged to be used by the party who are stationed there. Here
we remained all day. Captain Barelo had two beeves killed for
his and my men and charged nothing to either. Here he received
orders from the general to lead us through the wilderness to
Montelovez, in order that we should not approximate to the
frontiers of Mexico, which we should have done by the usual
route of Pattos, Paras, &c.

10th May, Sunday. Marched past one copper mine now diligently worked. At this place the proprietor had 100,000 sheep,
cattle, horses, &c. Arrived at the Cadena, a house built and
occupied by a priest. It is situated on a small stream at the pass
of the mountains called by the Spaniards the Door of the Prison,
from its being surrounded with mountains. The proprietor was
at Sumbraretto, distant six days march. This hacienda was obliged
to furnish accommodations to all travelers.

Marched at five o'clock and passed the chain of mountains due
east 12 miles, and encamped without water. Distance 31 miles.

11th May, Monday. Marched and arrived at Maupemie [Ma-
pimi] at eight o'clock, a village situated at the foot of mountains
of minerals where they worked eight or nine mines. The mass of
the people were naked and starved wretches. The proprietor of
the mines gave us an elegant repast. Here the orders of Salcedo
were explained to me by the captain. I replied that they excited
my laughter as there were disaffected persons sufficient to serve
as guides should an army ever come into the country.

Came on three miles further, where were fig trees and a fruit
called by the French La Grain, situated on a little stream which
flowed through the gardens and formed a terrestrial paradise.
Here we remained all day sleeping in the shade of the fig trees
and at night continued our residence in the garden. We obliged
the inhabitants with a ball, who expressed great anxiety for a
relief from their present distressed state and a change of government.

12th May, Tuesday. Was awoke in the morning by the singing
of the birds and the perfumes of the trees around. I attempted to
send two of my soldiers to town, when they were overtaken by
a dragoon and ordered back—they returned, when I again ordered
them to go and if a soldier attempted to stop them to take him
off his horse and flog him. This I did as I conceived it was the

duty of the captain to explain his orders relative to me, which he had not done, and I conceived that this would bring on an explanation. They were pursued by a dragoon through the town, who rode after them making use of ill language. They attempted to catch him but could not. As I had mentioned my intentions of sending my men to town after some stores to Captain Barelo, and he had not made any objections, I conceived it was acting with duplicity to send men to watch the movements of my messengers; I therefore determined they should punish the dragoons unless their captain had candor sufficient to explain the reasons for his not wishing the men to go to the town, in which wish I should undoubtedly have acquiesced; but as he never mentioned the circumstance I was guardedly silent, and the affair never interrupted our harmony.

We marched at five o'clock and came on 15 miles and encamped without water. One mile on this side of the little village the road branches out into three, the right hand one by Pattos, Paras, Saltelo, &c. being the main road to Mexico and St. Antonio. The road which we took leaves all the villages a little to the right, passing only some plantations; the left hand one goes immediately through the mountains to Montelovez but is dangerous for small parties on account of the savages. . . . In passing from Chihuahua to Texas by this route, you make in seven days what it takes you 15 or 20 by the ordinary one, but it is very scarce of water, and your guards must either be so strong as to defy the Apaches, or calculate to escape them by swiftness, for they fill those mountains, whence they continually carry on a predatory war against the Spanish settlements and caravans. . . .

14th May, Thursday. . . . This day the thermometer stood at 30° Raumauer, 99° 1-2 Fahrenheit and the dust and drought of the road obliged us to march in the night, when we came 15 miles and encamped without water—indeed this road which the general obliged us to take is almost impassable at this season for want of water, whilst the other is plentifully supplied. . . .

20th June, Saturday. Came on 16 miles in the morning—passed several herds of mustangs or wild horses, good land, ponds and small dry creeks, prairie, and woods alternately. It rained considerably. We halted to dry our baggage long before night. Distance 20 miles. . . .

24th June, Wednesday. The horses came up this morning; lost six overnight. We marched early and in 15 miles came to the river Angelina [in Texas], about the width of the Natchez, running N. & S. Good land on its borders—two miles further was a settlement of Barr and Davenport's, where were three of our lost horses—one mile further found two more of our horses where we halted for dinner. Marched at four o'clock, and at half past eight arrived at Nacogdoches—were politely received by the adjutant and inspector, and Captain Herrara, Davenport, &c. This part of the country is well watered but sandy; hilly soil—pine, scrub oak, &c. Distance 37 miles.

25th June, Thursday. Spent in reading a gazette from the United States, &c. A large party at the adjutant and inspector's to dinner. 1st toast, "The President of the United States." 2nd. "The King of Spain." 3d. "Governors Herrara and Cordero.". . . .

29th June, Monday. Our baggage and horses came up about ten o'clock, when we dispatched them on. . . . Marched ourselves at two o'clock, and arrived at the river Sabine by five. Here we saw the cantonment of the Spanish troops, when commanded by Colonel Herrara on the late affair between the two governments. Crossed the Sabine river and came about one league on this side to a little prairie, where we encamped. Parted with Lieutenant Guodiana and our Spanish escort. And here I think proper to bear testimony to the politeness, civility, and attention of all the officers, who at different periods and in different provinces commanded my escort (but in a particular manner to Malgares and Barelo, who appeared studious to please and accommodate all that lay in their power), also the obliging, mild dispositions evinced in all instances by their rank and file. On this side of the Sabine I went up to a house where I found 10 or 15 Americans hovering near the line, in order to embrace an opportunity of carrying on some illicit commerce with the Spaniards, who on their side were equally eager. Here we found Tharp and Sea, who had been old sergeants in General Wayne's army. Distance 15 miles. . . .

1st July, Wednesday. Finding that a horse of Doctor Robinson's, which had come all the way from Chihuahua, could not proceed, was obliged to leave him here. Yesterday and today passed many Choctaws, whose clothing, furniture, &c. evidently marked the superiority of situation of those who bordered on our frontiers to those of the naked, half-starved wretches whom we found hanging round the Spanish settlements. Came on and passed a string of huts, supposed to be built by our troops, and at a small run a fortified camp but a half mile from the hill, where anciently stood the village Adyes.

We proceeded on to a spring where we halted for our loads, and finding the horses much fatigued and not able to proceed, left them and baggage and proceeded on, when we arrived at Natchitoches about four o'clock P.M.

Language cannot express the gaiety of my heart when I once more beheld the standard of my country waved aloft!—"All hail," cried I, "the ever sacred name of country, in which is embraced that of kindred, friends, and every other tie which is dear to the soul of man!!" Was affectionately received by Colonel Freeman, Captains Strong and Woolstoncraft, Lieutenant Smith, and all the officers of the post.

Z. M. PIKE

The Mountain Men

[*Pike's report on New Mexico stirred American interest in the region. Since it was isolated from the rest of New Spain by mountains and deserts and was more than 1,500 miles from Mexico City, it suffered from a lack of manufactured goods, which Spanish traders were unable to supply. Although Spanish law prohibited outside traders within the imperial domains, a few Americans attempted to breach the barrier and were welcomed by goods-hungry settlers in Santa Fe, who were eager to exchange their silver, furs, hides, and mules for cloth, cutlery, tea, coffee, and sugar. But when the authorities in Mexico got wind of their activities, not even bribes could keep these early American traders from landing in jail at Chihuahua. In 1821, however, the situation changed, for in that year Mexico proclaimed its independence from Spain and opened Santa Fe to American trade.*

[*This news quickly spread among the fur traders in St. Louis and Independence, Missouri, which soon became a staging point for traders headed for the Southwest. One of the most influential organizers of the trade with Santa Fe was William Becknell. In 1821 he started from his home at Franklin, Missouri, with a string of packhorses loaded with trade goods and made his way across the plains to the Big Bend of the Arkansas and thence southwest by the site of Dodge City, across the Cimarron River, the northwestern Panhandle of Oklahoma and on to Santa Fe. This route, later known as the Santa Fe Trail, was followed by countless traders for the next 23 years, until the Mexican government in 1844 closed Santa Fe to Americans. Wagon trains setting out from Independence and other towns would organize for the trip across the plains at Council Grove, Kansas. There they would elect a train captain who was given authority over the safety of the caravan of covered wagons usually pulled by oxen but sometimes by mules. If attacked by Indians, the wagons were formed into a hollow square or circle and used for defense. This tactic worked, and hundreds of tons of merchandise were transported across the plains to Santa Fe in relative safety, though the caravans traversed territory swarming with Comanche, Kiowa, Kansas, and other warlike tribes.*

[The development of the Santa Fe trade stimulated a further interest in the West. The technique of mutual protection in wagon trains taught pioneers a way of moving into the West with the minimum danger from hostile Indians. Gradually traders, trappers, adventurers, and settlers filtered into the trans-Mississippi area. In 1828 William and Charles Bent and their partner, Céran St. Vrain, erected a trading post and private fortress on the headwaters of the Arkansas River east of the present site of La Junta, Colorado. Bent's Fort, as it was called, served for many years as a rendezvous and protection point for traders and explorers. William Bent married a daughter of an important chief of the Cheyenne tribe, a union which helped keep peace on the border. Bent's Fort was an important outpost until 1852. In that year the United States government offered to buy the fort but made such a low bid that William Bent in disgust blew up the adobe structure and erected another trading post farther down the Arkansas.

[The activities of St. Vrain and the Bents were typical of the enterprise of many Americans in the first third of the nineteenth

century. Hundreds of adventurers percolated into the wilds, along previously unexplored rivers, in search of beaver. These trappers were either employed by fur trading companies that flourished in this period or operated independently. In the first days of summer, after trapping through the winter and early spring, they would meet at some convenient spot for a rendezvous with agents of the Missouri Fur Company, organized by Manuel Lisa (with William Clark as a shareholder); the American Fur Company, organized by John Jacob Astor; or some other company. Two of the famous rendezvous points were Jackson's Hole and Pierre's Hole in the Yellowstone region. Indians, white trappers, and agents for the companies would meet for several weeks to smoke, drink, tell stories, and trade. Sometimes the rendezvous would end in a drunken brawl, after which the trappers—having sold their furs, obtained a supply of ammunition, sugar, and coffee, and squandered their money—would return for another year in the wilderness. These were the famous "mountain men" who blazed many trails into the Far West.

[One of the most notable of the mountain men was Jedediah Smith. From his home in New York state he moved to Missouri and in 1822 joined a fur-trading expedition headed for the Rockies. From this time until 1831, when he died at the hands of a marauding band of Comanches on the Santa Fe Trail, Smith explored countless western trails. He led the first overland expedition to California in 1826. With 17 companions in August of that year he set out from Bear River on the Utah-Idaho border, crossed southwest Utah, Arizona and southern California, and on November 27 reached the Franciscan mission of San Gabriel on the outskirts of what would one day be Los Angeles. These were the first Americans known to have crossed deserts and mountains from the east to reach Spanish California.

[Although Smith and his companions had no license to trap in Spanish territory and were subject to imprisonment, the Spanish governor let them go in peace. After hospitable entertainment by the friars of a mission outpost at Redlands, California, they departed on February 1, 1827, crossed the San Bernardino Mountains, went north to the Tehachapi Mountains and discovered a pass that led them into the San Joaquin Valley, where they found abundant game. Following the Stanislaus River into the western foothills of the Sierra Nevada, they searched for a pass.

Leaving the main party camped on the western slope, Smith and two colleagues finally made their way through the mountains and, after a journey of incredible hardship across the desert of Great Salt Lake, reached Bear Valley on July 3, 1827.

[Smith was so eager to return to the West that he waited only ten days to recuperate before organizing another expedition of 18 men to return to California. This time they encountered a series of misfortunes. While they were crossing the Colorado River in Arizona the Mojave Indians fell on them, killed ten of the party, and severely wounded another. To avoid arrest, Smith and five survivors skirted San Gabriel, though they left the wounded man and two others to seek refuge at the mission. After rejoining the remnant of the first expedition on the Stanislaus River, the party, now short of supplies, appealed to the Spanish mission at San Jose for help, only to get themselves arrested by the civil authorities at Monterey. American ship captains in the harbor paid their fines and obtained their release, taking their stock of beaver pelts in exchange.

[Smith and his colleagues then proceeded up the Sacramento Valley, entered Oregon, and crossed the Rogue River to reach the Pacific Coast at Coos Bay. On July 13, 1828, they were in camp on the Umpqua River when Umpqua Indians attacked. Smith and two companions were away from the camp and thus survived. All except one man in camp died at the hands of the savages. The survivor fled to the woods and eventually reached Fort Vancouver, a trading post of the Hudson's Bay Company. There Smith and his two companions also found safety. In exchange for hospitality shown them, Smith gave Dr. John McLoughlin, superintendent for the Hudson's Bay Company, information about the virgin territory they had explored and the rich harvest of beaver pelts that trappers could expect to reap in the Sierras.

[After wintering at Fort Vancouver, Smith and a single companion left in the spring of 1829 to journey across mountains and desert to reach the rendezvous at Pierre's Hole, on the west side of the Grand Tetons. He and his companion trapped enough beavers on the way to the rendezvous to turn a respectable profit. But Smith's greatest assets were the information he had acquired about trails across Utah, Nevada, Arizona, California, Oregon, Washington, Montana, Idaho, and Wyoming.

[*Smith was only one of several mountain men who were notable explorers. Another was Joseph Walker, whose name is perpetuated in Walker Pass in California, the Walker River in California and Nevada, and Walker Lake in Nevada. A Tennessee frontiersman, Walker learned so much about the topography of the Far West on trapping expeditions that he was able to serve as official guide to later exploring expeditions. For example, Captain Benjamin Louis Eulalie de Bonneville, a Frenchman in the United States army, employed Walker in 1832 to guide an expedition described by Washington Irving in* The Adventures of Captain Bonneville, U.S.A. *(1837).*

[*Perhaps the mountain man best remembered today is Kit Carson, who served as guide for John Charles Frémont in his exploring expedition of 1842 in the Rockies and, along with Thomas Fitzpatrick, another mountain man, joined Frémont's second expedition in 1843–44 which made a much more extensive exploration of the West. The exploring feats of the mountain men were not preserved in official reports, maps, and charts but in the memories of the men they guided. They became a part of the folklore of the West, and their deeds are still talked of by fishermen, hunters, and campers who continue to haunt their old trails in the parts of the Far West that have not yet been spoiled by civilization. Some of these mountain men have also had a resurrection as heroes in western fiction purveyed by television.*

[*After Pike's expedition an official exploration of the West was conducted in 1819–20 by Major Stephen H. Long on orders from John C. Calhoun, then Secretary of War. Long, a trained military engineer, had previously explored the Fox and Wisconsin river systems in the upper Mississippi Valley. At this time the War Department was planning to establish a fort at the confluence of the Yellowstone and Missouri rivers, with sufficient troops to keep the Indians in check and to drive out interloping British fur traders. A scientific study of the region by a group of specialists under Long's direction was part of the plan.*

[*Long organized a group of naturalists and geologists at Pittsburgh in the spring and early summer of 1819. "The object of the expedition," his orders read, "is to acquire as thorough and accurate knowledge as may be practicable of a portion of the country which is daily becoming more interesting but which is as yet imperfectly known. . . . You will enter in your journal everything*

*interesting in relation to soil, face of the country, water courses
and productions, whether animal, vegetable, or mineral.*"

[*The group traveled by steamboat from Pittsburgh to St. Louis.
After the acquisition of more equipment and supplies, they left
St. Louis on June 21, 1819, and proceeded up the Missouri as far
as Council Bluffs, which they reached on September 17. There
they pitched camp for the winter. In the spring they resumed
their journey and traveled up the Platte and South Platte until
they reached the Rockies at the end of June. Long discovered the
peak in Colorado that bears his name, and a little later members
of the expedition made the first ascent of Pike's Peak.*

[*Long divided his group and sent one party down the Arkansas
River while he led another down the Canadian River, which he
mistakenly believed to be the Red River. His discovery of the
confluence of the Canadian and Arkansas rivers corrected earlier
notions of the topography of the region. Both parties made a
rendezvous at Fort Smith and went from there to Cape Giradeau,
Missouri, where they were mustered out.*

[*The observations of Long and his specialists added to the
knowledge of the flora, fauna, and geology of the territory covered. Long, however, emphasized the barrenness of some of the
western lands and thus gave currency to the notion that a vast
desert existed in the interior, a not altogether erroneous description of portions of the country.*

[*One of the specialists on the journey was Edwin James, a
botanist and geologist, who compiled a report published in Philadelphia in 1823 as an* Account of an Expedition from Pittsburgh
to the Rocky Mountains . . . in . . . 1819 and '20 . . . Under
the Command of Major Stephen H. Long. *James' narrative em-
phasizes natural history. His descriptions of buffalo, for example,
show keen powers of observation. A few paragraphs from the*
Account *will give the flavor of the document and will indicate
why the report attracted interest:*]

Volume I

Chapter 18

During all the day on the 23rd [June, 1820] we traveled along the south side of the Platte, our course inclining something more toward the southwest than heretofore. . . . Large herds of bisons were seen in every direction; but, as we had already killed a deer and were supplied with meat enough for the day, none of the party were allowed to go in pursuit of them. . . .

On the following day we saw immense herds of bisons, blackening the whole surface of the country through which we passed. At this time they were in their summer coat. From the shoulders backward all the hinder parts of the animal are covered with a growth of very short and fine hair, as smooth and soft to the touch as a piece of velvet. The tail is very short and tufted at the end, and its services as a fly brush are confined to a very limited surface.

The fore parts of the body are covered with long shaggy hair, descending in a tuft behind the knee, in a distinct beard beneath the lower jaw, rising in a dense mass on the top of his head as high as the tip of the horns, matted and curled on his front so thickly as to deaden the force of the rifle ball, which rebounds from the forehead or lodges in the hair, causing the animal only to shake his head as he bounds heavily onward. The head is so large and ponderous, in proportion to the size of the body, that the supporting muscles, which greatly enlarge the neck, form over the shoulders, where they are imbedded on each side of elongated vertebral processes distinguished by the name of hump ribs, a very considerable elevation called the hump, which is of an oblong form, diminishing in height as it recedes so as to give considerable obliquity to the line of the back.

The eye is small, black, and piercing; the horns, which are black and remarkably robust at base, curve outward and upward, tapering rapidly to the tip. The profile of the face is somewhat convexly curved, and the superior lip, on each side, papillose within, is dilated and extended downward so as to give a very oblique appearance to the lateral rictus or gape of the mouth, considerably resembling, in this respect, the ancient architectural bas reliefs representing the heads of the ox. The physiognomy is menacing and ferocious, and the whole aspect of the animal is sufficiently formidable to influence the spectator who is, for the first time, placed near him in his native wilds, with certain feelings which indicate the propriety of immediate attention to personal safety.

The bison cow bears the same relation, as to appearance, to the bull that the domestic cow does to her mate; she is smaller, with much less hair on the anterior part of her body, and though she has a conspicuous beard, yet this appendage is comparatively short; her horns also are much less robust and not partially concealed by hair.

The dun color prevails on the coat of the bison, but the long hair of the anterior part of the body, with the exception of the head, is more or less tinged with yellowish or rust color. The uniformity of color, however, amongst these animals is so steadfast that any considerable deviation from the ordinary standard is regarded by the natives as effected under the immediate influence of the Divinity. . . .

They are the skins of the cows, almost exclusively, that are used in commerce; those of the bulls being so large, heavy, and difficult to prepare that this is, comparatively, seldom attempted.

That the bison formerly ranged over the Atlantic states there can be no doubt, and Lawson informs us that even in his time some were killed in Virginia. . . .

Aside from the vast herds of bisons which it contains, the country along the Platte is enlivened by great numbers of deer, badgers, hares, prairie wolves, eagles, buzzards, ravens, and owls. These, with its rare and interesting plants, in some measure relieved the uniformity of its cheerless scenery. We found a constant source of amusement in observing the unsightly figure, the cumbrous gait, and impolitic movements of the bison; we were often delighted by the beauty and fleetness of the antelope and the social comfort and neatness of the prairie dog.

This barren and ungenial district appeared, at that time, to be filled with greater numbers of animals than its meagre productions are sufficient to support. It was, however, manifest that the bisons, then thronging in such numbers, were moving toward the south. Experience may have taught them to repair at certain seasons to the more luxuriant plains of Arkansas and Red river. What should ever prompt them to return to the inhospitable deserts of the Platte, it is not, perhaps, easy to conjecture. In whatever direction they move, their parasites and dependants fail not to follow. Large herds are invariably attended by gangs of meagre, famine-pinched wolves and flights of obscene and ravenous birds. . . .

26th. . . . At evening we arrived at another scattering grove of cottonwood trees, among which we placed our camp immediately on the brink of the river. The trees of which these insulated groves are usually composed, from their low and branching figure and their remoteness from each other as they stand scattered over the soil they occupy, revived strongly in our minds the appearance and gratifications resulting from an apple orchard, for which from a little distance they might readily be mistaken if seen in a cultivated region. At a few rods distant on our right hand was a fortified Indian camp which appeared to have been recently occupied. It was constructed of such broken half-decayed logs of wood as the place afforded, intermixed with some skeletons of bisons recently killed. It is of a circular form, enclosing space enough for about thirty men to lie down upon. The wall is about five feet high, with an opening toward the east and the top uncovered.

At a little distance in front of the entrance of this breastwork was a semicircular row of sixteen bison skulls, with their noses pointing down the river. Near the centre of the circle which this row would describe, if continued, was another skull marked with a number of red lines.

Our interpreter informed us that this arrangement of skulls and other marks here discovered were designed to communicate the following information, namely, that the camp had been occupied by a war party of the Skeeree [Skidi or Wolf] or Pawnee Loup Indians, who had lately come from an excursion against the Cumancias [Comanches], Lipans, or some of the western tribes. The number of red lines traced on the painted skull indicated the number of the party to have been thirty-six; the position in which the skulls were placed, that they were on their return to their own country. Two small rods stuck in the ground, with a few hairs tied in two parcels to the end of each, signified that four scalps had been taken. . . .

Volume II

Chapter 18

General description of the country traversed by the Exploring Expedition, extracted from a report of Major Long to the Hon. J. C. Calhoun, Secretary of War, dated Philadelphia, January 20th, 1821.

.   .   .   .

V. Of the country situated between the Meridian of the Council Bluff and the Rocky Mountains.

We next proceed to a description of the country westward of the assumed meridian and extending to the Rocky Mountains, which are its western boundary. This section embraces an extent of more than four hundred miles square, lying between ninety-six and one hundred and six degrees of west longitude, and between thirty-five and forty-two degrees of north latitude.

Proceeding westwardly from the meridian above specified, the hilly country gradually subsides, giving place to a region of vast extent spreading toward the north and south and presenting an undulating surface, with nothing to limit the view or variegate the prospect but here and there a hill, knob, or insulated tract of tableland. At length the Rocky Mountains break upon the view, towering abruptly from the plains and mingling their snow-capped summits with the clouds.

On approaching the mountains no other change is observable in the general aspect of the country except that the isolated knobs and tablelands, above alluded to, become more frequent and more distinctly marked—the bluffs by which the valleys of watercourses are bounded present a greater abundance of rocks, stones lie in greater profusion upon the surface, and the soil becomes more sterile. If to the characteristics above intimated we add that of an almost complete destitution of woodland (for not more than one thousandth part of the section can be said to possess a timber growth), we shall have a pretty correct idea of the general aspect of the country.

The insulated tracts herein alluded to as tablelands are scattered throughout the section and give to the country a very striking and wonderful appearance. They rise from six to eight hundred feet above the common level and are surrounded in many instances by rugged slopes and perpendicular precipices, rendering their summits almost inaccessible. Many of them are in this manner completely insulated, while others are connected with the plains below by gentle acclivities leading from their bases to their summits upon one side or other of the eminence. These tracts, as before intimated, are more numerous but less extensive in the vicinity of the Rocky Mountains than they are further eastward; and in the former situation they are more strikingly characterized by the marks above specified, than in the latter. . . .

Immediately at the base of the mountains, and also at those of some of the insular tablelands, are situated many remarkable ridges, rising in the form of parapets to the height of between fifty and one hundred and fifty feet. These appear to have been attached to the neighboring heights of which they once constituted a part, but have at some remote period been cleft asunder from them by some extraordinary convulsion of nature which has prostrated them in their present condition. The rocky stratifications of which these ridges are principally composed, and which are exactly similar to those of the insulated tablelands, are distinctly marked and have various dips, or inclinations, from forty-five to eighty degrees.

Throughout this section of country the surface is occasionally characterized by water-worn pebbles and gravel of granite, gneiss, and quartz, but the predominant characteristic is sand, which in many instances prevails almost to the entire exclusion of vegetable mold. . . . In some few instances, however, sandy knobs and ridges make their appearance, thickly covered with red cedars of a dwarfish growth. There are also some few tracts clad in a growth of pitch pine and scrubby oaks; but in general nothing of vegetation appears upon the uplands but withered grass of a stinted growth, no more than two or three inches high, prickly pears profusely covering extensive tracts, and weeds of a few varieties, which, like the prickly pears, seem to thrive best in the most arid and sterile soils.

In the vicinity of the Rocky Mountains, southwardly of the Arkansa river, the surface of the country in many places is profusely covered with loose fragments of volcanic rocks. . . . But the volcanoes whence they originated have left no vestiges by which their exact locality can be determined. In all probability they were extinguished previously to the recession of the waters that once inundated the vast region between the Allegheny and Rocky Mountains. . . .

The Platte rises in the Rocky Mountains and, after an easterly course of about eight hundred miles, falls into the Missouri at the distance of about seven hundred miles from the Mississippi. It derives its name from the circumstance of its being broad and shoal, its average width being about twelve hundred yards exclusive of the islands it embosoms, and its depth in a moderate stage of water so inconsiderable that the river is fordable in almost every place. The main Platte is formed of two confluent tributaries of nearly equal size, called the North and South Forks, both of which have their sources considerably within the range of the Rocky Mountains. They unite about four hundred miles westward from the mouth of the Platte, having meandered about the same distance eastwardly from the mountains. Besides these the Platte has two tributaries of a respectable size, the one called the Elk Horn, entering a few miles above its mouth, and the other the Loup Fork, entering about ninety miles above the same place. The valleys of the Platte and its several tributaries are extremely broad and, in many places, possessed of a good soil. They gradually become less fertile on ascending from the mouths of the rivers on which they are situated, till at length they exhibit an arid and sterile appearance. . . .

The valley of the Platte, from its mouth to its constituent forks, spreads to the width of ten or twelve miles and forms a most beautiful expanse of level country. It is bounded on both sides by high lands, elevated twenty-five or thirty feet above the valley and connected therewith by gentle slopes.

The river in several places expands to the width of many miles, embosoming numerous islands, some of which are broad and considerably extensive, and all of them covered with a growth of cottonwood and willows. These are the only woodlands that make their appearance along the river; and in traveling westward these become less numerous and extensive till at length they entirely disappear. Copses and skirts of woodland again present themselves in the neighborhood of the mountains, but they are of small magnitude, and the trees they furnish are of a dwarfish growth. For a distance of nearly two hundred miles, commencing at the confluence of the North and South Forks and extending westwardly toward the mountains, the country is almost entirely destitute of woodland, scarcely a tree, bush, or even a shrub making its appearance.

The Platte is seldom navigable except for skin canoes requiring but a moderate depth of water, and for these only when a freshet prevails in the river. No attempts have ever been made to ascend the river in canoes for any considerable distance, the prevalence of shoals and the rapidity of the current discouraging such an undertaking.

Expansion and "Manifest Destiny"

[*The mountain men and explorers were not the only Americans who moved into the distant West during the first four decades of the nineteenth century. They were followed by adventurous settlers willing to risk Indian attacks, the miseries of hunger and thirst, the prospect of arrest by Spanish authorities, and countless other hazards in order to find fresh land and homesteads beyond the rim of civilization. Some of these emigrants were simply squatters who settled on land of their choice without any legal certification of their right to possess it. Others obtained from such authorities as might exist title to the land they occupied.*

[*The early filtration into Texas was both legal and extralegal. Early in the century American interlopers and Mexican dissidents tried to stir up trouble in Texas and to cut it off from New Spain as an independent principality. In 1812 a revolt led by an American and a Mexican made a promising start but was soon snuffed out. Again in 1821 another group led by an American, James Long, declared Texas a republic, but Long was killed before his republic could gain strength enough to survive. Before Mexico became independent of Spain, another American, Moses Austin, undertook to obtain legal permission to settle a colony of English-speaking emigrants in Texas. He died before he could carry his scheme to fruition, but his son, Stephen Austin, in 1823–24 finally succeeded in establishing legally a colony of Americans in Texas. Austin's emigrants and others of their kind ultimately succeeded in severing Texas from Mexico and joining it to the United States. As Ray Billington in* Westward Expansion *comments: "The fate of Texas, as of the entire Far West, was decided not by government officials in Washington, but by the expansive forces of the American frontier which were soon to bring the vanguard of American settlement into the northernmost province of Mexico." On March 2, 1836, Texas declared its independence of Mexico, and on March 1, 1845, President Tyler signed the resolution passed by the House and Senate to annex Texas.*

[By this time a notion was current in the United States that the nation had a "manifest destiny" to occupy the whole continent north of Mexico proper and south of Canada, from the Atlantic to the Pacific. Not all citizens of the United States were expansionists, but the recently elected President, James K. Polk, was an ardent advocate of the doctrine of manifest destiny.

[As American emigrants penetrated Texas, so they also filtered into California, where they often married Spanish-American heiresses and became owners of vast cattle ranches. Yankee ship captains, as related in Richard Henry Dana's Two Years Before the Mast, *developed a thriving business with California by exchanging manufactured products of New England for hides and tallow.*

[American emigrants also discovered the green and fertile valleys of Oregon, which, by 1845, had proved tempting enough to lure across the plains and mountains some 6,000 settlers. The early migrations to Oregon were led by men who combined a missionary zeal and a sound instinct for profit. A Massachusetts citizen named Hall J. Kelley had long advocated colonization in the Northwest and by 1831 was hoping to duplicate the settlement of Massachusetts Bay, with all of its Puritan virtues, in Oregon. Kelley induced Nathaniel J. Wyeth, a Cambridge businessman, in 1831–32, to lead a small party over what became known as the "Oregon Trail" to Fort Vancouver, the first group of American emigrants to use a route that grew increasingly important during the next two decades.

[In 1834 Wyeth led to Oregon a second party that included two missionaries, Daniel and Jason Lee, who stirred other like-minded Christians to undertake a mission to the Indians of the Northwest. One of the most notable of the Oregon missionaries was Dr. Marcus Whitman, a physician and businessman, from Wheeler, New York. In 1835 he made an exploratory journey to

the Northwest and returned to the East to marry. With his wife, a friend, Henry Spalding, and his wife, and two single men, Whitman returned to Oregon in 1836 over the Oregon Trail. The wives of the two missionaries were the first white women known to have made this overland journey. Dr. John McLoughlin, presiding genius of the Hudson's Bay Company, at this time ruled the region, but he welcomed the missionaries and allowed Whitman to establish a mission at Waiilatpu 25 miles from Fort Walla Walla and another at Lapwai. But McLoughlin induced most of the other missionaries and settlers to select the Willamette valley south of the Columbia for their homesteads. This locality, he reasoned, would inevitably fall to the United States, while the territory north of the Columbia, he hoped, would become Great Britain's.

[Whitman proved more useful as a guide to emigrants headed for Oregon than he did as a saver of Indian souls. Whitman was genuinely interested in the salvation of the Indians but made little headway. Ironically, he and his wife and 12 members of the mission in 1847 were massacred by Cayuse Indians who thought his treatment of their children for measles had caused their deaths.

[In 1843 occurred a great migration which Whitman helped to lead. More than a thousand men, women, and children, with some 5,000 head of livestock, set out from Independence, Missouri in the spring of that year. They used the Oregon Trail, which followed the course of the Platte River past Fort Laramie to the approach to the Continental Divide at South Pass, then on past Fort Bridger on the upper Green River, and thence to Fort Hall on the Snake River. Following the Snake to Fort Boise, the route turned north to Fort Walla Walla then followed the Columbia to Fort Vancouver. There the emigrants scattered to the south, principally in the Willamette Valley. As in Texas, emigrants to this frontier were solidifying their strength and would insure the possession of the territory by the United States.

[One of the most persistent expansionists in this period was Senator Thomas Hart Benton of Missouri who assisted a young second lieutenant, John C. Frémont, of the Corps of Topographical Engineers, in organizing an expedition which mapped Iowa Territory in the summer of 1841. Frémont had been a guest in the Benton house in Washington and had met Benton's daughter Jessie, with whom he eloped when parental permission was not forthcoming. Benton later forgave the couple, for he shared

Frémont's enthusiasm for the western country, and thereafter encouraged and helped his son-in-law to conduct exploring expeditions in the Far West.

[In the summer of 1842 Frémont explored the Wind River chain of the Rockies in Wyoming as well as the region from Fort Laramie to South Pass and the headwaters of the Green River in an effort to determine the best route to Oregon. He had Kit Carson as his guide. By October he was back in Washington, and his highly literate wife helped him prepare a report of the expedition which was published in 1843.

[In May 1843 Frémont led another and more extensive expedition to the Far West. He had as guide Thomas Fitzpatrick, who was later joined on the Arkansas River by Kit Carson. Again Frémont hoped to find an easier route for the Oregon Trail through Colorado but failed in this objective. He returned to the regular Oregon Trail and witnessed the great migration of 1843 headed for the Northwest. He led his own expedition through the Salt Lake region to Fort Hall and thence to Fort Boise, the Marcus Whitman mission on the Columbia River, the Dalles (rapids of the Columbia), and Fort Vancouver.

[This was not precisely virgin territory for an explorer, but Frémont returned by way of the Great Basin between the Sierra and the Rockies, which he explored with some care, and eventually reached Pyramid Lake in western Nevada. On January 18, 1844 he was on Carson River near the site of Virginia City, Nevada, and braved the wintry weather to cross the Sierra Nevada into the Sacramento Valley, which he reached in March. After a stop at Sutter's Fort, not far from the spot where gold was to be discovered four years later, he continued his journey southwest to Los Angeles and thence by the Spanish Trail to Santa Fe and on east by Bent's Fort and the Arkansas to St. Louis, which he reached in August, 1844. His second report appeared in print as President James K. Polk, also an ardent expansionist, took office. Thereafter Frémont was involved in the politics of the Mexican War and in other exploring expeditions, but the expeditions of 1842 and 1843–44 gained him the reputation of being "the Path-Finder of the West."

[The reports of these expeditions were printed together in 1845 as Senate Ex. Document 174, 2nd Session, Twenty-eighth Congress, with the title: Report of the Exploring Expedition to the

Rocky Mountains in the Year 1842 and to Oregon and North California in the Years 1843–44. By Brevet Captain J. C. Frémont. . . . *Thanks to the literary ability of his wife, Frémont's accounts of his explorations are highly readable and entertaining. Excerpts follow:*]

A Report of the Exploring Expedition to Oregon and North California in the Years 1843–44

Continuing down the river [the Fontaine-qui-bouit, or Boiling Spring], we encamped at noon on the 14th [July, 1843] at its mouth on the Arkansas river. A short distance above our encampment, on the left bank of the Arkansas, is a *pueblo* (as the Mexicans call their civilized Indian villages) where a number of mountaineers, who had married Spanish women in the valley of Taos, had collected together and occupied themselves in farming, carrying on at the same time a desultory Indian trade. They were principally Americans and treated us with all the rude hospitality their situation admitted; but as all commercial intercourse with New Mexico was now interrupted in consequence of Mexican decrees to that effect, there was nothing to be had in the way of provisions. They had, however, a fine stock of cattle, and furnished us an abundance of excellent milk. . . .

By this position of affairs, our expectation of obtaining supplies from Taos was cut off. I had here the satisfaction to meet our good buffalo hunter of 1842, Christopher Carson, whose services I considered myself fortunate to secure again; and as a reinforcement of mules was absolutely necessary, I dispatched him immediately, with an account of our necessities, to Mr. Charles Bent, whose principal post is on the Arkansas river, about 75 miles below Fontaine-qui-bouit. He was directed to proceed from that post by the nearest route across the country and meet me with what animals he should be able to obtain at St. Vrain's fort. I also admitted into the party Charles Towns—a native of St. Louis, a serviceable man, with many of the qualities of a good voyageur. According to our observations the latitude of the mouth of the river is 38° 15′ 23″; its longitude 104° 58′ 30″; and its elevation above the sea 4,880 feet.

On the morning of the 16th, the time for Maxwell's arrival having expired, we resumed our journey, leaving for him a note in which it was stated that I would wait for him at St. Vrain's fort until the morning of the 26th, in the event that he should succeed in his commission. Our direction was up the Boiling Spring river, it being my intention to visit the celebrated springs from which the river takes its name and which are on its upper waters, at the foot of Pike's peak. . . .

On the afternoon of the 17th we entered among the broken ridges at the foot of the mountains, where the river made several forks. Leaving the camp to follow slowly, I rode ahead in the afternoon in search of the springs. In the meantime, the clouds, which had been gathered all the afternoon over the mountains, began to roll down their sides, and a storm so violent burst upon me that it appeared I had entered the storehouse of the thunder storms. I continued, however, to ride along up the river until about sunset, and was beginning to be doubtful of finding the springs before the next day when I came suddenly upon a large smooth rock about twenty yards in diameter where the water from several springs was bubbling and boiling up in the midst of a white incrustation with which it had covered a portion of the rock. As this did not correspond with a description given me by the hunters I did not stop to taste the water, but, dismounting, walked a little way up the river, and, passing through a narrow thicket of shrubbery bordering the stream, stepped directly upon a huge white rock at the foot of which the river, already become a torrent, foamed along, broken by a small fall. A deer which had been drinking at the spring was startled by my approach, and, springing across the river, bounded off up the mountain.

In the upper part of the rock, which had apparently been formed by deposition, was a beautiful white basin overhung by currant bushes, in which the cold clear water bubbled up, kept in constant motion by the escaping gas and overflowing the rock, which it had almost entirely covered with a smooth crust of glistening white. I had all day refrained from drinking, reserving myself for the spring; and as I could not well be more wet than the rain had already made me, I lay down by the side of the basin and drank heartily of the delightful water. . . .

July 19. A beautiful and clear morning, with a slight breeze from the northwest; the temperature of air at sunrise being 57.5°. At this time the temperature of the lower spring was 57.8°, and that of the upper 54.3°.

The trees in the neighborhood were birch, willow, pine, and an oak resembling *Quercus alba* [white oak]. In the shrubbery along the river are currant bushes (*Ribes*), of which the fruit has a singular piney flavor; and on the mountainside, in a red gravelly soil, is a remarkable coniferous tree (perhaps an *Abies*), having the leaves singularly long, broad, and scattered, with bushes of *Spiraea ariaefolia*. By our observations, this place is 6,350 feet above the sea, in latitude 38° 52′ 10″, and longitude 105° 22′ 45″.

Resuming our journey on this morning, we descended the river in order to reach the mouth of the eastern fork, which I proposed to ascend. The left bank of the river here is very much broken. There is a handsome little bottom on the right, and both banks are exceedingly picturesque—strata of red rock, in nearly perpendicular walls, crossing the valley from north to south. About three miles below the springs, on the right bank of the river, is a nearly perpendicular limestone rock presenting a uniformly unbroken surface twenty to forty feet high containing very great numbers of a large univalve shell, which appears to belong to the genus *Inoceramus*. . . .

In contact with this, to the westward, was another stratum of limestone containing fossil shells of a different character. . . .

July 20. This morning (as we generally found the mornings under these mountains) was very clear and beautiful, and the air cool and pleasant, with the thermometer at 44°. We continued our march up the stream along a green sloping bottom, between pine hills on the one hand and the main Black Hills on the other, toward the ridge which separates the waters of the Platte from those of the Arkansas. As we approached the dividing ridge the whole valley was radiant with flowers: blue, yellow, pink, white, scarlet, and purple vied with each other in splendor. Esparsette was one of the highly characteristic plants, and a bright-looking flower (*Gaillardia aristata*) was very frequent; but the most abundant plant along our road today was *Geranium maculatum* [wild geranium], which is the characteristic plant on this portion of the dividing grounds.

Crossing to the waters of the Platte, fields of blue flax added to the magnificence of this mountain garden; this was occasionally four feet in height, which was a luxuriance of growth that I rarely saw this almost universal plant attain throughout the journey. Continuing down a branch of the Platte among high and very steep timbered hills covered with fragments of rock, toward evening we issued from the piney region and made a late encampment near Poundcake Rock, on that fork of the river which we had ascended on the 8th of July. Our animals enjoyed the abundant rushes this evening, as the flies were so bad among the pines that they had been much harassed. A deer was killed here this evening; and again the evening was overcast, and a collection of brilliant red clouds in the west was followed by the customary squall of rain. . . .

Reaching St. Vrain's fort on the morning of the 23d, we found Mr. Fitzpatrick and his party in good order and excellent health and my true and reliable friend, Kit Carson, who had brought with him ten good mules with the necessary pack saddles. Mr. Fitzpatrick, who had often endured every extremity of want during the course of his mountain life and knew well the value of provisions in this country, had watched over our stock with jealous vigilance, and there was an abundance of flour, rice, sugar, and coffee in the camp; and again we fared luxuriously. Meat was, however, very scarce; and two very small pigs, which we obtained at the fort, did not go far among forty men. Mr. Fitzpatrick had been here a week, during which time his men had been occupied in refitting the camp; and the repose had been very beneficial to his animals, which were now in tolerably good condition.

I had been able to obtain no certain information in regard to the character of the passes in this portion of the Rocky Mountain range, which had always been represented as impracticable for carriages, but the exploration of which was incidentally contemplated by my instructions with the view of finding some convenient point of passage for the road of emigration which would enable it to reach, on a more direct line, the usual ford of the Great Colorado—a place considered as determined by the nature of the country beyond that river.

It is singular that, immediately at the foot of the mountains, I could find no one sufficiently acquainted with them to guide us to the plains at their western base; but the race of trappers who formerly lived in their recesses has almost entirely disappeared— dwindled to a few scattered individuals—some one or two of whom are regularly killed in the course of each year by the Indians. You will remember that in the previous year I brought with me to their village near this post, and hospitably treated on the way, several Cheyenne Indians whom I had met on the Lower Platte. Shortly after their arrival here, these were out with a party of Indians (themselves the principal men) which discovered a few trappers in the neighboring mountains, whom they immediately murdered, although one of them had been nearly thirty years in the country and was perfectly well known, as he had grown gray among them.

Through this portion of the mountains also are the customary roads of the war parties going out against the Utah and Shoshonee Indians; and occasionally parties from the Crow nation make their way down to the southward along this chain in the expectation of surprising some straggling lodges of their enemies. Shortly before our arrival one of their parties had attacked an Arapaho village in the vicinity, which they had found unexpectedly strong; and their assault was turned into a rapid flight and a hot pursuit, in which they had been compelled to abandon the animals they had rode and escape on their war horses.

Into this uncertain and dangerous region small parties of three or four trappers, who now could collect together, rarely ventured; and consequently it was seldom visited and little known. Having determined to try the passage by a pass through a spur of the mountains made by the Câche-à-la-Poudre [Powder] River, which rises in the high bed of mountains around Long's peak, I thought it advisable to avoid any encumbrance which would occasion detention and accordingly again separated the party into two divisions—one of which, under the command of Mr. Fitzpatrick, was directed to cross the plains to the mouth of Laramie River, and, continuing thence its route along the usual emigrant road, meet me at Fort Hall, a post belonging to the Hudson Bay Company and situated on Snake River, as it is commonly called in the Oregon Territory, although better known to us as Lewis's Fork of the Columbia. The latter name is there restricted to one of the upper forks of the river. . . .

On the evening of the 8th [August] we encamped on one of these freshwater lakes which the traveler considers himself fortunate to find; and the next day, in latitude by observation 42° 20′ 06″, halted to noon immediately at the foot of the southern side of the range which walls in the Sweet Water valley, on the head of a small tributary to that river.

Continuing in the afternoon our course down the stream, which

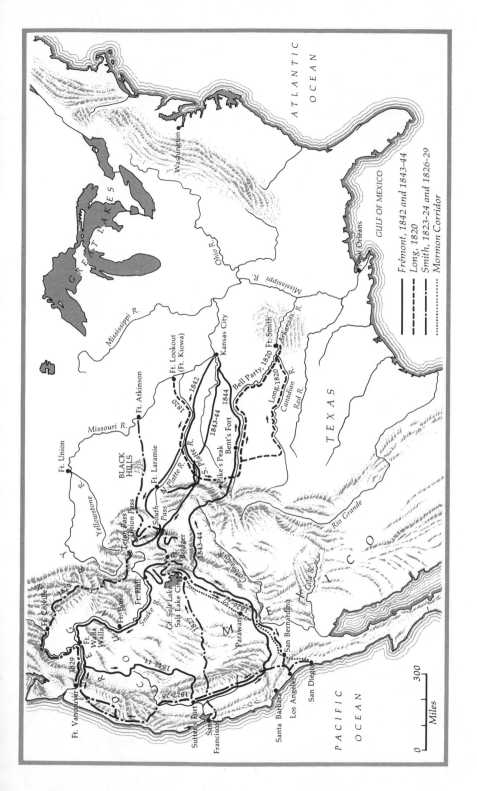

ATLANTIC OCEAN

GULF OF MEXICO

New Orleans

GREAT LAKES

Washington

Mississippi R.

Ohio R.

Susquehanna R.

Missouri R.

Ft. Union

Ft. Atkinson

Ft. Lookout (Ft. Kiowa)

Kansas City

Ft. Smith

Arkansas R.

Bell Party, 1820

Long, 1820

Canadian R.

Red R.

TEXAS

1842

1820

1843-44

1844

S. Platte R.

N. Platte R.

Bent's Fort

Pike's Peak

BLACK HILLS

Ft. Laramie

South Pass

Teton Pass

Union Pass

Yellowstone R.

Rio Grande

MEXICO

Gila R.

Colorado R.

1843-44

Ft. Bridger

Gt. Salt Lake

Salt Lake City

Parawan

San Bernardino

San Diego

Los Angeles

Santa Barbara

San Francisco

Sutter's Fort

1827-28

1824

1843-44

Snake R.

Ft. Hall

Ft. Boise

Ft. Walla Walla

Ft. Colville

Ft. Vancouver

1829

1826

OREGON

Columbia R.

PACIFIC OCEAN

Frémont, 1842 and 1843-44
Long, 1820
Smith, 1823-24 and 1826-29
Mormon Corridor

Miles
0   300

The Frontier Moves to the Far West

here cuts directly through the ridge forming a very practicable pass, we entered the valley; and, after a march of about nine miles, encamped on our familiar river, endeared to us by the acquaintance of the previous expedition; the night having already closed in with a cold rain storm. Our camp was about twenty miles above the Devil's Gate [in Natrona County, Wyoming], which we had been able to see in coming down the plain; and, in the course of the night, the clouds broke away around Jupiter for a short time, during which we obtained an immersion of the first satellite, the result of which agreed very nearly with the chronometer, giving for the mean longitude 107° 50' 07"; elevation above the sea 6,040 feet; and distance from St. Vrain's fort, by the road we had just traveled, 315 miles.

Here passes the road to Oregon; and the broad smooth highway, where the numerous heavy wagons of the emigrants had entirely beaten and crushed the artemisia, was a happy exchange to our poor animals for the sharp rocks and tough shrubs among which they had been toiling so long; and we moved up the valley rapidly and pleasantly. With very little deviation from our route of the preceding year, we continued up the valley, and on the evening of the 12th encamped on the Sweet Water, at a point where the road turns off to cross to the plains of Green River. The increased coolness of the weather indicated that we had attained a great elevation, which the barometer here placed at 7,220 feet; and during the night water froze in the lodge.

The morning of the 13th was clear and cold, there being a white frost; and the thermometer, a little before sunrise, standing at 26.5°. Leaving this encampment (our last on the waters which flow toward the rising sun), we took our way along the upland toward the dividing ridge which separates the Atlantic from the Pacific waters, and crossed it by a road some miles further south than the one we had followed on our return in 1842. We crossed very near the table mountain at the southern extremity of the South Pass, which is near twenty miles in width and already traversed by several different roads. Selecting as well as I could, in the scarcely distinguishable ascent, what might be considered the dividing ridge in this remarkable depression in the mountain, I took a barometrical observation which gave 7,490 feet for the elevation above the Gulf of Mexico. You will remember that, in my report of 1842, I estimated the elevation of this pass at about

7,000 feet; a correct observation with a good barometer enables me now to give it with more precision. Its importance, as the great gate through which commerce and traveling may hereafter pass between the valley of the Mississippi and the north Pacific, justifies a precise notice of its locality and distance from leading points, in addition to this statement of its elevation. . . . From this pass to the mouth of the Oregon is about 1,400 miles by the common traveling route; so that, under a general point of view, it may be assumed to be about halfway between the Mississippi and the Pacific ocean, on the common traveling route. . . .

August 16. Crossing the [Green] River, here about 400 feet wide, by a very good ford, we continued to descend for seven or eight miles on a pleasant road along the right bank of the stream of which the islands and shores are handsomely timbered with cottonwood. The refreshing appearance of the broad river, with its timbered shores and green wooded islands in contrast to its dry sandy plains, probably obtained for it the name of Green River, which was bestowed on it by the Spaniards who first came into this country to trade some 25 years ago. . . . Lower down, from Brown's hole to the southward, the river runs through lofty chasms, walled in by precipices of *red* rock; and even among the wilder tribes who inhabit that portion of its course I have heard it called by Indian refugees from the Californian settlements the Rio *Colorado.* We halted to noon at the upper end of a large bottom, near some old houses which had been a trading post, in latitude 41° 46′ 54″. At this place the elevation of the river above the sea is 6,230 feet. That of Lewis's Fork of the Columbia at Fort Hall is, according to our subsequent observations, 4,500 feet. The descent of each stream is rapid, but that of the Colorado is but little known, and that little derived from vague report. . . .

August 18. We passed on the road this morning the grave of one of the emigrants, being the second we had seen since falling into their trail; and halted to noon on the river, a short distance above. . . .

One of our mules died here, and in this portion of our journey we lost six or seven of our animals. The grass which the country had lately afforded was very poor and insufficient; and animals which have been accustomed to grain become soon weak and unable to labor when reduced to no other nourishment than grass. The American horses (as those are usually called which are brought to this country from the States) are not of any serviceable value until after they have remained a winter in the country, and become accustomed to live entirely on grass.

August 19. Desirous to avoid every delay not absolutely necessary, I sent on Carson in advance to Fort Hall this morning, to make arrangements for a small supply of provisions. . . .

August 20. We continued to travel up the creek by a very gradual ascent and a very excellent grassy road, passing on the way several small forks of the stream. The hills here are higher, presenting escarpments of particolored and apparently clay rocks, purple, dark red, and yellow, containing strata of sandstone and limestone with shells, with a bed of cemented pebbles, the whole overlaid by beds of limestone. The alternation of red and yellow gives a bright appearance to the hills, one of which was called by our people the Rainbow Hill; and the character of the country became more agreeable and traveling far more pleasant, as now we found timber and very good grass. Gradually ascending, we reached the lower level of a bed of white limestone, lying upon a white clay, on the upper line of which the whole road is abundantly supplied with beautiful cool springs, gushing out a foot in breadth and several inches deep, directly from the hill side.

At noon we halted at the last main fork of the creek, at an elevation of 7,200 feet, and in latitude, by observation, 41° 39' 45"; and in the afternoon continued on the same excellent road, up the left or northern fork of the stream, toward its head, in a pass which the barometer placed at 8,230 feet above the sea. This is a connecting ridge between the Utah or Bear River mountains and the Wind River chain of the Rocky Mountains, separating the waters of the Gulf of California on the east and those on the west belonging more directly to the Pacific from a vast interior basin whose rivers are collected into numerous lakes having no outlet to the ocean. From the summit of this pass, the highest which the road crosses between the Mississippi and the Western ocean, our view was over a very mountainous region whose rugged appearance was greatly increased by the smoky weather, through which the broken ridges were dark and dimly seen. The ascent to the summit of the gap was occasionally steeper than the national road in the Alleghenies; and the descent, by way of a spur on the western side, is rather precipitous, but the pass may still be called a good one. Some thickets of willow in the hollows below deceived us into the expectation of finding a camp at our usual hour at the foot of the mountain; but we found them without water, and continued down a ravine, and encamped about dark at a place where the springs again began to make their appearance but where our animals fared badly; the stock of the emigrants having razed the grass as completely as if we were again in the midst of the buffalo.

August 21. An hour's travel this morning brought us into the fertile and picturesque valley of Bear River, the principal tributary to the Great Salt Lake. The stream is here 200 feet wide, fringed with willows and occasional groups of hawthorns. We were now entering a region which for us possessed a strange and extraordinary interest. We were upon the waters of the famous lake which forms a salient point among the remarkable geographical features of the country and around which the vague and superstitious accounts of the trappers had thrown a delightful obscurity, which we anticipated pleasure in dispelling, but which, in the meantime, left a crowded field for the exercise of our imagination.

In our occasional conversations with the few old hunters who had visited the region it had been a subject of frequent speculation; and the wonders which they related were not the less agreeable because they were highly exaggerated and impossible.

Hitherto this lake had been seen only by trappers who were wandering through the country in search of new beaver streams, caring very little for geography; its islands had never been visited; and none were to be found who had entirely made the circuit of its shores; and no instrumental observations or geographical survey of any description had ever been made anywhere in the neighboring region. It was generally supposed that it had no visible outlet; but among the trappers, including those in my own camp, were many who believed that somewhere on its surface was a terrible whirlpool through which its waters found their way to the ocean by some subterranean communication. All these things had made a frequent subject of discussion in our desultory conversations around the fires at night; and my own mind had become tolerably well filled with their indefinite pictures, and insensibly colored with their romantic descriptions, which, in the pleasure of excitement, I was well disposed to believe and half expected to realize.

Where we descended into this beautiful valley, it is three to four miles in breadth, perfectly level, and bounded by mountainous ridges, one above another, rising suddenly from the plain. . . .

We continued our road down the river and at night encamped with a family of emigrants—two men, women, and several children—who appeared to be bringing up the rear of the great caravan. I was struck with the fine appearance of their cattle, some six or eight yoke of oxen, which really looked as well as if they had been all the summer at work on some good farm. It was strange to see one small family traveling along through such a country, so remote from civilization. Some nine years since, such a security might have been a fatal one; but since their disastrous defeats in the country a little north the Blackfeet have ceased to visit these waters. Indians, however, are very uncertain in their localities; and the friendly feelings, also, of those now inhabiting it may be changed. . . .

Crossing in the afternoon the point of a narrow spur, we descended into a beautiful bottom formed by a lateral valley which presented a picture of home beauty that went directly to our hearts. The edge of the wood, for several miles along the river, was dotted with the white covers of emigrant wagons collected in groups at different camps, where the smokes were rising lazily from the fires, around which the women were occupied in preparing the evening meal, and the children playing in the grass; and herds of cattle, grazing about in the bottom, had an air of quiet security and civilized comfort that made a rare sight for the traveler in such a remote wilderness.

In common with all the emigration, they had been reposing for several days in this delightful valley in order to recruit their animals on its luxuriant pasturage after their long journey and prepare them for the hard travel along the comparatively sterile banks of the Upper Columbia. . . .

August 25. . . . In about six miles travel from our encampment, we reached one of the points in our journey to which we had always looked forward with great interest—the famous Beer Springs [Soda Springs, Idaho] . . . , which is a basin of mineral waters enclosed by the mountains, which sweep around a circular bend of Bear River, here at its most northern point, and which from a northern, in the course of a few miles acquires a southern direction toward the Great Salt Lake. A pretty little stream of clear water enters the upper part of the basin from an open valley in the mountains, and, passing through the bottom, discharges into Bear River. Crossing this stream, we descended a mile below and made our encampment in a grove of cedar immediately at the Beer Springs, which, on account of the effervescing gas and acid taste, have received their name from the voyageurs and trappers of the country, who, in the midst of their rude and hard lives, are fond of finding some fancied resemblance to the luxuries they rarely have the fortune to enjoy. . . .

The extraordinary rapidity with which the buffalo is disappearing from our territories will not appear surprising when we remember the great scale on which their destruction is yearly carried on. With inconsiderable exceptions, the business of the American trading posts is carried on in their skins; every year the Indian villages make new lodges, for which the skin of the buffalo furnishes the material; and in that portion of the country where they are still found, the Indians derive their entire support from them, and slaughter them with a thoughtless and abominable extravagance. Like the Indians themselves, they have been a characteristic of the Great West; and as, like them, they are visibly diminishing, it will be interesting to throw a glance backward through the last twenty years, and give some account of their former distribution through the country, and the limit of their western range. . . .

September 6. Leaving the encampment early, we again directed our course for the peninsular butte across a low shrubby plain, crossing in the way a slough-like creek with miry banks, and wooded with thickets of thorn (*Crataegus*) [hawthorn] which were loaded with berries. This time we reached the butte without any difficulty, and, ascending to the summit, immediately at our feet beheld the object of our anxious search—the waters of the Inland Sea [Great Salt Lake], stretching in still and solitary grandeur far beyond the limit of our vision. It was one of the great points of the exploration; and as we looked eagerly over the lake in the first emotions of excited pleasure, I am doubtful if the followers of Balboa felt more enthusiasm when, from the heights of the Andes, they saw for the first time the great Western ocean. It was certainly a magnificent object, and a noble terminus to this part of our expedition; and, to travelers so long shut up among mountain ranges, a sudden view over the expanse of silent waters had in it something sublime.

Several large islands raised their high rocky heads out of the waves; but whether or not they were timbered was still left to our imagination, as the distance was too great to determine if the dark hues upon them were woodland or naked rock. During the day the clouds had been gathering black over the mountains to the westward, and, while we were looking, a storm burst down with sudden fury upon the lake and entirely hid the islands from our view. So far as we could see, along the shores there was not a solitary tree and but little appearance of grass; and on Weber's Fork, a few miles below our last encampment, the timber was gathered into groves and then disappeared entirely. As this appeared to be the nearest point to the lake where a suitable camp could be found we directed our course to one of the groves, where we found a handsome encampment, with good grass and an abundance of rushes (*Equisetum hyemale*). At sunset the thermometer was at 55°; the evening clear and calm, with some cumuli.

September 7. The morning was calm and clear, with a temperature at sunrise of 39°.5. The day was spent in active preparation for our intended voyage on the lake. On the edge of the stream a favorable spot was selected in a grove, and, felling the timber, we made a strong *corál*, or horse pen, for the animals, and a little fort for the people who were to remain. We were now probably in the country of the Utah Indians, though none reside upon the lake. The India-rubber boat was repaired with prepared cloth and gum, and filled with air in readiness for the next day.

The provisions which Carson had brought with him being now exhausted, and our stock reduced to a small quantity of roots, I determined to retain with me only a sufficient number of men for the execution of our design; and accordingly seven were sent back to Fort Hall under the guidance of François Lajeunesse, who, having been for many years a trapper in the country, was considered an experienced mountaineer. Though they were provided with good horses and the road was a remarkably plain one of only four days' journey for a horseman, they became bewildered (as we afterward learned) and, losing their way, wandered about the country in parties of one or two, reaching the fort about a week afterward. . . .

We formed now but a small family. With Mr. Preuss and myself, Carson, Bernier, and Basil Lajeunesse had been selected for the boat expedition—the first ever attempted on this interior sea; and Badeau, with Derosier and Jacob (the colored man) were to be left in charge of the camp. We were favored with most delightful weather. Tonight there was a brilliant sunset of golden orange and green which left the western sky clear and beautifully pure; but clouds in the east made me lose an occultation [a celestial observation]. The summer frogs were singing around us, and the evening was very pleasant, with a temperature of 60°— a night of a more southern autumn. For our supper we had *yampah*, the most agreeably flavored of the roots, seasoned by a small fat duck which had come in the way of Jacob's rifle. Around our fire tonight were many speculations on what tomorrow would bring forth, and in our busy conjectures we fancied that we should find every one of the large islands a tangled wilderness of trees and shrubbery, teeming with game of every description that the neighboring region afforded and which the foot of a white man or Indian had never violated.

September 9. The day was clear and calm; the thermometer at sunrise at 49°. As is usual with the trappers on the eve of any enterprise, our people had made dreams, and theirs happened to be a bad one—one which always preceded evil—and consequently they looked very gloomy this morning; but we hurried through our breakfast in order to make an early start and have all the day before us for our adventure. The channel in a short distance became so shallow that our navigation was at an end, being merely a sheet of soft mud with a few inches of water and sometimes none at all, forming the low-water shore of the lake. All this place was absolutely covered with flocks of screaming plover. We took off our clothes, and, getting overboard, commenced dragging the boat—making, by this operation, a very curious trail and a very disagreeable smell in stirring up the mud, as we sank above the knee at every step. The water here was still fresh, with only an insipid and disagreeable taste, probably derived from the bed of fetid mud.

After proceeding in this way about a mile we came to a small

black ridge on the bottom, beyond which the water became suddenly salt, beginning gradually to deepen, and the bottom was
sandy and firm. It was a remarkable division, separating the fresh
water of the rivers from the briny water of the lake, which was
entirely saturated with common salt. Pushing our little vessel
across the narrow boundary, we sprang on board, and at length
were afloat on the waters of the unknown sea.

We did not steer for the mountainous islands but directed our
course toward a lower one [Fremont Island], which it had been
decided we should first visit, the summit of which was formed
like the crater at the upper end of Bear River valley. So long as
we could touch the bottom with our paddles we were very gay;
but gradually, as the water deepened, we became more still in
our frail batteau of gum cloth distended with air and with pasted
seams. Although the day was very calm, there was a considerable
swell on the lake; and there were white patches of foam on the
surface which were slowly moving to the southward, indicating
the set of a current in that direction and recalling the recollection
of the whirlpool stories. The water continued to deepen as we
advanced, the lake becoming almost transparently clear, of an
extremely beautiful bright-green color; and the spray, which was
thrown into the boat and over our clothes, was directly converted
into a crust of common salt, which covered also our hands and
arms.

"Captain," said Carson, who for some time had been looking
suspiciously at some whitening appearances outside the nearest
islands, "what are those yonder?—won't you just take a look with
the glass?" We ceased paddling for a moment and found them
to be the caps of the waves that were beginning to break under
the force of a strong breeze that was coming up the lake. The
form of the boat seemed to be an admirable one, and it rode on
the waves like a water bird; but, at the same time, it was extremely slow in its progress. When we were a little more than
halfway across the reach two of the divisions between the cylin-
ders gave way, and it required the constant use of the bellows
to keep in a sufficient quantity of air. For a long time we scarcely
seemed to approach our island, but gradually we worked across
the rougher sea of the open channel into the smoother water
under the lee of the island, and began to discover that what
we took for a long row of pelicans ranged on the beach were

only low cliffs whitened with salt by the spray of the waves; and about noon we reached the shore, the transparency of the water enabling us to see the bottom at a considerable depth.

It was a handsome broad beach where we landed, behind which the hill into which the island was gathered rose somewhat abruptly; and a point of rock at one end enclosed it in a sheltering way. And, as there was an abundance of driftwood along the shore, it offered us a pleasant encampment. We did not suffer our fragile boat to touch the sharp rocks, but, getting overboard, discharged the baggage, and, lifting it gently out of the water, carried it to the upper part of the beach, which was composed of very small fragments of rock.

Among the successive banks of the beach, formed by the action of the waves, our attention, as we approached the island, had been attracted by one 10 to 20 feet in breadth, of a dark brown color. Being more closely examined, this was found to be composed, to the depth of seven or eight and twelve inches, entirely of the larvae of insects, or, in common language, of the skins of worms, about the size of a grain of oats, which had been washed up by the waters of the lake. . . .

Carrying with us the barometer and other instruments, in the afternoon we ascended to the highest point of the island—a bare rocky peak 800 feet above the lake. Standing on the summit, we enjoyed an extended view of the lake, enclosed in a basin of rugged mountains which sometimes left marshy flats and extensive bottoms between them and the shore and in other places came directly down into the water with bold and precipitous bluffs. . . . As we looked over the vast expanse of water spread out beneath us and strained our eyes along the silent shores over which hung so much doubt and uncertainty and which were so full of interest to us, I could hardly repress the almost irresistible desire to continue our exploration; but the lengthening snow on the mountains was a plain indication of the advancing season, and our frail linen boat appeared so insecure that I was unwilling to trust our lives to the uncertainties of the lake. I therefore unwillingly resolved to terminate our survey here and remain satisfied for the present with what we had been able to add to the unknown geography of the region. We felt pleasure also in remembering that we were the first who, in the traditionary annals of the country, had visited the islands, and broken, with the cheerful sound of human voices, the long solitude of the place. [Salt Lake had previously been discovered in 1824 by a party led by Jim Bridger.]

The Great Basin and the Mormons

[*This region of the Great Basin in what is now Utah soon attracted emigrants. Early explorers were fascinated by the phenomenon of the salt lake and were delighted at the game and grass on the Bear River which flowed into the lake, but much of the land appeared unpromising. Yet this was the domain that Brigham Young selected to be the refuge of the Church of the Latter-Day Saints, more generally known as the Mormons. This sect, founded by Joseph Smith, had suffered persecution from non-Mormons (whom they called Gentiles) and had been driven from Ohio to Missouri and finally to a city they founded in Illinois called Nauvoo. After the assassination of Smith on June 24, 1844, Brigham Young became the dominant figure in the church and a little later was elected its president. The bitter attacks of the Gentiles and the threat of mob violence convinced Young that members of his faith had to get out of the United States to be safe. Accordingly, in 1845 he promised that the Saints would leave Illinois with the coming of spring. In February 1846 the first band of 1,600 Mormons crossed the Mississippi River into Iowa, and others streamed into Iowa for the rest of the year. Young had not yet decided where his migrants would ultimately settle, but he intended to lead them farther west, beyond the confines of the United States. In the meantime they stopped at temporary camps in Iowa. In the locality of modern Omaha, Nebraska, Young established a large base which he named Winter Quarters. That became the staging area for the final trek west.*

[*In the summer of 1847 Young led an exploring group of 146 men and women in 73 wagons from Winter Quarters along the Oregon Trail to Fort Bridger, where Jim Bridger, another famous mountain man, tried to persuade them to head for the Willamette Valley in Oregon, but Young had decided upon settling somewhere in the Great Basin, then in Mexican territory. Pushing through the Wasatch Mountains and finally into what is now called Emigration Canyon, on July 24, 1847, the Pioneer Band looked out upon the valley of the Great Salt Lake. "This is the place," Young exclaimed, and the wagons rumbled down into the plain covered with sagebrush. Not everyone thought it a promising looking spot, but Young saw its potentialities. Camping beside a mountain stream, the Pioneer Band began the first permanent settlement in Utah, called by the Mormons "Deseret."*

[Young planned the migration of the faithful so carefully that he had advance parties plant corn and other food crops along the route so that succeeding emigrants could find food and forage on the journey. By the end of 1848, so successfully had he managed the migration that 5,000 souls had arrived at Salt Lake.

[But Young had not foreseen the result of the war with Mexico, which began with Congress' declaration on May 13, 1846, and ended with the Treaty of Guadalupe Hidalgo signed on February 2, 1848. From this conflict the United States gained possession of the remainder of the West, including, of course, the Kingdom of the Saints that Brigham Young had occupied in Deseret, changed by the United States to Utah.

[The clannishness of the Mormons, combined with their practice of plural marriages, produced a growing hostility from non-Mormons. The devotion to polygamy also created an enormous, and perhaps prurient, curiosity throughout the country as journalists wrote sensational stories about the Saints.

[With the discovery of gold in California in 1848 and the great migration to the West, which became a flood by 1849, interest in western routes became acute. Since many emigrants to California traveled by way of Salt Lake, concern and curiosity about the region increased. In 1849 the federal government ordered Captain Howard Stansbury of the Corps of Topographical Engineers, United States Army, to make an extensive survey of the Great Basin. With a party of 18 men he completed the task in 1850, and in 1852 he described the results in a government publication, Senate Document 3, *Thirty-second Congress, Special Session of Congress. This document was republished in the same year in London with the title* An Expedition to the Valley of Great Salt Lake of Utah. *Although much of the report provides strictly scientific and geographical observations, Stansbury included information about the natural resources of the region, the Indians, the Mormons and other matters of general interest. Brief excerpts follow:]*

Chapter 1

Before leaving Fort Leavenworth we were joined by a small party of emigrants for California who desired to travel in our company for the sake of protection, and who continued with us as far as Salt Lake City. This proved a fortunate arrangement, since we thereby secured the society of an excellent and intelligent lady, who not only by her cheerfulness and vivacity beguiled the tedium of many a monotonous and wearisome hour, but by her fortitude and patient endurance of exposure and fatigue set an example worthy the imitation of many of the ruder sex. . . .

At length, on the 31st day of May [1849], our preparations being completed, we commenced our journey, my own party consisting in all of eighteen men, five wagons, and forty-six horses and mules; while that of Mr. Sackett, our fellow traveler, contained six persons, one wagon, one traveling carriage, and fifteen animals. Lieutenant Gunnison, being too ill to travel in any other manner, was carried on his bed in a large spring wagon, which had been procured for the transportation of the instruments. The weather, in the morning, had been dark and lowering with occasional showers, but it cleared off about noon; the camp broke up, the wagons were packed, and we prepared to exchange, for a season, the comforts and refinements of civilized life for the somewhat wild and roving habits of the hunter and the savage. My party consisted principally of experienced *voyageurs* who had spent the best part of their lives among the wilds of the Rocky Mountains and to whom this manner of life had become endeared by old associations. We followed the "emigration road" (already broad and well beaten as any turnpike in our country) over a rolling prairie, fringed on the south with trees. . . .

Friday, June 1. . . . In the course of the afternoon we passed the traveling train of a Mr. Allen, consisting of about twenty-five ox teams, bound for the land of gold. They had been on the spot several days, detained by sickness. One of the party had died but the day before of cholera, and two more were then down with the same disease. In the morning early we had met four men from the same camp, returning on foot, with their effects on their backs, frightened at the danger and disgusted already with the trip.

It was here that we first saw a train "corralled." The wagons were drawn up in the form of a circle and chained together, leaving a small opening at but one place, through which the cattle were driven into the enclosed space at night and guarded. The arrangement is an excellent one and rendered impossible what is called, in Western phrase, a "stampede"—a mode of assault practised by Indians for the purpose of carrying off cattle or horses, in which, if possible, they set loose some of the animals and so frighten the rest as to produce a general and confused flight of the whole. To a few determined men, wagons thus arranged form a breastwork exceedingly difficult to be carried by any force of undisciplined savages. Occasional showers during the day. Evening clear and pleasant with a bright moon. Day's travel, twelve miles. . . .

Chapter 4

Monday, August 27. . . . Rather more than halfway between the cañon of Ogden's Creek and the north end of the valley a pass is found by which a crossing of the mountain into the Salt Lake Valley can be effected. The ascent of the western side is, for the first four or five hundred yards, very abrupt and rocky and would require a good deal of grading to render a road practicable; but after this, little or no labor would be necessary except to cut away the brush, which, in places, is quite thick. The length of the pass is about three miles, and the height of the range through which it makes the cut, from eight hundred to a thousand feet above the valleys on each side. The valley of Ogden's Creek, or Ogden's Hole (as places of this kind, in the nomenclature of this country, are called), has long been the rendezvous of the Northwest Company on account of its fine range for stock in the winter, and has been the scene of many a merry reunion of the hardy trappers and traders of the mountains. Its streams were formerly full of beaver, but these have, I believe, entirely disappeared. Some few antelope were bounding over the green, but the appearance of fresh "Indian sign" accounted for their scarcity. . . .

Descending the pass through dense thickets of small oak trees, we caught the first glimpse of the Great Salt Lake, the long-desired object of our search and which it had cost us so many weary steps to reach. A gleam of sunlight, reflected by the water, and a few floating, misty clouds, were all, however, that we could see of this famous spot, and we had to repress our enthusiasm for some more favorable moment. . . .

Emerging from the pass we entered the valley of the Salt Lake, and, descending some moderately high tableland, struck the road from the Mormon settlements to the lower ford of Bear River, whence, in two or three miles, we came to what was called Brown's Settlement and rode up to quite an extensive assemblage of log buildings, picketed, stockaded, and surrounded by out-buildings and cattle yards, the whole affording evidence of comfort and abundance far greater than I had expected to see in so new a settlement. Upon requesting food and lodging for the night, we were told to our great surprise that we could not be accom-modated, nor would the occupants sell us so much as an egg or a cup of milk, so that we were obliged to remount our horses; and we actually bivouacked under some willows within a hundred yards of this inhospitable dwelling, turning our animals loose and guarding them all night, lest, in search of food, they should dam-age the crops of this surly Nabal [Biblical character inhospitable to King David]. From a neighboring plantation we procured what we needed; otherwise we should have been obliged to go supper-less to bed. . . .

The following day we reached the City of the Great Salt Lake, and found that the train had arrived safely on the 23d and was now encamped near the Warm Springs on the outskirts of the city, awaiting my coming.

The result of the reconnaissance we had thus completed was such as to satisfy me that a good road can be obtained from Fort Bridger to the head of the Salt Lake; although I incline to the opinion that it should pass farther north than the route taken by me, entering the southern end of Cache Valley, probably by Blacksmith's Fork, and leaving it by the cañon formed by Bear River in making its way from that valley into the lake basin. . . .

Before reaching Great Salt Lake City, I had heard from various sources that much uneasiness was felt by the Mormon community at my anticipated coming among them. I was told that they would never permit any survey of their country to be made; while it was darkly hinted that if I persevered in attempting to carry it on, my life would scarce be safe. Utterly disregarding, indeed giving not the least credence to these insinuations, I at once called upon Brigham Young, the president of the Mormon church and the governor of the commonwealth, stated to him what I had heard, explained to him the views of the government in directing an exploration and survey of the lake, assuring him that these were the sole objects of the expedition. He replied that he did not hesitate to say that both he and the people over whom he presided had been very much disturbed and surprised that the government should send out a party into their country so soon after they had made their settlement; that he had heard of the expedition from time to time since its outset from Fort Leavenworth; and that the whole community were extremely anxious as to what could be the design of the government in such a movement. . . .

Upon all these points I undeceived Governor Young to his entire satisfaction. I was induced to pursue this conciliatory course, not only in justice to the government, but also because I knew, from the peculiar organization of this singular community, that, unless the "President" was fully satisfied that no evil was intended to his people, it would be useless for me to attempt to carry out my instructions. He was not only civil governor, but the president of the whole Church of Latter-Day Saints upon the earth, their prophet and their priest, receiving, as they all firmly believed, direct revelations of the Divine will, which, according to their creed, form the law of the church. He is, consequently, profoundly revered by all, and possesses unbounded influence and almost unlimited power. I did not anticipate open resistance; but I was fully aware that if the president continued to view the expedition with distrust, nothing could be more natural than that every possible obstruction should be thrown in our way by a "masterly inactivity."

. . . So soon, however, as the true object of the expedition was fully understood, the president laid the subject matter before the council called for the purpose, and I was informed, as the result of their deliberations, that the authorities were much pleased that the exploration was to be made; that they had themselves contemplated something of the kind, but did not yet feel able to incur the expense; but that any assistance they could render to facilitate our operations would be most cheerfully furnished to the extent of their ability. This pledge, thus heartily given, was as faithfully redeemed; and it gives me pleasure here to acknowledge the warm interest manifested and efficient aid rendered, as well by the president as by all the leading men of the community, both in our personal welfare and in the successful prosecution of the work.

The Gold Rush
to California

ON January 24, 1848, a workman named James Marshall, employed by Johann August Sutter, saw some shiny grains and specks in the tailrace of Sutter's sawmill at Coloma, California, about forty miles from Sacramento. Salvaging the glittering particles, Marshall discovered that they were gold brought down by the rushing waters of the American River. He reported his find to Sutter and they agreed to keep quiet about the discovery. Sutter was afraid that news of a gold strike would disrupt his labor force and bring in unwanted intruders. He little knew what was in store for the whole of California.

Despite the effort of Sutter to keep the discovery a secret, the news leaked out and soon everybody in Monterey was excited about gold on the American River. By the end of June, 1848, all Monterey was trying to get to the gold fields, and the reports of strikes were so sensational that word spread like a fire throughout California and to the East. By the end of 1849 would-be miners were converging upon California from all parts of the country as well as from Europe, South and Central America, the Hawaiian Islands, China, and Australia. Nothing like it had ever been seen in America.

Ships sailing around Cape Horn were loaded with passengers bound for San Francisco. A shorter sea route took passengers to the Isthmus of Panama, where they made a hazardous trip to the Pacific side. If they escaped fever they might hope to obtain boat passage up the Pacific coast. Every sort of craft that would float was pressed into service, and many a rotten tub foundered at sea with all hands. When vessels anchored in San Francisco harbor, it was a lucky captain who could retain a crew. In some instances every soul, including officers, deserted ship and headed for the gold fields, leaving the vessel to swing idly at anchor in the bay.

Most emigrants to California, however, traveled overland in ox-drawn wagons. Before the gold rush emigrants, lured by stories of the mild climate and fertile soil, had been filtering into California over various trails. Some gold seekers followed the route from Missouri to Santa Fe, then across what is now Arizona to the lower Colorado River and thence over the Cajon Pass to San Diego. From there they made their way north to the Sacramento Valley and the gold fields. Others followed the Oregon Trail as far as Fort Hall. From there they turned southwest, following the Humboldt River past the dreadful Humboldt and Carson "sinks," and thence along the Carson River to a pass in the Sierras. Still others attempted a shorter route south of Salt Lake across the Utah and Nevada deserts to the Sierra. Some had guides who could show them routes where they might find water and grass for their cattle. Others attempted to make the crossing with no other help than an inadequate map and a compass. Soon publishers were turning out "Emigrant Guides" which provided such geographical information and helpful advice as the compilers could assemble. One party in 1849, following an incompetent guide, got lost in a desolate waste that came to be known as Death Valley, where some of them perished. An account of this journey, published in 1894 by one of the survivors, William Lewis Manly, with the title *Death Valley in '49*, gives a dramatic account of the hardships on the trails to California.

In the hysterical rush to get to the gold fields many Easterners set out with inadequate equipment and little knowledge of what they would encounter. Hundreds of emigrants met disaster from Indians, weather, thirst, starvation, exhaustion, and disease. Epidemics of cholera ravaged wagon trains, and the victims were buried in unmarked graves beside the trails. Cattle died and their bones lined the routes followed by later emigrants, grim reminders of the misfortunes of travelers to the West. But no dangers were great enough to stem the human tide flowing westward. From Independence, Missouri, an endless stream of covered wagons rolled across the prairies. By the beginning of June, 1849, someone reported that some 40,000 emigrants and 12,000 wagons bound for California had crossed the Missouri River since spring. But that was only the beginning.

As these emigrants poured into California from overland and from the sea, they found no facilities to care for them and had to make the best of such crude shelters as they could improvise. In San Francisco and in Sacramento the usual habitations were tents, and men felt lucky to find shelter from the elements under any sort of cover. At the diggings on the American River and elsewhere in the mining region tents and shacks lined the watercourses.

The story of crossing the plains in '49 and of life in the gold fields provided grist for many a journalist. Newspapers throughout the world printed stories of the American West, and publishers eagerly grabbed the manuscript of any book describing the adventures of gold seekers. Some of these books still make fascinating reading. One of the best accounts of a trip across the continent was written by Alonzo Delano, an ailing resident of Illinois whose doctor convinced him that a trip across the plains would improve his health. A similar prescription had been given to Francis Parkman, and his *Oregon Trail* resulted. It was evidently a case of "kill or cure," and Delano set out in the spring of 1849. With prescient wisdom he decided that he would go out not to mine but to be a trader and sell goods to the miners. Though Delano himself did not get rich, some of the most prosperous emigrants in the Gold Rush were merchants and not miners. For example, the fortune of Collis Huntington had its beginning as a hardware and general store that catered to miners.

Delano's Narrative

[*Delano's narrative, published in 1854 and again in 1859 with the title* Life on the Plains and among the Diggings, *is valuable for its concrete detail in contrast to the generalities of some of the Gold Rush journals. Although he was conscious of writing a "literary" account, he did not sacrifice information to the literary ornamentation characteristic of the mid-nineteenth century. Excerpts from his narrative follow:*]

Chapter 1

. . . .

A company had been formed at Dayton, a few miles above Ottawa [sic. Present-day Dayton, Ohio, is south of Ottawa], under the command of Captain Jesse Greene, for the purpose of crossing the plains, and I resolved to join it. Our general rendezvous was to be at St. Joseph on the Missouri, from which we intended to take our departure. I had engaged men, purchased cattle and a wagon, and subsequently laid in my supplies for the trip, at St. Louis. My wagon I shipped by water to St. Joseph, and sent my cattle across the country about the middle of March to meet me at the place of rendezvous in April.

All things being in readiness, on the day first named [April 5, 1849] I bid adieu to my family and to Ottawa, and proceeded to St. Louis on the steamer *Revolution,* and there took passage for St. Joseph on the *Embassy.* The companions of my mess were Messrs. J. H. Fredenburg, Matthew Harris, and Eben Smith, from Ottawa—the two last I had engaged to take across the plains on condition of their assistance during the journey and half they should make for one year from the time we left home—a contract which was then common. We were joined on our trip up the river by a young man named Robert Brown, who was looking out for some opportunity of going to California and who was proceeding to St. Joseph for this purpose.

There was a great crowd of adventurers on the *Embassy.* Nearly every state in the Union was represented. Every berth was full, and not only every settee and table occupied at night, but the cabin floor was covered by the sleeping emigrants. The decks were covered with wagons, mules, oxen, and mining implements, and the hold was filled with supplies. But this was the condition of every boat—for since the invasion of Rome by the Goths, such a deluge of mortals had not been witnessed as was now pouring from the States to the various points of departure for the golden shores of California. . . .

A tedious passage of ten days brought us, on the 19th, to St. Joseph, where we learned that the Dayton company, which had preceded us, had left that day with the intention of moving up the river to some other point for crossing into the Indian Territory, where they would halt until the grass was sufficiently advanced to afford forage for our cattle, and which would give us ample time to overtake them before setting out from the land of civilization on our arduous journey across the plains. . . .

Chapter 2

May 3, 1849. Our company was well arranged and provided for the great journey before us. Every wagon was numbered, and our captain, with the concurrence of the members of the company, directed that each wagon should in turn take the lead for one day, and then, falling in the rear, give place to the succeeding number, and so on, alternately, till the whole seventeen advanced in turn. Every mess was provided with a portable light cooking stove, which, though not absolutely necessary, was often found convenient on account of the scarcity of fuel; each man was well armed with a rifle, pistol, and knife, with an abundant supply of ammunition, and each mess had a good and substantial tent. Each wagon was drawn by from three to six yoke of good cattle; and it was agreed that they should be prudently driven, for we could well anticipate the helplessness of our condition should our cattle give out on the plains, where they could not be duplicated. To prevent their being stolen by the Indians or straying at night, a watch was set while they were feeding; and at dark they were driven in and tied to the wagons, where they were constantly under the supervision of the night guard; and it is owing to this watchfulness and care, that we lost none by Indians throughout the trip.

Before sunrise the cattle were driven out to graze, and all hands were astir, and some engaged in that business of life, cooking breakfast. The wagons formed a circle, outside of which the tents were pitched, so that had thieves been disposed to get at our valuables, they would have been compelled to pass into the inner circle under the eyes of the guard; and in case of an attack the wagons would form a barricade. Anticipating a scarcity of fuel, the company, on leaving the timber of the Missouri, had thrown wood enough on the wagons to serve two days for cooking, and now before each one the smoke gracefully curled in active preparation for wooding up the engine of life. Brown was installed cook, the other boys agreeing to perform his duty as night watch. Henderson drove our cattle, and Smith made himself generally useful, in collecting fuel, pitching and striking the tent—in fact, all had their respective duties to perform. About nine o'clock the camp was broken up, the tents put into the wagons, the cattle driven in and yoked, and our second day on the plains commenced.

The country was rolling prairie; with the Little Namaha [i.e., Nemaha, in Nebraska] on the right, four or five miles distant, and no timber in sight except on the banks of the stream. Our route was traced mainly by marking the course of the hollows and little streams which diverged to the right or left, keeping such ridges as appeared to divide the waters which flowed into the Great or Little Namaha. Old Mr. Greene, the father of our worthy captain, from his experience in traversing the western prairies acted as our chief pioneer, and he was rarely at fault, although, at times, it was extremely difficult to determine the true ridge, from the evenness of the ground and the windings of the hollows.

About ten o'clock I had walked in advance of the train about a mile, and was a little behind Mr. Greene, who was accompanied by Mr. Fredenburg, on the pony, when suddenly two strangers came in sight upon an eminence, having three mules and ponies. On seeing us, they halted and gazed for a few moments, and then took a direction as if to cut off a circuitous bend, which our train was making, without approaching us. Messrs. Greene and Fredenburg, desiring to make some inquiries, galloped across the plain and intercepted them.

These men told them that they belonged to a company of a hundred wagons which had started out from Old Fort Kearny two weeks before and had gone about forty miles on the plains when the grass failed and the company were compelled to stop, and that they were then returning to the settlements for some additional supplies. After getting some directions, the parties separated, each continuing their several routes.

About two hours afterward we were met by two white men and an Indian who were in pursuit of these men. It appeared that the two men belonged to no company of emigrants and their story of the hundred wagons was a sheer fabrication. They had stolen their animals from an Illinois company at Fort Kearny and were making their escape. Their pursuers, suspecting the Indian to be accessory to the theft, forced him to go with them in pursuit. At night the two men returned to our camp having overtaken the thieves, who, on seeing that they were pursued, jumped from their animals and made their escape in the timber on the bank of the creek. When they were running off, the Indian asked permission of his companions to mount a fine pony for the purpose of intercepting the rogues. One of them dismounting from his recovered animal, the Indian mounted and set off in pursuit at a round gallop and soon disappeared behind a hill. After waiting some time for his reappearance, they chanced to look in another direction and saw the outline of the Indian making off with their pony, a new saddle, and an overcoat which had remained on the saddle. It was now too late to think of overtaking the red runaway, and they had to submit to their loss with the best grace they could, cursing their own credulity, but giving the Indian credit for his ingenuity. . . .

Chapter 7

June 25. Our road still lay along the peculiar and interesting valley of the Sweet Water [in Wyoming]; but at this point we left the river, and for ten miles there was neither grass nor water, and the deep sand and dust made the traveling extremely laborious. Long trains of wagons and of animated life, as usual, varied the wild scenery; and had it not been for excessive weariness of long travel we should have enjoyed it with infinite zest. . . .

During our drive in the early part of the day, on gaining a slight elevation, we obtained a view of the lofty Wind River Mountains, covered with snow, at an apparent distance of thirty or forty miles. They are much higher than those of the Sweet Water, and present a magnificent appearance. On the north side of the road stood a bare, isolated rock of granite, sloping like a roof, which, though not as large as Independence Rock [also on the Sweetwater], was something of a curiosity from its immense size. In the bare granite range on the right was a mountain rock many miles distant which resembled a castle with a dome, and it looked like the stronghold of some feudal baron of olden time; but as we passed on, it soon changed its appearance to a shapeless, broken mass of granite. At night we again reached the river, where a new road had been made through a singularly gloomy gorge in the northern mountains through which the river flowed. It was reported to be the best road, although it was necessary to ford the river four times; but it was said that by this route we should avoid a heavy sand road, and we therefore thought we would take it. The grass, though not abundant, was passably good. Distance, fifteen miles.

June 26. We crossed the river at the first ford and entered the rocky gorge through which the river flowed and proceeded about a mile to the second ford. A narrow pathway had been cut in the bank, capable of admitting but one wagon at a time, and the ford was so deep that every wagon box had to be raised about six inches from its bed to prevent the water from flowing in. The ford was crooked and bad, and a large number of teams were in advance of us, which would detain us till noon before our turn would come to cross. Under the circumstances we judged it best to return and take the old road, which was described as being sandy and hard. We accordingly faced about, and on reaching the road and leaving the river we found about four miles of sand road, but the rest of the way was good and the distance was no greater. We gained time, for on reaching the point where the two roads united, at a distance of eight miles, we found ourselves meeting trains which had been a day ahead of us, and they represented that the road by the gorge was not good, and that the river had to be crossed four times by deep and bad fords, which delayed them. The day was excessively warm, the dust deep, and the cloud which arose from the passing trains rendered traveling extremely unpleasant.

. . . Some of the boys, thinking that water could be easily obtained, took a spade and, going out on the wild grass, commenced digging. About a foot from the surface, instead of water they struck a beautiful layer of ice, five or six inches in thickness. Many trains were passing at the time, and all stopped and supplied themselves with the clear, cooling element, and buckets were brought into use to supply ourselves with frozen water for our supplies. This natural icehouse is not only a great curiosity in itself but, from its peculiar situation in this dry, barren, sandy plain, is justly entitled to be called the diamond of the desert. To the unsophisticated this may look like a traveler's tale, but it is easily explained upon natural principles. We were now at an elevation of about six thousand feet. The morass was either a pond or a combination of springs, covered with turf or swamp grass; and at this high altitude the temperature of winter is very severe, converting the water of the morass to solid ice. Although the sun of summer is intensely hot in those mountain valleys, the turf and grass intercept the intensity of its rays and prevent the dissolution of the ice, on the principle of our domestic icehouses; thus a kind Providence affords a necessary and indispensable comfort to the exhausted traveler in these dry and barren regions.

We were now on a plain, sixteen miles distance to water. The sage here attained a great growth, being as high as my head and the trunk frequently six inches in diameter. I observed a new species of prairie dog, or, it may be, a connecting link between the prairie dog and ground squirrel. They are about the size of the latter with much the shape of the former, and burrow under the sage bushes, to which they fly on the least alarm. We found them so numerous at some of our encampments that we could knock them over with sticks, and the boys amused themselves in killing them with pistols. They were very fat and oily, but, on being parboiled and roasted, were quite good. . . . Antelope were plenty, and droves of mountain sheep, or ibex, were upon the hills. We made about six miles on the sixteen-mile stretch when we encamped, with none but alkaline water and scarcely any grass, and it required all our care to keep our cattle from straying in search of food and to prevent them from drinking the fatal water. Drive, eighteen miles.

Chapter 13

.   .   .   .

August 26. The Sierra Nevada—the snowy mountain so long wished for, and yet so long dreaded! We were at its base, soon to commence its ascent. In a day or two we were to leave the barren sands of the desert for a region of mountains and hills where perhaps the means of sustaining life might not be found; where our wagons might be dashed to atoms by falling from precipices. A thousand vague and undefined difficulties were present to our imaginations; yet all felt strong for the work, feeling that it was our last. Yet the imagined difficulties were without foundation. Instead of losing our wagons and packing our cattle; or, as some suggested as a last resort for the weary, mounting astride of an old ox and thus making our debut into the valley of the land of gold—we were unable to add a single page of remarkable adventure across the mountains more dangerous than we had already encountered.

A drive of four miles brought us to the baked, dry bed of a

lake [perhaps Humboldt Lake, Nevada], which I estimated to be twenty miles in circumference, surrounded on three sides by the mountains. Toward the upper end of this lake the Sierra Nevada seemed to decrease much in height, and we could see even beyond the plain over which our road lay that it seemed to blend with other hills on our right, and a low depression appeared, as if an easy passage might be made in that direction—even easier than at the point where we crossed—where the bed of the lake was about five miles wide and the ground smooth and level as a floor. About a mile from the base of the mountain and on the bottom land of the lake were many acres of fine grass, with a fine mountain brook running through it, which sank as it reached the bed of the lake; and a little way from our place of halting there were perhaps an hundred hot springs, which induced us to call this Hot Spring Lake.

It was now only eight miles to the Pass, and, the grass being excellent, the company halted for noon with the intention of driving on in the afternoon to the crossing. I availed myself of the opportunity to make an excursion to the mountains, not only with a view of gratifying my curiosity, but hoping a chance shot might add something in the way of flesh to our larders. At the foot of the mountain I was joined by two young men from a Missouri train, and we commenced the ascent. On the sides of the mountain we saw a species of nectarine growing on dwarf bushes not more than twelve or eighteen inches high; but they were sour and acid, not yet being fully ripe. In the ravines were an abundance of wild black cherries, but those were not very good. Pines grew to a great height, and we were refreshed by their cooling shade.

I had preceded my companions along the border of a deep ravine, and was about fifty rods in advance when the ravine terminated in a perpendicular wall of rock, hundreds of feet high, around which there appeared to be a craggy opening, or passage. While I was gazing on the towering rock before me, I momentarily changed my position, when the front part of my coat was grazed by something passing like a flash before me. Glancing at the base of the rock, I saw two naked Indians spring around a jutting, and I comprehended the matter at once. I had been a mark, and they had sent an arrow which grazed my coat, but without striking me. I instantly raised my rifle and discharged it at the flying Indians, and sprang behind a tree. The noise of my piece soon brought my companions to my side, and going cautiously to the rock, a few stains of blood showed that my aim had not been decidedly bad; but we saw nothing more of the Indians. . . .

Chapter 14

.   .   .   .

September 9. It was reported that it was twenty miles to the next water; we therefore started early in the morning. We found the road good, and at the distance of fourteen miles there was a little grass. It was understood that the train would drive the twenty miles, which would bring us to the first tributary of Feather River; and with Colonel Watkins I had walked to the fourteen-mile point.

As the train did not come up, however, I concluded to go on alone to the branch. The whole distance was finely wooded with magnificent pines. Occasionally volcanic rock protruded above the ground, and the soil was discolored with ochre. It was nearly sunset when I descended a steep pitch to a small valley through which flowed the Feather Creek. While I sat near a camp, patiently awaiting the arrival of my company, with an anxious longing for a crust of hard bread, the shades of night began to darken, and no train appeared. The prospect of no supper and a bed without blankets were rising before me, producing no very pleasant feelings, when a gentleman approached and, stopping before me a moment, observed,

"You are alone."

"Yet, I am in advance of my train, which was to come to this place; but I fear something has detained them."

"No matter," he replied; "I want you to go with me and spend the night at our camp. Come," said he, as I hesitated, knowing that none were well supplied with provisions; "you must go and share what we have. No excuse—no ceremony."

I followed him, and such as they had I freely shared, and the evening was whiled away in such pleasant conversation as well-bred and well-educated gentlemen know how to introduce. Gentle reader, if there is any mystery in all this, it may be explained by saying they were Odd-Fellows; yet in all my journey, when circumstances have taken me from my own train, I have never, in a single instance, been denied the rites of hospitality; and although at this time, when our route had been lengthened nearly three weeks—when every individual had scarcely supplies enough for himself, and when a single meal was an item of consideration, the courtesy of a civilized land was extended, and the weary and hungered were not denied the enjoyment of hospitality, such as Messrs. Cox and C. C. Lane, of Flemingsburgh, Kentucky, extended to me.

The train did not come up. It appeared that, as they came to the fourteen-mile halt, a beautiful lake [Honey Lake, California] had just been discovered a mile and a half east of the road, and that they had driven to it, where, finding luxuriant grass, they had concluded to lay up all day. Distance, twenty miles.

September 10. That branch of Feather River where I spent the night is a Rocky Mountain stream of ice-cold water, about two rods wide. In the small valley in which we lay another creek nearly as large gushed out at the base of the mountain. We had expected, on reaching Feather Creek, to find auriferous indications [i.e., signs of gold], but the formation was a kind of greenstone along the stream, and trap-rock in the mountains, with neither quartz nor slate.

The train came up early, and we went on. Ten miles over a rough road brought us to a paradise in the mountains which is the principal head of the main fork of Feather River. A low, broad valley [Mountain Meadows, California] lay before us, probably twenty miles or more in length and ten miles or more in width, apparently enclosed by high, pine-covered mountains. Into this flowed the mountain creek already named, through a deep gorge in the hills. A mile above, where the road led into the valley, was a curiosity indeed. At the very base of the hill the water gushed forth, forming at once a stream of crystal clearness and cold as ice, six rods wide and eight feet deep. In fact it was an underground river which had burst into the light of day, of sufficient capacity to float a small steamboat. From a little height we could trace its serpentine course through the tall grass of the valley for two or three miles, until it united at nearly right angles with Feather River, which moves with a slow, even current through the broad bottom, a clear, beautiful and navigable river. Many miles below it entered the mountains through a high, rocky, and almost impassable cañon, being joined, however, by another affluent of

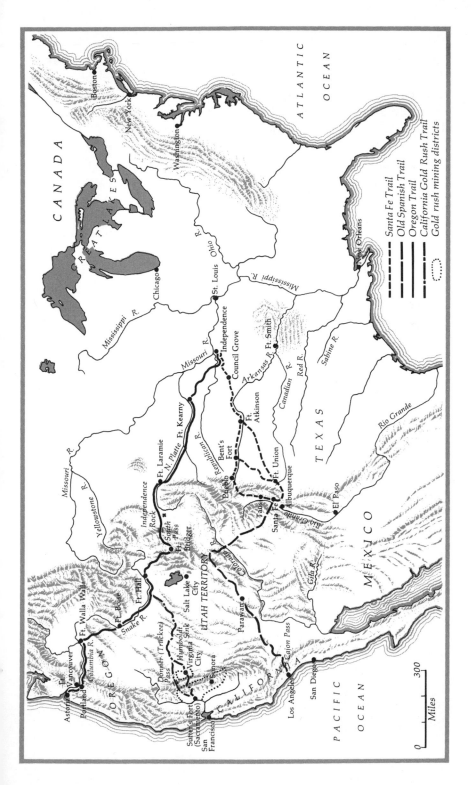

Routes Westward: The Santa Fe, Oregon, Old Spanish, and Gold Rush Trails

nearly the same size flowing from the northeast through a broad
lateral valley, and then, by a long series of rapids and falls, after
a circuitous course of between two and three hundred miles it
emerged from the foot of hills, through a rough cañon, into the
broad valley of the Sacramento.

From the indications along the edges, this valley is overflowed
by the rains of winter and the melting snow of spring—thus making a broad but shallow mountain lake of from sixty to eighty
miles in circumference. Ducks, swans, and wild geese covered its
waters, and elk, black-tailed deer, and antelope were numerous
on the bottoms; while the tracks of the grizzly bear, the wolf, and
cougar were frequent on the hills. We halted for the night on this
beautiful bottom, after a drive of sixteen miles.

. . . About one o'clock, we reached the western side of the
valley, where there was an encampment of a hundred wagons
laying over to recruit their cattle, for it was known that it was
seventy miles to Lawson's [Lassen's House] in the valley of the
Sacramento, and also, that fifty miles of the distance was over a
rough, mountain desert, destitute of grass and water. Lawson
[Peter Lassen] himself had passed the day before with an exploring party, and had left directions what course we were to take
to reach the valley, as well as a table of distances to water, which
was posted on a tree by the roadside above our camp. Distance,
ten miles.

September 12. We were now in the valley of plenty. Our poor
teeth, which had been laboring on the filelike consistency of pilot
bread, had now a respite, in the agreeable task of masticating
from the "flesh pots" of California.

As we determined to lay over during the day, our wagon master,
Traverse, concluded to butcher an ox, and the hungry Arabs of
our train were regaled with a feast of dead kine. Feeling an aristo-
cratic longing for a rich beef steak, I determined to have one.
There was not a particle of fat in the steak to make gravy, nor
was there a slice of bacon to be had to fry it with, and the flesh
was as dry and as hard as a bone. But a nice broiled steak, with a
plenty of gravy, I would have—and I had it. The inventive genius
of an emigrant is almost constantly called forth on the plains, and
so in my case. I laid a nice cut on the coals, which, instead of
broiling, only burnt and carbonized like a piece of wood, and when

one side was turned to cinder, I whopped it over to make charcoal of the other. To make butter gravy, I melted a stearin candle, which I poured over the delicious tit-bit, and, smacking my lips, sat down to my feast, the envy of several lookers-on. I sopped the first mouthful in the nice looking gravy, and put it between my teeth, when the gravy cooled almost instantly, and the roof of my mouth and my teeth were coated all over with a covering like hard beeswax, making mastication next to impossible.

"How does it go?" asked one.

"O, first rate," said I, struggling to get the hard, dry morsel down my throat; and cutting another piece, which was free from the delicious gravy, "Come, try it," said I; "I have more than I can eat (which was true). You are welcome to it." The envious, hungry soul sat down and, putting a large piece between his teeth, after rolling it about in his mouth awhile, deliberately spit it out, saying, with an oath, that

"Chips and beeswax are hard fare, even for a starving man."

Ah, how hard words and want of sentiment will steal over one's better nature on the plains. As for the rest of the steak, we left it to choke the wolves.

We were successful in killing ducks, and our evening meal was more palatable. At night a hunter came in and reported that he had seen an outcrop of slate on a mountain bordering the valley below, and from his description we thought there were indications of gold, and a small party was organized for prospecting the following morning.

September 13. How long we might be out in prospecting we could not tell, but putting up a two days' supply of bread and coffee, a party of six of us started off, under the guidance of the hunter, to the mountain, while the train took the road toward Lawson's, after cutting grass to be used on the desert. Three miles traveling brought us to a lofty mountain, and about midway up its sides was a small outcrop of light gray slate, standing about ten degrees from a vertical position, the dip in the rock being to the southeast. We made some slight excavations and washed some of the earth but obtained nothing, and concluded to return to the road in a diagonal direction so as to save distance in overtaking the train. Three of the party, Hittle, Tuttle and Jackson, took a different direction and crossed a ridge to the valley below, when they became bewildered and were out all night. This little prospecting tour was the origin of a report to emigrants behind that there was good gold diggings near, and at one time a party of forty men started out and spent several days in searching for the lucky mines. . . .

Chapter 16

[*September 26.*] We had driven half of the previous night to reach our resting place; and we now learned that we were within three miles of Sacramento City and Sutter's Fort. After a frugal dinner of hard bread and water, Doctor Hall, Mr. Rood and myself doffed our soiled garments and, after assuming habiliments more in accordance with civilized life, we set out for town, leaving our cattle and wagon in the care of Mr. Pope. Taking off our clothes on reaching the ford, we waded across the American, a clear and beautiful stream about four hundred feet wide, and reached the city of tents about four o'clock in the afternoon. And here I found myself more than two thousand miles from home in a city which had risen as if by enchantment since I had crossed the Missouri, a stranger, way-worn and jaded by a long journey, half famished for want of even the necessaries of life, practicing domestic economy to the fullest extent, with every prospect before me of continuing in the practice of that useful science; for, on examining the state of my treasury, I found myself the wealthy owner of the full sum of four dollars!—enough to board me one day at a low-priced hotel. And I had come in the pleasant anticipation of raising a full supply of provisions, which would cost not less than two hundred dollars. . . .

Sacramento City, at the period of which I write, contained a floating population of about five thousand people. It was first laid out in the spring of 1849 on the east bank of the Sacramento River, here less than one-eighth of a mile wide, and is about a mile and a half west of Sutter's Fort. Lots were originally sold for $200 each, but within a year sales were made as high as $30,000. There were not a dozen wood or frame buildings in the whole city, but they were chiefly made of canvas stretched over light supporters; or were simply tents, arranged along the streets. The stores, like the dwellings, were of cloth, and property and merchandise of all kinds lay exposed, night and day, by the wayside, and such a thing as a robbery was scarcely known. This in fact was the case throughout the country, and is worthy of notice on account of the great and extraordinary change which occurred. There were a vast number of taverns and eating houses, and the only public building was a theatre. All these were made of canvas.

At all of the hotels and groceries gambling was carried on to a remarkable extent, and men seemed to be perfectly reckless of money. Indeed, it seemed to have lost its value, and piles of coin and dust covered every table and were constantly changing hands at the turn of a card.

At high water the river overflows its banks, and a notice of a dreadful disaster of this kind will appear hereafter. For a mile along the river lay ships, barges, and various water craft, laden with merchandise and provisions. Trade was brisk, and prices exorbitantly high.

On the north side of the city is a large and deep slough, in which cattle frequently mire and perish, and at this time the effluvia arising from their putrid carcasses was almost insufferable. A little beyond the slough the American River empties into the Sacramento. This river is not navigable for vessels. The Sacramento River, though affected by the tide, is pure and sweet, and generally is better to drink than the water of the wells, some of which are slightly brackish.

On the first day of October, all things being in readiness, Pomeroy and myself, taking Mr. Pope, with McNeil's cattle, set out for *somewhere,* but with no definite location in view. Arrived at Bear River, we encamped under the trees on the bottom, and, after turning out our cattle and cooking our suppers, we placed our provision chest at our heads, and, spreading our blankets, were soon asleep despite the howling of the cayotes all around us. On awaking in the morning we discovered that the thievish animals had been at our bedside in the night, and had actually taken the cloth which covered our provisions and dragged it across the road without awaking us. . . .

Chapter 27

With regard to the resources of California, Nature has indeed been bountiful, and if they are properly developed no state in the Union can present a greater amount of real wealth. California extends from about the thirty-second to the forty-second degree of latitude, and embraces within this space of ten degrees almost every variety of climate. It is a country of mountain and plain, but its greatest area is mountainous. On the east the Sierra Nevada, with its everlasting snows, stretches from one end of the state to the other, presenting peaks from ten to fourteen thousand feet above the level of the ocean; and on its western borders the Coast Range is bounded entirely by the Pacific Ocean. Between the Sierra and the Coast Range lay the valleys of the San Joaquin and Sacramento, making one continuous plain five hundred miles in length, while many minor valleys in the foothills of the Sierra, and probably in the Coast Range also, make collectively a large area of arable land.

. . . In my opinion there is arable land enough in these mountain valleys, if properly cultivated, to supply the whole mining population with vegetables, fruit, and grain, while the larger valleys can raise enough not only to supply its population and that of the cities, but also a surplus for exportation. I have been induced to change my preconceived opinion with regard to the agricultural capacities of the country by actual demonstration. On my first arrival very little farming was done. Nearly all the vegetables, flour, and grain were derived from foreign ports, and little had been done to develop the agricultural capacities of the country. The long droughts seemed to render it impossible for grain to grow without irrigating the parched earth, where the grass withered and became crisp under the burning sun; but the energy of man soon demonstrated that California had its regular seasons as well as the Atlantic States, and that grain put into the ground in season to have the benefit of the winter and spring rains grows rapidly in the prolific soil and matures long before the summer sun withers it; and that crops are as sure in California as on the Atlantic coast.

Two years produced an important change: vegetables were produced in sufficient quantities not only to supply the demand, but the prices were infinitely reduced, and their importation ceased; and it was found that small grains thrived well and yielded three-fold what they do at home.

. . . In the South the grape is cultivated with infinite success; peaches grow in perfection, and I cannot see why apples will not succeed well in certain districts of the mountain valleys.

In the mountains water power is abundant for all mechanical purposes, and the noble pines, made into lumber, will form a source of wealth equaled only by its mineral treasures. It is true there has been a vast deal of individual suffering, more, perhaps, than usually occurs in the settlement of a country. . . .

The climate is delightful and salubrious. Although the days in summer are hot, yet the evenings are cool; and the laborer, though exhausted by the heat of the day, is refreshed with a good night's sleep, without the sultriness of the Atlantic summers; and the dryness of the atmosphere in summer soon withers the vegetation, and prevents the malaria of damper climates. . . .

In conclusion, I beg leave to say that there are many subjects of which it would have given me pleasure to speak. . . . The most that I can hope for is that the reader may find amusement and understand some of the trials encountered by the early emigrants to California, especially by the miners, whom I know to be an honorable and intelligent class of people.

The Gold Fields

[*One of the earliest firsthand accounts of the gold fields was written by Edward Gould Buffum and published in both Philadelphia and London in 1850 with the title* Six Months in the Gold Mines. *Buffum was a young army lieutenant whose company was mustered out in Los Angeles in 1848. Like other members of his military unit, he joined the rush to the gold fields when the news of the discovery at Sutter's Mill reached them.*

[*Buffum's narrative was both informative and entertaining. In fact it served as a useful guide to inexperienced emigrants who had little knowledge of how to go about the recovery of gold. Buffum gave precise details of the two types of mining common*

*at this time, the "dry diggings" and the "wet diggings." Excerpts
from his account follow:*]

Introduction

On the 26th day of September, 1846, the 7th Regiment of New
York State Volunteers, commanded by Colonel J. D. Stevenson,
sailed from the harbor of New York under orders from the Secretary of War to proceed to Upper California. The objects and
operations of the expedition, the fitting out of which created some
sensation at the time, are now too well understood and appre-
ciated to require explanation. This regiment, in which I had the
honor of holding a lieutenant's commission, numbered, rank and
file, about seven hundred and twenty men, and sailed from New
York in the ships *Loo Choo, Susan Drew,* and *Thomas H. Perkins.*
After a fine passage of little more than five months, during which
we spent several days pleasantly in Rio [de] Janeiro, the *Thomas
H. Perkins* entered the harbor of San Francisco and anchored off
the site of the town then called Yerba Buena, on the 6th day of
March, 1847. The remaining ships arrived soon afterward.

Alta [Upper] California we found in quiet possession of the
American land and naval forces—the "stars and stripes" floating
over the old Mexican *presidios* [garrisons]. There being no immediate service to perform, our regiment was posted in small
detachments through the various towns.

The now famous city of San Francisco, situated near the extreme
end of a long and barren peninsular tract of land which separates
the bay of San Francisco from the ocean, when first I landed
on its beach was almost a solitude, there being not more than
twelve or fifteen rough houses and a few temporary buildings for
hides to relieve the view. Where now stands the great commercial metropolis of the Pacific, with its thirty thousand inhabitants,
its busy streets alive with the hum of trade, were corrals for cattle
and unoccupied sandy hills.

With the discovery of the gold mines a new era in the history
of California commences. This event has already changed a com-
parative wilderness into a flourishing state, and is destined to
affect the commercial and political relations of the world. Between
California as she was at the period of the cession to the United

States and as she is at this time there is no similitude. In two short years her mineral resources have been developed and she has at once emerged from obscurity into a cynosure upon which nations are gazing with wondering eyes. Her mountains and valleys, but recently the hunting grounds of naked savages, are now peopled with a hundred thousand civilized men; her magnificent harbors crowded with ships from far distant ports; her rivers and bays navigated by steamboats; her warehouses filled with the products of almost every clime, and her population energetic, hopeful, and prosperous.

Chapter 3

. . . So long as manual labor is employed for washing gold, the "cradle" is the best agent to use for that purpose. The manner of procuring and washing the golden earth was this: The loose stones and surface earth being removed from any portion of the bar, a hole from four to six feet square was opened, and the dirt extracted therefrom was thrown upon a rawhide placed at the side of the machine. One man shoveled the dirt into the sieve, another dipped up water and threw it on, and a third rocked the "cradle." The earth, thrown upon the sieve, is washed through with the water, while the stones and gravel are retained and thrown off. The continued motion of the machine and the constant stream of water pouring through it washes the earth over the various bars or rifflers to the "tail," where it runs out, while the gold, being of greater specific gravity, sinks to the bottom, and is prevented from escaping by the rifflers. When a certain amount of earth has been thus washed (usually about sixty pans full are called "a washing"), the gold, mixed with a heavy black sand which is always found mingled with gold in California, is taken out and washed in a tin pan until nearly all the sand is washed away. It is then put into a cup or pan, and when the day's labor is over is dried before the fire, and the sand remaining carefully blown out. This is a simple explanation of the process of gold washing in the placers of California.

At present, however, instead of dipping and pouring on water by hand, it is usually led on by a hose or forced by a pump, thereby giving a better and more constant stream and saving the labor of one man. The excavation is continued until the solid rock is struck, or the water rushing in renders it impossible to obtain any more earth, when a new place is opened. We found the gold on the Yuba [River] in exceedingly fine particles, and it has always been considered of a very superior quality. We inquired of the washers as to their success, and they, seeing we were "green horns" and thinking we might possibly interfere with them, gave us either evasive answers or in some cases told us direct lies. We understood from them that they were making about twenty dollars per day, while I afterward learned, from the most positive testimony of two men who were at work there at the time, that one hundred dollars a man was not below the average estimate of a day's labor.

On this visit to Foster's Bar I made my first essay in gold digging. I scraped up with my hand my tin cup full of earth and washed it in the river. How eagerly I strained my eyes as the earth was washing out and the bottom of the cup was coming in view! and how delighted, when, on reaching the bottom, I discerned about twenty little golden particles sparkling in the sun's rays, and worth probably about fifty cents. I wrapped them carefully in a piece of paper and preserved them for a long time —but, like much more gold in larger quantities which it has since been my lot to possess, it has escaped my grasp, and where it now is Heaven only knows. . . .

Sutter's Fort is a large parallelogram of adobe walls, five hundred feet long by one hundred and fifty broad. Portholes are bored through the walls, and at its corners are bastions on which cannon are mounted. But when I arrived there its hostile appearance was entirely forgotten in the busy scenes of trade which it exhibited. The interior of the fort, which had been used by Sutter for granaries and storehouses, was rented to merchants, the whole at the annual sum of sixty thousand dollars, and was converted into stores where every description of goods was to be purchased at gold-mine prices. Flour was selling at $60 per barrel, pork at $150 per barrel, sugar at 25 cents per pound, and clothing at the most enormous and unreasonable rates. The principal trading establishment at this time was that of Samuel Brannan & Co. Mr. Brannan informed me that since the discovery of the mines over seventy-five thousand dollars in gold dust had been received by them. Sutter's Fort is in latitude 35° 33′ 45″ N., and longitude 121° 40′ 05″ W.

With all our worldly gear packed in an ox wagon, we left Sutter's Fort on the morning of the 1st of December, and, traveling about seven miles on the road, encamped in a beautiful grove of evergreen oak to give the cattle an opportunity to lay in a sufficient supply of grass and acorns preparatory to a long march. As we were to remain here during the day, we improved the opportunity by taking our dirty clothing, of which by that time we had accumulated a considerable quantity, down to the banks of the American Fork, distant about one mile from camp, for the purpose of washing. While we were employed in this laborious but useful occupation, Higgins called my attention to the salmon which were working up the river over a little rapid opposite us. Some sport suggested itself; and more anxious for this than labor, we dropped our half-washed shirts and started back to camp for our rifles, which we soon procured and brought down to the river. In making their way over the bar the backs of the salmon were exposed some two inches above water; and the instant one appeared, a well-directed rifle-ball perforated his spine. The result was that before dark Higgins and myself carried into camp thirty-five splendid salmon, procured by this novel mode of sport. We luxuriated on them and gave what we could not eat for supper and breakfast to some lazy Indians who had been employed the whole day in spearing some half dozen each. There is every probability that the salmon fishery will yet prove a highly lucrative business in California.

Next morning we packed up and made a fresh start. That night we encamped at the "Green Springs," about twenty-five miles distant from Sutter's Fort. These springs are directly upon the road and bubble up from a muddy black loam, while around them is the greenest verdure—the surrounding plain being dotted with beautiful groves and magnificent flowers. Their waters are delicious.

As the ox team was a slow traveler and quarters were to be looked for in our new winter home, on the next morning Higgins and myself were appointed a deputation to mount two horses we had brought with us and proceed post-haste to the "dry diggings." We started at 10 A.M. and traveled through some beautiful valleys and over lofty hills. As we reached the summit of a high ridge, we paused by common consent to gaze upon the landscape and breathe the delicious air. The broad and fertile valleys of the Sacramento and San Joaquin lay stretched at our feet like a highly colored map. The noble rivers which lend their names to these rich valleys were plainly visible, winding like silver threads through dark lines of timber fringing their banks, now plunging amid dense forests, and now coming in view sparkling and bright as the riches they contain; the intermediate plains, here parched and browned with the sun's fierce rays, there brilliant with all the hues of the rainbow and dotted with the autumnal flowers and open groves of evergreen oak. Herds of elk, black-tailed deer, and antelope browsed near the mountain sides, on the summit of which the eagle builds his eyry.

The surrounding atmosphere, fragrant with delightful odors, was so pure and transparent as to render objects visible at a great distance, and so elastic and bracing as to create a perceptible effect on our feelings. Far in the distance the massive peak of Shasta reared its snow-capped head from amid a dense forest fourteen thousand feet into the sky.

We arrived at what was then called Weaver's Creek about dusk. About a dozen log houses, rudely thrown together and plastered with mud, constituted the little town which was to be our winter home and where we were to be initiated into the mysteries, pleasures, and sufferings of a gold digger's life. A pretty little stream, coursing through lofty oak and pine-covered hills and on whose left bank the settlement had been made, was the river that had borne down the riches which we hoped to appropriate to our private uses.

It was a beautiful afternoon when we reached it. The sun was just declining, and, resting upon the crest of the distant Sierra Nevada, seemed to cover it with a golden snow. The miners were returning to their log huts with their implements of labor slung over their shoulders, and their tin pans containing the precious metal in their hands. We learned that the "dry diggings" for which we had started were three miles further into the mountains, that there was a great scarcity of water, and that but very little could be accomplished before the commencement of the rainy season. Finding some old friends here, who generously offered us a "chance" upon the mud floor of their log cabin, we remained with them for the night, and, stretching our blankets upon the floor and lighting our pipes, were soon engaged in an interesting conversation on the all-absorbing topic.

Next morning our party arrived with the team, and from the representations of our friends, we concluded to remain at Weaver's Creek, and pitched our tent on the banks of the stream. Our teamster's bill was something of an item to men who were not as yet accustomed to "gold-mine prices." We paid three hundred dollars for the transportation, about fifty miles, of three barrels of flour, one of pork, and about two hundred pounds of small stores, being at the rate of thirty dollars per cwt. This was the regular price charged by teamsters at that time, and of course there was no alternative but to pay, which we did, although it exhausted the last dollar belonging to our party. But there before us, on the banks of that pretty stream and in the neighboring gorges, lay the treasures that were to replenish our pockets, and the sigh for its departure was changed by this thought into a hope that our fondest wishes might be realized in our new and exciting occupation.

Chapter 4

The day after our arrival, in anticipation of the immediate commencement of the rainy season (a time dreaded by strangers in all California, and particularly in the northern region), we determined to build a log house, and were about to commence operations when we received an offer for the sale of one. We examined it and found a little box of unhewn logs, about twenty feet long by ten wide, which was offered us at the moderate price of five hundred dollars. The terms, however, were accommodating, being ten days' credit for the whole amount. With the reasonable expectation that we could pay for our house by gold digging in a less time than it would require to build one, we purchased it, and ere nightfall were duly installed in the premises.

Our party now consisted of ten, . . . [including] a man by the name of Russell, the same of whom Dana speaks in his *Two Years Before the Mast,* and who had persuaded us to allow him to join us. . . . We were a queer-looking party. I had thrown aside all the little ornaments of dress and made my best bow before the gold-digging public in red flannel and corduroy. Bob was the only member of the concern who retained what he had always in his own land considered his peculiar ornament. Right glad would he have been to rid himself of it now, poor fellow, but it was too indelibly stamped to allow of removal. It was a broad piece of blue tattooing that covered his eye on one side, and the whole cheek on the other, and gave him the appearance of a man looking from behind a blue screen. Our partnership did not extend to a community of labor in gold digging, but only to a sharing of the expenses, trials, and labors of our winter life.

The "dry diggings" of Weaver's Creek being a fair specimen of dry diggings in all parts of the mining region, a description of them will give the reader a general idea of the various diggings of the same kind in California. They are called "dry" in contra-distinction to the "wet" diggings, or those lying directly on the banks of streams and where all the gold is procured by washing. As I before said, the stream coursed between lofty tree-clad hills, broken on both sides of the river into little ravines or gorges. In these ravines most of the gold was found. The loose stones and top earth being thrown off, the gravelly clay that followed it was usually laid aside for washing, and the digging con-tinued until the bottom rock of the ravine was reached, com-monly at a depth of from one to six feet. The surface of this rock was carefully cleared off and usually found to contain little crevices and holes, the latter in miner's parlance called "pockets," and in which the gold was found concealed, sparkling like the treasures in the cave of Monte Cristo. A careful examination of the rock being made, and every little crevice and pocket being searched with a sharp-pointed knife, gold in greater or less quan-tities invariably made its appearance.

I shall never forget the delight with which I first struck and worked out a crevice. It was the second day after our installation in our little log hut, the first having been employed in what is called "prospecting," or searching for the most favorable place at which to commence operations. I had slung pick, shovel, and bar upon my shoulder and trudged merrily away to a ravine about a mile from our house. Pick, shovel, and bar did their duty, and I soon had a large rock in view. Getting down into the excavation

I had made and seating myself upon the rock, I commenced a careful search for a crevice and at last found one extending longitudinally along the rock. It appeared to be filled with a hard, bluish clay and gravel, which I took out with my knife, and there at the bottom, strewn along the whole length of the rock, was bright, yellow gold in little pieces about the size and shape of a grain of barley. Eureka! Oh how my heart beat! I sat still and looked at it some minutes before I touched it, greedily drinking in the pleasure of gazing upon gold that was in my very grasp and feeling a sort of independent bravado in allowing it to remain there. When my eyes were sufficiently feasted, I scooped it out with the point of my knife and an iron spoon, and, placing it in my pan, ran home with it very much delighted. I weighed it, and found that my first day's labor in the mines had made me thirty-one dollars richer than I was in the morning.

The gold, which, by some great volcanic eruption, has been scattered upon the soil over an extensive territory, by the continual rains of the winter season has been sunk into the hills until it has reached either a hard clay which it cannot penetrate, or a rock on which it rests. The gold in the hills, by the continual rains, has been washing lower and lower until it has reached the ravines. It has washed down the ravines until it has there reached the rock, and thence it has washed along the bed of the ravines until it has found some little crevice in which it rests, where the water can carry it no farther. Here it gathers, and thus are formed the "pockets" and "nests" of gold, one of which presents such a glowing golden sight to the eye of the miner and such a field for his imagination to revel in. How often, when I have struck one of these, have I fondly wished that it might reach to the centre of the earth and be filled as it was at its mouth with pure, bright yellow gold.

Our party's first day's labor produced one hundred and fifty dollars, I having been the most successful of all. But we were satisfied, although our experience had not fulfilled the golden stories we had heard previous to our reaching the placers. Finding the average amount of gold dug on Weaver's Creek at that time to be about an ounce per day to a man, we were content so long as we could keep pace with our neighbors. There is a spirit of emulation among miners which prevents them from being ever satisfied with success whilst others around them are more successful. We continued our labors for a week and found, at the end of that time, our whole party had dug out more than a thousand dollars; and after paying for our house and settling between ourselves our little private expenses, we were again on a clear track, unencumbered by debt, and in the heart of a region where treasures of unknown wealth were lying hidden in the earth on which we daily trod.

The Frontier in Alaska

THE dream of an empire in America, such as England, France, and Spain had acquired, inspired Peter the Great, Czar of Russia, to draw up plans, shortly before his death in 1725, for explorations in the Arctic to see whether Siberia was joined to the American continent. To lead this expedition he chose Vitus Bering, a Dane, who had long served in the Russian navy. As Bering's assistants the Czar appointed another Dane, Martin Spanberg, and a Russian, Alexander Chirikov. After incredible efforts and hardships, Bering and Chirikov finally in 1741 sailed into waters that now bear Bering's name and later sighted land in southern Alaska. Bering probably landed on Kayak Island, and on the way back to his base in Kamchatka he discovered some of the Aleutian Islands. Plagued by calamities and weakened by scurvy, he made a landing on an uninhabited island off the Kamchatka coast and there on December 19, 1741, he died. But his discoveries gave Russia a claim to Alaska.

Late in the eighteenth century Russia began to exploit the fur trade in Alaska. In 1796 the Russian Fur Company was chartered, and henceforward it became the principal agency for Russian penetration of the country. Under the leadership of Alexander Baranov, managing director of the company, the fur trade flourished. He founded Sitka in 1802 and for many years governed from a wooden "castle" in that stockade. The Russians made no effort to develop any other resource in Alaska except furs and fossil ivory from mammoth tusks.

In 1846 the Western Union Telegraph Company obtained permission from the Russian government to make a survey for a proposed telegraph line that could connect North America with

Europe. The line would run from Oregon through British Columbia and Alaska, thence by cable across Bering Strait, and on across Siberia to tap a European line in Russia proper. In 1865 actual work began and continued until 1868, when the successful completion of a cable across the Atlantic rendered the more expensive overland line unnecessary.

The acquisition of Alaska by the United States had been bruited before the Civil War but nothing came of these early suggestions. In 1867, however, Russia indicated a willingness to sell the whole region to the United States. The fur trade had fallen on evil days, and Russia was willing to part with a portion of the world that was distant and now profitless. Almost single-handedly, William H. Seward, then Secretary of State, managed to engineer the purchase for $7,200,000 and miraculously get the treaty ratified by the Senate, for many in the government and out thought the purchase a ridiculous extravagance. Newspapers printed satirical pieces and cartoons poking fun at "Seward's Ice Box." Not until gold was discovered in the Klondike more than 20 years later did the public become reconciled to the purchase.

Whymper's Travels

[*One of the best early descriptions of Alaska, previously called Russian America, was written by a member of the Western Union surveying party, Frederick Whymper, an Englishman, who was both artist and author. He had come out to Victoria, British Columbia, in 1862 and joined the Alaska surveying party in a spirit of adventure. His book, published in London in 1868 with the title* Travel and Adventure in the Territory of Alaska, *was widely read. It was brought out in New York in 1869 and again in 1871 and had a Paris edition in French translation in 1871. Vividly written and illustrated with sketches by the author, the book gave Americans the first readable account of the land they had acquired.*

[*Whymper was in Sitka on October 18, 1867, when the Russians formally transferred Alaska to the United States. Excerpts from his description of the new country follow:*]

Chapter 6

The recent acquisition of Russian America by the United States Government is one of the events of our day. Four hundred thousand square miles of territory have been, under the name of "Alaska," added to the already vast domain of Uncle Sam, and Russia has rid herself of an isolated possession of dubious value.

The purchase was not allowed to be completed quietly. On its announcement the people of the United States were, in fact, taken by surprise; there was much hostile criticism and strong political opposition. That has now for the most part passed away, and American enterprise has begun to develop the resources of the country. . . .

Russia has naturally done much toward the exploration of her colony; and some of her naval officers hold a deservedly high rank as geographers. Lisiansky, Kotsebue, and Lütke are names as familiar to men of science as to navigators. Among our own countrymen, Moore, Kellet, Collinson, and McClure, when engaged in the search for Sir John Franklin, also examined some portions of the coasts, while Captain Bedford Pim, who made some extensive land trips, is well remembered at some of the (late) Russian posts. But, with the exception of the one visit paid by a Russian, Zagoskin, until our expedition commenced its work, the interior of the country had been little visited except by the traders of the Russian American Fur Company; and much valuable information has been hitherto locked up in their archives. By the recent treaty all the documents relating to the territory were to be handed over to the United States Government. Let us hope that they may, in the interests of geography, receive a thorough investigation.

The treaty between Russia and the United States establishes the eastern and southern boundary lines as arranged by Russia and Great Britain in 1825. The western line includes the whole of the Aleutian Islands; Attu is distinctly named as the most westerly island ceded. The northern boundary is only limited by the ice and snow of the Arctic.

In 1865 the Western Union Telegraph Company of America, the largest corporation of its kind in existence, commenced the explorations for a proposed overland telegraph, which, by means of a cable via Bering Straits was to unite the Old and New World. . . .

It is needless to state that an expedition employing several hundred explorers, who examined six thousand miles of country on both sides of the Pacific—from Fraser River [in British Columbia] to Bering Straits, and thence southward to the Amur [in northeastern Asia]—has added something to our knowledge of those countries. In point of fact, five volumes like the present would hardly give a fair idea of the amount of travel undertaken. Much of the information acquired is in the hands of the Telegraph Company, and much more in the possession of individuals and is virtually lost to the world. I have confined myself almost exclusively to the narration of my own experiences, ranging over nearly two and a half years. . . .

Our expedition had a military organization, and to each man was assigned a special duty. . . . Several collectors for the Smithsonian Institution at Washington accompanied us, among the principal of whom were Messrs. Dall, Rothrock, Bannister, and Elliot. Major Kennicott, besides being selected on account of his previously acquired knowledge of the country, was the appointed director of the scientific corps.

The men selected by Colonel Bulkley were nearly all young, and hardly one beyond the prime of life. He more than once said that no old man (or old woman either) should serve on his expedition, and he could have hardly found a better place than San Francisco for the selection of active and "live" men. There, nearly everyone has been more or less a traveler and knows something of the many acquirements valuable in a new country.

Doubtless Colonel Bulkley's preference for youth, activity, and "go" is that of Americans generally. Here in England I have sometimes thought that youth was considered more of a crime than a recommendation, and that you were nowhere until you had—like old port—acquired "body" and "age"!

Chapter 7

On the 30th July, 1865, I bade a final adieu to Victoria, joined the W. U. Telegraph Company's steamer *Wright* and the following day we were en route for Sitka, the then capital of Russian America.

Our voyage, made in calm summer weather, was not specially eventful. . . . After threading Johnstone Straits we passed to the north of Vancouver Island and outside Queen Charlotte's Island. I mention this fact because there is well known to be an "inside passage" threading the archipelago of islands north of Vancouver Island. In winter it may possibly be the better route, but it is of a difficult and tortuous nature.

On the 8th August we reached the intricate and rock-girt shores of Sitka Sound, and soon came to an anchor immediately abreast of the town of Sitka. The harbor, though small, is commodious, and the water is usually as smooth as a millpond. It is in lat. 57° 2′ 45″ N., long. 135° 17′ 10″ W.

Sitka, or New Archangel, is as yet the only "city" in the country and therefore deserves some little notice. Formerly it was exclusively the headquarters of the Russian American Fur Company, but has now become a town of some life and will probably much increase in size.

The island on which Sitka is built is one of a group or archipelago discovered in 1741 by Tschirikoff [Chirikov], the companion of Bering, who, unlike that brave commander, lived to return from his adventurous voyage, the third and last of an important series. . . . At the date of our visit, a palisade or stockade divided the Russian and Indian habitations, and no native, unless working in some private house, was allowed in the town after dark. . . .

The town is situated on a low strip of land, the Governor's house rising on a rocky height a hundred feet or so above the general level. Snow-capped and peaked mountains and thickly wooded hills surround it, and Mount Edgecumbe on Crooze [Kruzof] Island immediately opposite the town, an extinct volcano of eight thousand feet in height, is the great landmark of this port—the most northern harbor on the Pacific shores of America. The coloring of the town is gay, and the surroundings picturesque. The houses yellow, with sheet-iron roofs painted red; the bright green spire and dome of the Greek Church; and the old battered hulks, roofed in and used as magazines, lying propped up on the rocks at the water's edge, with the antiquated buildings of the Russian

Fur Company, gave Sitka an original, foreign, and fossilized kind of appearance.

Landing at the wharf and passing a battery of ancient and dilapidated guns, we first saw the stores and warehouses of the Company, where furs of the value of £200,000 were sometimes accumulated. Sitka in itself had but a moderate Indian trade but was the headquarters of the company, whence the peltries of twenty-one different stations were annually brought. After passing the Governor's house, which is perched on a rock and only reached by a steep flight of stairs, we found the bureau and workshops of the company and a number of the better class of houses of employes. On the left of the street a shrubbery, the "Club Gardens," with summer houses, card and supper rooms, and swings for the children, and a little further the Greek Church with its dome and spire of oriental style overshadowing a plainer Lutheran structure within a few steps of it, attracted our attention. Then came the "Clubhouse" occupied by unmarried servants of the company, the schoolhouse, from which scholars of promise were sent to St. Petersburg, and the hospital, a very neat and clean building. Beyond these were a few dozen cottages and shanties, and then—the woods! with the one promenade of the place running through them.

Sitka enjoys the unenviable position of being about the most rainy place in the world. Rain ceases only when there is a good prospect of snow. Warm sunny weather is invariably accompanied by the prevalence of fever and pulmonary complaints, and rheumatism is looked upon as an inevitable concomitant to a residence in the settlement. Doubtless the miasma arising from damp and decaying vegetable matter is one reason why Sitka is more unhealthy in fine weather than in wet, a fact which was constantly stated to us by the inhabitants. The winter is by no means severe, the thermometer rarely standing below 20° Fahr.

A vast deal of nonsense has been published and republished in the newspapers of the United States relative to the agricultural resources of their new acquisition. The reader may take my word for it that the culture of a few potatoes and other vegetables is all that has been done in this way, and that the acres of barley mentioned in some of these high-flown paragraphs are purely mythical. There is not an acre of grain in the whole country. . . .

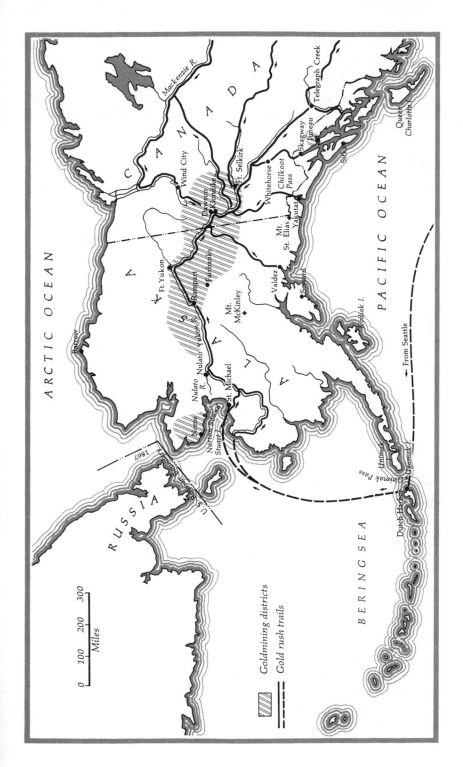

Early Alaskan Routes

The white and half-breed population of Sitka was about eight hundred, but has risen since the American occupation to about two thousand persons. A company of Russian infantry formed the garrison, and the soldiers were allowed to work for the [Russian American] Company, receiving extra pay.

The Russian American Company, formed on the model of our Hudson's Bay Company, commenced its existence as a chartered corporation in 1799, but had existed as a body of traders and merchants long before that date. Between the two fur companies there have been disputes. Latterly the coast, as far as the Chilkat River, had been leased by the former to the latter company for trading purposes. The most valuable station of the Russians, without exception, was the Island of St. Paul (Pribilof Group in Bering Sea), which yielded the larger part of the sea otter obtained by them.

In the neighborhood of Sitka extensive fisheries existed, and from 100,000 to 150,000 salmon were annually exported to the Sandwich Islands and elsewhere. Immediately on the arrival of a boatload of fish at the wharf, a number of the poorer women, some of them Indians, arranged themselves in two long lines and very rapidly cleaned and gutted the salmon. A few buckets of water were then thrown over the heap, and they were carried to the vats and put in brine at once. Each woman took as her share a large fish weighing 20 or 30 lbs., and worth—just nothing! It is said that the salmon is so abundant in the streams in the springtime that they impede the passage of boats, and that when a strong southeast wind comes it drives them ashore, where they lie in piles putrifying.

The Kalosh Indians seen at Sitka inhabit the coast between the Stikine and Chilkat rivers. At the date of our visit large numbers were absent, but in winter they are said to congregate to the number of 2,500. The Chilkat Indians also come to Sitka. . . .

We shall not readily forget the reception given us by the residents of Sitka, who seemed bent on making up for the absence of the Governor, Prince Maksutoff. Russian hospitality is proverbial, and we all somewhat suffered therefrom. The first phrase of their language acquired by us was *"Petnatchit copla"* (fifteen drops). Now this quantity—in words so modest—usually meant a

good half tumbler of some unmitigated spirit, ranging from Co-
gnac to raw vodka of a class which can only be described by a
Californian term as "chain lightning," and which was pressed
upon us on every available occasion. To refuse was simply to
insult your host. Then memory refuses to retain the number of
times we had to drink tea, which was served sometimes in tum-
blers, sometimes in cups. I need not say the oft-described samovar
was in every household. Several entertainments—balls, suppers,
and a fête in the club gardens—were organized for our benefit, and
a number of visitors came off daily to our fleet of four vessels—
strangely enough the only ones in harbor, though the company
owned many sailing vessels and steamers. We found the Russians
there living on terms of great intimacy with their domestics. The
latter almost invariably addressed their masters and mistresses
by their Christian names, and often by abbreviations thereof.
Thus a gentleman by name "Ivan" (John) would be so called
by his servants; and his wife whose name was Maria but by her
husband known as Molly would be so addressed by the servants,
to the great scandal of propriety.

But Sitka in the hands of the Russian Company and Sitka in
those of its new owners are already very different things. An
Anglo-Russian newspaper, to be printed in double columns, is
projected and is to appear this spring (1868). Town "lots" are
held at fabulous prices; for a small log house 10,000 dollars
(£2000) is asked, and I should not be surprised to learn that
salmon was half a dollar a pound, that a dozen "saloons," hotels,
barbers' shops, and "lager bier" cellars had been started, or especially that the Sitka waterworks were a great success! Every
"correspondent's" letter from thence, and I have read a score,
agrees in one fact, "that our aqueous supply evinces no sign of
failure!"

In the "good old Russian times" there were, it is said, about 180
church holidays to the year; now they will be confined to Christmas and New Year's days, Washington's birthday and the 4th of
July (Independence day). But if the enlightened citizens of the
country choose to avail themselves of the privilege, they can enjoy
two Sundays each week. Owing to the fact that the Russians came
eastward and we came westward, there is of course a day's difference where the two meet, and their Sunday in Sitka falls on

our Saturday. "The San Franciscan," says a California newspaper, "who arrives at Archangel on Friday night, according to his reckoning, will find the stores closed and business suspended on the following morning, and so will lose not only that day, but the next, too, if his conscientious convictions and the force of habit are only strong enough. On the other hand, the pious Alaskan merchant who belongs to the Greek Church will look with horror on the impious stranger who offers to trade or swap jackknives on Sunday, but who on Monday morning suddenly assumes a clean shirt, black broadcloth, a nasal twang, and that demurely self-satisfied air which is our national idea of a religious demeanor.". . .

A San Francisco company leased from the Russians the privilege of obtaining ice from St. Paul's, Kodiak Island. The Americans, as it is unnecessary perhaps to remark, use ice at table to a far greater extent than we do, and in the Atlantic States it is sold at an almost nominal price. California, about the warmest State in the Union, naturally consumes a large quantity of ice. It is cut from an artificial lake which has an area of forty acres. The laborers are all Aleuts (Aleutian islanders) and are principally engaged for three or four months of winter, while the ice is firm, in cutting it up and storing it for summer consumption. The larger part of this luxury is consumed in San Francisco, but it finds its way to Mexican, Central, and even South American ports. Kodiak, which is included in the purchase, is therefore by no means an unimportant acquisition.

The formal transfer of Russian America to the United States authorities took place on October 18th, 1867. It is said that the Russian flag showed great reluctance to come down, and stuck on the yardarm of the flagstaff. . . .

Chapter 8

. . . .

On the 3rd September [1865], when tacking and trying to make Ounimak Pass or passage between Ounimak [Unimak] and Ougamok [Ugamak], two of the Aleutian Islands, we caught a glimpse through the opening mists of the volcano of Chichaldinskoi [Shisaldin]. This mountain is, on the authority of Lütke, 8,935 feet in height [actually 9,387 feet], and is situated on Ounimak Island. It has a very graceful form. Near it is a second mountain of less elevation, with a jagged double summit, of very odd and irregular appearance. On the evening of the 4th Chichaldinskoi loomed out very distinctly, and when the clouds cleared from it we could see smoke issuing from a large cleft near the summit. In Ounimak Passage a second volcano over 5,000 feet in height was seen, and Captain Scammon observed during the night the fire of one on Akutan Island. The whole chain of the Aleutian Islands is volcanic. They deserve an expedition to themselves.

We arrived in Norton Sound on the 12th September, having experienced very rough weather in Bering Sea; in fact, during part of the time we had to "lay to." Approaching for the first time these northern coasts of Russian America, we observed with surprise the dried-up and sunburnt appearance of everything on shore. The hills varied much in color, from shades of crimson and red to tints of brown and yellow. The summer in this country, though short, is intensely warm while it lasts; late in the season hot days alternate with frosty nights, and the vegetation is much affected thereby. We went into the Sound carefully taking soundings, and indeed it was very necessary as our later experience will show. We arrived off the Island of St. Michael's [probably Stuart Island in Norton Sound] at 10 A.M. on the 13th, and found that our steamer had already called there and had again started for Bering Straits. . . .

Chapter 16

· · · · · · · · · ·

Nulato is the most inland and also most northern of all the Russian Fur Company's posts; on Zagoskin's authority it is in lat. 64° 42′ 11″ N., and long. 157° 58′ 18″ W. (of Greenwich). It is on the north bank of the Yukon and is situated on a flat stretch of comparatively open land, bounded on the southwest by the Nulato River, a tributary of the Yukon,—a stream one of whose mouths is at least seventy yards in width.

A smaller stream, also falling into the great river, bounds this open patch of land on the northeast. Trees of good average growth and sufficiently large for building purposes are to be found in the woods at a moderate distance from the fort, and the soil, a rich vegetable mold with clay underlying, though swampy in spring, might possibly be turned to some account. Luxuriant grass and innumerable berries grow up and ripen in the brief summertime.

The post resembles those before described, and differs only in having two watchtowers. It is surrounded by a picket, and during our stay the gate was always shut at night, and Indians excluded when present in large numbers. Before our arrival a "watch" had been kept regularly at night for reasons that will afterward appear. The log building occupied by us formed a part of one side of the fort square. The windows of our room were of seal gut, and, as the days were now about two hours in length, our light inside was none of the best. We slept wrapped up in fur-lined blankets and skins on a platform raised about two feet above the floor, which latter we had caulked with moss and covered with straw and skins. Even then, although our room was generally warm enough, the floor was sometimes intensely cold. I once hung up some damp cloth to dry; near the rafters it steamed; within a foot of the ground it froze firmly, with long icicles hanging therefrom. The air near the floor has shown a temperature of $+4°$ when the upper part of the room was $+60°$ or $+65°$ Fahr.

Our supply of water was obtained from a hole kept constantly open—or as open as nature would allow it to be—through the ice of the Yukon, at a distance of a quarter of a mile from the post. The "water sledge" was one of the institutions of the place, and a large barrel was taken down and filled with water—and a good deal of broken ice—and brought back for the supply of the station. It was generally dragged by men, and sometimes by Indian women, as it would have taken more dogs than the place possessed to move it. It may very naturally be asked, "Does not a river like the Yukon freeze to the bottom?" and the answer is, most emphatically, "No; excepting only in extremely shallow places." We saw ice nine feet thick and upwards, but it was not produced by the natural process of gradual freezing and thickening, but had been forced up on other ice before the river was completely and firmly frozen. I think an average of five feet of ice will form where there is sufficient depth of water. Its universal covering of snow has, doubtless, the effect of preventing the formation of extremely thick ice; the current of the river has the same effect.

I have before mentioned the Indian mode of fishing through holes in the ice, but had not been prepared to see it practiced on the large scale common on the Yukon. Early in the winter large piles or stakes had been driven down through the ice to the bottom of the river; to these were affixed traps, consisting simply of a wicker-work funnel leading into a long basket not unlike the eel pots to be seen on the Thames, but on a larger scale. Oblong holes above them were kept open through the ice by frequent breaking, and sometimes a great number of "white fish" and a large black fish known by the Russians as *Nalima* [turbot or ling] were taken, and we fell in for a share. The last named is mainly used for dog feed, but its very rich and oily liver was much eaten by the Russians and was not despised by us. . . .

The effect of intense cold on our stores in the magazine was a very interesting study; our dried apples were a mass of rock and had to be smashed up with an axe, our molasses formed a thick black paste, and no knife we had would cut a slice of ham from the bone till it was well thawed in our warmer room. Our preserved meats would, with a continuation of those times, have been preserved forever and would have made, as Kane says, excellent "canister shot." After purchasing grouse or hares from the Indians, they would remain, uneaten, for a month or longer period in as good condition as ever, and there was no fear of their getting too "high" in that climate.

Our coldest day for the whole season occurred in December [1866]. On the 26th of November the thermometer fell suddenly from the comparatively moderate temperature of $+2°$ to $-18°$, and continued lowering steadily—day by day—till it reached (on the 5th December) $-58°$ Fahr., or *ninety degrees below freezing*. But the weather was lovely; no wind blew or snow fell during the whole time, and we did not feel the cold as much as at many other times. Meantime the barometer rose rapidly and stood at slightly above thirty inches on our coldest day. . . .

[*December*] *21st*. Our shortest day, the sun rose at 10:40 A.M., and set soon after 12:30 P.M. The *interval* is given correctly, but we had no "Greenwich time" to go by, and, therefore, it is only the duration of sunlight that is to be depended upon.

25th. Merry Christmas! not the first by a good many that I had spent away from home and kindred. We all tried to be jolly and were moderately successful, yet there was a slight "back current" of regret and a tinge of melancholy in our proceedings. We decorated our room with flags and Indian trading goods and spruce-fir brush in place of holly; got out the newest and brightest of our tin plates and pewter spoons, raised a big fire of logs—in the oven! and Dall set to work vigorously in the manufacture of gingerbread and pies, but it could not quite put out of mind the dear ones at home and what we well knew they were about.

. . . About five o'clock in the afternoon, the table, neatly covered with cotton drill and set out with the "plate" provided by the company in the shape of iron mess kettles, tin platters, and cups, was ready, and we sat down to a repast—to use a Californianism—of a "high-toned and elegant nature."

BILL OF FARE

SOUPE À LA YUKON.

ARCTIC GROUSE—ROAST.

ALASKA REINDEER MEAT.

NULATO CRANBERRY SAUCE.

CALIFORNIA (PRESERVED) PEAS AND TOMATOES.

DRIED-APPLE PUDDING.

PIES.   GINGERBREAD À LA DALL.

ICED CHEESE.

COFFEE.   TEA.

ICED WATER.

Winding up with a limited supply of rum punch, and pipes *ad libitum!*

Not a bad dinner of itself; the iced cheese was a novelty I can recommend; only the traditional pudding was missing.

We passed the evening singing and reciting. Dall read an original poem; and I brought out a MS. story (still there!), entitled the "Missing Mummy!"

27th. Just as we were turning in for the night a fine auroral display in the N.W. was announced, and we all rushed out to witness it from the roof of the tallest building in the fort. It was not the conventional arch but a graceful, undulating, ever-changing "snake" of electric light, evanescent colors, pale as those of a lunar rainbow, ever and again flitting through it, and long streamers and scintillations moving upward to the bright stars, which distinctly shone through its hazy, ethereal form. The night was beautifully calm and clear, cold, but not intensely so, the thermometer at +16°. A second one was seen by us on the 13th January (1867), which had the arched form but not of that exact nature which has been so often represented; and later we witnessed other displays, though not so frequently as we had expected. . . .

Chapter 18

Although snow covers the ground and the rivers are frozen for nearly eight months of the year in northern Russian America, winter can hardly be said to exist for that time. As early as April 5th a thaw occurred, and, though it again got cooler, it proved to us that spring was fast approaching. On the 9th flies made their appearance, the courtyard of the post became a swamp, and, on the 10th, I found the willows and smaller trees budding. . . .

From the 11th to the 25th of April the weather got cooler, with slight falls of snow. After the latter date, however, the thermometer rarely fell below freezing point, and, by comparison with our winter experiences, it seemed quite warm. On the 28th of the same month, the first goose from the south arrived. . . .

On the 5th May the Nulato River made a decided breakup; it had shown many signs of it before, but its ardor had been nipped in the bud. This time it burst in good earnest, and on the 12th it opened still more and ran out on the *top of the Yukon ice* for more than a mile *up* the great river. In many places the rain had bared the ice from its usual covering of snow; it is, without doubt, a powerful agent in breaking up these great rivers. The general effect was mess and confusion; the ice dirty and mixed with logs and debris, and the water, in tortuous streams, running all over its surface. Several persons belonging to the fort, who had been shooting on the island opposite, had much difficulty in getting back; and Ivan, the *"bidarshik,"* almost came to grief, getting wedged in between loose ice and up to his neck in water. He was rescued by canoes from the fort. Indians have been carried away and drowned by an unexpected breakup of the river, and the fish traps are invariably swept away.

On the 12th [May], mosquitoes made their first appearance, and on the 13th the swallows arrived and were flitting round the fort or building under the eaves of the roof. The indefatigable Kuriler bagged six geese and, the following day, ten more. The weather was now so warm and sunny that we felt enervated and oppressed by it.

19th. First real breakup of the Yukon, the ice coming down in a steady flow at the rate of five or six knots an hour. For several days afterward this continued and was an exciting scene after the monotony of the winter. A constant stream of broken ice passed the station, now surging into mountains as it met with some obstacle, now grinding and crashing on its way and carrying all before it. Whole trees and banks were swept away before its victorious march, and the river rose some fourteen feet above its winter level. On the 22nd a quantity of "black ice," i.e., ice discolored by some very dark-looking earth, went by. By the 24th, the river was beginning to clear. . . .

All was now activity: the Russians preparing for their spring trading excursion, Dall and myself for our projected trip, and Mr. Dyer for his journey down the river to its mouths. . . . The river was still full of ice and driftwood, and navigation was difficult. The only way of ascending the stream was by keeping near, generally *very* near the banks. We had frequently to cross and recross the stream to get into quieter water, and at such times exerted ourselves specially so that we might not lose much by the operation. As it was, we usually drifted down half a mile or so.

How shall I, in few words, describe this immense stream, one that our men were wont to compare with the Mississippi! At Nulato, which is 600 miles above its mouths—as before stated—it is from bank to bank one mile and a quarter wide, while in other places it opens out into lagoons four to five miles in width, studded with innumerable islands. Our explorers have traveled up it 1,800 miles. Its tributaries—to be hereafter mentioned—would be large rivers in Europe, and I can therefore understand the proud boast uttered by a native of its banks, and translated for our benefit, "*We* are not savages, we are Yukon Indians!" . . .

Chapter 21

.   .   .   .

Whilst stopping in Plover Bay [August 1867] some of our men found a keg of specimens preserved in alcohol belonging to one of our Smithsonian collectors. Having had a long abstinence from exhilarating drinks, the temptation was too much for them, and they proceeded to broach the contents. After they had imbibed to their hearts' content and become "visibly affected thereby," they thought it a pity to waste the remaining contents of the barrel, and, feeling hungry, went on to eat the lizards, snakes, and fish which had been put up for a rather different purpose! Science was avenged in the result, nor do I think they will ever repeat the experiment. . . .

Chapter 22

That Russian America is likely to prove a bad bargain to the United States Government I cannot believe. The extreme northern division of the country may, indeed, be nearly valueless; but the foregoing pages will have shown that, in the more central portions of the territory, furs are abundant and that the trade in them, which may probably be further developed, must fall into American hands. The southern parts of the country are identical in character with the neighboring British territory and will probably be found to be as rich in mineral wealth; whilst the timber, though of an inferior growth owing to the higher latitude, will yet prove by no means worthless.

The fisheries may become of great value. There are extensive cod banks off the Aleutian Isles and on many other parts of the coast. Salmon is *the* commonest of common fish in all the rivers of the North Pacific and is rated accordingly as food only fit for those who cannot get better. In Alaska, as in British Columbia, the fish can be obtained in vast quantities simply at the expense of native labor. To this add the value of salt (or vinegar), barrels, and freight, and one sees the slight total cost which would be incurred in exporting to benighted Europe that which would there be considered a luxury. . . .

The Aleutian Islands, besides having some commercial importance, yielding, as they still do, the furs of amphibious animals to a large amount, have many points of interest. On nearly all of them active or passive volcanoes exist, and on one or two geysers and hot springs have been discovered. There are records of very severe shocks of earthquake felt by the Russian traders and natives dwelling on them.

Conclusion:
A Nation in Motion

FROM the earliest times Americans have been a nation in motion as they have probed and searched the continent. From the time of Captain John Smith onward, curiosity about the interior sent explorers upon countless expeditions. The West held an enduring fascination that lured men of many types to follow its trails—sometimes to fortune, sometimes to disaster. Danger and hardship never deterred the stream of adventurers who discovered the excitement of a journey toward the setting sun decades before Horace Greeley advised young men to go West. The attraction of the West has lasted through the nation's history; even today hordes of migrants continue to swarm to California in search of some inexplicable recipe for comfort, health, prosperity, happiness.

For decades during the nineteenth century discontented men of various classes comforted themselves with the belief that they could improve their lot by packing up and moving to greener pastures somewhere on the western horizon. During the first half of the nineteenth century migrants leapfrogged across the Great Plains to California and the lush, green valleys of Oregon. But after the Civil War, when many Americans were uprooted and restless, and foreign immigration increased the pressure for land, even the High Plains between the one-hundredth meridian and the Rockies, previously designated as "the Great American Desert," began to receive increasing numbers of settlers, first cattlemen and then farmers.

Farmers accustomed to areas of plentiful rainfall gradually learned to adapt to the conditions of the semiarid plains, where they utilized the techniques of "dry-farming" or developed irrigation projects to supply water to parched fields. New investigations of the High Plains showed that regions reported by earlier explorers to be uninhabitable could be grazed or farmed profitably. The tragic elimination of the Plains Indians, and the buffalo on which they subsisted, left extensive territories open to settlement in the last quarter of the nineteenth century. On much of this land, owned by the Federal government, a farmer could obtain free 160 acres merely by "homesteading" it, that is, by putting on it "improvements" (a habitation of some sort) and cultivating it. Free land in the West attracted many foreign immigrants as well as farmers from the worn-out lands in the East. In the two decades from 1870 to 1890 the population in the country west of the Mississippi increased from 6,877,000 to 16,775,000.

The Superintendent of the Census in 1890 reported that settlements had so penetrated even the wildest parts of the country that no longer was a consistent frontier line discernible. That report of the passing of an official frontier gave rise to a famous essay, "The Significance of the Frontier in American History," by the historian Frederick Jackson Turner. Turner's essay, published in 1894, maintained that up to that time, "American history has been in a large degree the history of colonization of the Great West. The existence of an area of free land, its continuous recession, and the advance of American settlement westward, explain American development." He insisted that this repeated penetration of unsettled territory resulted in a constant "return to primitive conditions on a continually advancing frontier line and a new development in that area. American social development has been continually beginning over again on the frontier. This perennial rebirth, this fluidity of American life, this expansion westward with its new opportunities, its continuous touch with the simplicity of primitive society, furnish the forces dominating American character."

Turner credited frontier conditions with the development of the spirit of self-reliance, independence, and courage that made up what he called the "American character." He also believed that the frontier had helped inspire enthusiasm for democratic principles in government. Although Turner himself set forth his views as tentative, they quickly became gospel for a whole school of historians who came after him.

Reappraisals of the history of frontier society in our time have modified many of the more dogmatic views of the influence of the frontier held by Turner's disciples. Nevertheless, the existence of a great continent into which the population could expand, of almost illimitable sources for adventure and profit, had an enormous impact upon Americans. The impact even extended to foreign visitors who came for adventure and returned to write about the wonders of the new country—and sometimes to comment upon the crudeness of its inhabitants.

The existence of fresh lands in the West, whether free or for purchase, exerted a continual fascination for Americans. Always the possibility existed of "moving out West" to something better. Far-off pastures frequently looked greener to restless or dissatisfied men and women, and a constant stream has always been moving westward, even to our own day, as witness the great influx into California since World War II. We have been a restless and a constantly moving people, frequently without deep roots in any locality. Mobile and ready to travel, we have been ever ready to listen to the call of adventure or the siren song of real-estate promoters. Our ancestors traveled on foot, by horseback, or in ox-drawn wagons; the motor car and the airplane have now given us faster and easier means of transport. But American restlessness remains an innate characteristic.

Although ribbons of concrete now span the continent and millions move at mortal speeds between the Atlantic and the Pacific, we continue to yearn for fresh trails and new roads. Part of our current malaise is caused by frustration over the drying up of sources of adventure in the great outdoors. Rock festivals in open fields are a sorry substitute for hunting buffalo and grizzlies, probing unknown ranges in the Rockies or panning gold from the riverbeds of California or the Yukon. But even though little virgin territory remains to be explored and exploited, many of us remain pathfinders and explorers. We still search for areas not too thickly populated, for streams where trout still leap to a dry fly, where one can still follow the trails of Jedidiah Smith or Joseph Walker and forget smog, pollution, and the less attractive members of the genus *Homo sapiens*. The zeal for exploration and discovery has not yet died in us.

Index